CANADA

BEFORE

CONFEDERATION

A STUDY IN HISTORICAL GEOGRAPHY

CANADA BEFORE CONFEDERATION

A STUDY IN HISTORICAL GEOGRAPHY

R. COLE HARRIS & JOHN WARKENTIN

CARLETON UNIVERSITY PRESS
Ottawa, Canada
1991

© Carleton University Press Inc. 1991

ISBN 0-88629-137-2

Printed and bound in Canada

Published originally by Oxford University Press

Carleton Library Series   166

Canadian Cataloguing in Publication Data
  Harris, R. Cole
    Canada before Confederation

  (The Carleton library ; 166)
  Includes bibliographical references and index.
  ISBN 0-88629-137-2

    1. Canada—Historical geography.   I. Warkentin,
  John, 1928-   . II. Title. III. Series.

  FC179.H37 1991   911'.71   C91-090047-7
  F1027.5.H37 1991

Distributed by: Oxford University Press Canada
                70 Wynford Drive
                Don Mills, Ontario
                Canada. M3C 1J9
                (416) 441-2941

Cover design: Y Graphic Design

Acknowledgements

Carleton University Press gratefully acknowledges the support extended to
its publishing programme by the Canada Council and the Ontario Arts
Council.

TABLE OF CONTENTS

LIST OF FIGURES

INTRODUCTION TO THE CARLETON LIBRARY EDITION

It is hard to believe that some seventeen years have elapsed since Canada's two leading historical geographers, Richard Colebrooke Harris and John Warkentin, produced *Canada Before Confederation: A Study in Historical Geography*. What years they have been!

The 1970s were heady times for historical geography. The decade had opened with Cole Harris, Quixote-like astride his "historical geographical mule," tilting at contemporary trends in geography. His mission was to provoke debate and reflection on the current condition and future prospects of the discipline.[1] Arguing in favour of a perspective that nurtured "a habit of seeing together the complex of factors that make up the character of places, regions or landscapes,"[2] he looked to the future with confidence:

> If I read the signs aright, geography is again in a period of rapid flux from which the outcome is still unclear. Certainly the last decade has shown the historical geographical mule to be a stubborn beast, and my strong hunch is that the next will reveal its fertility to even the most sceptical.[3]

He was soon to be proven correct. Across the Atlantic, British historical geographers produced a series of volumes that displayed new methodologies and theoretical perspectives.[4] Our colleagues "to the south of the line" demonstrated their confidence in the vibrancy of historical geography by launching *The Historical Geography Newsletter* in December, 1971 and by publishing their own collection of current research in the field.[5]

Closer to home the decade opened with a salvo of fine scholarship.[6] Peter Goheen's *Victorian Toronto* and Eric Ross's *Beyond the River and the Bay*, both published in 1970, served as symbolic statements of contrasting perspectives within the discipline as well as demonstrations of rigorous and imaginative scholarship. The following year, Conrad Heidenreich took as his theme in historical geography the "reconstruction and interpretation of past landscapes" and applied it with much success to seventeenth century Huronia. Jim Gilmour, while making no explicit reference to historical geography, effected an historical interpretation of Ontario's nineteenth century industrial economy. Also in 1972, Jim Lemon's *The Best Poor Man's Country* explored the historical geography of early Pennsylvania from the perspective of the interplay of society and land within cultural and social contexts. And in 1974, there were two more fine studies by Canadian historical geographers: John Mannion's *Irish Settlements in Eastern Canada* explored the transfer, adaptation, and retention of Irish material culture in Canada, while Arthur Ray's *Indians in the Fur Trade* did much to explain the ecological and cultural mechanics of the fur-trade prior to 1870. These, together with other works, were fine vindications of Cole Harris' faith in his colleagues and his discipline.

As if to dispel any lingering doubts concerning the vitality of historical geography, two other ventures served to cement the recent gains. First, in 1975, the *Journal of Historical Geography* came into being, declaring that its purpose was to "reflect progress in the area of study known as historical geography."[7] Secondly, in the summer of that year, the Ontario Historical Geographers hosted the "British-Canadian Symposium on Historical Geography" and so commenced a series of exchanges that was to evolve through several ever-lengthening regionally-inclusive acronyms into the ecumenical ICHG.[8] This "International Conference of Historical Geographers" has come to be the pre-eminent intellectual forum and "bonding-event" for the discipline.

It was in this context of a strong and vital historical geography that *Canada Before Confederation* appeared in 1974.[9] It was the third in the "Andrew H. Clark Historical Series in the Historical Geography of North America" published by Oxford University Press. It had been preceded by Donald Meinig's *Southwest: Three Peoples in Geographical Change 1600-1970* and David Ward's *Cities and Immigrants: A Geography of Change in Nineteenth Century America*.[10] In his foreword to these earlier volumes, Andrew Clark had offered his definition of that "little cultivated field of American historical scholarship—that which is usually called historical geography or geographical history."[11] It is interesting to recall what the doyen of North American historical geography considered the discipline to be at that time:

> We prefer to think of them as studies of changing geography or of geographical change. Those of us engaged in the enterprise are, for the most part, professional geographers and, although our major readership must be among historians, and it is to them that we mainly address ourselves, our central and vital concern with place, location, and interaction or diffusion through space clearly identifies us in our own profession.[12]

For Clark, the emphasis upon "place" as the experienced manifestation of "location" was mediated by an analysis of temporal and spatial processes: it was the study of "geographical change." Harris and Warkentin's study went beyond this conceptualization. For them, geography was a "synthesizing field" that attempted to better understand how humans have occupied the land. This requires an appreciation of the regional variety of the earth's surface and of the culturally influenced interaction between societies and their environments.

The study of landscape was central to this focus. For Harris and Warkentin, landscapes came into being as "human creations" and as imprints of human action; and "to understand something of them is to understand something of their creators."[13] Maitland-like, they deciphered the superimposed impressions on their Canadian palimpsest; and like Margaret Atwood, they viewed time

> as having a shape, something you could see, like a series of liquid transparencies, one laid on top of another. You don't look back along time but down through it, like water. Sometimes this comes to the surface, sometimes that, sometimes nothing. Nothing goes away.[14]

Their emphasis, therefore, was on understanding the human experience of occupying and organizing the land and not with the aseptic world of spatial or temporal process. Of course, it was understood that these relationships were dynamic. Indeed, this was the essential theme running through their study: how profoundly different colonial enclaves, a culturally diverse population, an essentially localized sense of community, and non-complementary regional economies produced sectional rather than central identities. And for Harris and Warkentin, this conjunction of regional and centralizing forces was central to this enterprise of interpreting the development of Canada.

But how was all this received in 1974? Principles of fairness dictate that I should start with my own evaluation then. My geography belonged more to the world of C. Darryl Forde, Emrys Bowen, Estyn Evans, and Clifford Darby than to that of Hartshorne, Christaller, and von Thunen. Not unexpectedly, therefore, Harris and Warkentin's concern with people, land, places, and regions was a welcome reassertion of themes that were central to my own appreciation of what was at the core of the discipline.

Perhaps it was an exercise in self-indulgence, therefore, but my review reflected my own preferences.[15] I appreciated their grappling with understanding the essential character of each of the major regions of Canada through discussions of the ways by which society organized space, developed the natural resources, and nurtured human communities. I waxed poetic in my approval of the way in which the specifics of people, products and processes were not allowed to detract from their treatment of the quintessential regional expressions of time and place. And I praised their use of landscape:

It is in the landscape that subtle differences are discerned which distinguish between the attitudes and values of French and English in Quebec or those of English, Irish and Americans in Ontario. While it may be argued that the landscape analysis is at its best in identifying the distinctive material elements of the cultural history of any area, it cannot be denied that it is at its most exciting when attempting to infer the non-material dimensions. By using this device of landscape, the authors bring to their otherwise standard historical approach an interesting interpretation, if not critical analysis, of some two centuries of Canadian development.

For me, at least, the authors had succeeded in their stated objective, the provision of "a comprehensive and deliberately provocative synthesis."

How did others react to *Canada Before Confederation*?[16] Predictably, the prophets had some trouble getting appreciated in their own country. The review in the *Journal of Historical Geography* did praise Harris and Warkentin for being "lucid, provocative and descriptive," but complained that the book "makes neither for a fully satisfactory interpretative mono-graph nor for a textbook," and concluded that it will "never be regarded as a new interpretation of Canada." Thankfully, this review also praised the work as "a haven of sanity" from "cryptic numeric tautology" and the "new historical geography based on mathematical precision and the aridity which so frequently follows it."

Others, however, were more laudatory. Irene Spry in the *Geographical Journal* found it to be "a masterly and stimulating analysis of the forces that had shaped the character and quality of Canadians and their country on the verge of the adventure of Confederation." J.M.S. Careless in the *Canadian Historical Review* considered it to be "a survey but a thorough, scholarly one; a succinct, lucid, solidly based account of human settlement and change," and concluded with a final accolade, "it should sell well and long; at least it deserves to!" Wreford Watson, writing in the *Scottish Geographical Magazine*, declared it to be "not only an outstanding study of Canada but a distinguished work in historical geography". C.M. Johnston's review in the *American Historical Review* praised the study for "an impression of the early development that departs refreshingly from some of the customary approaches to Canadian history." He did, however, take the authors to task for their treatment of Confederation, "essentially a political and constitutional event, as a landmark in the social, economic, and cultural growth of Canada." Finally, Peter Goheen in the *Geographical Review* shared this concern with the elevation of Confederation to symbolic prominence and argued for the need to consider continentalism as an accompaniment to regionalism in the nation's history. Like others, however, he closed with approbation:

> The authors must be commended, on the other hand, for what they have achieved. They have provided us with several splendid essays of regional interpretation, and they have created a synthesis that will guide the student and stimulate and provoke the scholar. The book is a welcome contribution.

But that was then. What about now? How will a reprint of the 1974 work fare in 1991? In 1974, Harris and Warkentin pricked us with all their hope that "readers who reject parts of our interpretation will do the research to prove us wrong." This challenge was certainly not the only spur, but much was subsequently produced by many researchers, as is demonstrated by Graeme Wynn's recent masterly compilation and assessment of the now substantial number of publications by Canadian historical geographers.[17]

Also, much scholarly water has flowed under the theoretical bridge since 1974. The list is an imposing one: phenomenology, existentialism and humanism; semiotics and iconography; new ethnography, and hermeneutics; structuration and structuralism; post-modernism and deconstructionism. As Giles Gunn summarized it,

> now the air is filled with talk about the anxiety of influence, the hermeneutic circularity of understanding the deconstruction of metaphors, the semiotics of discourse, the intertextuality of experience, and the demystification of signs.[18]

Rather than considering landscape as a repository of material culture, or relics of past societies, we are now suspicious of them as mere reflexive products of some super-organic culture. Attention is now directed to revealing the social and cultural priorities that produced such landscapes and the interactions that take place between people and their landscapes. Thus, we are now reading landscape as an ideologically charged text. It is "a terrain of metaphor," replete with meaningful signs and symbols that are being interpreted through the devices of carnival, spectacle, theatre, and chronotopes.[19]

Running through all of this, however, is a continued commitment to understanding people, places, and landscapes. This is still the foundation of what many of us do, even though we may be posing our questions differently as our approaches are informed by contemporary theoretical developments. But the essential questions are the same.

In particular, writing in 1991 at this crucial juncture in Canadian affairs, I am struck by how historical geographers' concerns for national and regional identities and with peoples' sense of place can contribute much to the current debate about a Canada "after" or even "without" the principles of Confederation. Indeed, in 1974, Cole and John closed their volume on a

Canada "before" Confederation with an interpretive essay regarding what was a pressing problem then. They assayed an overview of the character and ethos of the nation which emerged at Confederation from the synthesis of the diverse regional heritages and their very last paragraph concluded,

> In these ways, Confederation posed a challenge to British North Americans of an altogether different order from the clearing of fields, the building of industry, the defense of narrow identities, or even the creation of a ringing Canadian mythology. Basically, it was the challenge to find a way to balance scale and identity, that is, to find a way to live as human beings within the modern world, a quest still reflected in the tensions of Confederation today.[20]

Plus ça change, plus la même chose.

Brian S. Osborne
February, 1991
Kingston.

References

[1] Cole Harris, "Reflections on the Fertility of the Historical Geographical Mule" (Toronto: University of Toronto, Department of Geography, Discussion Paper No. 10, November, 1970).

[2] *Ibid.*, p. 14.

[3] *Ibid.*, p. 32.

[4] Alan R.H. Baker, John Hamshere and John Langton, editors, *Geographical Interpretations of Historical Sources: Readings in Historical Geography* (Newton Abbot, Devon: David and Charles Publishers Ltd., 1970); Alan R. Baker, editor, *Progress in Historical Geography* (Newton Abbot, Devon: David and Charles Publishers Ltd., 1972); H.C. Darby, editor, *A New Historical Geography of England* (Cambridge: Cambridge University Press, 1973).

[5] Ralph E. Ehrenberg, editor, *Pattern and Process: Research In Historical Geography* (Washington: Howard University Press, 1971).

[6] Peter H. Goheen, *Victorian Toronto 1850-1900* (Chicago: University of Chicago, 1970); Eric Ross, *Beyond the River and the Bay* (Toronto: University of Toronto Press, 1970); Conrad Heidenreich, *Huronia: A History and Geography of the Huron Indians 1600-1650* (Toronto: McClelland and Stewart Ltd., 1971); James M. Gilmour, *Spatial Evolution of Manufacturing: Southern Ontario 1851-1891* (Toronto: University of Toronto Press, 1972); James T. Lemon, *The Best Poor Man's Country: A Geographical Study of Early Southeastern Pennsylvania* (Baltimore, Maryland: Johns Hopkins Press, 1972); John J. Mannion, *Irish Settlements in Eastern Canada: A Study of Cultural Transfer and Adaptation* (Toronto: University of Toronto Press, 1974); Arthur J. Ray, *Indians in the Fur Trade: Their Role as Hunters, Trappers and Middlemen in the Lands Southwest of Hudson Bay, 1660-1870* (Toronto: University of Toronto Press, 1974).

[7] "Editorial," *Journal of Historical Geography*, Vol. 1, no. 1 (1975), p. i.

[8] Brian S. Osborne, editor, *The Settlement of Canada: Origins and Transfer—Proceedings of the 1975 British-Canadian Symposium on Historical Geography* (Kingston: Queen's University, 1976).

[9] R. Cole Harris and John Warkentin, *Canada Before Confederation: A Study in Historical Geography* (New York: Oxford University Press, 1974).

[10] D.W. Meinig, *Southwest: Three Peoples in Geographical Change 1600-1970* (New York: Oxford University Press, 1971); David Ward, *Cities and Immigrants: A Geography of Change in Nineteenth Century America* (New York: Oxford University Press, 1971).

[11] Andrew H. Clark in Ward, *op. cit.*, p. v.

[12] *Ibid.*

[13] Harris and Warkentin, *op. cit.*, p. vi.

[14] Margaret Atwood, *Cat's Eye* (Toronto: McClelland and Stewart, 1988), p. 3.

[15] Brian S. Osborne, review of *Canada Before Confederation* in *Humanities Association Review*, Vol. 27 (1976), pp. 202-203.

[16] This discussion refers to the following reviews of *Canada Before Confederation*: J.M.S. Careless, in *The Canadian Historical Review*, Vol. LVII (1977), pp. 168-170; Peter G. Goheen, in *The Geographical Review*, Vol. 65 (1975), pp. 540-542; F.C. Innes, in *Journal of Historical Geography*, Vol. 1 (1975), pp. 117-118; C.M. Johnston, in *American Historical Review*, Vol. 80 (1975), p. 1069; Irene M. Spry, in *Geographical Journal*, Vol. 144 (1978), pp. 344-345; Wreford Watson, in *Scottish Geographical Magazine*, Vol. 92 (1976), pp. 65-66.

[17] Graeme Wynn, "Introduction," in *People, Places, Patterns, Processes: Geographical Perspectives on the Canadian Past*, Graeme Wynn, editor (Toronto: Copp Clark Pitman Ltd., 1990), pp. 1-37.

[18] Giles Gunn, *The Culture of Criticism and the Criticism of Culture* (Oxford: Oxford University Press, 1987), pp. 21-22.

[19] Dennis Cosgrove, "A Terrain of Metaphor: Cultural Geography 1988-89," *Progress in Human Geography*, Vol. 13 (1989), pp. 566-575; Mireya Folch-Serra, "Place, Voice, Space: Mikhail Bakhtin's Dialogical Landscape," *Society and Space*, Vol. 8 (1990), pp. 255-274.

[20] Harris and Warkentin, *op. cit.*, p. 329.

PREFACE TO THE CARLETON LIBRARY EDITION

Texts have their own lives after they leave their authors' pens. Such has been the case with *Canada Before Confederation*, which John Warkentin and I wrote in the late 1960s and early 1970s, and which now, somewhat to our surprise—and to our considerable pleasure—is being republished by Carleton University Press in the Carleton Library Series. Whether in the life of an academic discipline or of a country, twenty years is a considerable time; we would not write *Canada Before Confederation* today as we wrote it twenty years ago. Yet, as Brian Osborne remarks in his generous introduction, our interest in people, places and landscapes would remain as strong as ever, and would now be reinforced by a widespread interdisciplinary insistence on the interdependence of societies and territories. An account of European coping with non-European places is central to understanding New World societies, and the particular shape of that coping in northern North America is central to understanding Canada. We would probably still write a book that ended with a political event—Confederation—because now it seems even more important to understand Canada before that venture began. Ours is not a linear history five hundred years long. It is, rather, a story of geographical fragments with, to be sure, some bonds among them and some underlying elements of common structures. Perhaps such Canadian realities are particularly accessible to a geographer's gaze. *Canada Before Confederation* was one attempt to write a geographical synthesis at the scale of the country, the *Historical Atlas of Canada* is another, and John and I would both hold that the country requires more.

Cole Harris
U.B.C., Valentine's Day, 1991

PREFACE

More than sixty years ago, when Hugh Egerton wrote the preface to the second volume of an *Historical Geography of Canada* (part of Sir Charles Lucas's series *Historical Geography of the British Colonies*), he owned that, whatever the term historical geography had meant to Sir Charles, the volumes in the series were histories, albeit histories laying particular stress on the influence of physical factors such as climate and landform on the course of events. This is still a common and rewarding view of the way geography may be linked to history, but as it is only a part of our view of historical geography, we might well begin by explaining what we mean by the term. Geography is a synthesizing field, concerned, as one geographer has said, with "the varying character of the surface of the earth as the home of man." Geographers seek to understand the actual settled land (the landscape, some geographers would say), the differing character of the earth's surface (regional variety), and the complex, interlacing relationships between man and land. Only one aspect of this last concern is the influence of physical nature on man, and geographers now recognize that most of even these physical influences are filtered by man's heavy cultural conditioning. Algonkians and Europeans lived in the same St. Lawrence lowland, experienced the same landforms and much the same climate, but responded to common influences in radically different ways. And man also creates his environments: the landscape of present-day Southern Ontario is largely the product of human activity, which in turn influences the people who live in it. To a considerable extent man is a captive of his own creations.

When a geographer expresses interest in the theme of man and land he is thinking of these many relationships, not simply of the influence on the course of human events of a highly abstract nature conceived as separate from and uninfluenced by man.

Historical geographers have the same interests that other geographers have except that they tend to ask questions about the past. They too are interested in the regions and landscapes of human life and in the enormous theme of man and land, but are more likely to examine the villages and trading patterns of the Hurons or the relationship between the building of the Grand Trunk Railway and the growth of Toronto in the 1850s than the effect of the St. Lawrence Seaway or the proposed jumbo airport on Toronto. Of course, the historical geographer cannot ignore man nor can he treat him as one member of an equation. The regions and landscapes an historical geographer studies are human creations; to understand something of them is to understand something of their creators. This is precisely the fascination of geography; it is an approach to the study of man, and it is characteristic of this approach that it brings the imprint of man on the surface of the earth to the center of attention. Because historical geographers are so inevitably bound up with the study of man they must be, to a considerable extent, social or economic historians. Moreover, history and geography share a common interest in synthesis, which makes the literature in each field mutually accessible and complementary. The difference between history and historical geography is a difference in emphasis: a geographer's interest in the imprint of man on land, in the regions and landscapes of human life, and, growing inevitably out of this, his interest in the theme of man and land brings to the center of his attention considerations that most historians relegate to the peripheries.

This historical geography of Canada treats the area that became Canada from the time of modern European contact at the end of the fifteenth century to Confederation in 1867. It is concerned with the European rather than the indigenous inhabitants of Canada, partly because of our incompetence to comment on the geography of Indian or Eskimo life, but also because, for better or for worse, the developments in this period that transformed the geography of Canada were triggered by Europeans. We end with Confederation out of prudence. Thereafter, forces relating to urbanization and industrialization loomed much larger. Neither of us has made a study of these general trends, and the geographical literature of this period of Canadian development is still almost non-existent—an impossible base, we thought, for the conjecture that would be forced upon us. The decision to terminate the study at Confederation, is partly the choice of a well-known date that fits all our regions fairly well, but we have also considered that Confederation and its promise of inter-colonial railways symbolized a general shift in the scale of Canadian life and for this reason agreed that an important political date could logi-cally conclude a geographical study. We are also mindful of the stresses in Confederation today, which seem to suggest that an examination of what we were when that adventure began would not now be amiss.

Bibliographies at the end of each chapter indicate, as far as brief indi-cation is possible, the sources used in the preparation of each chapter. The text has not been footnoted, with the exception of Chapter 6, The Western Interior: 1800-1870, which is based largely on primary sources in the Hudson's Bay Company archives.

In writing this book we have relied on our own research, on the small published literature on the historical geography of Canada, on the work of many economic and social historians, and on a rapidly growing body of B.A., M.A., and Ph.D. theses on aspects of the early geography of Canada. Five years ago this book probably could not have been written, and even today there are enormous gaps in our understanding of the early geography of Canada that only research will fill. An early decision we had to make was not to write a book that reiterates the need for re-search on topic after topic. Rather we have attempted to write a compre-hensive and deliberately provocative synthesis. At this stage in the geo-graphical study of early Canada there is not a large enough pool of solid work to warrant a cautious interpretation, and we hope that read-ers who reject parts of our interpretation will do the research to prove us wrong.

The conception and general organization of the book is the work of both of us, but each of us has been responsible for specific chapters. Chapter 5 (The Atlantic Region) and Chapter 6 (The Western Interior) are by John Warkentin, the rest of the book is by Cole Harris. Each of us has approved the work of the other, but the research and writing have been undertaken independently. While responsibility for the book is ours, the contributions of colleagues in geography and history have been so numerous that in retrospect the book appears as the composite undertaking of a great many people. The following have our special thanks: Grant Head, Conrad Heidenreich, and Eric Ross, who com-mented on the introductory chapter; Louise Dechêne, W. J. Eccles, and

Jean-Pierre Wallot, whose critiques of the chapters on French Canada were invaluable; Jim Cameron, Michael Cross, Peter Ennals, Louis Gentilcore, James Lemon, Frances Mellen, James Simmons, C. F. Whebell, and Graeme Wynn, without whose assistance the chapter on Ontario could hardly have been written; Ian Brookes, Andrew Clark, David Erskine, and Graeme Wynn, who provided insight and special knowledge on the Atlantic region; Barry Kaye and A. R. Ray, who commented on the chapter on the Western Interior; Richard C. Harris Sr. who, knowing his native province far better than does his son, did much of the research for the chapter on British Columbia; Margaret Ormsby, J. L. Robinson, Bill Ross, and Keith Ralston, who made helpful suggestions on it; and Allan Smith, who commented on the conclusion. The assistance of the National Archives in Ottawa, through its excellent service in the manuscript and map divisions and the special study space that it provided has been much appreciated by us both. The Governor and Committee of the Hudson's Bay Company kindly permitted access to their archives and granted permission to publish redrawn versions of maps in their collection.

Vancouver and Toronto   R. C. H.
November 1973   J. W.

FOREWORD

The second largest country in the world is in no danger of running out of territory or of many of the basic resources that its relatively small population uses. There is, however, surprisingly little of the kind of land on which Canadians are able or willing to live. It may well be that most Canadians, residing as they do in the mosaics of squalor and grandeur that are the Canadian cities, have a less than lucid perception of the role of the vast territories in Canada's past or present. I am by no means sure that the conventional political, social, and economic histories of the country can clarify that role without assistance. Early on, Canadian historiography had a great infusion of geographical blood from Harold Innis and some of his students, but much of that spirit has since been diverted into more limited and esoteric channels. The blossoming of a new, meticulously researched historical geography in the past quarter-century, however, has given us the opportunity to look at Canada in a new way, by viewing the country's changing geography throughout the years.

The two authors of *Canada Before Confederation: A Study in Historical Geography* have spearheaded much of the new kind of study of geographical change that has made the writing of this book possible. In their preface they cogently argue that history and geography share a common interest in synthesis, and in this first roughing-out of a framework for the study of Canada's historical geography on a national scale, they have combined the two disciplines with considerable skill.

Professor Harris received much of his education in his native province by the Pacific, and, after further study in France and the United States, he taught for many years at the University of Toronto. Now on the faculty of the University of British Columbia, he divides his interests between his home region, where his English roots are deeply set, and French Canada. His ground-breaking *The Seigneurial Regime in Early Canada: A Geographical Study* his been followed by extensive research on Québec after the Conquest. Professor Warkentin, a son of one of Manitoba's vigorous Mennonite communities, teaches at York University in Metropolitan Toronto and has broadly catholic interests in his native country, where he received all of his education. His wide interests are reflected in his editing of the Canadian Association of Geographers' authoritative compendium: *Canada: A Geographical Interpretation*. But his major interests are in the continental interior, especially in its scientific exploration throughout the years; his concern is with the information that the explorers took with them and with the feedback from their activities that helped to shape the changing view of the geography of North America in the rest of the world (see *The Western Interior of Canada: A Record of Geographical Discovery 1612-1917*).

Rough Rock Lake   Andrew Hill Clark
Minaki, Ontario
July 1973.

CANADA BEFORE CONFEDERATION

1 THE EUROPEAN PENETRATION

OF CANADA

The northeastern coast of North America was visited by Norsemen at the beginning of the eleventh century and perhaps by European fishermen four and a half centuries later. The major rediscovery came late in the fifteenth century when explorers searching for a direct sea route to Asia touched land. Like Columbus, John Cabot believed that his landfall in 1497 on the coast of either Cape Breton Island or Newfoundland had brought him to "Cathay," or northern China. Cabot went down with his ship in 1498 while on a second voyage to establish a spice trade in the newly discovered lands. But during the next decade the Corte Real brothers, João Fernandes, and perhaps John Cabot's son Sebastian explored parts of the northeastern North American coast without finding any trace of the Chinese empire. With the negative results of these voyages Europeans began to suspect that the newly discovered land lay between Europe and Asia. The conceptual discovery of North America was being made, and with it the search began for a passage through the new land to Asia. In 1524 Giovanni da Verrazano, sailing for France, made the first continuous voyage along the coast between Florida and Cape Breton; a few months later Estévan Gomez repeated the feat for Spain, and the Englishman John Rut may have sailed along the same coast in 1527. These voyages established that a fairly continuous coastline lay between the landfalls of Columbus and Cabot (see Fig. 1-1). There were still gaps in the map of the coast, each of which could prove to be the entrance to a western ocean, but after Verrazano and Gomez the principal search for a water route to the Orient was directed farther north.

By this time placer gold had been found in the Caribbean, gold and silver ornaments and plate were flowing to Spain from the conquered Aztec and Inca empires, and the search for a route around the new lands was overshadowed by a rush to explore them. In 1534 Francis I, king of France, authorized Jacques Cartier "to discover certain islands and lands where it is said that a great quantity of gold and other precious things is to be found." The results of the three Cartier voyages over the next eight years and of an attempt at colonizing by the sieur de Roberval, Cartier's associate in the Canadian venture, were considerable: discovery of the Gulf of St. Lawrence and of the St. Lawrence River; an impression of the Indians and of the agricultural potential of the St. Lawrence valley; experience with a northern winter; and the belief that the St. Lawrence might provide a river route to Asia. But the cargo of gold and diamonds Cartier took back to France proved to be iron pyrites and quartz crystals, and because the French still viewed the new lands in Spanish terms, their interest waned. The explorations of Cartier belong with those of Coronado and De Soto; all three penetrated deeply into the continent but none of them found the gold they sought. They did reveal enough of the new land to make it clear that there were no new Mexicos or Perus ripe for the plucking.

Much of the newly discovered land was discouragingly bleak. Cartier found not "one cartload of earth" along the north shore of the Gulf of St. Lawrence, and the coasts of Labrador and Newfoundland were generally no more inviting. "I think," wrote Cartier, "that this is the land which God gave as his portion to Cain." A severe continental climate, the bitter Labrador current, and the scouring effects of recent continental glaciation had created a coastline along the eastern rim of the Canadian Shield that is still among the least settled in the middle latitudes. Cartier was much more impressed with the south shore of the Gulf of St. Lawrence—especially where he touched on Prince Edward Island—and with the St. Lawrence valley. To the south, perhaps along the coast of North Carolina, Verrazano was sufficiently enchanted with the land to name it Arcadia; but in the sixteenth century, plantation crops and gold whetted European interest in North America, and not even the promise of a New World Arcadia could attract settlers.

The one northern resource that held European interest came from the off-shore waters. John Cabot had noted that the seawaters around Newfoundland were swarming with fish, and within four or five years of his first voyage (if not before it) English, Breton, and Portuguese fishermen sailed there regularly to fish for cod. They were attracted by an immense fishing ground in the shallow waters over the continental shelf where the mixing of arctic and subtropical currents provides nutrients for the vast quantities of plankton needed to support a large fish population. The impetus to exploit the Newfoundland grounds came from European demands for protein. At the beginning of the sixteenth century, the population of Europe and the prices of agricultural products, particularly cereals, were rising rapidly. Farmers converted meadows and pastures to arable (plowland) to take advantage of the cereal prices, real wages were dropping, and a cheap substitute for meat was in demand. The techniques of fishing in the North Atlantic and the necessary seamanship already had been developed; and it was little more difficult, for example, for a Portuguese fisherman to sail to Newfoundland than to Iceland. When the fish resources of the northwestern Atlantic became known, much of the manpower of the fishery swung westward to connect one of the world's largest concentrations of edible fish to the European market. The Spanish fleet to the northwest Atlantic in 1553 was reported to be 200 vessels strong, in 1578 it was described as "above 100 sail"—two-thirds the size of the French fleet—and early in the next century the English fishery in Newfoundland waters employed several thousand men each year.

The cod fishery was conducted by fishermen operating out of scores of ports around much of the North Atlantic rim. Considered as a whole, the fishery became an approximately radial system focused on a relatively small area of the western Atlantic, principally on the banks (the shallower parts of the continental shelf) off Newfoundland and Nova Scotia and the adjacent inshore waters. Over-all control of the fishermen was possible neither in the many small ports from which they sailed nor on the fishing grounds where they came most closely together. Consequently the fishery was extremely divisive. It was international rather than national, competitive rather than monopolistic, and its regulation was always extremely difficult. The pre-emptive system whereby the first captain in a port became its admiral for the season and distributed fishing rights was widely and successfully resisted, particularly by fishermen who were not English. The system had no impact at all on the many fishermen who made the round trip from Europe with little or no contact with the land. When settlement of the mainland began, fortifications were taken and retaken, settlements were razed and rebuilt. The balance between the principal competitors was constantly shifting. An individual fishing crew sailing from home port to fishing ground and back again had little contact with other fishermen, and it was largely for this reason that West Country English and Irish folk cultures survived for generations in adjacent outports in Newfoundland.

Focused as it was on the continental shelf, the cod fishery had little landward momentum. As long as a wet cure was used—the cod headed, split, gutted, stored in the hold between layers of salt, and dried in the home port in Europe—many of the fishing ships made the round trip without landing in the New World. Yet early in the English and French fisheries, perhaps even before 1550, a more efficient dry cure was also used. Drying took place on shore where the cod were headed, split, lightly salted, and laid out to dry on a cobble beach or on wooden platforms. This technique required timber each year for drying platforms (flakes) and landing stages. On shore the crews required firewood, bark for constructing temporary shelters, and dinnage (dry branches and twigs) to protect the fish they dried from condensation and leaks in the hold. As a result the coastal forests were quickly stripped. In the 1580s a young Hungarian who accompanied Sir Humphry Gilbert to St. John's harbor (Newfoundland) had noted a forest—undoubtedly the spruce, fir, birch, and poplar tangle of the boreal forest—that was almost too dense to walk in. By 1622 it was noted that "the woods along the coasts are so spoyled by the fishermen that it is a great pity to behold them, and without redress undoubtedly will be the ruine of this good land. For they wastefully bark, fell and leave more wood behind them to rot than they use about their stages although they employ a world of wood upon them." Forest fires started by the fishermen were probably even more damaging. Although the influence of Europeans on the native flora and fauna of the northeastern rim of North America may have been almost as devastating as in the islands and perimeter of the Caribbean, it was at least confined to a narrow belt of land along the shore. The continental penetration of the fishery was slight.

In most ways the cod fishery was the antithesis of the fur trade, a continental enterprise that led to the first European penetration of Canada. The fur trade brought Europeans and natives together as the fishery had not, it tended toward monopoly and the standardization of technology and culture over wide areas. It led to an extensive knowledge of inland areas, and the structure it created extended the full breadth of the northern continent.

Through the fishery the Europeans had come into contact with the

Beothuk Indians of Newfoundland, "evil folk" whom the fishermen detested and hunted. Undoubtedly fishermen had also encountered Algonkian and Eskimo peoples in the Gulf of St. Lawrence, but the rarity of European trade goods dating earlier than the late sixteenth century in Algonkian sites and the absence of such goods from Iroquoian sites in Ontario indicate how rare these contacts were in the century after Cabot's voyage. At this time three broad linguistic groups lived in northeastern North America: Eskimos, distinct in physical race as well as culture, who lived in an area extending from the north shore of the Gulf of St. Lawrence near the Strait of Belle Isle along the Labrador coast and westward through the Arctic to the mouth of the Mackenzie River; Algonkians, a mixed group of peoples united chiefly by linguistic affiliations, who lived in a broad belt from the present Maritimes and New England to the Rocky Mountains; and Iroquoians, who occupied much of the St. Lawrence valley and the land immediately north and south of Lake Erie and Lake Ontario. European explorers and traders had few dealings with the Eskimos before the late nineteenth century; but the Algonkians and Iroquoians were caught inescapably in the European penetration of the northern half of the continent. The Algonkians were scattered for the most part in small bands of a few to a hundred or more families at river or lakeside around the watery southern fringe of the Canadian Shield. They were migratory, a hunting and fishing people whose birch-bark canoes in summer and toboggans and snowshoes in winter gave them great mobility in a land of rushing streams, lakes, and prolonged cold. The Iroquoians lived in palisaded agricultural villages of up to several thousand inhabitants. The women cultivated corn, beans, and squash in fields the men had cleared, and the men traded surplus corn and other items, fished, hunted, and fought their neighbors. This way of life created some of the highest population densities in pre-Columbian North America. There were perhaps 25,000 people between Lake Simcoe and Georgian Bay in the villages of the Huron Confederacy, more in the villages of the Neutrals and Petuns to the south and west, and perhaps 12,000 people immediately south of Lake Ontario and Lake Erie in the five "nations," which together constituted the League of the Iroquois.

The tribes and clans in which most of these peoples lived were tied together in an intricate web of relationships created by the demands of war and trade. War was an adventure, a skill in raiding was a source of prestige. When a man was killed, members of his family demanded pay-

ments or took revenge on the family of the killer; these blood feuds disrupted intertribal relations for generations. Prisoners of war were often
tortured to death to revenge some earlier killing. Trade, which took place
between military allies, was usually inaugurated and maintained by
elaborate ceremony, speech-making, and the exchange of presents and
hostages. Once a family or clan had established connections and opened
a route of trade, the route was its property. Among the Iroquoians these
arrangements were controlled by the confederacy and any change in the
trading pattern threatened the intertribal military structure. In this
tangle of intertribal relations European fur traders played an increasing
and only partially comprehending role in the last half of the sixteenth
century.

In 1534 Cartier had traded a few furs; by the middle of the sixteenth
century the fur trade had become an established adjunct to the cod
fishery. In the last decade of the century a succession of Frenchmen
obtained exclusive (but in fact usually overlapping and unenforceable)
privileges in the fur trade, and by the end of the century both English
and French showed some interest in settling the St. Lawrence valley.
Their motives were mixed. The Englishman Edward Hayes, who accompanied Sir Humphry Gilbert on his last voyage to Newfoundland and
wrote a full account of it, argued that a settlement in the St. Lawrence
valley could be built up on the profits of the fur trade to provide a base
for a river connection with the Pacific. The Huguenot Chauvin de Ton-
netuit, who established a short-lived settlement at Tadoussac at the
mouth of the Saguenay in 1600, was a fur trader. The effort by the Sieur
de Monts, a Huguenot who had been granted New France in 1604, to
establish a colony in Acadia was influenced by Champlain's interest in a
report of mines in the area and by the latter's hope that a route to the
Orient might be found there. These motives may have been weighed
when De Monts decided—again on Champlain's advice—to move the
colony to the St. Lawrence, but undoubtedly the first objective was to
establish a base for the fur trade in a promising area where competition
could be controlled.

The founding of Québec on the St. Lawrence River in 1608 established the French on one of the four principal Atlantic entries to North
America. Of the others the Mississippi was too far south to tap the best
furs, but the entries by the Hudson River and Hudson Bay were soon to
draw on much of the same hinterland as did the St. Lawrence. The low
heights of land that facilitated expansion out of the St. Lawrence basin
also increased the competition within it. The principal advantages for

French fur traders along the St. Lawrence were close contact with the Algonkians and their skills, and plentiful supplies of white birch for canoes. Cartier had been stopped at the Lachine rapids in 1534, as were his great-nephew Jacques Noël in 1585, and Champlain when he first visited Canada in 1603. But by 1610 Champlain had sent a French lad to live with the Algonkians along the lower Ottawa, an act which from the Indian point of view provided a hostage and an indication of French good will, and from that of the French, an eventual interpreter and an informant on Indian lore. The traders were beginning to acquire a knowledge of the Indians and of Indian skills that would permit them to move far into the interior. In 1613 Champlain explored the Ottawa River and in 1615–16 he spent the winter in Huronia. The French had formed an alliance with the Algonkians and the Hurons that guaranteed the hostility of the League of the Iroquois, and was to lead to almost a century of intermittent warfare; but given Champlain's interest in the fur trade and exploration, he had no choice but to side with the Indians whose situation and skills could open the west to him. By the time of Champlain's death in 1635, Frenchmen had seen Lake Michigan and Lake Superior (see Fig. 1-1), Jesuit priests had lived with the Hurons for years, and the technical basis of the St. Lawrence fur trade for the next 200 years had been laid.

The St. Lawrence trade depended on Indians for hunting, trapping, and preparing furs, and on Indian skills and customs for much of the actual conduct of the trade. The coureurs de bois (independent French traders), who became common in the interior after the Iroquois League defeated the Huron in 1649, relied on Indian woodlore to survive in the bush. The birch-bark canoe became their vehicle. The French accepted the importance of ceremony, presents, and the military implications of trading alliances, and this sensitivity to the Indian concept of trade gave them a great advantage over their European competitors. Perhaps they had borrowed so much because the independence of Indian life attracted them, or because as seventeenth-century Catholics they were more concerned to proselytize among the Indians than were the Protestants; but primarily, it was because, to be successful, St. Lawrence traders had to be mobile enough to strike out into the interior. Away from the protection of the palisade they had to know how to deal with the Indians and, in a strange environment, to rely on Indian knowledge and skills. The basic techniques of the St. Lawrence fur trade did not change when Scots, Englishmen, and New Englanders gained control of it in the 1770s.

In committing themselves to the St. Lawrence River and the birch-

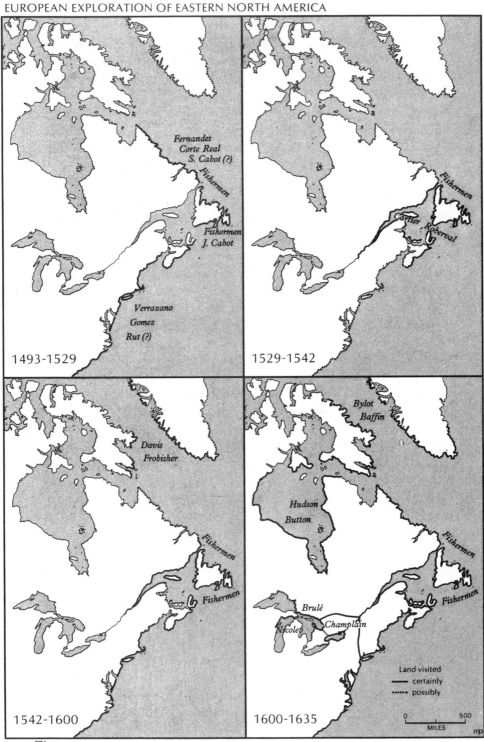

1493-1529

Fernandes
Corte Real
S. Cabot (?)

Fishermen

Fishermen
J. Cabot

Verrazano
Gomez
Rut (?)

1529-1542

Fishermen

Cartier Roberval

1542-1600

Davis
Frobisher

Fishermen

Fishermen

1600-1635

Bylot
Baffin

Hudson
Button

Fishermen

Brulé

Nicolet

Champlain

Fishermen

Land visited
—— certainly
····· possibly

0   600
MILES

mp

Figure 1-1.

bark canoe, the French developed a linear trading pattern that was inherently expansionistic, vulnerable to outside competition, and internally monopolistic. The axis of the fur trade extended from the French channel port to Québec, and from there westward up the St. Lawrence and Ottawa rivers, to branch eventually in an increasingly complex pattern as it approached the source of furs. Over the years the axis lengthened until at the end of the St. Lawrence trade in the early nineteenth century, Montréal was roughly a midpoint. For more than a century there was a divide at Michilimakinac—one branch turning south into Lake Michigan, the other northwest into Lake Superior—and through much of the French regime there was an illegal but substantial seepage southward from Montréal. But the over-all linear structure which had emerged even in Champlain's day was maintained until the collapse of the St. Lawrence fur trade in 1821.

Furs were quickly hunted out along the axis of the trade; and the easiest way to find more, even without the pressure from traders around Hudson Bay and at Albany, was to push farther into the interior. Such expansion created a fragile lifeline that could be easily cut. The Iroquois repeatedly stopped the flow of furs to Montréal by sealing off the Ottawa River route; similarly, more than a century later in 1819, employees of the Hudson's Bay Company crippled the Montréal-based Northwest Company (the Nor'westers) by seizing the wintering partners and their furs as they made the Grand Rapids portage on the Saskatchewan River. Because of the linear structure a single, well-planned move could have devastating effect, and for this as much as for reasons of logistics, interior forts were soon an essential part of the St. Lawrence trading system. Internally the linear pattern favored monopoly control. The late sixteenth-century monopolies for trade in the Gulf had been unenforceable, but as soon as the trade moved into the river, monopoly privileges acquired their intended bite. Although there were frequent periods of competition in the long life of the St. Lawrence trade, the drift was back toward monopoly. The final violent struggle early in the nineteenth century between the Northwest and the XY companies grew out of the inability of a linear, continental trading structure to support competition.

While this structure was taking shape along the St. Lawrence, English interest revived in the Northwest Passage. In 1576 the swashbuckling gentleman privateer, Martin Frobisher, sailed in quest of it, and in the next fifty years a dozen voyages—most of them characterized by unbelievable hardship and courage—revealed the outlines of Hudson Bay and of the long ice-clogged passage between Baffin Island and Greenland. When Luke Foxe sailing in 1631 for London merchants and Thomas James sailing in the same year for Bristol competitors agreed—contrary to several tantalizing previous reports—that there was no current from the west in Foxe Channel, Englishmen finally concluded that the North-west Passage did not exist, and to all intents and purposes they dropped the search for it for over 200 years. Yet the most northerly of the Atlantic entries to North America had been discovered and mapped, and when the Canadian traders Médard Chouart, sieur des Groseilliers, and Pierre Esprit Radisson told a curious Stuart court that the route by the Bay led to the best furs in North America and could be exploited at great profit, enough geographical information was at hand to make their scheme plausible. The English had tasted the profit of the fur trade in 1629 when the adventurer David Kirke and his brothers captured Québec, and subsequently in Acadia from 1654 to 1670, and there had been a good deal of theorizing at court about the importance for the imperial economy of controlling trade routes and of balancing southern with northern territories. On both these counts the Canadians' proposal was attractive. A probing voyage in 1668 brought a handsome return, and in 1670 the Hudson's Bay Company came into existence with its governor and associated merchant adventurers made proprietors of Rupert's Land, the vast drainage basin of Hudson Bay.

In its first year the Company built a fort at the mouth of the Rupert River, and had several forts in James Bay and others as far west as the Churchill River before the end of the century. Despite great individual feats of exploration, particularly Henry Kelsey's exploration of the Saskatchewan in 1690 and William Stewart's journey to Great Slave Lake in 1730, the Company did not carry the fur trade to the interior. Fort Henley, built a hundred miles up the Albany River in 1743, was abandoned twelve years later, and but for sporadic attempts to re-establish this fort, the Company did not budge from its "sleep by the frozen sea" until the 1770s. The massive and ineffective fort built at Churchill early in the eighteenth century symbolized a defensive marine orientation, and a pattern of trade that in many ways was the opposite of that from the St. Lawrence.

The drainage basin of Hudson Bay is four times as large as that of the St. Lawrence, and a few forts on the Bay could draw furs from most of this vast area. Each river-mouth fort commanded a different fur region, and a roughly radial trading pattern developed, focused on the Bay and drawing furs in a wide arc from what is now central Québec to the Keewatin District of the Northwest Territories. As any one route produced only a fraction of the total trade of the Bay, the incentive to push inland was less than along the St. Lawrence. Were the trade interrupted at one fort, there would still be trade at the others, and until competition extended around much of the perimeter of the Hudson Bay drainage basin, the Company did not have to move inland. In the St. Lawrence trade a challenge to a single fort or route far in the interior would elicit a lightning response, but as Pierre Radisson and Médard Chouart had told the English Restoration court, the Bay was better placed for the fur trade, and Company factors could wait at bayside for the natural drain of the late spring thaw to bring an annual supply of furs.

Partly for this reason, relations between Company employees and the Indians were not nearly as close as those between the Indians and the St. Lawrence traders. Moreover, most Company employees were cautious and prudent Presbyterians from the Orkney Islands, sound managers of their own property and dependable employees, but temperamentally a world apart from the Indians or even the French Canadians. Many of them had been hired on three-year contracts and had come to the Bay in their early middle age. They had had no boyhood experience with canoes, and knew no Indian languages. For many years the Company frowned on their cohabitation with Indian women. In the late seventeenth century and throughout much of the eighteenth century Company employees usually remained aloof from the Indians, rarely learning Indian languages fluently or mustering the bravado or rhetoric that Indians admired and St. Lawrence traders possessed in good measure. Much of the trade at the Bay was conducted through a hole in a fort wall after little or no ceremony. It is noteworthy that the Company's first attempt to establish an inland post ended when Indians surprised and murdered the traders.

In the first forty years of the Bay trade, control of forts fluctuated between French and English, and intense international competition might have continued much longer had it been easier to reach the Bay. The forts themselves were vulnerable to marine attack, and as each commanded a different hinterland, the spatial structure of the trade did not favor a monopolistic organization. The bottleneck, however, was the entrance to the Bay through Hudson Strait, and in the long run, English experience with this difficult route and skill in high-latitude sailing protected their monopoly.

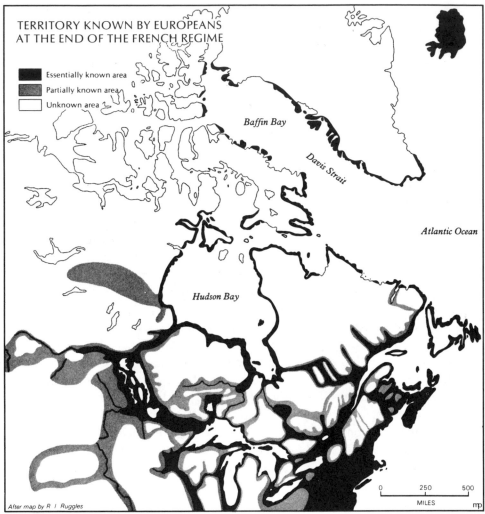

Figure 1-2.

While employees of the Hudson's Bay Company sat by the Bay, traders from the St. Lawrence had broken through the Shield to the northern plains. In the late 1730s they built three forts on Lake Winnipeg, and in the 1740s and 1750s built several more on the Saskatchewan River. These were well-planned moves, based on a growing knowledge of the interior (see Fig. 1-2), which took them over 2000 canoe-miles from Montréal. There in the heart of the continent they tended to trade light goods for light valuable furs such as marten and otter; they still took large quantities of the best beaver, but heavier goods and the heavier bulkier furs, including most of the beaver, were traded at the Bay. To some extent the land-based and expansionistic system of the Canadians, and the maritime and defensive system of the English were complementary. Yet by this time Canadian traders were encroaching on most of the perimeter of the Hudson Bay drainage basin, and the Hudson's Bay Company slowly responded to their challenge. In 1735 Anthony Henday returned to the Bay with more than sixty canoes and a great wealth in furs from the upper Saskatchewan. Similar expeditions followed in the 1760s, and in 1774 the Company built Fort Cumberland on the Saskatchewan. By the 1790s its posts on Rainy Lake, Lake of the Woods, and Lake Winnipeg lay athwart the trading lifeline from Montréal. During this expansion from the Bay, the York boat, a broad keel boat that drew approximately three feet and carried up to four tons of freight, became a mainstay of interior travel from the Bay. Although slower and much heavier than a canoe, it was more rugged and stable, required less skill to handle, and reduced costs when portages were few. Neither fast nor mobile enough for the St. Lawrence trade, the York boat was well suited to builders from the Orkney Islands who were not skilled canoemen, who did not have ready supplies of birch bark, and who traveled relatively short distances inland.

Even so, at the end of the eighteenth century the value of the St. Lawrence trade was several times that of the Bay. In 1779 Peter Pond had crossed from the Saskatchewan to the Mackenzie drainage basin, garnering some 80,000 prime beaver skins from Chipewyan and Slave Indians near Lake Athabaska. Ten years later Alexander Mackenzie descended the Mackenzie River to the Arctic Ocean, and in 1792 he followed the upper Fraser and Bella Coola rivers to the Pacific. The St. Lawrence fur trade had expanded into the last major untapped source of furs on the continent. In so doing its lifeline had become almost 3000 miles long, several times the distance from Hudson Bay to the same trading area. This expansion had been achieved by a superb organization run with dash and ruthlessness. Roads were built around portages on the Ottawa River, a canal at Sault Ste-Marie, and ships supplemented canoes on Lake Superior. The supply base at Michilimakinac was moved forward to Grand Portage on Lake Superior at the mouth of the Pigeon River route to the Lake of the Woods and Lake Winnipeg, and after 1802–3 to Fort William. Pemmican and wild rice from the Rainy River —Lake of the Woods area replaced corn as the portable staple of the voyageurs (canoemen in a fur brigade, usually French Canadians). Wintering partners returned in the spring to Grand Portage, exchanged furs for bales of trade goods, and were off in a few days for the northwest. Yet the locational advantage clearly lay with the trade through the Bay, which could be supplied directly by sea and which lay much closer than the St. Lawrence to the prime fur areas. By 1810 the Hudson's Bay Company was reorganizing for a major push into the Athabaska region, even recruiting voyageurs in Canada; and the difference between the skill of its traders and those from the St. Lawrence had diminished greatly. In this deteriorating situation, Lord Selkirk, who had strong financial interests in the Bay Company, planted a settlement in 1812 of Irish and Scots directly across the supply route of the Northwest Company. Nor'westers and settlers soon clashed, and in 1816 the massacre of twenty settlers at Seven Oaks provoked extensive legal battles that threatened to damage both companies. All the while the volume of furs passing through Montréal declined steadily until the merger of the two companies in 1821 virtually stopped the flow in this channel. Always expansionistic and vulnerable to outside competition, the trade out of Montréal collapsed when it ran out of fresh territory to exploit and faced aggressive competition from the Bay.

By the time the St. Lawrence trade was absorbed into the Hudson's Bay Company, the fur trade had established a British presence across the northern half of North America. In so doing it gave some resistance to the northward territorial expansion of the United States. The boundary agreements of 1783, 1818, and 1846 that created most of the present border between Canada and the United States reflected the negotiated balance at each date between the American perception of settlement opportunities and the British interest in the fur trade. Where American settlement, or American perception of the opportunity for settlement, preceded the boundary treaty, as in the Middle West or in the Oregon country, former fur-trading territory passed to the United States. Elsewhere, the land opened up by the trade from the St. Lawrence and Hudson Bay remained in British hands. The principal waterways in this territory had been discovered and used. Four major physiographic regions— the St. Lawrence–Great Lakes lowland, the Canadian Shield, the plains, and the cordillera—had been revealed. In a general way the nature of the Canadian climate was known. Agriculture had been attempted successfully at many forts. An extensive land use based on a single dominant resource had established that the northern half of North America was of some value, and that Europeans could live in it. It had opened half a continent and set a stage for subsequent developments. When other land uses were contemplated the discovery and utilization of the Canadian land proceeded in ways that often effaced any physical traces of the fur trade. There remained the territory of the fur trade—a vast, diverse area that had been organized in one transcontinental system but that would not necessarily fit into another.

Bibliography

There is a large and often excellent literature on the topics summarized in this short chapter, and this bibliography suggests only a few of the more important, accessible materials of general interest. An over-all survey by geographers is in the A. H. Clark–D. Q. Innis article "The Roots of Canada's Geography," in John Warkentin (ed.), *Canada: A Geographical Interpretation* (Agincourt, Ont.: Methuen Publications, 1968), pp. 13–56. Another useful survey article, "The Northern Approaches to Canada," by T. J. Oleson and W. L. Morton is in the *Dictionary of Canadian Biography*, vol. I (Toronto: University of Toronto Press, 1966), pp. 16–21. Taken together, the essays on individual explorers in this volume comprise a substantial contribution to the study of early Canadian exploration. Samuel Eliot Morison's *The European Discovery of America: The Northern Voyages, A.D. 500–1600* (New York: Oxford University Press, 1971) presents a comprehensive account of all the voyages across the Atlantic to the New World before 1600. Harold Innis's study, *The Cod Fisheries: The History of an International Economy* (New Haven: Yale University Press, 1940) remains a monumental work; those who find Innis's detail and style overpowering should read at least the introduction and conclusion. The fur trade now has an enormous bibliography, but there is still no more provocative introduction to this subject than Harold Innis, *The Fur Trade in Canada: An Introduction to Canadian Economic History* (New Haven: Yale University Press, 1930). A more recent survey is in E. E. Rich, *The Fur Trade and the Northwest to 1857* (Toronto: McClelland and Stewart, 1967), while *Beyond the River and the Bay* (Toronto: University of Toronto Press, 1970) by Eric Ross is a charming and illuminating picture of the geography of the northwestern fur trade early in the nineteenth century. Much more specialized is Bruce Trigger's excellent article, "The French Presence in Huronia," *Canadian Historical Review* 49 (June 1968), 107–

41, which treats a pivotal area of the early fur trade and describes a particularly significant instance of the cultural dislocation which the European presence almost everywhere forced on the Indians. The *Manitoba Historical Atlas* (Historical and Scientific Society of Manitoba, 1970), a facsimile collection edited by John Warkentin and Richard Ruggles, is a starting point for a study of the exploration and mapping of the western interior. The cartographic imagination of the West is treated by Richard Ruggles in "The West of Canada in 1763: Imagination and Reality," *The Canadian Geographer* 15 (1971), 235–61.

2 THE FRENCH IMPACT

IN CANADA AND ACADIA

Both Acadia, the colony centered on the Bay of Fundy, and Canada, the colony along the lower St. Lawrence, began as fur-trading ventures. The connection of the early fur trade with the cod fishery, the superior quality of furs to the north, the strength of the Spanish to the south, and the territorial claims based on the explorations of Jacques Cartier led French traders to a northern approach to North America. Both colonies lay along the edge of the boreal forest, near the northern limit of agricultural land, and within the territory of migratory bands of Algonkian Indians. Canada was admirably placed for the fur trade, but neither colony could grow sugar and other low-latitude crops, or even some of the crops of northwestern France. Most Frenchmen who had heard of Canada and Acadia must have perceived of them much as Voltaire once described Canada, that is, as so many acres of snow, and neither colony attracted many settlers.

In the century and a half that it was a French colony, about 10,000 immigrants came to Canada, and no more than 500 to Acadia. Of those who emigrated to Canada, almost 4000 were *engagés* committed, much as were the indentured servants in Virginia, to several years of service to the men who had engaged them. Approximately 3500 were soldiers released from military service. Toward the end of the French regime, 1000 prisoners—salt smugglers for the most part—were sent to Canada, and in the late 1660s as many women had been shipped out to marry. At most, 500 immigrants had come on their own. All but a handful of these settlers were French. They came from all the provinces of France, but

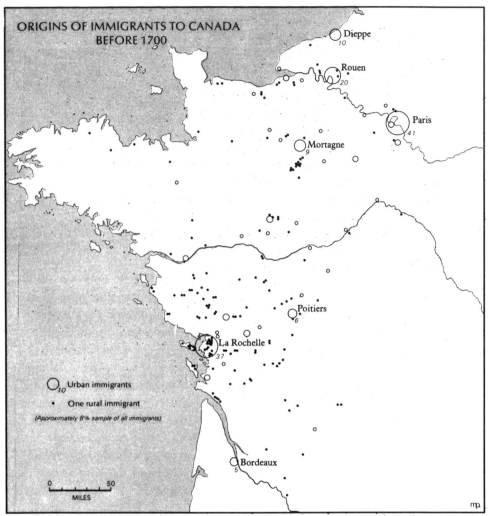

Figure 2-1.

particularly from the west (see Fig. 2-1). More than half of them came
from south of the Loire River, and most of this group from the old provinces of Aunis, Saintonge, and Poitou in the immediate hinterland of La
Rochelle, the principal port of embarkation for Canada. Not more than
one-fifth of the immigrants were Normans. Most of the Acadians came
as engagés, but some were demobilized soldiers or were castoffs from
the Atlantic fishery. There is no evidence that Canadians and Acadians
came from different parts of France.

Just over half of the immigrants were urban people. Paris and La Rochelle alone contributed about 20 per cent of the immigrants, and substantial numbers came from every important town in or near the valley of the lower Seine. Immigrants from south of the Loire were much more likely than those from farther north to have grown up in agricultural villages or hamlets; even so, about half of these rural people were artisans, not farmers or farm laborers. Probably fewer than one-quarter of all the immigrants to Canada had had much previous agricultural experience. Whether rural or urban, most of them were poor, drawn from the lower ranks of French society. They were the sons and daughters of artisans, laborers, farmers, or small shopkeepers. In most cases their security in this modest station of life had been threatened—perhaps by a father's premature death, perhaps by sisters and brothers all with claims on the family patrimony, perhaps by failure to find a job or a husband. Prisoners, girls from the Paris orphanages and poorhouses, and the considerable percentage of soldiers and engagés recruited from among the landless unemployed were available to emigrate precisely because they were already dislocated from their niche in French society. And most of them came to Canada because they were sent. Immigration grew out of official policy decisions rather than individual excitement over the lure of a new land. This was especially true after 1663 when the king's ministers, anxious to hasten Canadian settlement, inaugurated a much more broadside approach to colonization than had been characteristic of the years when Canada was administered by the Company of New France. After 1663 most immigrants crossed the Atlantic as individuals; before that time the nuclear family had been the common unit of immigration and the social and economic status of the immigrants had been somewhat higher.

The people who came to Canada found themselves in a more continental location than any other area of European settlement in eastern North America before the nineteenth century. The colony could not be reached by sea in winter; even in summer it lay almost a thousand shoal-ridden and often foggy miles from the open ocean. Immediately to the north was the Canadian Shield, thirty miles away at Montréal, but less than five at Québec. The hills of the southern edge of the Shield rise only 1000–2000 feet above the St. Lawrence lowland, and were easily penetrated by canoe along the Saguenay, St-Maurice, and Ottawa rivers; but they marked the northern limit of the St. Lawrence valley and, until the end of the eighteenth century, the northern limit of agriculture. To

the south, a little farther away and a little gentler, lie the hills of the
Appalachian highlands. Between the Shield and the Appalachians is the
narrow band of the lower St. Lawrence valley, an area of gently dipping
sedimentary rock overlaid by the sand and clay deposits of the Champlain Sea, which covered the valley in immediate post-glacial times. In
many parts of the lowland these deposits were reworked into shoreline
bars, dunes, and terraces as the Champlain Sea retreated. Cutting
through the middle of the plain is the St. Lawrence River, the second
largest river by volume in North America. Even above Québec it frequently is a mile or more wide, and below the city it widens rapidly
toward the Gulf. At Québec, the river is incised some 200 feet into the
lowland shales, but from Trois-Rivières to Montréal its banks are low.
Beyond Montréal lie the Great Lakes and the heart of the continent
which the French soon learned to reach by birch-bark canoe.

Acadia was a maritime cul de sac without a continental hinterland.
Most of the uplands of the Nova Scotian peninsula and the Fundy shore
of New Brunswick were ice-scoured, hard rock massifs without agricultural potential. The Micmac hunted there and traded furs to the French
settlers in the region (the Acadians), but there was no great river and
little incentive to draw the Acadians themselves inland. Almost all of
them lived at the edge of the tidal marshland within smell of the salt.
Although the Acadians were frequently neglected by both the French
and the English, their location close to the banks fishery and to an axis
of the North Atlantic trade meant that they were never isolated.

For Frenchmen who rarely, if ever, had handled an ax, the forest set
the new land most sharply apart from the old. Open areas—occasional
beaver meadows, a few acres of Indian clearing at Montréal, the tidal
meadows along the lower St. Lawrence and at several points around the
Bay of Fundy—were rare. The Canadian and Acadian forests lay in a
narrow transition zone between the vast broadleaf forests to the south,
and the even more extensive and predominantly coniferous boreal forest.
Around Montréal and in the valley of the Richelieu River an extension
of the American oak–hickory forest comprised a wide variety of deciduous species. Between Lac St-Pierre (the widening of the St. Lawrence
east of Trois-Rivières) and Québec, a beech–maple association included
hemlock, pine, and spruce among its common species; along the lowland
east of Québec, yellow birch and the conifers became more common.
Many lowland species disappeared rapidly along the edge of the Shield
where the forest was predominantly spruce, fir, poplar, and birch.

Throughout the lowland were local climaxes of black spruce and tamarack on poorly drained soils. Around the Fundy shore was a spruce–fir association; farther inland, spruce, pine, and hemlock; in some areas, an association dominated by sugar maple, yellow birch, and fir. Probably most of these forests were not mature, having been burned by lightning fires or by fires set intentionally or accidentally by the Indians. Near the end of the French regime a Canadian *intendant* (the official in charge of civil government) wrote that the Indians were still not easily discouraged from burning the forest to drive game.

Because of the difficulty of clearing the forest, the few open areas assumed an importance out of all proportion to their size. The first meadows and pasture in Canada were the natural grasses along the St. Lawrence, and in Acadia the more extensive marshlands became the focus of almost all settlement. Built by the slow accretion of silt carried by the surging 40-foot tides of the Bay of Fundy, the marshes supported peat mosses, cotton grasses, sedges, horsetails, and willow herb just above the high-water line and a tough, low cord grass below it. Natural pasture and hay were abundant, and when the Acadians had built the log and sod dikes and sluice gates (*aboîteaux*) that let fresh water out and prevented the re-entry of the sea, the marshes also produced twenty to twenty-five bushels of wheat per acre for many years in succession without manuring or deep plowing.

Winters in Canada and Acadia were far more severe than in France. The January mean temperature in Québec and Montréal (10° F) is twenty-five degrees lower, and around the Bay of Fundy fifteen degrees lower than that in Paris. From five to eight feet of snow fell in Acadia each winter, slightly more fell along the lower St. Lawrence, and from mid-December to mid-April, two or more feet of snow lay on the ground. The Bay of Fundy was ice-free, but the St. Lawrence was frozen for three and a half months. Ships from France could not ride out the winter in Canada, and because they had to allow for any early freeze in the fall and to wait for the Gulf of St. Lawrence to clear of pack ice in the spring, the colony was cut off from France for at least six months each year. Summers were more similar to those in northern France. The July means at Montréal (70° F) and Québec (68° F) were both slightly above the Paris mean for the month, while the July mean around the Bay of Fundy was slightly below it. In the face of these climatic differences settlers were uncertain for years about the crops that could be grown successfully. Pear, peach, and walnut trees were killed along the lower St. Lawrence by low winter temperatures. A short growing season of 150 days at Montréal and 130 at Québec made it difficult to ripen Indian corn. The slow-ripening wheats brought over from seventeenth- and early eighteenth-century France did not ripen properly in the shorter summers along the lower St. Lawrence. This was even more true in Acadia where lower summer temperatures strongly favored pasture and livestock. Yet European food preferences were deeply ingrained, and wheat was widely grown in both areas.

The soils of the St. Lawrence lowland had formed out of the clays, sands, and shoreline gravels left by the Champlain Sea. A brown forest soil, easily the most fertile that was accessible to early settlers, developed under the oak–hickory association; a soil less rich in nutrients but still suitable for agriculture was associated with the mixed forest; and a podzol, essentially sterile for agricultural purposes, developed under the coniferous forest of the Shield. Of many azonal soils only the boggy soils on parts of the Montréal plain were fertile when drained. All in all, the soil resources of the lower St. Lawrence were meager. Between the Shield to the northeast and the Appalachian highlands to the south was little enough land, and much of it comprised agriculturally unproductive azonal soils. The Montréal plain was the only substantial area of good soil, but large parts of it had to be drained. The Acadian marshlands were fertile when diked, but the upland soils behind were thin, rocky, and highly podzolized. Only with ample manuring, liming to counteract their acidity, and much labor could they be brought into generous production, and the Acadians rarely bothered to do so.

The Indian population density in Canada and Acadia was no higher than one person for each ten square miles of forest and lake. As noted in the previous chapter, all the Indians in these areas in the seventeenth century spoke Algonkian tongues and lived in small bands practising a migratory, hunting, fishing, and gathering economy. They were expert canoemen, and their use of snowshoes and toboggans on frozen waterways gave them fair mobility even in the dead of winter. Each band was under a chief but, unlike the Iroquois, the Algonkians possessed no larger tribal or intertribal political organization. The Iroquois lived south and west of Canada in what is now upstate New York and Southern Ontario. They were an agricultural people, and their population density was much greater than that of the Algonkians. Their numbers, combined with their intertribal political organization and their strategic location athwart important fur routes, made them a decisive presence.

Acadia

French settlement of the land around the Bay of Fundy began to take on an air of permanence only in the early 1630s. The years following De Monts's establishment on the coast of Maine in 1605 and at Port Royal in 1606 had been a time of intense and often vicious rivalry among French fur traders. On top of this, the English freebooter Samuel Argall sacked the tiny fort at Port Royal in 1613; and in 1628 the Scottish adventurer William Alexander established a settlement there. Yet in 1632 the Treaty of St-Germain-en-Laye recognized French territorial claims to Acadia. Agricultural settlement really began shortly thereafter; and before mid-century the first dikes were built on the marshes at Port Royal. When in 1654 Port Royal was again taken by the English, more than 200 people lived in the settlement. A few of them returned to France after the English takeover, but 350 French-speaking settlers, almost all Acadians by birth, lived along the marshes at Port Royal when the French regained control in 1670.

Throughout these early years, the fur trade drew Acadians and Micmac, the dominant Algonkian people in Acadia, into regular contact. A good deal of French blood was absorbed into the Indian community; a little Indian, probably, into the Acadian. Acadians became adept with birch-bark canoes and snowshoes and probably relied even more heavily on Indian lore about dyes, herbal remedies, and edible roots and berries than did the Canadians. As the Acadians perfected the techniques of farming the marshlands and agriculture became more important to them, the territory and economy of Acadians and Micmacs, although interrelated, became increasingly distinct. Perhaps for this reason, the relationship between a European and an indigenous culture in Acadia was as harmonious as anywhere in North America.

The year after the French regained control of Acadia, a small group led by a prosperous Port Royal farmer established a settlement at Beaubassin at the head of the Chignecto arm of the Bay of Fundy, and a decade later another group left Port Royal for the marshes on Minas Basin. By the end of the century there were several settlements around the head of the Bay (see Fig. 2-2), and the population there was larger than at Port Royal. As undiked marshland was still available in the Port Royal settlement, the preference of Port Royal's younger and more adventurous inhabitants for a location at the head of the Bay appears to

Ile St-Croix. The French settlement at Ile St-Croix is Acadia 1604-5 as depicted in Champlain's *Voyages*. Even in this tiny beginning a rigid French geometry was quickly imposed.

be associated with the desire to be well located for the fur trade (particularly at Beaubassin) and to be accessible without official interference to traders from New England, as much as it was with the attraction of the marshes around the Bay of Fundy. Perhaps the return of French civil authority restricted the freedom of people long accustomed, as one Frenchman put it, "to decide everything for themselves," and they reacted by moving away. Certainly the New England connection had become critical to the Acadians, providing the means for them to exchange furs, feathers, wheat, and livestock for molasses, sugar, brandy, and many essential manufactures that were beyond the scope of Acadian crafts. Often the New Englanders paid in cash, and before the construction of Louisbourg they were the principal source of specie in Acadia. When the governor of Acadia moved to the St. John River in the 1690s he found the Acadians unwilling to supply his garrison for fear of annoy-

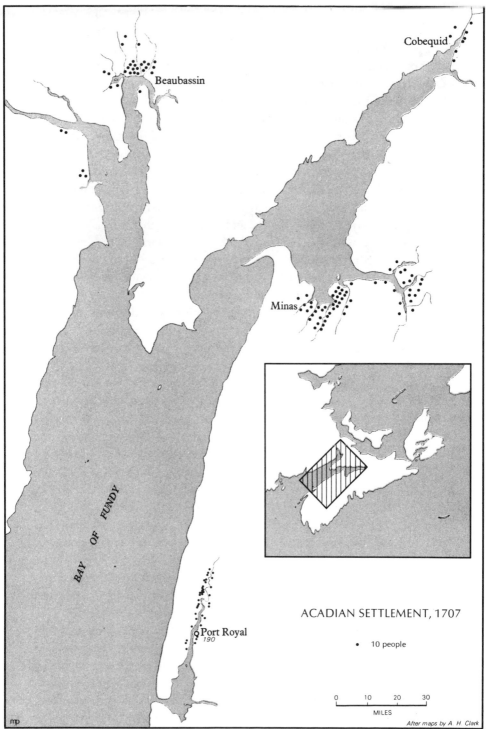

Cobequid

Beaubassin

Minas

BAY OF FUNDY

Port Royal
190

ACADIAN SETTLEMENT, 1707

• 10 people

0   10   20   30
        MILES
After maps by A. H. Clark

mp

Figure 2-2.

ing the New Englanders. Except at Port Royal, officials were powerless
to stop the Yankees from putting in along the coast, and rarely were the
Acadians induced by their threats to buy the more expensive goods that
were intermittently available at the fort.

In 1710 the English captured Port Royal for the final time; and their
sovereignty was confirmed by the Treaty of Utrecht in 1713. English
officials as much as the French before them resented the trade with New
England, which reduced the sale of English manufactured goods and
jeopardized the garrison's provisioning, but, like the French, they could
contain it only at Port Royal. Although the population density increased
on all the marshlands, growth was most rapid on those at the head of
the Bay of Fundy, in Minas Basin, and in Chignecto Bay. Cape Breton
Island remained with the French, who began the fortress of Louisbourg
in 1720. Until the English increased the pressure on them to take the
oath of allegiance in the early 1750s, Acadians did not move to Cape
Breton Island, where the population consisted almost entirely of fishermen scattered along the east coast and the military and merchant establishment of Louisbourg. At mid-century there may have been just over
10,000 Acadians around the Bay of Fundy, another 2500 French-
speaking residents on Cape Breton Island, a sprinkling in fishing stations
along the southeastern shore of Nova Scotia, and a few on Isle St-Jean
(Prince Edward Island). Settlement clustered around the marshlands
of the Bay (see Fig. 2-2), but there was no town and, with the possible
exception of the concentration of troops and administrators around the
fort at Port Royal, no compact village. Within these clusters houses generally were spaced more closely than along the St. Lawrence. Figure 2-3,
taken from Mitchell's survey of the Annapolis River settlement in the
1730s, shows a string of tiny hamlets. The documents that would clarify
the matter were probably lost in the 1750s, but it appears that hamlets
including several farmhouses were the common unit of settlement
throughout the Acadian marshlands. The impetus for such settlements
may have been the need to pool labor to build the dikes; and some hamlets probably were extended family or kin groups as the names on
Mitchell's map—Godet's Village, Village Denis, and so forth—suggest.

In principle, Acadian land was held *en seigneurie* and within seigneuries was subconceded as in Canada. There is no evidence, however, that
a regular cadastral system ever emerged, that seigneurs ever collected
more than a fraction of the charges to which they were legally entitled,
or that, with the possible exception of one seigneurie at Beaubassin, they
provided any of the mills, roads, and courts which were their responsi-

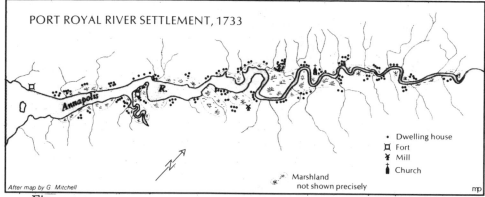

Figure 2-3.

bility. As they had known no other land system in France, the Acadians probably accepted that land was held from a seigneur to whom payments were due. Before 1710 and occasionally thereafter, they made seigneurial payments, often, one suspects, no more than the nominal *cens,* a token payment indicating that land was held from a seigneur and that in uncertain times would seem to provide some guarantee of possession. There were a few notaries before 1710, and priests tried to take their place thereafter, but only a drastically simplified version of French customary law and a few traces of the seigneurial system can ever have existed in Acadia.

Acadian houses were wooden and perhaps most usually were built of posts driven into the ground (*pôteaux* or *pieux en terre*) to make a palisade-like structure that was chinked with clay and eventually covered with boards, or they were built of roughly squared logs laid horizontally and pegged to vertical timbers at the corners and at intervals along the walls (*pièce sur pièce*). Thatch, bark, shingles, or boards were needed for roofing. As in Canada, there were several farm buildings, with stock and farm family living under separate roofs. No one who saw and commented on these buildings was very favorably impressed. One new arrival at Port Royal had to have the church pointed out to him, "as otherwise I would have taken it for a barn." Along the lower St. Lawrence the fusion of the medieval tradition of the stonemasons and the baroque tastes of churchmen and royal officials created a distinctive church architecture, but in Acadia where the official hold was tenuous and artisans trained in France were virtually absent, there was no comparable development.

The Acadians' over-riding occupation was farming. Wheat and peas were their principal field crops, although only at Minas was wheat as dominant as along the lower St. Lawrence. Every farm included a plot of vegetables: cabbages and turnips were particular favorites, and a heavy soup of cabbage, turnip, and pork slices was daily fare in winter. Most farms had a small orchard of cherry, pear, and apple trees. "Port Royal," said a visitor in the early 1690s, "is a little Normandy for apples," although contrary to Norman practice few trees were grafted, and the quality of fruit must have been low. The Acadians drank some cider, but less of it than a "beer" made of new spruce tips, molasses, and yeast. Almost all farmers kept sheep and pigs and many had horses, but undoubtedly cattle were the most important livestock and accounted for most of the Acadian agricultural surplus. There were more cattle per farm on the great marshlands at Beaubassin than anywhere else, and fewer stock and a smaller output of grain per farm at Port Royal. The relative poverty of the Port Royal farmers may have been associated with the smaller area of marshland at their disposal, but more likely with the ability of French or British officials in the fort at the mouth of the Annapolis River to give teeth to their ban on trade with New England. At Beaubassin and in the Minas Basin, where New Englanders traded unchecked each summer, the largest farms contained up to 50 head of cattle, 100 sheep, 20–30 hogs, a few horses, and 40–50 acres of arable. With kitchen gardens and orchards close to their houses and stock and grain fields on the marshes, the Acadians ate well and produced a surplus. Although both French and English officials considered them indolent, they, like the Canadians, achieved a far higher standard of living than all but the most privileged French peasants. Only at Port Royal were there references to poverty.

Acadian agriculture depended on the marshlands, which the New Englanders who replaced the Acadians after 1755 never learned to utilize as effectively. Central to the Acadian success was the dike and within it the aboîteau, or sluice gate, both probably brought to the Bay of Fundy from the coastal plains of Aunis and Poitou. In 1700 the French trader Dièreville described the aboîteau and its mountings as follows:

> Five or six rows of large logs are driven whole into the ground at the points where the tide enters the Marsh, and between each row other logs are laid, one on top of the other, and all the spaces between them are so carefully filled with well-pounded clay, that the water can no longer get through. In the centre of this construction, a Sluice is con-

trived in such a manner that the water on the Marshes flows out of its own accord, while that of the Sea is prevented from coming in.

The Acadians neither manured nor rotated their fields, but as a combination of storm and spring tide would occasionally breach the dikes, providing a fresh layer of silt, there was probably no need to do so. Dièreville reported that the diked lands were worked in common; and settlement in hamlets also suggests that Acadian agriculture had a collective aspect. Although many fields were not enclosed, collective agriculture in Acadia probably rested on the need for labor to build and maintain the dikes and to dig the drainage ditches rather than, as in Europe, on the timing of field rotations and grazing rights.

Many of the Acadians caught fish in traps at the river mouths, and a few young men drifted into the Atlantic fishery when times were bad. Although they required a great deal of wood for buildings and sluice gates, and became quite proficient woodsmen, the Acadians rarely exported wood, perhaps because oak (used for ship's timbers) was uncommon. By the eighteenth century they were building small ships to be used for trade and fishing. Sawmills and gristmills were scattered through the settlements; and there were blacksmiths, wheelwrights, carpenters, coopers, and a number of other artisans, most of whom combined their trades with farming.

By the 1720s Acadians were sailing their own small ships to Louisbourg and occasionally to Boston; and for more than thirty years before 1755 their exports to Louisbourg probably surpassed those to New England. Acadian, French, and even New England ships carried cattle, grain, furs, and a host of items around the Nova Scotian peninsula to Louisbourg. Perhaps more often, goods were taken across the isthmus to Baie Verte and Tatamagouche on Northumberland Strait where they were picked up by ships from Louisbourg. The English at Port Royal feared that as many as 500–700 cattle, 2000 sheep, and a good many thousand bushels of wheat were exported to Louisbourg each year; in some years the trade may actually have approached these proportions. Frequently the Acadians were paid in specie which they eventually used to buy manufactures from the New Englanders. In this way much of the money that the French poured into Louisbourg worked its way into the English seaboard colonies.

The Acadians themselves had shown a good deal of commercial skill in turning an accessible location that was a severe military disadvantage into a clear economic asset. They became a small cog in the trading

world of the North Atlantic, and this connection plus their skill in draining the marshes around the Bay of Fundy enabled them to supply
amply their relatively simple needs and wants. They were neglected by
the mother country and cut off from institutions of government and law
and from most of the intellectual currents of their day. Priests became
important leaders, but it was probably the bonds of blood and need in
the many tiny hamlets that dotted the edge of the marshlands that held
Acadian society together. Then, in 1755 at the onset of the Seven Years
War, the English rounded up and deported as many of the Acadians as
they could catch. Settlers from New England soon moved onto their upland clearings and farmed their marshlands. When some of the Acadians
trickled back in the 1760s, the cultural landscape they had created was
almost gone.

Canada

THE SETTLEMENT OF THE ST. LAWRENCE LOWLAND

From 1608 when Samuel de Champlain established a small fort at Québec until 1663 when young Louis XIV revoked the charter of the Company of New France, Canada was an outpost of the fur trade. No more
than 2500 Europeans lived along the St. Lawrence in 1663, half of them
in the fortified villages of Québec, Trois-Rivières, and Montréal and
almost all the rest within a few miles of these places. The Company of
New France, created in 1627 and required by charter to grant seigneuries and bring out colonists, was far more interested in trade than in
colonization, and no more than ten of the seventy seigneuries it conceded had any settlers in 1663. For this failure the Company lost its
charter, and Canada became a crown colony. Jean Talon, the first royal
intendant, arrived in 1665, and in the next thirty years some 5000 immigrants followed. Immigration and a high rate of natural increase led to
a population of more than 11,000 before the end of the century. Almost
all settlers lived within a mile of the river—most on the north shore and
within twenty-five miles of Québec or Montréal—but a few lived along
the shore near Trois-Rivières (see Fig. 2–4). Otherwise the banks of the
St. Lawrence were almost as unsettled as they had been at the beginning
of the century.

The fur trade rather than agriculture had drawn settlers up-river from
Québec. Trois-Rivières was located at the mouth of the St-Maurice fur
route, Montréal at the junction of the Ottawa River with the St. Law-

rence and, because of the Lachine rapids, at the point of trans-shipment from boat to canoe. For twenty years after the founding of Montréal in 1642, its annual fair was the principal fur market in Canada, but a good deal of trading also took place in the farmhouses along the river. A governor noted that settlement was dispersed because of "the desire of each one of the habitants to be ahead of the others in order to obtain more furs," and many complained that farmhouses in the Montréal area were really cabarets—that is, that their owners were trading liquor to the Indians. In the last four decades of the seventeenth century many habitants left the St. Lawrence lowland on unauthorized trading expeditions. This was the great age of the coureurs de bois who, contrary to many edicts, roamed through the Great Lakes basin and beyond to the Mississippi and traded their furs wherever the price was best—often to the English on Hudson Bay, at Albany, or across the Appalachians in Carolina. The percentage of the population engaged in this trade is still to be ascertained, but it must have been high. At the end of the century perhaps half the adult males living west of Trois-Rivières had spent some time in the fur country, although few men had broken entirely with their base on a farm along the lower St. Lawrence.

Farming developed slowly. Champlain noted in the late 1620s that only one and one-half acres had been cleared for cultivation at Québec; and many more years passed before most habitants were primarily farmers. Most immigrants undoubtedly turned reluctantly to farming. Almost a third of seventy-one rotures (farm lots) in a parish on the Ile d'Orléans had changed hands within five years of concession; of the twenty-three rotures in Charlesbourg (one of the villages which Jean Talon laid out in 1666) thirteen had changed hands within twelve years, and some had had several owners. This rate of turnover was considerably lower than the average for newly granted land in Ontario and the American Middle West in the early nineteenth century, but it alarmed the intendant, who issued an ordinance forbidding settlers to sell concessions before putting up a building and clearing two arpents (one arpent = five-sixths of an acre) suitable for cultivation with a mattock. The sale of a roture or two on which a plot of land had been cleared and a hut built enabled many settlers to earn a meager living. Yet many others who were totally unfamiliar with farming and had no experience in clearing preferred to sell land rather than to clear and farm it. Land was cleared much more slowly than in nineteenth-century Ontario, where settlers had previous experience with the forest or access to more than a century

St-François, Ile d'Orleans. A view north from the Ile d'Orleans across some of the oldest farmland in Canada. The house in the foreground dates from the French regime; the higher row of well-separated houses on the other shore (the côte de Beaupré) comprises the côte, or rang, of early settlement. Long lots extend back to the Canadian Shield, which is but a farm's length from the river. The Public Archives of Canada.

of accumulated lore about the techniques of clearing. Before long, however, the rate of sales dropped—few new settlers came from France—and when the labor requirements of the fur trade were met, there was no other way for most immigrants to live than to settle down to farm.

Farming took place on rotures that had been conceded by the seigneur. The legal trappings of the seigneurial system had been established in Canada when the Company of New France received by the terms of its charter most of eastern North America "en toute propriété, justice, et

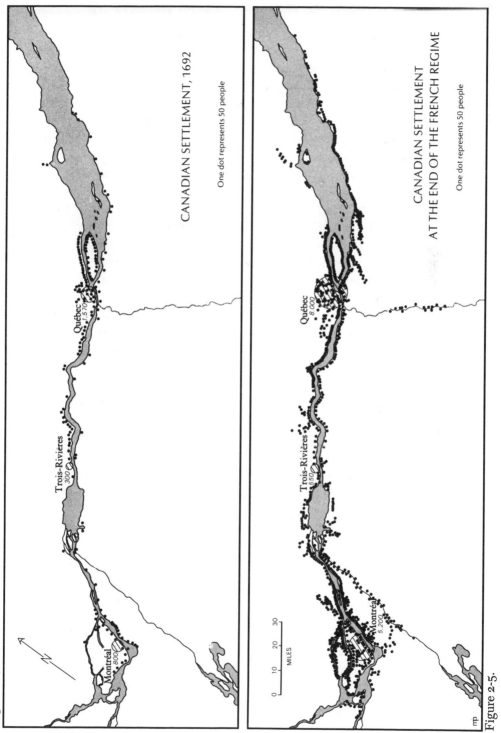

Figure 2-4.

CANADIAN SETTLEMENT, 1692

One dot represents 50 people

Québec
1,570

Trois-Rivières
300

Montréal
800

N

Figure 2-5.

CANADIAN SETTLEMENT
AT THE END OF THE FRENCH REGIME

One dot represents 50 people

Québec
8,000

Trois-Rivières
550

Montréal
5,200

0   10   20   30
MILES

mp

seigneurie," and was legally obliged to subenfeudate. The Company granted most of the St. Lawrence lowland en seigneurie. The Intendant Talon and his successors withdrew some of the larger of these seigneuries and conceded others, and at the end of the seventeenth century some 150 seigneuries were available for rural settlement. All farming was on this land. Royal officials forbade settlement farther west on the ground that as long as farmland was available for the asking within the seigneuries, settlement to the west could only complicate the problem of policing the fur trade. To the north and south of the seigneurial grants the land was poor or inaccessible.

In the last sixty years of the French regime no more than 4000 immigrants came to Canada, a few trickling into the colony almost every year. Population growth depended largely on natural increase. In 1712, some 20,000 people lived in Canada. Settlement had spread out along the river from the towns and was beginning to turn up some of its navigable tributaries. Because most settlers choosing between otherwise equivalent lots chose the one closer to a town, the river frontage near the towns filled up first. Unsettled riverbank midway between Montréal and Québec was due partly to poor drainage, or to sandy soils and difficult access to the river around the shores of Lac St-Pierre, but principally to remoteness from the two principal centers. Opposing the centripetal force of the towns was the attraction of unoccupied land along the river. The river was the connection between the farms and the outside world, and as long as river frontage was available within thirty or forty miles of a town, the habitants preferred it to almost any interior location. Only near Québec and Montréal and along the Chaudière River were there many settled farms lots away from navigable water—even by the end of the French regime.

In 1739, the year of the last census taken during the French regime, more than 40,000 people lived in Canada, most of them farmers. The fur trade extended almost 2000 canoe-miles west of Montréal to Lake Winnipeg and the Saskatchewan River. As the route lengthened, it became more difficult for one man to participate in both farming and trading, and the occupations of coureur de bois and farmer were tending to become separate and permanent. Moreover, the manpower requirements of the fur trade were increasing less rapidly than the Canadian population. These circumstances and improving markets favored the expansion of agriculture. Throughout the seventeenth century the only markets for the surplus from Canadian farms were the few townsmen in Québec and Montréal (many of whom had their own gardens) and, to an even smaller extent, the flotillas of canoes outfitted for the fur trade. At the beginning of the eighteenth century, wheat was overproduced, prices were low, and many farmers were discouraged from clearing more land. Then in 1709, crop failures in western Europe opened the market in the French West Indies to Canada. Fairly regular exports began, the price of wheat rose, and clearing proceeded more rapidly than ever before. Each summer the intendant prepared an assessment of the likely harvest and an inventory of existing food reserves, and on the basis of this calculation forbade, limited, or opened exports. When exports were permitted peddlers, merchants, and ship captains looking for a return cargo toured the countryside buying grain and flour; for two decades after 1720 from 4000–8000 barrels of flour and several hundred thousand pounds of biscuits were exported almost every year as well as, in the best years, more than 4000 barrels of peas, meat, and a good many horses. Then in 1742 and for several years thereafter, harvests were poor; and as they improved the Seven Years War was brewing. Merchant shipping in the long difficult route out of the Gulf of St. Lawrence was always vulnerable to attack. The last eighteen years of French rule were marked by an agricultural depression that considerably slowed the rate of clearing and debilitated the entire colony.

From 1740 to 1760, when Canada finally fell to the British, the population increased again by half to about 65,000. Nearly one-fourth of the people lived in Québec, Montréal, and Trois-Rivières, the highest level of urbanization at that date in any North American colony. The rest were distributed as shown in Figure 2-5. A row of settlements stretched for 200 miles along the north shore, another, somewhat longer, along the south. Peter Kalm, the Swedish agronomist who visited Canada in 1749, described its settlement fairly accurately as two rows of whitewashed farmhouses straggling along the river; but to understand the settled landscape of Canada toward the end of the French regime it is necessary to look at these lines of settlement in considerably more detail.

THE DETAILED SETTLEMENT PATTERN

At larger magnification the lines of settlement appear as shown in Figure 2-6. In some areas there were farmhouses every 200 or 300 yards for miles along the river; in others, tributary streams, stretches of infertile land, or the pattern in which farm lots had been conceded interrupted the côtes (lines). There were few nodes of settlement anywhere. Churches, gristmills, manor houses, the part-time farmers who operated forges—all

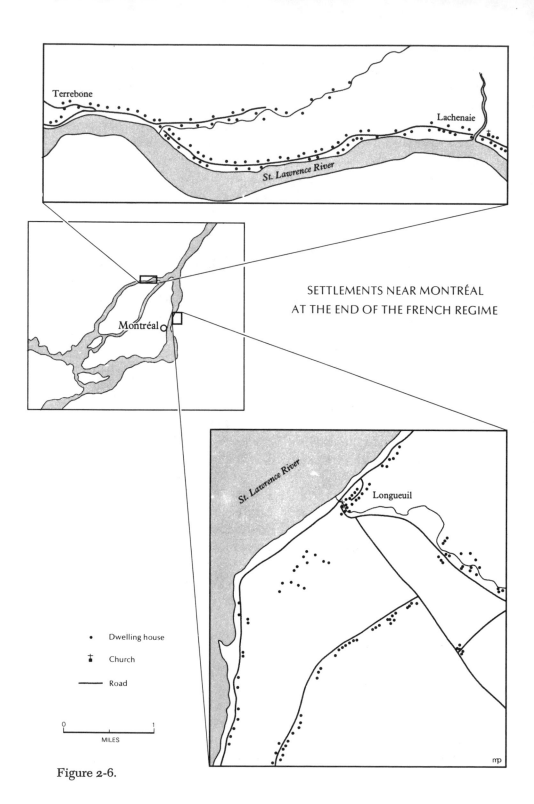

SETTLEMENTS NEAR MONTRÉAL
AT THE END OF THE FRENCH REGIME

Terrebone

Lachenaie

St. Lawrence River

Montréal

St. Lawrence River

Longueuil

•   Dwelling house

✝   Church

——   Road

0   1
    MILES

Figure 2-6.

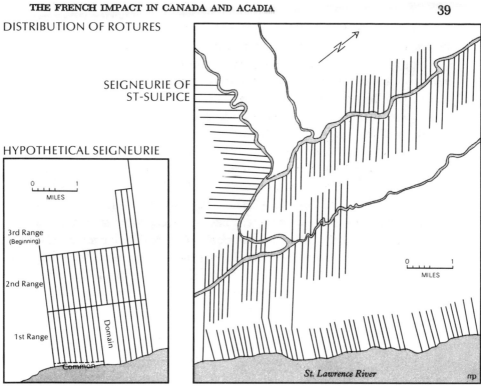

DISTRIBUTION OF ROTURES

SEIGNEURIE OF
ST-SULPICE

HYPOTHETICAL SEIGNEURIE

Figure 2-7.

were scattered along the côtes. At the end of the French regime there were, besides Québec, Trois-Rivières, and Montréal, only six nucleated villages and four hamlets in Canada.

Underlying the côtes was the cadastral system of the colony. In the 1630s a few seigneurs had begun conceding rotures. The oldest surviving roture contract (1637) describes a long, thin lot near Québec; even now this shape—a long lot—is characteristic of farms along the lower St. Lawrence. Most Canadian rotures were fifty to one hundred arpents in size and approximately rectangular in shape with a common ratio of width to length of 1:10. Within a seigneurie, the first rotures were usually conceded in a row along the river; then in parallel series behind the first row. Where a navigable tributary of the St. Lawrence crossed the seigneurie, rotures were conceded along it as along the main river. Some of these patterns are shown in Figure 2-7.

Long lots appeared in Louisiana, in Wisconsin, at Vincennes in Illinois, around Fort Detroit, along the Red River, and in several other places where the seigneurial system was never introduced. In Canada the king's ministers and some seigneurs opposed the long-lot system for several years and never standardized it by official edict. The long lot appears, then, less as an imposition from above than as the preference of the settlers. Possibly this preference was a direct European inheritance. Street, or dike, villages (*Waldhufendörfer, terroir en arête de poisson*) with elongated farms extending at approximate right angles from them appeared in the Netherlands, in Germany, and in northwestern France in the twelfth and thirteenth centuries, and still existed in the seventeenth. Some of the settlers in Canada may have come from a part of France where this settlement pattern had survived. More striking, however, is the similarity between conditions in seventeenth-century Canada and in much of northwestern France five centuries before. Both were pioneer areas where land was being cleared and settled, where a single line of transportation—whether river or road—provided the connection with the outside world, and where individual settlers were not entirely free to select and to demarcate their own agricultural land.

In 1666 and 1667 the Intendant Jean Talon, acting on instructions from Colbert, attempted to introduce a cadastral system based on compact, nucleated settlement and encouraged seigneurs to do the same. For years thereafter governors and intendants, supported by the church and apparently by many of the seigneurs, favored village settlement. The king's ministers in France were convinced that until the habitants settled in villages it would be easy for the Iroquois "to slit their throats." Officials in Canada urged that nucleated settlements would be easier to administer. Yet Talon's villages were not quickly settled, and when land in them was eventually cleared, the houses were set well back on the lots, not around the central square. Undoubtedly, nucleated settlements had not appeared because the habitants did not want to live in them.

Because the St. Lawrence was the artery of travel in early Canada, almost all settlement was along its banks. Officials and some seigneurs favored the establishment of riparian villages; the habitants preferred isolated farmhouses on their own river lots. Central to the official interest in villages was the idea of control; by the same token the habitants reacted against such control in favor of a loosely structured, independent way of life. Clearly, a man was much more on his own on a farm lot than in a riverside village, for with the forest at every back door and the river at every front door, unobtrusive movement along the St. Lawrence was easy, and virtually impossible for government officials, seigneurs, or churchmen to control. Immigrants had come to a vast, sparsely settled land, had recognized that traditional authorities could be bypassed there, and had seized the opportunity. But why had they done so? One of the reasons, almost certainly, was their involvement—often illegally, and in competition with their seigneur—in the fur trade. For a frequently illegal and clandestine activity like the fur trade, an isolated pattern of settlement from which the individual could slip away unobserved had many advantages. Moreover, Indian and habitant mixed in the fur trade; and the Indians' mobility, arrogance, rhetoric, and disdain for routine were admired and emulated. It is also possible that settlers from French villages may have remembered the oppressive influence of a seigneur or curé and sought to avoid it in Canada. For those who had been con-scripted into the army, jailed, or summarily shipped to Canada as en-gagés, their brushes with authority had been painful. And if, as it appears, most settlers had been uprooted sometime before they came to Canada, then restiveness—or at least the need to forage for themselves—had been part of their life in France. Further, it must be remembered that immigrants came as individuals or as members of nuclear families rather than as members of communities, that they came from many different parts of France, and that half of them had been urban people. Many of them had never been part of tight communities, and immigration itself was a highly individualizing process. In 1683 the Intendant Demeulles claimed that immigrants came to Canada to "escape their crimes"; that they betook themselves to isolated spots to indulge their "vicious ways." Although his comment seriously distorts their motives, Demeulles may have been right in assuming that the restless, independent temperament of the Canadians had many of its roots in France and in the character of Canadian immigration.

If the habitants avoided villages for these reasons, then, of the alternatives, the long lots gave frontage on a major transportation route (whether river or road) to a maximum number of settlers. Even today, lines of closely spaced farmhouses have a gregarious feel—as if, in rejecting village for côte, the habitants had struck a balance between their wishes to associate with their fellows and to be isolated from authority. Also of some significance were the ease and cheapness with which the long lots could be surveyed and the ready access to the river for fishing, for in the early years food was often in short supply.

By the eighteenth century the relative importance of the fur trade had declined, Canadian seigneurs had proved not to be a domineering class, and most of the population was native-born. The habitants' aversion to nucleated settlement had waned. The ten villages and hamlets in Canada in 1760 had all been settled since 1700, and by the 1750s some habitants were requesting their seigneurs to establish others. Eight petitions reached the intendant, each containing similar proposals: that the village serve as a market place, as a center for artisans, and as an entrepôt between farm and town. Even so, at this date most habitants were content to live on their own farms, and had never considered living anywhere else. Apparently they did not find occasional trips to town for supplies and services too inconvenient. Because settlement was spread along the transportation routes, it was relatively easy to keep in contact with the town. Moreover, some specialization of function existed within the côte. If a habitant could not repair a broken cart wheel, one of his neighbors probably could. Another had a forge and did odd jobs for the habitants nearby. The côte, neither tightly agglomerated nor dispersed, made such loose association easy; to the degree that the côte included some of the characteristics of nucleated settlement, villages were redundant.

In Canada as in seventeenth-century France the seigneurie had little influence on settlement patterns. Lines of farmhouses usually crossed seigneurial boundaries without a break, and the seigneurial manor was never the focus for roads or settlement. Many habitants had contact with their seigneur only on St. Martin's Day (November 11), when they paid their *cens et rentes;* because of the laxity of management, others did not see him or his representative for years; still others had no idea who he was. Most of the seigneurs lived in town, and only a few of them had been colonizers, such as Pierre Boucher, who in the 1670s brought a few settlers to his seigneurie on the south shore opposite Montréal island, or the Jesuits, who placed settlers on land near Trois-Rivières. Generally, however, the seigneurial system had neither expedited colonization nor shaped the way of life of the rural community.

In seventeenth-century France the seigneurie had become essentially a fiscal institution that directed part of the peasants' income to the seigneurial elite, but in early Canada only a few seigneurs were able to make any money at all from their land. To be sure, all seigneurs were entitled to charge a *cens* (hence the word *censitaire* for one who paid it), a token payment indicating that land was held *en roture* (that is, it could not be sub-granted); a *rente,* an annual payment in cash or kind intended to be a real source of revenue; and a banal charge fixed at one-of the rural community. Certainly the parish had little bearing on settlement patterns until well into the nineteenth century.

In many areas the kin group had emerged as an extra-family social unit by 1700. The first nuclear families in a seigneurie were unrelated, and there was a good deal of spatial mobility in the early rural population. (Some sons, however, settled near the parental roture, often on additional rotures their father had acquired for that purpose.) When the population was low and there was little immigration, a côte that had been settled for two or three generations could be dominated by only a few surnames. In Lotbinière, a seigneurie forty miles from Québec on the south shore, there were forty-nine families in 1724, some fifty years after the first settlement there. Of these families eight were Lemays and twenty belonged on the paternal side to one of the four principal families in the seigneurie. There was a tendency for related families to live close together along the côte, but kin groups were not visible in the landscape as they apparently were in Acadian hamlets. The inter-relatedness of nearby families, however, had an important bearing on the social force of the côte, providing an alternative to the social structuring of village and parish.

FARM BUILDINGS

Each established farm centered around a cluster of small buildings. Besides the farmhouse there was likely to be a barn with a central threshing floor and adjoining bays for storing hay and grain (*grange*); a small stable for horses (*écurie*); another for cattle (*étable*); a shed; an outdoor oven; and perhaps several other small buildings with specific functions. Of the main building types in France, the *maison bloc*, in which family and livestock lived under one roof, and the *maison cour*, in which the two were separated, only the latter came to rural Canada. The house was usually placed within a few yards of a road or path along the river, or on the brow of a terrace marking a shoreline of the post-glacial Champlain Sea, and the grange, écurie, and étable, fifty to a hundred yards behind.

At first these buildings were wooden. The first farmhouses were built of posts driven into the ground with a thatch, plank, or bark roof, and a dirt floor. Later in the century the French construction technique known as *pièces sur pièce* (see p. 29) became more common. There were also buildings of heavy planks placed horizontally on a post frame (*en bois*

Table 2-1. Seigneurial revenue (in livres)

Source of revenue	10 newly settled families	20 newly settled families	20 established families	50 families	100 families	500 families
	Probable return					
Cens	1.5	3	6	15	30	150
Rente	60	120	240	600	1200	6000
Fishing rights	...	...	...	100	200	400
Common pasture	20	40	40	100	200	1000
Lods et ventes	25	50	100	250	500	2500
Sales of rotures	...	...	...	...	100	500
Interest	...	...	...	...	100	500
Banalities						
Revenue	100	200	400	1000	2000	10,000
Expenditure	500	500	500	500	1000	5000
Net profit or loss	—400	—300	—100	500	1000	5000
TOTAL	—293.5	—87	286	1565	3330	16,050

fourteenth of the grain ground, for the use of the gristmill. If a tenant disposed of his land, the seigneur was also entitled to the *lods et ventes* of one-twelfth of the sale price of a roture. But most seigneuries were settled slowly and as Table 2–1 indicates, sparsely settled seigneuries were economic liabilities. Government officials had favored low charges for Canadian rotures in the hope that settlers would be attracted from France; if a seigneur disregarded the intendant and charged more for his land, as he could, prospective censitaires simply went elsewhere. In a largely unsettled colony there was ample opportunity for censitaires to pick and choose.

A seigneur needed at least twenty families on his land to cover the annual expenses of the gristmill he was expected to provide, and forty to fifty before he could begin to live more comfortably than most of his censitaires. Because of the low population and the large number of seigneuries, most owners had far fewer settlers than this, even at the end of the French regime. Moreover, because of the size of Canadian families and the modified system of partible (divided) inheritance, lay seigneuries in Canada often were left to many heirs. In these circumstances the considerable expense of bringing settlers from France was not repaid in the seigneur's lifetime. In order to settle their land most seigneurs had to attract established settlers, and might hope to do so either by reducing annual charges or by providing superior milling facilities. In choosing the first alternative, however, they risked future revenue; in choosing the second they committed themselves to a considerable outlay that might bring no return. Thus the seigneur's role in the settlement process was notably passive. In this sense the seigneurial system bore much the same relationship to colonization and settlement in Canada during the French regime that English common law and the township survey bore to colonization and settlement in Upper Canada (Ontario) in the nineteenth century.

The role of the parish is more obscure. Almost all the habitants were Catholics, and although they disregarded many sacerdotal orders—the order, for example, to refrain from selling liquor to the Indians—and understood little of church dogma, there is no reason to suggest that they were irreligious as a class. In most areas they were served by itinerant priests who spent no more than three or four weeks a year in any one place, and until the bishop's decision in 1722 to establish resident priests in rural parishes, the direct influence of church and parish on the life of the rural community must have been slight. In some places a parish organization had been created years before the arrival of a curé. Church wardens were elected, sites for a cemetery or a new roof for the chapel were discussed in meetings of the parish vestry (*la fabrique*), and occasionally tithes may have been collected in advance of a priest's visit. Yet until resident priests (curés) were introduced, such organization within a parish was intermittent and haphazard. There are enough indications of habitants refusing to pay the tithe, of curés appealing to their bishop for another posting, and of parishes reverting to the earlier system of itinerant priests to make it clear that a curé was often an unwelcome imposition. Several possible reasons may be suggested: reaction against the tithe, although it had been fixed at only one twenty-sixth of the grain harvest and, as such, was rarely an onerous charge; reaction against French priests, who knew and understood little of rural life in Canada; reaction against the moral strictures of many Canadian priests who, for example, took the dimmest view of the habitants' fondness for drink and their frequently promiscuous behavior. There is some evidence that the parish was beginning to become an important social institution toward the close of the French regime, but little evidence that it was a fulcrum

Eglise St-Laurent. One of the finest parish churches of the French regime, demolished one hundred years ago to make way for a larger church. The Public Archives of Canada.

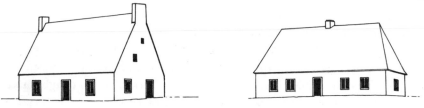

Figure 2-8. Farmhouses, Early Eighteenth Century
Substantial farmhouses of these types were being built by prosperous farmers by the beginning of the eighteenth century, if not earlier. The walls were usually fieldstone and mortar, the roofing thatch or boards. The Québec house (right) is of Norman origin. The common house of the Montréal region (left) is found, with minor variations, in much of northwestern France. Houses of the "Montréal" type were built throughout Canada; it is not certain that they were particularly characteristic of the Montréal area. (Drawings by Peter Ennals)

de charpente); buildings of mud and straw mortar (*torchis*); and—roughly similar to English Tudor—buildings of half-timber construction usually filled in with *torchis*. At the beginning of the eighteenth century, fieldstone houses began to appear in the countryside; and by the end of the French regime they were perhaps the most common type of house near Québec and Montréal.

A common assumption is that farmhouses near Québec were of Norman design and that the heavier, squarer houses near Montréal reflected the traditions of the provinces of Maine and Anjou as well as the pressure of Iroquois attack. The two types are shown in Figure 2-8. There were, however, many variations in these forms, and the regional pattern of house types in early Canada and the extent of borrowing of specific French styles are far from clear. Probably many of the buildings in early Canada drew on the folk architecture of Aunis and Poitou, although the years of constructing in wood must have blurred the settlers' memories of specific French house styles. Simply because an habitant from one region in France was likely to have a wife from another, and possibly an engagé from a third, and because his neighbors were of similarly diverse backgrounds; several folk traditions must have fused in the rural buildings of early Canada. On the other hand, building bees were unknown along the lower St. Lawrence in the seventeenth and early eighteenth century, and farmhouses were often the work of hired artisans, a few of whom had learned their trade in France. Perhaps partly for this reason

Canadian innovations were slow to appear. For example, although field-stone houses often had walls more than two feet thick and steeply pitched roofs (up to 65° to the horizontal), it would be misleading to ascribe such construction to the severity of winter and the depth of snowfall. Thatched roofs had to be steeply pitched to be watertight, and thick walls were associated with the method of construction especially when stone and mortar were dumped between plank frames, as was often done in Canada. An official claimed that with firewood in abundance the habitants suffered less from winter than their counterparts in the milder climate of northwestern France; and certainly major adjustments of vernacular house styles to the Canadian climate did not appear until late in the eighteenth century. Along the lower St. Lawrence as in many other parts of the New World, house styles were among the most enduring elements in the cultural landscape.

Granges, or barns, on the other hand, were much larger than their French counterparts, and were almost always built of wood because wooden buildings were considered drier and warmer than those of stone. The size of a barn—not uncommonly fifty to seventy feet by some twenty-five—grew out of the need for enough hay to tide stock over a long winter. A large door on the long side of the building opened onto a central threshing floor bounded by a storage bay on either side. Occasionally one of the bays was used for stock, although the grange-étable only became common in the nineteenth century. In size and interior arrangement, if not in the steep pitch of the roof or in the slight flare of the eaves, the Canadian barn closely resembled the "English" two-bay barn, the most common barn in early nineteenth-century Ontario.

Farmhouse, barn, and outbuildings made a building complex that reflected a considerably higher standard of living than that of the peasant in northwestern France. The smallest houses were only about fourteen by sixteen feet. Most were larger, often twenty by thirty feet with three or four rooms on the ground floor and a spacious attic above. Although there were regional differences in size and in construction materials—for example, farmhouses near Trois-Rivières were generally small and constructed of wood and thatch—within a given côte farm buildings were strikingly similar. Even seigneurial manors were often almost indistinguishable from the neighboring farmhouses. Nor was there a sharp difference between rural and urban houses. Most town houses had a cellar, and a fire wall extending above the roof at either gable, but in size and line they resembled rural houses. After the conquest, English visitors and officials sometimes lamented a lack of the picturesque in the French-Canadian farm complex, but their judgment reflected a different aesthetic tradition. In choice of site, and in the economy, symmetry, and simple elegance of line and form, early Canadian vernacular architecture was the best that there has been in Canada.

AGRICULTURE

Even by the still-medieval standards of agriculture in France and most of the rest of Western Europe in the seventeenth and early eighteenth century, the farmland that spread along the lower St. Lawrence toward the end of the French regime, looked ragged and unkempt. Many fields were spotted with stumps, fallow land was often untended or plowed only in the fall, many pastures were little better than fields of weeds, and —especially in the first years after clearing—minor constituents of the forest flora sprouted through the crops. This sloppy agricultural practice was less a reflection of the outmoded techniques of French agriculture and of the urban background of many settlers than of the basically different conditions under which agriculture was practised on the two sides of the Atlantic. In France at the beginning of the seventeenth century, land was scarce and expensive and agricultural labor plentiful and cheap, but in North America the relationship was reversed. A peasant farming ten arpents in northwestern France usually practised a three-course rotation of crops: rye or wheat in a field one year; barley, oats, or peas the next; and fallow the third. There was a delicate balance between the size of his holdings, his farm techniques, his requirements for haulage, the feed his farm produced and the number of his livestock, the size of his household, and his surplus. A change in any part of the system could undermine his narrow margin of viability. For this reason and because agriculture was the collective responsibility of the village, individual systems of agriculture changed slowly, and those changes which increased the productivity of land tended to lead to smaller holdings. In the New World farmers sought to maximize returns from labor rather than from land. Elaborate crop rotations, heavy manuring, and the selective breeding of cattle—all labor-intensive practices that increased or conserved the productivity of land—all but disappeared. In Canada, as throughout the thirteen English colonies, land was usually cropped for several years in succession and then allowed to revert to bush, or was farmed in the simplest two-course rotation. In most parts of the colony three-course rotations were rare or nonexistent. Because the forest was used for pasture and breeding uncontrolled, the quality of stock had deteriorated and manure was rarely available. European visitors—especially those acquainted with the use of fodder crops and elaborate crop rotations—derisively compared North American agriculture to that of medieval Europe. Indeed, approximate European parallels for early North American agriculture may have existed before A.D. 1000 in much of Europe; after A.D. 1050 in areas of new settlement; in areas of severe depopulation after the epidemics and wars of the fourteenth century; and around the fringes of the ecumene as late as the seventeenth and eighteenth centuries. In each case, as in North America, the population pressure on the land was relatively low.

An abundance of land is a necessary precondition for the development of extensive agriculture, but it is not an entirely sufficient explanation for it. For a good many years after a settler took a roture, clearing rather than farming was his first concern, and because much of his labor went into clearing he had to devise an agricultural system that could produce some food with a minimum of effort. Moreover, intensive agriculture on the best European model required a substantial acreage in feed crops to maintain the sizable herds or flocks which, in turn, supplied manure for the arable. In North America the urban market for livestock products was small and export opportunities were limited; most farmers kept only enough stock to supply their own needs and to make occasional sales in the towns. Thus they had no opportunity to rotate feed crops with cereals. They rarely collected manure, and even when they did, the supply would have been only enough to fertilize an acre or two a year. In northwestern France a farmer with a cow or two, and ten or fifteen arpents of land had no choice but to cultivate as intensively as he knew how; along the lower St. Lawrence it was uneconomical for an habitant with thirty to fifty cleared arpents to practise more than the most elementary two-course rotation or to manure most of his land. Such extensive agriculture could yield high returns per man; it was neither better nor worse than more intensive farming but a different system which worked well in a forested setting where land was plentiful and the market for livestock or feed crops was limited.

In 1750 Peter Kalm noted that Canadian rail fences resembled those in Sweden but missed the far more important point that individual holdings were enclosed. At this time most of the agriculture in northwestern France was still practised in open fields; that is, it was a collective rather than an individual responsibility. Although enclosure decrees were common in the 1770s, agricultural individualism in northern France emerged strongly only with the Revolution. In Canada it was as old as the colony's agricultural beginnings and perhaps an inevitable corollary of the dismemberment of the rural community. Open-field cultivation depended on a web of custom known to every villager, and the uprooted life in France of most immigrants to Canada as well as the mixing of traditions along the lower St. Lawrence militated strongly against it. Different village traditions would not easily combine in a harmonious open-field system and, as it was, a large part of the immigrants were city-bred and knew nothing of open-field life in France. The dislocation associated with New World settlement had the effect of accelerating on one side of the Atlantic a process of social change that was slowly gaining momentum on the other.

Yet traces of open-field practice began to appear. Seigneurs set aside common pastures, usually natural meadows along the river, which were used to capacity until well into the nineteenth century. Fences were not always put up and cowherds were fairly common. As long as the riparian meadows were the principal pasture, only the front of a roture needed to be fenced, although several ordinances on the subject suggest that habitants often neglected to build even this short fence. Fences did not seem necessary to farmers who were clearing land or growing the same crop without rotation. But as new crops were introduced, fences between adjacent properties became essential. In 1725 the Sovereign Council, in an effort to encourage the sowing of winter wheat, ordered all habitants who had not already done so to erect fences, and in the meantime to tend their livestock throughout the year. By the end of French rule virtually all farm boundaries and most fields were enclosed, and rail fences, each set of rails supported at either end by a pair of closely spaced posts, stood as visible evidence of a profound social and agricultural change.

Canadian agricultural practice, then, was sloppy and extensive even by French standards, and was the product of individual rather than collective decisions. Wheat rather than rye was the principal crop everywhere except at the extreme eastern end of the colony where the growing season was less than one hundred days. It was frequently observed that three-quarters of the land in crops was in wheat, and that in a given year about half the cleared land was arable. Immediately after clearing, land was often in wheat for many years in succession; later a

degenerate form of convertible husbandry (several years of cereals followed by pasture or by untended fallow) or wheat–pasture–wheat became the common rotations, the pasture often no more than a field of
weeds. There is some evidence of more elaborate rotations on lands the
seigneurs had reserved for their own use, and on some habitant farms.
Although almost all habitants kept a few cattle, sheep, and pigs, and
one or two horses, fields were rarely manured. Consequently, seed-yield
ratios were low; after 1700 a ratio of 1:6 was average for the colony and
was no lower only because of the high yields on newly cleared land.
Peas, oats, and barley were grown in addition to, but not in rotation
with, wheat. A few habitants grew maize but none grew potatoes. In the
1720s the intendant attempted to encourage the cultivation of hemp by
raising its price to three times that in France. Production jumped from
200 pounds in 1722 to more than 44,000 in 1727; by 1730 more than
200,000 pounds of low-quality hemp filled the warehouses in Québec.
When the intendant cut the price of hemp, most farmers gave up the
crop. Almost all farms had a kitchen garden with the common French
vegetables, herbs, tobacco, and a few apple trees. Most of the cleared
land not planted in any given year was in meadow or pasture, or in
the process of reverting to bush.

Although the farms on the richer soils near Montréal tended to carry
the most stock and to produce the most wheat, and those near Trois-
Rivières to be the poorest in the colony (see Fig. 2-9), there was little
regional differentiation in agricultural practice along the lower St. Lawrence. Within a given côte some habitants were better off than others,
but the extremes were not great. As far as we know, this was not typical
of village life in seventeenth- and eighteenth-century France. In many
French villages only one or two peasants, usually tenants on the lord's
domain, were prosperous, and only about a dozen owned enough land to
get by. Most of the villagers held less than enough land to live on and
supplemented their income as day laborers or artisans; some were almost
landless and destitute. In Canada, on the other hand, a settled roture
along a côte usually contained approximately twenty-five acres of cleared
land. Of these, some ten acres were in wheat; perhaps one acre each in
peas, oats, and barley; and a fraction of an acre in fruit trees and garden.
The rest of the land was in meadow or in the untended fallow that
passed for pasture. Such a farm usually produced a small surplus. Assuming a yield of some ten bushels per acre, it grew approximately a
hundred bushels of wheat, of which roughly fifteen bushels were re-

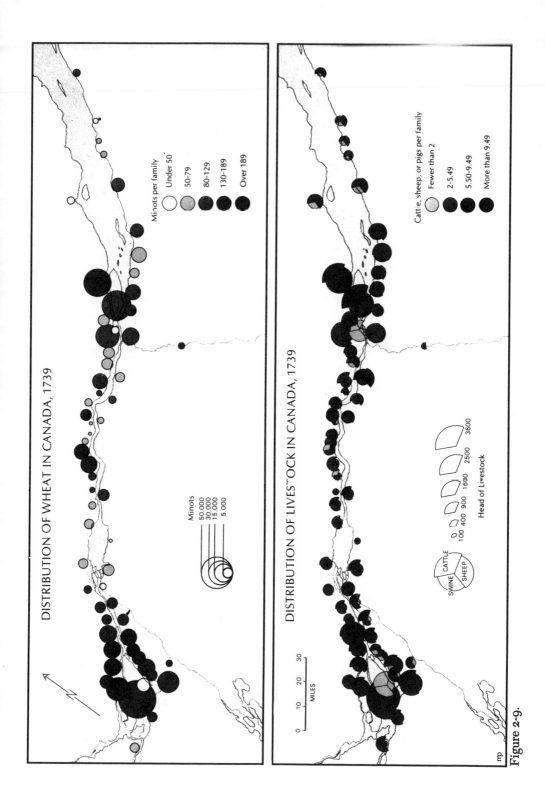

DISTRIBUTION OF WHEAT IN CANADA, 1739

Minots per family
Under 50
50-79
80-129
130-189
Over 189

Minots
50,000
30,000
15,000
5,000

DISTRIBUTION OF LIVESTOCK IN CANADA, 1739

Cattle, sheep, or pigs per family
Fewer than 2
2-5.49
5.50-9.49
More than 9.49

SWINE   CATTLE
SHEEP

Head of Livestock
100 400 900 1600 2500 3600

MILES
0 10 20 30

Figure 2-9.

tained for next year's seed, seven to pay milling charges and four as tithes. Two or three bushels may have been used to pay the cens et rentes. About two-thirds of the crop was left for domestic consumption or sale. Depending on the size of the farm family, a few bushels of wheat, a pig or a calf, and some butter or vegetables could be sold almost every year. Farms were smaller wherever land had been settled only a short time, although in some of the older settled seigneuries, a few habitants owned as much as one hundred acres of cleared land. Except for a handful of farms on seigneurial domains, such holdings were the largest farms in Canada, and probably produced a marketable surplus of approximately 150 bushels of grain, a few lambs and calves, a pig, and some dairy products, fruits, and vegetables.

Part of the explanation for the similarity of farms along the lower St. Lawrence is undoubtedly that all immigrants had started to farm at much the same level, and that there had been insufficient time for a great income differentiation to develop; but probably more important was the leveling influence of the *Coutume de Paris* and the uncertain market for the colony's agricultural surplus. The concern of the Coutume de Paris, which together with the statutes, edicts, and ordinances issued in Canada comprised the civil law of the colony, was for the family rather than for the individual. Central to it was the premise that land was a scarce and valuable resource in which all members of the family had a natural right to share. When a censitaire married, his property was held conjointly with his wife (the *communauté des biens*); when he died it passed in equal portions to his progeny, and his widow had rights to half the revenue from his property. During his life the *légitime* (a child's right to an inheritance) gave his children rights to half the family land; and, by the provisions of the *retrait*, sales could be annulled if they interfered with either the légitime or the communauté des biens. As long as land values were low, these protective measures were irrelevant, but as land was cleared and acquired a value equal at least to the labor costs of clearing it, the influence of the Coutume de Paris began to come into play. Farms which could support two families were subdivided at their owner's death. Large accumulations of cleared land rarely passed intact through successive generations of censitaires. Even at the end of the French regime almost every young censitaire began to farm with either an uncleared roture or at most a farm of average size, and all the checks built into the Coutume made it difficult for him to enlarge his holding. Had there been a large, assured market for his produce which justified the hiring of expensive farm laborers, he might have enlarged his holding, but even in the years of greatest rural prosperity in Canada (1720–42) a farm of one hundred cleared arpents was close to the limit.

SECONDARY INDUSTRY

At the beginning of royal government, Jean-Baptiste Colbert, the French intendant de finance, planned to diversify the Canadian economy, and Jean Talon's instructions contained explicit directions in this regard. During his short intendency Talon established a shipyard and brewery in Québec, a tannery across the river in the seigneurie of Lauzon, and an ironworks on the St-Maurice near Trois-Rivières; promoted a wood-tar and timber operation fifty miles downstream from Québec at Baie St-Paul; and instigated the cultivation of hemp throughout the colony. The heart of Colbert's plan was the shipyard, which he hoped would provide a local market for timber, wood-tar, iron, hemp, and canvas as well as the ships that would enable Canadians to participate in the Gulf of St. Lawrence fishery and the West Indian trade. But these ambitious plans collapsed in the early 1670s when Talon left the colony, and France, increasingly preoccupied with European concerns, cut back the amount of capital it sent to Canada.

For years secondary industry other than milling remained almost stagnant, suffering from under-capitalization and a lack of skilled labor and markets. Some wood-tar was made at Baie St-Paul, and masts were cut there, although they often rotted on the beach while awaiting the special ships (*flûtes*) that could transport them to France. The ironworks on the St-Maurice functioned intermittently. One enterprising seigneur, attempting to establish a weaving industry, turned to the fluff of cottonwood seeds and buffalo hair for raw materials when supplies of wool and flax were inadequate. Shipbuilding was resumed more successfully as agricultural exports rose. In 1723, private builders in Québec completed six merchant ships and two warships; in the next decade one hundred small vessels, almost all of them well under forty tons, were launched there.

Then in 1738, after toying with the idea for years, the king's ministers in France decided to construct ships of the line in Canada; and committed as much money to the project during the next nine years as they had for the construction of Louisbourg. Inspectors marked the best trees in the oak–hickory forest around Lake Champlain, and in winter, gangs of up to one hundred men followed to cut the timber. The logs were rafted down the Richelieu and St. Lawrence rivers to Québec. The small shipyards just north of Québec on the St-Charles River were rebuilt for ships of 500–700 tons, far larger vessels than any built in the English colonies to the south, and another mammoth shipyard opened in the city's lower town. Some 200 men worked there under the direction of a master shipbuilder and several skilled laborers sent over from France. Twelve warships, the largest of them more than 700 tons, were built between 1740 and 1750. Two were completed in the following years, and the hull of a third lay in the lower town yard when Wolfe's army arrived at Québec in 1759.

Long before 1750 it was apparent that this massive shipbuilding undertaking was in serious difficulty. The cost of labor was twice as high as in France, and Canadian laborers tended to be jacks-of-all-trades, but masters of none. By the 1740s all of them could handle an ax, but to shape and fit the parts of a man-of-war was another matter. Often they would not submit to the twelve- to sixteen-hour days worked in the shipyards. "As he is a Canadian, he prefers his liberty to being subjected to a clock," wrote the Intendant Bigot of a blacksmith who wanted to leave the yard. Canadian restiveness increased after 1742 when poor harvests made farming more attractive by increasing the value of wheat and bread more rapidly than that of labor. Because the fortunes of agriculture and industry were interconnected, the instability of the agricultural base was a fundamental industrial problem. Partly for this reason the industrial infrastructure was lamentably weak. Hemp, wood-tar, canvas, and iron were all produced in Canada, but their quality was often marginal. Most iron fittings for ships were imported while excellent bulk iron from the forges on the St-Maurice was shipped to France. Usually these supporting industries were maintained by price subsidies and collapsed when the subsidies were removed because of the overproduction of inferior goods.

Moreover, the forest resource had been incorrectly appraised. Ships of the line required huge timbers and masts which rarely could be obtained in Canada. The larger trees were old and usually were rotten at the center. Although a great deal of timber was rejected at the shipyards, undersized or slightly rotten timbers were frequently used, and Canadian-built ships acquired a poor reputation in France. Of the hundreds of ships built at Québec in the nineteenth century, only a handful were as large as those built by the French in the 1740s. As was likely to happen when decisions about North American development were taken in

Europe, the European need and the North American resource did not quite fit.

All in all, Colbert's vision in the 1660s of a diversified Canadian economy had not been realized by the end of the French regime. Canadian resources other than furs were neither distinctive nor valuable enough to justify the difficulty of transporting them to France, and the Canadian market for secondary manufactures could be supplied more cheaply from France. Only the rural service industries protected from French competition by high shipping costs had enjoyed some enduring success. By 1760 gristmills were scattered forty to fifty families apart along the côtes, their exact sites determined by the small tributary streams that provided power for watermills, or by the promontories on which windmills were built. The latter were wooden or stone towers fifteen to twenty feet high and ten to twelve feet in diameter; the former were low structures indistinguishable at a distance from the small farmhouses. These small mills could produce a steady revenue if farms on the surrounding lots were well established. The largest gristmills, such as one in Beaupré and another in Terrebonne, were more than one hundred feet long and three stories high, with granaries in the top floors and several pairs of water-powered millstones below. In 1739 Canada had seventy sawmills; they too yielded a small but fairly steady revenue.

THE TOWNS

Underlying all of this, and in many ways linking it together was the commercial activity of the towns—but of the first Canadian towns we know very little. Commercial, administrative, and military rather than industrial functions undoubtedly were their lifeblood, and commercial considerations (those of the fur trade) largely determined their location. Québec was located at the head of navigation for large sailing ships, and the site had the secondary advantage of controlling the river. Both Montréal and Trois-Rivières were at the junction of important canoe routes into the interior. Because the Ottawa River led to a larger trading hinterland than the St-Maurice, Montréal rather than Trois-Rivières commanded more of the interior trade. Québec, the point of contact with Placentia in Newfoundland, with Louisbourg, with the West Indies, and with France, was the port of the colony. The principal trade of Canada flowed past rather than through Trois-Rivières, which remained a village throughout the French regime.

At the end of French rule, with some 8000 people in Québec and just

Québec from Point Levy. The city at the time of the English conquest. A large hull is under construction in the shipyard below the fort. The Public Archives of Canada.

over 5000 in Montréal, almost a quarter of the Canadian population was urban. This proportion of townsmen, higher than in any of the English colonies to the south, had not changed since the early days of royal government. In large part it reflected the considerable size of the governmental and particularly the military bureaucracy, and numerous troops and clerics. Equally important for urban growth were the commercial requirements of the fur trade. A heavily capitalized and highly organized trading empire that spread over much of the continent required a sizable urban base, and because of the linear nature of the St. Lawrence trading operation, its North American base was concentrated in Québec and Montréal. In the seventeenth century, Indians came to trade at the annual fair in Montréal, and throughout the French regime furs and trade goods were stored in warehouses lining the waterfronts of the two towns. Immediately behind the warehouses were most of the shops and markets, which were established in Québec in 1675, in Montréal a year later. The goods traded in these markets in the eighteenth century suggest that the towns filled an important role as rural service centers, taking over some of the functions that might have gone to rural villages. By 1744 almost 350 skilled laborers and artisans representing more than thirty different occupations lived in Québec. Most of them were carpenters, furniture-makers, stone masons, coopers, blacksmiths, tailors, and rope-makers, but there were also gunsmiths, clock-makers, wig-makers, tinsmiths, silversmiths, and sculptors. This skilled labor force served the activities of the port and shipyards, the surrounding countryside, and a sizable group of prosperous administrators and merchants.

From the river the spires of the baroque churches, the residences of religious orders and of governors and intendants, and the lines of stone warehouses along the waterfront gave the towns an impressive appearance, but like most towns of the day in western Europe, from within they seemed less distinguished. Until well into the eighteenth century, pigs rooted among the refuse that was dumped in the narrow streets. Uncobbled streets became quagmires after heavy rains. Fires were common until an intendant's ordinance forbade the use of thatch as a roofing material. By the end of the French regime many urban buildings were stone, and their roofs board. Visitors likened Québec to a French provincial capital. Montcalm considered that it had a more fashionable society than Montréal, a rougher frontier town that people from Québec tended to feel had been contaminated by Indian values. In contrast with the countryside, the commercial and social life in the more confined and accessible spaces in the towns appears to have been closely regulated. Ordinances almost every year established the price of bread, meat, salt, and wheat; set regulations for weighing and measuring or for the length of time that goods could be displayed in the market; or admonished the young for various improprieties. Tradesmen complained that their activities were more closely circumscribed than in France. As the same complaint was never heard in the countryside, one can speculate on the different social implications in Canada of rural and urban life. Far better than speculation would be some solid studies of these early Canadian towns.

A traveler on the lower St. Lawrence toward the end of the French regime would have been charmed, as was Peter Kalm in 1750, by the straggling lines of simple, whitewashed farmhouses; the church steeples visible for miles along the river; the narrow bands of bright green where the land was cleared; the forest, reaching the river in some places and in others cut back almost a mile; and over the forest the profile of the Laurentians or the Appalachian highlands. It is a striking view today, but in the 1750s, long before urbanization and industry transformed the architecture and population pressure pushed the forest out of sight, the landscape must have had a wild and pristine quality that is now lost. Had the traveler been familiar with the landscape of northwestern France, he would have found much to perplex him: a general feel of rough prosperity with a total absence of wealth; no manor house that a rich French nobleman would have deigned to occupy; a virtual absence of villages; a weak influence on settlement patterns of such loci of authority and power as the church or the manor; a similarity of farmhouses; rail fences between individual properties; an extreme untidiness of cultivated land. Had he reflected on these matters, he might have concluded that the people who created the Canadian landscape were no longer French, and that to understand much of what he saw he would have to understand the nature of this distinctive society.

In France the wealth of the king, the nobility, the clergy, and much of the bourgeoisie depended on the rent of land. The labor of the peasant mass (about half of their gross product, paid in taxes and other charges each year) created the wealth of the few. French customary law, indeed the whole structure of French society, reflected the primacy of land as a source of wealth; and when Frenchmen came to Canada where land was almost free and the revenue from it nonexistent for years, the mortar which had held French society together was suddenly cracked. This new state of affairs was given tacit recognition by the Royal Edict of 1685 which permitted the nobility in Canada to engage in industry and commerce, activities which were closed to their class in France. Seigneurs in Canada became fur traders, soldiers, or administrators; little of their wealth came from the land. They still applied for seigneuries because a seigneurial grant imparted status to its holder. Indeed, there is evidence that in the upper levels of Canadian society a sense of rank was a central social value, but it was not a value that had grown out of the realities of Canadian life. Many seigneurs held their seigneuries only as status symbols, hoping that they would never be forced into the expense of developing them. Manor houses, when they were built, were usually as unpretentious as the neighboring farmhouses; seigneuries were rarely social or economic units on the land, or seigneurs more than passive agents in the settlement of land.

Moreover, the few Frenchmen who had crossed the Atlantic to Canada were not a cross section of French society. There were almost no intellectuals or aristocrats among them, few of the bourgeoisie, and just as few prosperous farmers. For the most part, Canada had been settled by the poor and dispossessed: girls from Paris poorhouses, landless laborers pressed into the army and sent to Canada as ordinary soldiers, people of similar background sent out as engagés, and a few petty criminals. The French roots of most of these people in particular villages and towns of France are now extremely difficult to trace because they were already uprooted, outsiders to the mainstream of French life, even before they crossed the Atlantic. And most immigrants came to Canada as individuals or as members of a temporary social structure, such as a poorhouse or an army, in which they never intended to spend their lives, and which were irrelevant to the settlement of Canada. In the emptiness of the country, where the fur trade was an alternative to farming, and the opportunity for strict official control was extremely slight, the individualism and self-reliance of these Frenchman was perpetuated and intensified. Theirs was not the individualism of the Puritan, but an insouciance and bravado born, most probably, of their Roman Catholicism, their association with the Indians, their modest prosperity, their isolation from official control, and their loose fit in France as in Canada within the formal institutions of French society.

For anyone accustomed to peasant life in France, life along the Canadian côtes would have seemed extraordinarily independent. Canadian settlement had not developed in villages, the parish was only slowly crystallizing even at the end of French rule, and agriculture was not a collective activity. Many men were as much at home in a canoe on Lake Superior or the Ohio River as on a farm lot along the lower St. Lawrence. Farm lots frequently changed hands, and a great many habitants had, in the course of their lives, lived in several seigneuries. Eventually, weak communities based on ties of kin and neighborhood developed in the côtes, but free of many of the constraints, of the exactions, of the need to create a common front against a hostile world—that is, against almost everything from outside the village—that bound a French village tightly together.

In France, village, parish, seigneurie, and central government all laid heavy charges on the peasants. The royal taille, originally an overlord's right to exact from a vassal whatever he needed when he needed it, had been commuted to an annual payment; but in Canada it and most other royal charges were discontinued as the king and his ministers sought to create conditions favorable to immigration. Habitants were expected to work two days each year on the king's roads, but there were no royal roads until well into the eighteenth century. Far from increasing the habitants' burden, the presence of the king's ministers considerably lightened it. The government could not impose itself on the habitants, but it offered certain services—inexpensive regional courts, for example, or the right of free appeal to the intendant. In operating hospitals, orphanages, and poorhouses the religious orders did the same. Such support only increased the independence of the habitants, who were not forced to compensate for an oppressive officialdom by a tighter social organization at the local level.

Although Canadian rural society was loosely structured, it would be wrong to conclude that the people who shaped the landscape of the lower St. Lawrence were the frontiersmen of American legend. The machinery of control had come to Canada, and if its authority could rarely be imposed, it could always be turned to and frequently was. Moreover, the Canadians were extremely fond of convivial pursuits— they were not found striking out into the wilderness to establish a farm miles ahead of the vanguard of settlement. They often left as young men for the wilderness—for the profit and excitement of the fur trade—but most of them returned to their côtes along the St. Lawrence. Finally, the drive for material success was less than in the English colonies. Most habitants lived well enough. In coming to a colony where land was abundant and the charges for it were low, it was not too difficult, at least by the second generation, to achieve a higher living standard than that of most French peasants. The habitants were not forced into the interminable round of work that many French peasants undertook merely to stay alive or that many New Englanders followed out of the compulsion of the Puritan ethic.

Bibliography

Although there is a vast literature on early Canada and Acadia, very few studies shed much light on the topics discussed in this chapter. The most useful source on Acadia is now A. H. Clark, *Acadia* (Madison: University of Wisconsin Press, 1969). Of many general histories of early Canada, W. J. Eccles, *The Canadian Frontier: 1534-1760* (New York: Holt, Rinehart and Winston, 1969), is probably the best, and contains much of interest to a historical geographer including an excellent bibliography. Eccles's article "The Social, Economic, and Political Signifi-cance of the Military Establishment in New France," *Canadian Histori-cal Review* 52 (March 1971), 1-22, should be read in conjunction with his book. The several attempts by sociologists to describe early Cana-dian society are as provocative as they are factually uncertain. A helpful entrée to this literature is a volume of essays, *French Canadian Society*, Carleton Library, No. 18 (Toronto: McClelland and Stewart, 1964). See also the article by Sigmund Diamond, "An Experiment in Feudalism: French Canada in the Seventeenth Century," *William and Mary Quar-terly* 3rd series, vol. 18 (Jan. 1961). The economic history of the French regime has not been well treated, but an important start is Jean Ham-elin's *Economie et société en Nouvelle France* (Québec: Laval Univer-sity Press, 1960). On more specialized topics see R. C. Harris, *The Sei-gneurial System in Early Canada: A Geographical Study* (Madison: University of Wisconsin Press, 1966), and by the same author, "The French Background of Immigration to Canada before 1700," *Cahiers de Geographie de Québec* (Fall 1972). Also, Louise Dechêne, "L'evolu-tion du régime seigneurial au Canada, le cas de Montréal aux XVIIe et XVIIIe siècles," *Recherches Sociographiques* 12 (mai–août 1971), 143–83; Georges Gauthier-Larouche, *L'évolution de la maison rurale Lauren-tienne* (Québec: Laval University Press, 1967); and Jacques Mathieu, *La Construction navale royale à Québec, 1739–1759* (Québec: Laval University Press, 1971). One of the best of the eighteenth-century travel accounts, and by far the best of its kind on early Canada, is Peter Kalm's delightfully informative diary of his Canadian travels: Adolphe B. Ben-son (ed.), *Peter Kalm's Travels in North America*, vol. 2 (New York: Dover Publications, 1966). Some of the maps relevant to a study of early Canada are published by Marcel Trudel, *Atlas de la Nouvelle-France, An Atlas of New France* (Québec: Laval University Press, 1968).

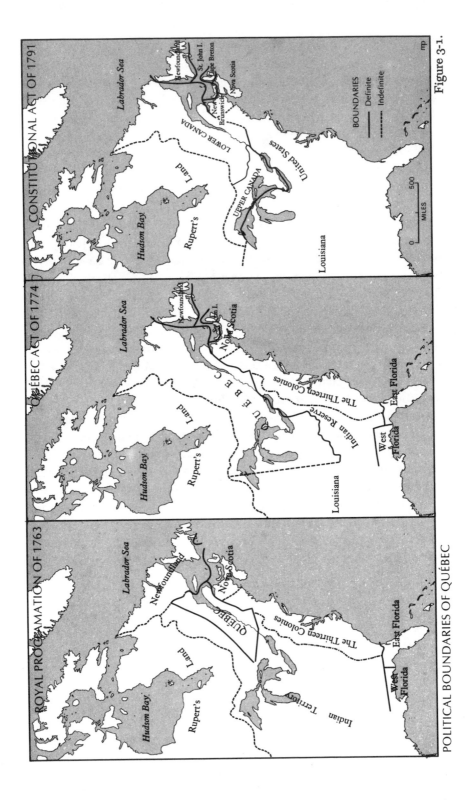

ROYAL PROCLAMATION OF 1763

Labrador Sea

Hudson Bay

Rupert's Land

Newfoundland

Nova Scotia

QUÉBEC

The Thirteen Colonies

Indian Territory

West Florida

East Florida

QUÉBEC ACT OF 1774

Labrador Sea

Hudson Bay

Rupert's Land

Newfoundland

Nova Scotia

St. John I.

QUÉBEC

Indian Reserve

The Thirteen Colonies

Louisiana

West Florida

East Florida

CONSTITUTIONAL ACT OF 1791

Labrador Sea

Hudson Bay

Rupert's Land

Newfoundland

St. John I.

Cape Breton

Nova Scotia

New Brunswick

LOWER CANADA

UPPER CANADA

United States

Louisiana

BOUNDARIES

—— Definite

---- Indefinite

0   500

MILES

POLITICAL BOUNDARIES OF QUÉBEC

Figure 3-1.

mp

3 QUEBEC IN THE CENTURY

AFTER THE CONQUEST

During the French regime, Canadians were connected by the fur trade to the continental interior and by immigration and the colonial elites to France, but after 1760 these external ties withered quickly. By the 1820s, in the minds of many French Canadians, the St. Lawrence River had become almost an inland sea, and their world the wedge of land between the Shield and the Appalachians. Faced with Pontiac's uprising in the west and with a welter of conflicting claims to the trade and territory of the interior, the British in 1763 had set the Great Lakes basin aside as an Indian reserve open to all licensed traders, and in so doing had defined Canada as the narrow trapezoid shown in Figure 3-1. This decision, however, had altered neither the pattern nor the volume of the St. Lawrence fur trade, and the Québec Act of 1774 redrew the boundaries of Canada to bring the colony's political and economic territories into closer accord. Then, in 1783, British and Americans negotiated a political boundary that divided the St. Lawrence trading hinterland into British and American territory. Soon thereafter Loyalist settlers along the upper St. Lawrence were clamoring for an elected assembly and for the use of English civil law. The simplest administrative solution to their demands, embodied in the Constitutional Act of 1791, seemed to be to divide Canada into two colonies. A political territory, Lower Canada, was created along the lower St. Lawrence, outside of which French Canadians had no special rights.

Within this contracted political space, economic and political power was in the hands of English-speaking people. Immigration from France had stopped. For most French Canadians, France was a totally inaccessible and, especially after the Revolution, an increasingly alien land. By 1800 nearly all the important merchants were of British background, the relative importance of the fur trade was rapidly declining, and French Canadians were cut off from direct commercial ties with the external world. Equally isolated from power within Québec, and feeling the threat of an expanding English-speaking, Protestant population, French-Canadian life folded inward around its own institutions and myths. Because urban life had been so largely taken over by the English speaking, the rural seigneurial lowlands became the heartland of French Canada. Local communities strengthened, and institutions that had been weak during the French regime became more prominent. Ideas from the outside world still filtered into these rural areas, but the ethos of French-Canadian life had become essentially protective.

Although French-Canadian life folded inward, the French-Canadian population increased more than ten times in one hundred years. During the first half of the eighteenth century the Canadian birth rate averaged approximately 50 per thousand per year, but rose to more than 55 in the early 1760s as soldiers were demobilized and the marriage rate increased. From this high, the birth rate declined to just under 50 in the first two decades of the nineteenth century, rising again to almost 55 at mid-century. In epidemic years the death rate reached 45 per thousand, but usually it was under 30 in the eighteenth century and under 25 by the middle of the nineteenth century. War, poor harvests, or a drop in the price of wheat or wood affected the number of marriages and hence the birth rate within only a limited range. Without decisive Malthusian checks, the population doubled approximately every twenty-six years. In spite of a significant annual drain to New England after 1820, there were some 850,000 French Canadians in Québec in 1861.

In the mid-1760s there were not more than 500 English-speaking residents of Canada, but by 1790, after the coming of the Loyalists, perhaps one-fifth of the population of the British territory along the St. Lawrence and north of the Great Lakes was English speaking. After the division of this territory into Upper Canada and Lower Canada, land-seekers from New England continued to trickle into the Appalachian highlands southeast of Montréal (the Eastern Townships). A larger surge of English-speaking immigrants, part of the movement triggered by industrial and agricultural change in the British Isles, came after 1815. In 1847 alone some 90,000 immigrants arrived at Québec, and in the forty years after 1815 almost a million people landed in British North American ports. Although most of those disembarking at Québec went on to Upper Canada or to the United States, some stayed, and in 1861, 22 per cent of the total population in Lower Canada—260,000 people—were not French Canadians.

Here were two quite different populations: the one French speaking and Catholic, enclosed in the close knit of the rural community and acutely aware of its minority position within the British Empire and North America; the other English speaking and predominantly Protestant, a rich, powerful, and substantially urban minority in Québec, but a closely connected part of the British Empire and of the mainstream of nineteenth-century North American settlement. At the center of nineteenth-century French-Canadian life was the rural community, whereas the English-speaking immigrants in Québec, having recently experienced the dislocation of movement and, in many cases, of early British industrialization tended to share the increasingly individualistic values of the nineteenth-century world. These two dominant cultures coexisted in Québec, sometimes harmoniously, sometimes abrasively, but except in a few families and in a few local areas, they did not merge. A cultural divide, reinforced by the distribution of wealth, power, and patronage ran through the towns, differentiated many rural areas, and lay behind much of the colony's political life.

The existence along the lower St. Lawrence of two groups of people, each with its own traditions and outlooks, created almost endless legal confusion—much of it over land tenure. In 1762 Governor Murray granted seigneuries to two British officers, but in 1763 a Royal Proclamation established English law throughout the colony, and supplementary instruction to the governor stipulated that crown land would be granted in freehold. Yet the seigneurial system and French customary law continued to be observed along the lower St. Lawrence, and there were few if any freehold grants of crown land before 1774. In that year the Québec Act officially re-established French civil law in Canada, and instructions sent in 1775 stipulated that henceforth crown land would be granted in the seigneurial tenure. When the Loyalists objected to this tenure, the government proposed to waive all cens et rentes for ten years, but eventually sidestepped the problem by issuing location tickets which vaguely stipulated that the holder would receive title to his lot when certain improvements had been made. The Constitutional Act of 1791 allowed petitioners for crown land in Lower Canada to obtain it in freehold, and the secret instructions accompanying the Act specified that future grants should be made in freehold only. Thereafter there were

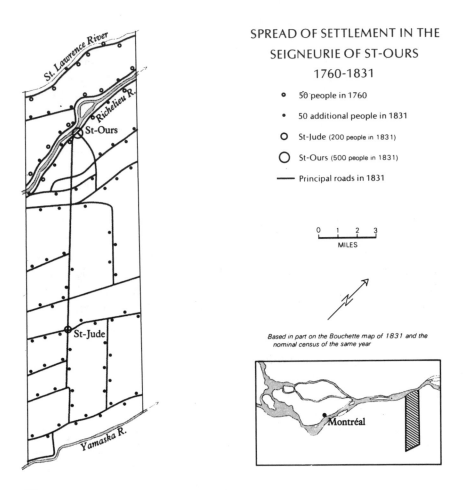

SPREAD OF SETTLEMENT IN THE
SEIGNEURIE OF ST-OURS
1760-1831

- ∘ 50 people in 1760
- • 50 additional people in 1831
- O St-Jude (200 people in 1831)
- ⬭ St-Ours (500 people in 1831)
- —— Principal roads in 1831

0   1   2   3
MILES

Based in part on the Bouchette map of 1831 and the
nominal census of the same year

Figure 3-2.

two distinctive systems of land tenure in Québec and, with minor exceptions, no further seigneurial grants of crown land. There matters rested until 1854 when, after years of heated debate, the seigneurial system was legally abolished. In fact abolition changed relatively little. Most censitaires could not reimburse their seigneur for the value of their rotures and continued to pay a rent (the annual interest charge against the value of their property) while the government compensated the seigneurs for the loss of the lods et ventes and the banal mill rights. If anything, seigneurial revenue rose. Yet it became much easier for the merchants to speculate in land, to control timber reserves, and to build mills at water power sites within the seigneuries. Indeed, the seigneurial system had been legally annulled largely to achieve these ends.

As the population of Lower Canada rose, the seigneuries filled up first, largely because most of the best land in the colony lay within them, but also because a good deal of township land was withheld by speculators or was too highly priced for most French Canadians and because French Canadians hesitated to settle among English-speaking people and on freehold. The cultivable land in many seigneuries was occupied by 1800 and in almost all seigneuries by the 1830s (see Fig. 3-2). When all the arable land in a rural area was settled, newcomers became rarer, local kin groups strengthened, and the rural society became even more enclosed. Farms were subdivided, and the number of landless laborers and artisans increased. Some were absorbed in villages nearby, but eventually many more moved away.

As early as 1810 a few French Canadians began to push into the Shield. They were soon followed in far greater numbers by both Protestant and Catholic Irish who settled relatively fertile lacustrine and fluvial pockets and then began to occupy the thin, stony tills that covered the uplands. Frequently the Irish combined farming and logging, but when the forest was denuded and the upland fields proved infertile, most of them drifted away. But the French Canadians stayed, some occupying the abandoned fields while others pushed beyond the fringe of Irish settlement to squat on unsurveyed land further north. Most of the French Canadians had come as single men or in nuclear families, but in the 1850s and 1860s some larger groups came into the wilderness, led by devoted priests, the most famous of whom, curé Antoine Labelle, once declared his ambition to replace every spruce with a colonist. The price of these attempts to preserve religion and culture and to encourage economic development was continuing rural poverty. By 1870 a second drift away from this unproductive land began.

While some French Canadians were settling in the Shield, others moved south into the United States or into the Eastern Townships of Québec, where they mingled with and began to displace settlers from New England. The other major outlet lay in the cities of Lower Canada, principally Montréal and Québec. French Canadians brought strong backs to the cities but few urban skills, and they usually became low-priced laborers working for English employers, or artisans dependent on the wages of other French Canadians.

The evolution of Québec after 1760 can no longer be described as a unitary process within a single region. The rest of this chapter examines developments in the seigneurial lands, the Shield fringe, the Eastern

Townships and the towns before considering, in conclusion, the implications of geographical change in Québec since the end of French rule.

The seigneurial lands

SETTLEMENT PATTERNS

During the French regime labor was relatively scarce and dear, and land abundant and cheap, but as the population rose along the St. Lawrence this relationship was gradually reversed. As the principal landholders the seigneurs benefitted while the censitaires grew poorer. An agricultural crisis in the 1830s affected both groups, reducing many censitaires to poverty and slowing the growth of seigneurial revenue, but by the 1850s the revenue from almost all seigneuries was many times higher than it had been a century before. In large part this increase was a by-product of population growth—many more censitaires were paying dues—and of the timber trade, which made an economic asset of much uncultivable land; but in many seigneuries, with the principal exception of those owned by the church or the crown, per capita charges were also rising. By the early nineteenth century most lay seigneurs had increased the rate of the cens et rentes in new roture contracts and were demanding payment in wheat rather than in capons as was common during the French regime. Even Louis-Joseph Papineau, the political leader of French-Canadian nationalism in the 1820s and 1830s, conceded rotures in his Ottawa valley seigneurie at a rate one-third above the highest charge levied during the French regime, and required most of the payment in wheat, a crop that could not be grown in most of his holdings. When wheat sold at six livres a bushel, an average price in the early nineteenth century, and well above the average price during the French regime, the censitaires paid more than five sols an arpent; when, in 1814, wheat sold at fourteen livres a bushel, they paid more than ten sols. Although such a payment was several times higher than any during the French regime, it is a moot point whether an intendant would have disallowed these rentes. The old rate had been increased only fractionally (higher payments reflecting primarily the rising price of wheat). Moreover, the low charges during the French regime reflected the abundance of land and the scarcity of colonists, conditions which had changed radically.

As seigneurial revenues increased, seigneurs paid more attention to their land. Many appointed agents who collected the dues, kept account books more regularly, and saw to it that roture contracts were standard-ized and printed. Some seigneurs, despairing, as one Englishman put it, of collecting more from "those tinkering habitants with no pay," sold the back rents to collectors at discounts of 25 to 50 per cent. Occasionally they took indebted censitaires to court. Withdrawn rotures were put up for auction and usually bought for next to nothing by the seigneur, who discouraged other bidders by requiring them to settle the back rents immediately. He could then let out the roture to a sharecropper or sell it on terms. Partly, however, out of concern for his censitaires' plight, partly because of the cost and inconvenience of litigation, no seigneur sued more than a small fraction of his debtors. Court action was under-taken to make an example of a few and thereby to goad the many into paying. Some seigneurs began requiring prospective censitaires to im-prove a roture and to pay the annual dues for several years before they issued a contract, a procedure that was unheard of before 1760. By such methods they collected a fair percentage of what they were owed; even so, it was as difficult, one bailiff explained to his seigneur, to collect from the habitants as to get blood from a stone.

During the French regime many seigneurs had been involved in the government, the army, or in commerce and had neglected their sparsely settled lands. But as the English took over the towns, a seigneurie often became its owner's principal support. The fine manor houses built in the early nineteenth century reflect both the rise in seigneurial revenue and the French-Canadian retreat from urban life and commercial values. Some of the finest manors, to be sure, were built by English-speaking seigneurs, for a good many seigneuries had passed into English hands in payment for debts, by marriage, or by purchase (see Fig. 3-3). Many of these seigneurs were involved in commerce or government, and considered their land as a speculative sideline or as an investment ex-pected to yield a steady 5 per cent per year. Others were charmed by the image of life on the land as a seigneur—a squire surrounded by his tenantry—and raised their families in the seigneurie. Such families were fluently bilingual and, although strongly attached to the British Empire, had moved some way into French-Canadian life. Perhaps the girls at-tended the Ursuline School in Québec and later married French Canadi-ans. More of the English seigneurs viewed their holdings as a peaceful retreat from a more hectic urban life, and in times of stress, as when some speculation in timber or grain had gone awry, they were wont to live there. The seigneurie was always a socially acceptable safety valve for

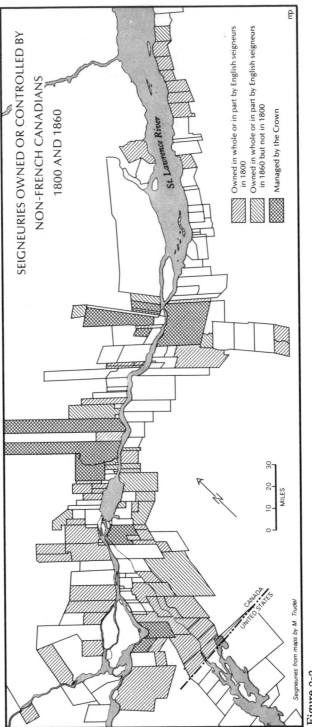

SEIGNEURIES OWNED OR CONTROLLED BY
NON-FRENCH CANADIANS
1800 AND 1860

St. Lawrence River

Owned in whole or in part by English seigneurs
in 1800

Owned in whole or in part by English seigneurs
in 1860 but not in 1800

Managed by the Crown

MILES
0   10   20   30

CANADA
UNITED STATES

Seigneuries from maps by M. Trudel

Figure 3-3.

many urban problems. "What shall I do," the daughter of an English seigneur wrote from Québec to her aunt in the seigneurie, "all the girls are getting married but me and here I am with no beau, not even an admirer. I think if I am not successful in this winter's campaign I shall have to accept your former offer of taking me to the seigneurie . . . for between ourselves the market, as Papa calls it, is greatly overstocked."

Whoever the seigneur, the settlement pattern remained based on the long lot and côte, or rang (range), as a côte was more commonly called in the nineteenth century. With seigneurs paying more attention to their properties, and settlement moving away from the irregular outline of the river, the orientation and dimensions of lots and rangs became more nearly standardized. Yet seigneurs adjusted their concessions to fit major topographic features, and cadastral patterns in the seigneuries rarely bore the inflexible geometrical stamp of those in the townships. Accompanying the move away from the river was a great increase in carting and a decline in local river traffic. Roads became the focus of settlement and some houses in river-front lots were moved back from the river to gain direct access to a road. In single-rang settlements a road ran along the front of each rang with houses on one side and the back, or trait carré, of the previously conceded rang on the other (see Fig. 3-4). In the double rang, which became more common, houses were built on either side of the road, thus increasing the density of local settlement and reducing the road mileage by one-half. In many seigneuries by the early 1800s there were six or seven double rangs along roads roughly parallel to the river, linked by one or two crossroads with no settlement along them.

As population pressure rose the density of settlement in the rangs increased. In any system of partible inheritance the size of individual holdings is in an almost constant state of flux, but as long as land was abundant along the lower St. Lawrence, rotures that were divided among many heirs tended to work back into the hands of one of them. As soon as land became scarce, the permanent subdivision of rotures began, and in a few seigneuries near the towns—Beaupré or the Ile d'Orléans for example—this process was well underway before 1760. Although population pressure in the early nineteenth century greatly increased the number of small rotures, the extent of subdivision was less than has sometimes been suggested. In Lotbinière, for example, the median size of rotures belonging to farmers declined from 130 arpents in 1831 to 110 in 1841 and to just over 90 in 1861—still a substantial farm. Such subdivi-

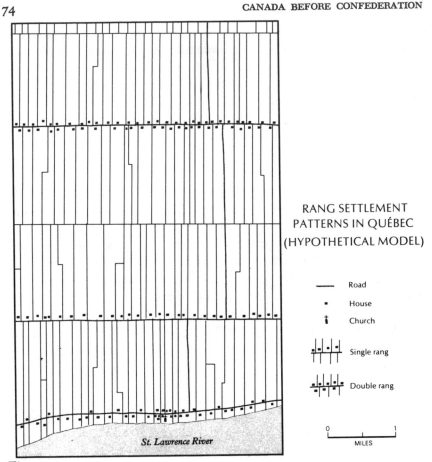

RANG SETTLEMENT
PATTERNS IN QUÉBEC
(HYPOTHETICAL MODEL)

—— Road

▪ House

✝ Church

Single rang

Double rang

0   1
MILES

Figure 3-4.

sion did mean that farmhouses were more closely spaced, in some areas
no more than one hundred yards apart. It also became common for two
or even three families to live under one roof. Some men farmed, others
were carpenters or worked in sawmills, and the boys hired themselves
out as day laborers when they could or worked around the farm.

The emergence of villages shortly after the conquest also contributed
to the rising rural population density. In 1777 there were almost as many
villages or hamlets on Montréal Island as there had been in the whole
colony at the end of the French regime. Near Québec most of the villages that are now strung along the côte de Beaupré and around the
Ile d'Orléans appeared as tiny hamlets before the end of the eighteenth
century; in 1815 when the surveyor general, Joseph Bouchette, drew the

most detailed map of the colony since Governor Murray's map of 1762, there was a village or hamlet in almost every settled seigneurie. There- after the establishment and growth of central places proceeded even more rapidly, particularly during the depths of the agricultural crisis of the 1830s.

In some cases a seigneur divided a portion of his domain or of a roture into village lots and in so doing usually laid out a market square and a rectangular grid of streets. More often, villages grew haphazardly along the road on either side of a church as farmers sold bits and pieces along the front of their rotures. Farmhouses and barns were scattered through these villages which tailed off almost imperceptibly into the normal rangs. Occasionally the rang thickened at a crossroads or near a gristmill, and in the 1820s and 1830s dormitory villages developed at sawmills. Some of these places became important enough to become centers of

Beauport. A common village scene in nineteenth-century Québec. Roof shapes indicate that most of the houses were built in the early part of the century. Houses were often oriented with respect to the sun, the river, or property lines rather than to the road.

parishes. Villages served the rural community in several ways: they provided the elderly with a place to live close to church and curé; they were
centers for the artisans, grain merchants, and shopkeepers who provided
an exchange between town and farm; and they grouped professional
services—those of curé, doctor, notary, and perhaps schoolteacher and
surveyor. The seigneurial manor or bailiff's residence was sometimes
part of a village but more commonly was located just outside it, a presence in but not a part of the village.

The reasons for the sudden appearance of the village in the latter
part of the eighteenth century are not altogether clear, but tentatively
it may be suggested that the early village was a creation of both the
parish and the grain trade, whose formative influence did not work in
concert until that time. Curés had not been established until at least the
1720s in most rural parishes; these early parishes were weak social units
which strengthened only near the end of the French regime at a time of
agricultural depression. The strengthening of the parishes was offset by
the weakness of the rural economy, and, although in the 1750s some
seigneurs had requested permission to lay out villages, the impetus to
establish them was not there. There was a serious shortage of priests
after the conquest, but in parishes still served by curés they were more
likely to be seen as links with a familiar tradition than, as so often had
been the case during the French regime, as unwelcome additions from
outside. At the same time broader economic connections within the
British imperial system led to the resumption of the grain trade which,
by the 1770s, had attained a greater volume than at any time during
the French regime. In this situation hamlets and villages appeared,
serving as entrepôts in the grain trade and as parish centers. The
first village artisans came from outside the parish, but as population
pressures increased, villages attracted the sons of local farmers; in many
villages the number of artisans increased greatly during the worst years
of the agricultural crisis. Except where the village was closely associated
with the timber trade, it had become by this date a reflection of agricultural ills rather than commercial vitality. In the 1850s and 1860s
mixed farming and rural industry expanded, and the village economy
again became more solidly based.

Most villages grew up around a church, its location depending on an
assessment of least travel time in the parish, on the advantages of a
commanding site, and on the strong pressure politics of the rangs. No
matter raised more heat in the rural community than the choice of a

church site—the prestige of a rang, travel time, and a clear commercial opportunity for artisans were involved. The bishop had the final say. He would usually approve unanimous recommendations, but these were rare. Almost invariably he received lengthy petitions favoring different sites; after he made his decision he invariably received another round urging him to change his mind. Preference was given most often to first-rang locations because the earlier church or chapel had been located there and because that rang, the oldest, had a special status as the hearth of the parish. The upshot of these pressures was usually that parish churches and associated villages were located about six to eight miles apart along the river. When there were several rangs, other churches and villages were similarly spaced in the interior. When two villages were much more closely spaced, the origin of one of them was frequently associated with sawmilling.

Villages constituted a new element in the social fabric, and they always stood somewhat apart from the rural communities that surrounded them. Initially most of villagers were newcomers to the parish, some of them from the towns, sometimes one or two of them English. Later when villages began to absorb more of the local population, the move to them was often the first step away from family, kin group, and rang. For a great many young French Canadians this may have been a difficult step, for a rural community was a maze of blood relationships. Of the 560 families in Lotbinière in 1861, the husband or wife in 110 of them was a Lemay, while the ten leading surnames in Lotbinière were represented in the husband or wife of 319 families. In only seventeen cases had the surnames of both partners been introduced to Lotbinière since 1842. In some cases a family was associated with a particular rang—in 1782 the Lemays were a family of the first rang, and the Hamels of the second—and the social structure of kin group and rang reinforced each other, but as time went by relatives tended to spread more widely. Because of the subdivision of parental rotures, two or three siblings often lived on adjacent farms, but other relatives were scattered for miles around, and there is every reason to suppose that the range of kin-group relationships included a good many of them. Within kin groups and the rangs was a strong tradition of mutual aid, and both the increasing consanguinity of the population and the nineteenth-century appearance of gatherings such as building bees suggest that this tradition had strengthened since the French regime.

The seigneur had become an important figure in the rural community. He or his agent was usually present in the seigneurie, a great many habitants were in debt to him, and his relative wealth and power —usually much greater than during the French regime—often set him off as an important figure. In decisions over such matters as the location of a church or a school he often played a prominent role, frequently exerting a strong influence on the local curé. Yet there was no more reason for the seigneurie itself to constitute a social unit than there had been during the French regime. Habitants still paid their dues when they could or when a collector threatened. Perhaps their picturesque custom of planting a Maypole in front of the seigneurial manor had become a little more common than during the French regime; otherwise, the round of their activity was not affected by the seigneurie.

Territorially and numerically, the largest social unit was undoubtedly the parish. In many cases surnames and kin-group affiliations changed sharply across parish boundaries, an indication of the frequency of intra-parish marriages and of the social round within a parish. It appears that the parish had strengthened considerably since the French regime, particularly early in the nineteenth century. With the decline of the fur trade and the increasing scarcity of land, the rural population had become much less mobile. There was considerable movement out of the St. Lawrence lowland or into the towns, but less than formerly between riverine parishes. Then too, the presence and influence of a curé became more widely accepted. There were still cases in which the habitants preferred a missionary to a resident priest, probably most often because of the cost of supporting a priest but also because a priest might interfere with the decidedly boisterous way of life in certain areas. Finally, more civil functions were performed in the parish. By the middle of the nineteenth century an inspector of roads and bridges, an inspector of the poor, and several fence and ditch viewers were elected in the parish; and a small land tax was levied for the maintenance of parochial schools with assessors of land, a tax collector, and a clerk elected to administer it.

BUILDINGS

After 1760 the house styles discussed in Chapter 2 gradually evolved into the distinctively French-Canadian house illustrated in Figure 3-5. Although a direct outgrowth of earlier styles, this house differed from them in the following principal respects: a more gently pitched roof with eaves overhanging as much as five feet, dormer windows and more fenestra-

Figure 3.5. French-Canadian House Types, 1820 and 1850
Right, a fairly typical farmhouse built around 1820. Note particularly the overhang of the eaves, the gentler pitch of the roof (as compared to houses of the French regime), and the slight elevation of the main floor. Such houses were of field stone, frame or *pièce-sur-pièce* construction.

Left, a substantial house dating from the 1850s. Such a house might be built by a prosperous farmer, notary, doctor, merchant, or, frequently, by a parish for its curé. Note the considerable elevation of the main floor and the fenestration. (Drawings by Peter Ennals)

tion, a porch along the front and often along the back of the house, and a main floor raised several feet above the ground. Many of these changes were adaptations to the Canadian climate—the overhang to protect the facade and to some extent the porch from rain, sleet, and snow, the additional windows to improve ventilation on a hot summer day, the cellar to serve as storage space in winter and as a cool kitchen in summer—but it is not clear why they appeared so late. Perhaps improvements in winter heating made possible by the increased use of stoves in the early nineteenth century led to the construction of airier houses, structures that tended to be more comfortable in summer. Here and there round log cabins with interlocking corners had been introduced from New England, but otherwise techniques of construction had not changed since the French regime. Some of the ornamentation around windows and doors was borrowed from the architectural modes of the day—a Georgian or neo-classical transom for example, or Victorian gingerbread around the dormers and the gable ends.

As seigneurial revenues rose, manor houses became a distinctive element in the rural scene. Some were larger versions of the French-Canadian vernacular house, but French as well as English seigneurs built handsome Georgian and neo-classical manors. The grounds around French-Canadian manors were sparsely adorned, but the English sense of the picturesque was likely to be expressed in winding avenues, vine-

Le vieux manoir à d'Autray. The nineteenth-century manor house was a good deal larger than its predecessors, and often departed completely from the French-Canadian architectural tradition. This neoclassical building is an import from the south, the American temple house. The Public Archives of Canada.

covered walls, and in the composed naturalness of an English garden. English seigneurs were also fond of paths through the woods leading, preferably, to a carefully constructed romantic view. "Ann," an English seigneur instructed his wife, "must lead the Ladies thro my Groves and thickets, particularly the Serpentine walk to the old Mill—the view of the river and the noise of the rapids, even in a state of nature, beggars description . . . if any vessels are at the hangard [wharf] they will add to the Scene." A few French Canadians copied the English taste for landscape; somewhat to his father's annoyance, one of Louis-Joseph Papineau's sons wanted to lay out an English park in the family seigneurie of Petite-Nation.

The major change in farm buildings was the consolidation of grange, écurie, and étable into a single structure. This was a long and still relatively low barn, with livestock kept on the ground floor and a ramp on one side leading to a hayloft above. Adoption of this style probably reflected the architectural influence of New England and the Eastern Townships—a ramp with a passage underneath it, for example, was common in the townships but virtually absent in Upper Canada—and coincided with the shift from cereals to livestock and mixed farming that took place after 1830. These barns were usually located well behind the farmhouse, but from a distance their size and whitewashed brightness made them the dominant buildings in the rang.

The parish church was the most striking building in rural Québec, the one that in early nineteenth-century sketches and etchings was the hallmark of the French-Canadian landscape. Frequently located on a bluff overlooking the river, on a beach ridge of the former Champlain Sea, or at a bend in the road so that there was a terminal view of the church from both directions, the church loomed over the village, its single, double, or occasionally triple spires making it visible from most of the parish. The parishioners contributed labor, money, and materials, but architecturally the church was only partially and, as time went on, only indirectly a product of folk culture. The bishop usually provided the plan, and with the rise of French-Canadian nationalism in the early nineteenth century, these plans were intended to evoke the parish church of the French regime. Even Louis XVI classicism, introduced belatedly to Québec in the 1820s by Jerome Demers, director of the Seminaire de Québec, and his protégé Thomas Baillairgé, blended with a concept of the traditional church. At their best these hybrids were singularly successful, and they have been well described by architectural historians.

AGRICULTURE

For fifty years after 1760 clearing proceeded more rapidly in the seigneurial lowlands than ever before. Only 75,000 arpents had been cleared in 1724 and just over 200,000 in 1739. During the next twenty years agricultural depression and war held back the rate of clearing. Then in 1784 the census reported more than 1,500,000 arpents of cleared land, an overly high figure but one that at least indicates the magnitude of the assault on the forest. West of Trois-Rivières, unbroken forest was no longer visible from the river, and the present extent of clearing virtually had been reached in many seigneuries by the end of the eighteenth century. The spate of clearing is explained partly by the return of peace and the growing rural population, and partly by the increased opportunity for agricultural exports within the British Empire. There were wide variations in prices and in volume of agricultural imports from year to year, but generally agriculture was more profitable in the last three decades of the eighteenth century than ever before, and the habitants were clearing land to take advantage of the opportunity.

The English introduced several new crops, among them potatoes, but the habitants' agricultural system was slow to change. Wheat and untended meadow or pasture were still the dominant land uses and were combined in the same loose system of convertible husbandry (see Chapter 2, pp. 51–52). This style of husbandry horrified Englishmen who had any knowledge of the improved farming practices of their day, and in 1789 the governor, Lord Dorchester, organized an agricultural society in the hope of modernizing it. The society, composed largely of English-speaking merchants and professional men, began ambitiously by sending agricultural instructions to local militia captains and parish priests, but soon found that, if read at all, the instructions were "almost totally and shamefully neglected." The feeling that the habitants were insouciant and shiftless grew. Yet the conditions which favored extensive agriculture during the French regime (see Chapter 2, pp 49–51) had not changed late in the eighteenth century, and by farming as he did an habitant was able to devote most of his energy to clearing while producing an agricultural surplus. Had he adopted the more intensive methods recommended by the agricultural society, his yields per arpent would have risen spectacularly, but he would have had less cleared land with a smaller percentage planted in wheat. His income, at least in the short term, probably would have fallen, or he would have worked harder and longer for little additional reward.

Rising prices and a fairly steady market for wheat tended to improve average rural living standards and to increase the range between the prosperous and the poor. As we have noted, sporadic opportunities for agricultural exports during the French regime and a system of partible inheritance had kept the size of individual farms below one hundred cleared arpents. Commercial ties within the British Empire weakened one of these checks on farm size. A few farmers combined an inheritance, a good marriage, and hard work to create substantially larger farms—up to almost 200 cleared arpents—than those farmed by their predecessors before 1760. At the same time, some of the merchants or professional men in the villages were buying land nearby; not uncommonly one of the largest farms in the parish belonged to the local notary, the merchant, or even the parish priest. This process of economic and perhaps social differentiation had barely begun in many seigneuries by the end of the eighteenth century, but in others there were a few relatively prosperous individuals, precursors of a larger group in the nineteenth century.

Wheat exports reached their peak in 1802–3 and declined rapidly thereafter. Although the price of wheat rose sharply during the Napoleonic wars, little French-Canadian grain was exported, and when wheat rusts and the hessian fly ravaged crops in the 1830s, Lower Canada became an importer of wheat. Behind the decimation of the wheat crops lay an extensive agricultural technology perpetuated at a time of increasing population pressure. Because French Canadians gave little attention to their cultivated land, fields were choked with weeds, and their grain contained a variety of weed seeds that made for dirty, often ill-tasting flour. As early as 1771 superfine flour from New York had been offered for sale in Québec. As grain cultivation expanded in upstate New York, the Ohio valley, and Upper Canada, the low quality wheat and flour produced in Lower Canada became vulnerable to competition from these areas. Often, however, Québec farms simply did not produce a surplus. Before 1800 the rate of land clearing had more than kept pace with population growth, but in the nineteenth century it did not. According to the 1831 census there were then well under four arpents of arable and pasture per person in Lower Canada. The colony was running out of agricultural land. Moreover, seed-yield ratios were also falling because there was less fresh, recently cleared land. An unresponsive agricultural system had become extremely vulnerable to competition and to natural calamities of the sort that would strike in the 1830s.

Population pressure did increase the local demand for wheat, hay, and livestock, and those who were able to supply this market strengthened their relative economic position. For example, seigneurs compounded their role as creditors by selling within their seigneuries more of the wheat and flour they obtained from the banal gristmill and the cens et rentes. There was some local sale for hay, and a growing market in the towns and villages for dairy products and meat. In 1831 twenty-

one, or one-fifth, of the first rang farms in Lotbinière contained more
than one hundred cleared arpents each; only one of them was still a
traditional wheat farm. Although most of these large farms produced a
wheat surplus, cattle or sheep were the principal products. More prosperous than the farmers were the notary (who was also the seigneurial
agent) the surveyor, and the innkeeper—each of whom owned a large
mixed farm. Apart from an occasional seigneur, there was still no real
wealth in the rural community, but the relatively prosperous group that
had begun to emerge late in the nineteenth century strengthened and
grew larger as the agricultural crisis deepened.

For most of the rural population, however, the failure of their principal food crop was an unmitigated disaster. In Lotbinière the wheat
harvest of about 23,000 bushels in 1831 had dropped to just over 300
bushels in 1841. Millers pleaded that there was no grain to grind, and
that they could not possibly pay the annual rent for the mill. One mill
not far from Québec was rented for £90 in 1820, £80 in 1830, and
£40 in 1839, and still the tenant miller remained heavily in debt. Rural
living standards fell to their lowest point in the nineteenth century, a
level comparable to the worst years of crop failure during the French
regime. In the villages as on the farms potatoes became the dietary
staple. The number of stock declined as animals were slaughtered and
game again became an important food. Subsistent and part-time farming became much more common.

Recovery began in the 1840s and continued in the 1850s. Wheat was
again widely grown—but as a subsistence crop on small acreages that
gave extremely low seed-yield ratios, often no higher than 1:2 or 1:3.
On most farms about half of the cleared land was in pasture, the rest in
meadow and in field crops, usually oats. The drift away from wheat and
toward livestock had begun well before the agricultural crisis of the
1830s, but the transition was hastened by the crisis to the point where
the mixed farm, essentially similar to that in present-day Québec, had
become widespread before 1860.

Farming practices varied from region to region. Near Montréal where
land values were higher, oats, peas, and wheat were the chief field
crops and occupied almost half of the cleared land. Although there was
a potato patch on almost all farms, the highest potato acreages were in
areas of Irish settlement. Cattle were the principal livestock on most
farms, but in some areas sheep (below Québec) and horses (near
Montréal) were more important. More striking than these regional dif-

ferences were those between French-Canadian and English-Canadian farms. In most cases the latter carried more and better stock and concentrated on a particular type of animal. There were sheep and pigs, for example, on almost all French-Canadian farms, but many English-speaking farmers specializing in dairy or beef cattle had none of these animals. Yields of every important crop, except perhaps potatoes, tended to be substantially higher on the generally larger English farms. They used more machinery and their farms not infrequently produced more than 2000 pounds of butter and as much or more cheese. It was the rare French-Canadian farm that produced 1000 pounds of butter, and in the 1860s there were still no cheese factories in French-Canadian areas.

Although French-Canadian agriculture had shifted from wheat to mixed farming, no corresponding change in agricultural technique had occurred. Selective breeding was rare, fields were not rotated, seed was not renewed, and it was little more common than it had always been for a farmer to manure his land. Crops of the agricultural revolution, such as turnips or mangle wurzel, had made almost no inroads. In response to the wheat failure and to changed market conditions, French-Canadian farmers had changed the emphasis but not the nature of their traditional agricultural system.

In an earlier age traditional techniques were better suited to the Canadian situation than many observers had realized, but by the mid-nineteenth century, when land was scarce and the market for livestock products was sizable, they had become archaic. Almost certainly their persistence is attributable to the following factors. In many rural areas society had become so insulated that farmers were not aware of new agricultural practices. In Lotbinière, for example, only twenty-five of the almost 4000 people in the seigneurie in 1861 were not French Canadians born in Lower Canada; in only seventeen families were both husband and wife new to the area since 1842. There were agricultural societies in most counties and agricultural fairs in Québec and Montréal, but membership in the societies was confined to a prosperous and frequently English few who had little influence on the habitants. A few seigneurs attempted to introduce new crops, and it is possible that their domains were centers for the diffusion of some agricultural techniques. Habitants were hindered in updating their agricultural practices by a shortage of breeding stock, of dealers selling improved or new seeds, and even of marketing agents for new crops. Without such facilities, enthusiasm for change was translated only slowly into practice. Finally, little cash or credit for agricultural experimentation was available. For most habitants along the lower St. Lawrence, indebted to their seigneur and local merchants, an uncertain investment in better stock or expensive machinery, or a trial planting of a new crop was sheer foolhardiness. In short there was great inertia built into traditional agricultural practice, and it endured in Québec long after the 1860s.

THE TIMBER TRADE

Immediately after 1760 the timber market in the British West Indies was supplied from New England and that in the British Isles principally from the Baltic. Timber continued to be cut around Lake Champlain, along the north shore of the St. Lawrence below Québec, and in many other parts of the colony. Exports of wood in various forms fluctuated from between 5 and 20 per cent of the total value of exports, but in the British market Canadian wood accounted for less than 1 per cent of the imports from the Baltic. The American Revolution brought no sudden improvement; Yankee traders in the British West Indies were replaced by Yankee smugglers, and a growing population in Nova Scotia and New Brunswick created another vigorous competitor with better access than Canada to the West Indian market. For Canada the decisive change came only in 1808 when Napoleon's continental blockade drastically reduced the amount of timber entering the British Isles from the Baltic, leading British timber merchants to turn to the North American colonies. From 1808 to 1812 exports from Québec of all categories of wood increased sharply; squared pine, the principal export, increased by thirteen times. By 1814 the British parliament had increased the tariff on foreign wood to sixty-five shillings a load. Although this protective tariff was reduced in 1821 to fifty-five shillings and was cut again in the 1840s as the British government moved toward free trade, a strong Canadian forest industry had been built up within this system of colonial preference. It remained competitive in the British market as the protective tariff was withdrawn. Moreover, by the late 1840s the burgeoning cities of the American Northeast and Middle West were creating a vast market for sawed lumber. Although in the first half of the nineteenth century the fortunes of the timber trade were by no means uniformly bright, an export staple had been found to fill some of the vacuum created in Lower Canada by the almost simultaneous collapse of the fur and grain trades.

From the seigneurs' point of view the timber trade enormously increased the value of their unconceded land, contributed to a rapid rise in revenues, and provided for many of them their principal point of contact with the commercial life of the colony. They began policing their timber reserves closely, and were quick to prosecute for illegal cutting. Some refused to concede land en roture until it had been logged. Others applied to convert their unconceded lands to freehold, hoping to avoid the logging restrictions written into some seigneurial title deeds, and to make their land a more attractive purchase for English-speaking timber merchants. Seigneurs of both cultural groups built sawmills providing seasonal work for as many as eighty men in the mill and for as many in the bush. Usually they contracted to sell wood to a Québec or Montréal timber merchant. Often these sales became a seigneur's principal source of revenue, while exploitation of the forest enhanced his role in the rural community. He was not only the man from whom land was held but he was also the principal employer.

For many habitants, work in the forests and sawmills provided a cash income, an alternative to emigration, and a stage in the transition from an agricultural to an industrial life. As timber rafts became common on the St. Lawrence, each with a crew of twenty or thirty men, the river again became important in French-Canadian life. It became common for young men, many of whom held a roture, to work in the woods during the winter, and for some of them to take part in the timber drives; the villages that developed around the sawmills were composed of landless laborers. The availability of such work during the worst years of the agricultural crisis probably reduced the size of the rural exodus, but it also created a dependence on off-the-farm employment. If the local forests had been cut, as frequently was the case by the early 1850s, the opportunity to return to full-time agricultural life was rare. A few men were absorbed in the small shipyards, foundries, tanneries, and other small industries that were becoming increasingly common in rural Québec. Many more drifted into the towns or left the St. Lawrence lowland altogether.

The shield fringe

Late in the 1790s British surveyors began to divide the land immediately north of the seigneuries into townships. These townships were approximately 100 square miles, and most of them eventually were divided in 11 ranges, each comprising 28 rectangular 200-acre lots with a ratio of width to length of approximately 1:2.5. In principle, lots were open to individual settlers on payment of a nominal registration fee, but even before they were properly surveyed, many of the townships passed into the hands of a few individuals who held land as a speculation or offered it at prices of from two to five shillings an acre. In 1818 the government half-heartedly attempted to correct these abuses by issuing location tickets which entitled a settler to occupy the land until he had met the conditions of settlement and could obtain legal title; that is, until he had built a house and lived in it for three years and had cleared and cultivated four acres of land for each 200 acres granted. Yet as these grants were rarely inspected, the engrossment of land was still relatively easy. In 1826 the government decided to sell lands at public auction, the price to be paid in four annual installments; and it provided for poor settlers by allowing them to acquire title to land for annual interest payments ("constituted rents") of 5 per cent of the estimated value of the land. In the late 1830s annual payments were replaced with outright cash sales. Settlers who left the St. Lawrence lowland for the Shield thus encountered a fairly uniform cadastral system, but a welter of methods of obtaining and paying for land. Little land was free. Even when no initial payment was required, as in the seigneuries that extended into the Shield, there were annual charges to be met on land offered for a constituted rent or sold on credit by a speculator.

Settlement of the townships north and west of the St. Lawrence lowland began in the Ottawa valley in the early 1800s. New Englanders arrived first, followed by a few Scottish and English settlers, then by Ulstermen and Irish Catholics, and a little later by French Canadians. Many of the New Englanders, the Scots, and the English brought capital, but almost all the Irish and the French Canadians were destitute. Individually or in nuclear families they drifted up the Ottawa valley in search of land or a shanty job, and if they stayed in Québec, they usually came to rest on a rocky, logged-over lot in the Shield rim of the Ottawa lowland.

Elsewhere in the Shield the pattern was much the same. Where settlement began in the 1820s and 1830s, usually in conjunction with the timber trade, the Irish were often the first to occupy the land; where it began after 1840 French Canadians predominated. The Irish who had settled the small pockets of relatively fertile fluvial or lacustrine soils often stayed on; those who settled on the thin stony tills that cover most of the southern rim of the Shield ultimately wandered off to the logging camps, to the lowland towns, or to the United States. Frequently their

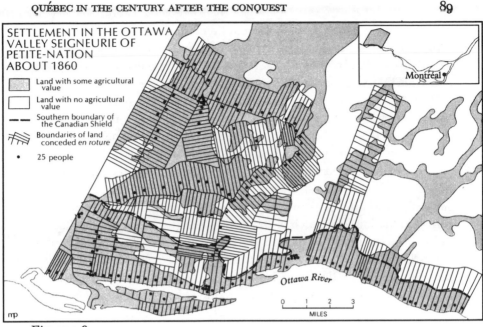

Figure 3-6.

farms were reoccupied by young French Canadians who were unable to find a farm in the older lowland settlements or who lacked the skills to practise a trade. Even in the late 1850s and 1860s, when several energetic priests backed by colonization societies in Montréal sought to preserve faith and culture by establishing agricultural sites well back in the Shield, the groups they led were made up of individuals and nuclear families drawn from here and there in the older parishes, rather than communities or even kin groups.

The regularity of the survey in the Laurentian townships was more than offset by the rough topography of the Shield and the scattered distribution of agricultural pockets; consequently the large-scale pattern of settlement in the Shield was considerably less regular than in the lowland. Still, by dividing their lots longitudinally and settling close to the roads, French Canadians re-created short, often isolated rangs almost wherever they settled in the Shield. English-speaking settlers were more dispersed, as they divided their fields into approximate squares and built their houses well back from the roads. The houses of English-speaking settlers who had come with some capital could be recognized at a glance, but both the Irish and the French Canadians built tiny cabins with a central chimney and a door in the middle of the long side. Some of the Irish adopted pièce sur pièce construction, while some of the French Canadians built cabins with interlocking flush corners, a construction technique that had come to Québec from the south.

Most Shield farms were small-scale, subsistence operations. Frequently a settler cleared only ten or fifteen acres after as many years on the land; on this small clearing, whether Irishman or French Canadian, he grew an acre or two of wheat—growing season permitting—two or three acres of oats, perhaps one acre of potatoes and peas, and another of barley and rye. Almost always he had at least one cow and two or three pigs and often a horse and a small flock of sheep. These animals grazed in the bush for much of the year; their manure was not collected and fields were not rotated. Such methods applied to the thin, sour soils of the Shield soon led to even lower yields per acre than in the older seigneurial lands. On the other hand, a few large farms, most of them owned by English-Canadian settlers, produced hay, oats, meat, and potatoes for sale to the lumber camps. Usually these farms had 20–30 acres in oats, several more in potatoes, and 40–80 acres in meadow or pasture. They carried up to 50 head of cattle, as many sheep, 5–10 horses, and 20 pigs. In the St-Maurice Valley even larger farms were operated by the lumber companies.

Most of the men and boys who worked the many subsistence farms scattered through the Shield fringe of Québec sought off-the-farm employment in the logging camps or sawmills. In 1806 the first timber raft was floated down the Ottawa River, and soon timber was being cut along all the major rivers of the southern rim of the Shield. As elsewhere in North America, the assault on the forest was marked by wasteful cutting and forest fires, until, by 1860, marketable white and red pine were becoming scarce throughout the great arc of land from the north shore of the St. Lawrence near Québec to the upper Ottawa River. Almost none of the capital or entrepreneurs in the timber trade were French Canadian. The largest firms were British concerns that had shifted their operations from the Baltic to the British North American colonies after Napoleon's continental blockade and the ensuing preferential tariff to aid colonial timber. Competing vigorously, although usually on a smaller scale, were a number of New England merchants, and by mid-century a rapidly increasing proportion of the timber merchants were English Canadians. Many of the mansions built in Montréal toward the middle of the nineteenth century were connected with the timber trade. The labor force was overwhelmingly Irish or French Canadian. Men worked from dawn to dusk, six days a week, for an average monthly wage of some ten dollars in the 1820s and twelve to fourteen dollars by 1860. Many of these men farmed during the summer; others were part of a floating male population that drifted among the logging camps and sawmills. Almost always there were more men than jobs; consequently wages were low and many employers were able to dispel the notion that jobs were a right by not hiring the same men in successive seasons.

Squared timber for naval construction was the basis of the early trade. Logs were squared in the woods, hauled by oxen or horses over the snow to the nearest watercourse, and floated after the spring breakup in rafts or cribs to the St. Lawrence River and on to Québec. As the market expanded for deals—heavy planks three or four inches thick—sawmills appeared close to the logging camps, and round logs were floated there for sawing. With the loss of the preferential tariff in 1846 and the rise of an American market for lumber in the 1850s, sawmills became larger and more complex. In general, the shift from the hand-squaring of timber to sawmilling increased the economies of scale, and led to larger corporate structures exerting control over larger territories. The early years of the trade had been characterized by intense, ruthless competition among rival firms, by frequent illegal encroachments on timber reserves, by timber stealing in the spring drives, and by brawling, often exacerbated by ethnic differences, among rival camps. These practices declined with sawmilling and with monopoly control in the larger river basins.

A seasonal laborer in the logging camps earned some fifty dollars for a winter's work, rarely enough to pay off his accumulated debts. He usually owed the local shopkeeper, who was often a New Englander, for supplies and seed. The laborer often sold grain to him in the fall; if the laborer used his own supply over the winter, in the spring he bought from the shopkeeper at a higher price. A seigneur or land speculator was also likely to be a creditor. Because few Irish or French-Canadian settlers could pay cash for land, they faced annual payments for their lots whether they settled in a seigneurie or a township. These charges and compound interest could quickly accumulate in ten or fifteen years to a debt of one to two hundred dollars. With the scarcity of jobs and agriculture a subsistence operation for many years, debt was inevitable, and in both the seigneuries and the townships most settlers lived with the fear that their land would be confiscated at any time. Indeed, confiscations were common, although not nearly so widespread as the almost universal indebtedness of the population made legally possible.

Because of their poverty, many quite populous parishes in the Shield had no resident priest. The tithe (one twenty-sixth of the grain crop) was not enough to support a curé and, although many parishes subscribed an additional sum for his maintenance, they usually failed to pay after he arrived. Usually the new curé would leave in a year or two, complaining perhaps, as one of them did, of "scratching among the stumps" for a livelihood. For a few years the parish would be served intermittently by a missionary priest, then there would be another subscription, another curé, and often another precipitous departure. In one seigneurie the habitants agreed to tithe in potatoes, but when the new curé arrived in a buggy pulled by two horses, many habitants refused to pay either tithe or subscription. The priest explained to the bishop that the buggy was old and had cost only a few dollars. "The mistake," he said, "is that I had it varnished, and that gives an appearance of luxury." Similarly, the habitants were slow to build schools and were even slower to send their children to them. The Education Act of 1841 established a monthly fee of one shilling and three pence per child which indigent parents could ill afford. Moreover, they were illiterate themselves, and they saw no real need to educate their children. Most French-Canadian and many Irish children in the Shield were not receiving even a year or two of schooling until late in the 1850s. The New Englanders, the Scots, and the English, on the other hand, strongly supported the school acts, and often had established schools on their own initiative. Because they were literate, relatively prosperous, competitive, and possessed a strong civic sense, they tended to fill most of the important civic offices created by the municipal laws of the 1840s and 1850s.

Fifty years after the push northward out of the St. Lawrence lowland began, a major segment of the boreal forest had been cut or burned and most of the pockets of cultivable land in the knobby hills of the Shield had been settled. The settlers eked out a living by intermittent, poorly paid work in the logging camps or the sawmills and by farming their patches of stony land. Debt was inescapable. Without education, without the support of extended family connections, with the parish still an embryonic institution, and with the seigneur or speculator a threatening creditor, most settlers were defenseless against economic exploitation. The Irish, with no emotional or nationalistic ties to the colonizing venture, usually were quick to leave, but the French Canadians lingered until their prospects became as bleak as those of any white rural people in mid-nineteenth century North America. The worst forms of sharecropping in the American South differed in organization but not in result. The pathetic irony of the habitants' position was revealed in the 1870s when some of the settlers who had been led into the Shield to find a haven for language, culture, and religion began emigrating to the United States to escape the debts that their years in the Shield had heaped upon them.

The Eastern Townships

Although colonization societies extolled the climate and soils of the townships lying between the seigneuries and the American border (the Eastern Townships), the rolling Appalachian highlands in this region were, in fact, only moderately suitable for agriculture. Valley bottoms were poorly drained, the uplands rocky, and little of the land was level. At higher elevations the growing season was too short for wheat. Still, soils were better there than in the Shield fringe, the over-all agricultural potential was much higher, and the Eastern Townships were an obvious area for French-Canadian agricultural expansion. Yet the first settlers in the area were Loyalists, and many more Americans came north in search of land after 1791, when the government of Lower Canada lifted its ban on settlement along the border. By 1817 approximately 20,000 people, most of them from northern New England, lived in the Eastern Townships. Newspapers from Vermont rather than from Québec or Montréal circulated there. For years the only regular mail service came from the south. Masonic lodges appeared early in the century. Until well into the 1820s when British Wesleyans first appeared, Methodists in the townships were ministered to by itinerant American preachers. Although politically a part of Lower Canada, the early settlers in the townships were tied socially and economically to New England; a governor of Lower Canada stated that they had so little contact with the lower St. Lawrence that they seemed hardly to belong to the colony.

Movement southward into the townships began with a trickle of English and Scottish settlers after 1815 and accelerated after 1830 as both Irish immigrants and French Canadians spilled out of the St. Lawrence lowland. From the middle of the century colonization societies were being formed to counteract the drain of young French Canadians to New England, and their literature extolled in emotional patriotic tones the

advantages of settlement in the Eastern Townships. The previous generation of French-Canadian nationalists had viewed the New Englanders in the townships with suspicion and jealousy, and French-Canadian
members in the Legislative Assembly had balked at voting money to
improve the road connections between the townships and the St. Lawrence lowland. One consequence of this defensive nationalism had been
to make the townships more accessible to New Englanders than to
French Canadians. This and the preference of the French Canadians
for lands held in seigneurial tenure, their fears that they could not compete economically with the New Englanders and might be culturally as-
similated by them, and their lack of capital to buy good land from the
speculators delayed their occupation of the townships until long after
the New Englanders were established and relatively prosperous. When
French Canadians did settle in the Eastern Townships they, like those
who settled in the Shield, came as individuals or as members of nuclear
families after relatively short moves from adjacent seigneuries. Few
brought any capital. They settled first in townships immediately south
of the seigneuries, and from there they or their descendents spread into
the areas previously settled by New Englanders. By 1851 the northern
townships were more than 50 per cent French Canadian and those along
the American border approximately 10 per cent. In 1871 the figures were
80 and 25 per cent respectively.

Much of the land in the Eastern Townships was granted to a leader
who, with many associates, acquired a large tract of land. Unlike the
proprietors of the early New England townships, however, this group
had no social or administrative importance in a new community, but
rather was a device by which one person could acquire much more land
than he could individually. The leader, who was usually an important
merchant, a member of the Executive or Legislative Council, or an army
or militia officer, selected his associates carefully, paid all the patenting
expenses, and paid off the associates (who surrendered their tracts of
land) with a small cash consideration and perhaps 200 acres of land for
each of them. Thus the New Englanders settled as individuals, and their
farms were well dispersed. Often they were well back from the road, frequently on higher, well-drained ground supporting a deciduous forest
that could be converted into potash. Depending on the terrain, a farm
family could be half a mile or more from its nearest neighbor. Perhaps it
was partly to counteract this isolation that the New Englanders were
inveterate joiners of associations, and that bees of all kinds, for tasks

ranging from clearing the forest to paring apples were an important part of their rural life. Industrial, service, and artisanal activities, on the other hand, were concentrated in central places which by the 1840s and 1850s were more common in the Eastern Townships than anywhere else in Québec. Some of these agglomerations were crossroad settlements, others grew up around waterpower sites that had attracted a sawmill or a gristmill. Often they were laid out around greens, and only rarely did they form the elongated street-village characteristic of the French Canadians. The settlements created by the New Englanders drew a much sharper distinction between farm and village life than did those of the French Canadians, a distinction that grew out of the New Englanders' greater commitment to commercial values and hence to a more efficient form of settlement for a particular commercial task.

Initially the New Englanders in the Eastern Townships built with round or squared logs, but by mid-century well over half of them lived in frame houses. Few had houses of brick or stone. Almost invariably the frame houses were clapboard and painted white; many were constructed with a gable end facing the road, and a shed at the other end connecting with the stable. Occasionally there was a covered connection from the house to the barn through shed and stable. Where possible the barns were built into a hillside with entry to the loft by means of a ramp at the gable end. Almost every hamlet had at least one church, usually a trim frame building of simplified Gothic or neoclassical line. The main street in the larger towns was lined with two- and three-story brick facades incorporating the neoclassical and Italianate motifs characteristic of mid-nineteenth century main-street architecture in much of northeastern North America. French Canadians, on the other hand, brought the architectural tradition that has been described above. Where the two groups abutted in the townships, two totally different traditions of vernacular architecture contributed to one of the most visible breaks in the cultural landscape of northeastern North America.

For several decades after the beginning of settlement in the townships, the principal markets for agricultural products were the local distilleries and tanneries that took potatoes and hides, and the incoming settlers who occasionally bought grain and livestock. In the 1830s and 1840s, as roads to Montréal improved, the raising of livestock (mostly beef cattle and sheep at first and later dairy cattle) became the focus of commercial agriculture. By the mid-1830s most of the cleared land in the townships was in meadow or pasture. Oats was the most important grain, and wheat, rye, buckwheat, and Indian corn were also grown, but in most farms grain crops accounted for not more than 10 to 15 per cent of the cleared acreage. Pasture was usually permanent, but meadow and grain crops were rotated. Because of the favorable ratio of meadow to grain fields, farmers could separate two or three years of grain crops on a given field by some ten years of meadow, and consequently grain yields in the Eastern Townships were almost twice as high as in the St. Lawrence lowland. Many Eastern Township farms carried excellent breeding stock, and the average quality of livestock in the townships soon became far higher than in the seigneuries. From time to time agricultural writers claimed that farmers spent too much time clearing and not enough tending their land, but meadow and pasture were well suited to the rolling terrain of the townships, as were livestock products to the Québec and Montréal markets. By any measure the English-Canadian farmers in the townships were the most prosperous in Lower Canada.

In the 1850s a large farm in the townships contained some 300 acres of cleared land. Of this at least 100 acres were in pasture, perhaps 30 were in grains, and the rest was meadow. Such a farm produced several hundred bushels of oats and perhaps 150 tons of hay, carried 50–60 cattle, as many as 20 horses, and a sizable flock of sheep. In the 1860s many individual township farmers were marketing more than 2000 pounds of butter and as much or more cheese each year. The colonization societies argued that French Canadians could do as well, and their literature gave many examples of habitants who had prospered in the townships. Yet French-Canadian successes were rare. Coming into the area relatively late and with little or no capital, French Canadians tended to occupy the poorer land. Frequently they were unaware of the importance of good breeding stock which, in any event, they could seldom afford. Because most of them could not read French, much less English, they could not follow the agricultural journals. When a French Canadian did become relatively prosperous, his farm usually was divided among several offspring. Thus income as well as culture divided New Englanders and French Canadians in the townships. Often the French Canadians worked part time in the sawmills or as summer laborers on farms on both sides of the border, leaving their farms to be tended by the women and children. This part-time attachment to farming usually preceded a move to a town in New England or the Eastern Townships.

By the 1850s the townships were alive with small-scale industrial activities. In some townships there were eight or ten sawmills; several asheries; gristmills; carriage shops; tanneries; foundries producing stoves, plows, and other agricultural implements; and many other small operations. Almost all of this activity was located at waterpower sites, and frequently the gristmill, carriage shop, or foundry was the focus of a hamlet or village. Although some industries served the entire region, most of them produced for a single county or less. When railways connected the townships more closely to outside manufactures, small mills became obsolete and industry gradually declined. Although many French Canadians in the townships were artisans or laborers, management was overwhelmingly English speaking.

The towns

The level of urbanization in Québec declined from 1760 until about 1830 when a rise began which has continued, with minor interruptions, to the present. During most of the French regime 25 per cent of the Canadian population lived in Québec, Montréal, or Trois-Rivières, but by 1825 only 10 per cent of the total population of Québec was urban; in 1851, the share rose to 13 per cent, and in 1871 to 15 per cent. There was a sharp difference in this respect between French- and English-speaking groups. In 1825, 35 per cent of the English Canadians but only 5 per cent of the French Canadians lived in Montréal, Québec, or Trois-Rivières. Whereas the French-Canadian urban population had little more than doubled in the sixty-five years between the conquest and 1825, it increased at least seven times in the next forty-five years as a net migration to the towns replaced the long drift of French Canadians away from the towns during the 1830s and the 1840s. By 1871 about 15 per cent of the French Canadians were urban, and French Canadians were in the majority in each of the three principal cities.

The de-urbanization of French-Canadian society before 1830 apparently reflected the concentration of commercial power in non-French-Canadian hands. The declining relative size of the urban population as a whole may be explained as an adjustment to the abnormally high level of urbanization during the French regime, a corollary of the importance of the military, the bureaucratic establishment, and the fur trade in a numerically small colony. After 1830 population pressure began to force French Canadians off the land, and some of them went to the towns where, although their economic prospects were not bright, they had some chance of earning a living.

Montréal, with more than 25,000 people, was slightly larger than Québec in 1825, a third larger in 1851, and almost twice as large (107,000 people) in 1871. Both cities were still primarily commercial centers, and the emerging dominance of Montréal reflected its greater attraction for commerce. Some of Montréal's advantage grew out of its central location in the largest area of productive agricultural land in Lower Canada, but much more depended on its relative proximity to the burgeoning markets of the Great Lakes basin. Early in the nineteenth century, Montréal's canoe connection to the west was giving way to a shorter, stronger connection by boat and road. The spate of road and canal construction along the St. Lawrence after the union of the two Canadas in 1840 and the building of the Grand Trunk Railway in the next decade increased the volume of Montréal's trade with the interior. Steamboats on the lower St. Lawrence heightened the city's importance as a port. Increasingly the commerce of the St. Lawrence flowed past Québec. Probably it is also important that—at least by the early 1800s—Montréal was the financial heart of the St. Lawrence trading system. By 1842 four banks had their head offices there; the city was also better served than Québec by brokerage and insurance firms. The relationship between financial power and urban growth in Lower Canada has not been studied adequately, but it is likely that the financial ascendancy of Montréal was more nearly a cause than an effect of accelerated urban growth. Finally, the industrial structure of the two cities was quite different. The nine shipyards in Québec at mid century employed almost 1500 men, considerably more than the number employed in all other manufacturing. In Montréal the industrial labor force was scattered among foundries, boot and shoe factories, distilleries, breweries, tobacco factories, brickyards, soap and candle factories, and a host of other small industries. Few individual firms employed more than 50 workers and the largest single employer, a foundry making steam engines, employed only about 250. This diversified production gave to Montréal a more flexible industrial structure than that of Québec and a broader base for urban growth as well.

In 1825 there were five villages with populations between 1000 and 2000, thirteen more between 500 and 1000, and many smaller villages and hamlets. Trois-Rivières had fewer than 3000 inhabitants. The iron works on the St-Maurice River, a few miles north of Trois-Rivières, employed several hundred men, and there were sawmills in some of the villages, but almost all of these nucleations were essentially local rural service centers. During the French regime there was no hierarchy of

Montréal Harbor, the heart of the commerce of the St. Lawrence and of English-Canadian commercial life in nineteenth-century Québec. The Public Archives of Canada.

central places along the lower St. Lawrence, and even in 1825 such a hierarchy was barely adumbrated in the relationship between Montréal or Québec, the village, and the farm. In the period between 1831 and 1871 the number of small central places increased several times, although after Montréal and Québec, no city had more than 10,000 people, and only eight had between 2000 and 10,000 people. The number of villages between 500 and 1000 people had increased from thirteen to

eighty-one. Most of the villages were rural service centers, and in some
of them there was manufacturing. Both functions were combined in the
larger towns. With the head office of the Bank of the Eastern Townships,
Sherbrooke had undoubtedly become a regional center in the townships,
and Sorel and Trois-Rivières may have been equally important in their
areas. Apparently an urban hierarchy had emerged, but the limited development of centers of intermediate size suggests that the importance
of Montréal and Québec depended largely on their trade connections
outside the province. The subsistent agriculture of habitant Québec did
not require an elaborate urban structure. Significantly, an urban hierarchy was most fully developed in the Eastern Townships.

Internally, urban territory was segregated functionally and ethnically,
although unlike the late nineteenth-century city, many sharp differences
in urban land use were common within relatively small areas. Take, for
example, the Montréal central business district in the 1840s. The waterfront was lined with warehouses and the offices of merchants, importers,
shipping companies, and shipping agents. There were also hotels, boardinghouses, taverns, and shops—but not nearly so many as along the parallel street one block to the northwest, which catered more to the needs
of seamen and stevedores. Although almost all of the city's leather merchants were on the same street, merchant offices were less common there
than along the waterfront. Slightly farther inland were the offices of insurance agents, stockbrokers and bill brokers, and lawyers—men who
served the port but who did not need to be located directly on the waterfront. Two full blocks inland was Montréal's principal retail avenue,
Notre Dame, containing most of the better stores and serving the city
rather than the waterfront. Another block to the north, St. James Street
was already established as a center of finance. Head offices of banks and
insurance companies located there as well as architects, lawyers, and a
few quality shops. The fifth major east-west street from the waterfront
marked the northern edge of the central business district. Shops, artisans, and many light industries such as brass foundries, candle-makers,
and carriage-makers were located there. The larger foundries were at
the mouth of the Lachine Canal just west of the central business district,
and several important factories, notably Molson's Brewery and Macdonald Brothers' tobacco factory, were located along the waterfront to the
east. Although the cliff dividing the lower and upper town in Québec
distorted the pattern, the general sequence of functional change away
from the waterfront was much the same as in Montréal. The lower town

contained the merchant offices, warehouses, shops, boardinghouses, and taverns; the upper town, most of the lawyers and the better shops.

In both Québec and Montréal in the 1840s the central business district was predominantly English speaking. In Montréal, then as now, the percentage of French Canadians increased toward the northeast, and in a few streets at the eastern margin of the central business district there was a clear French-Canadian majority. In total, however, French Canadians in Montréal's three central wards were only 32 per cent of the population, whereas in the city as a whole they were 43 per cent. There were French-Canadian streets in the lower town of Québec, others that were English speaking, and many more that were mixed; but the majority of the population was English speaking. In the Québec upper town, where there was a waiting list for pews in the Anglican cathedral, the English-speaking majority was even larger. In Québec's three central wards, 37 per cent of the population was French Canadian; in the city as a whole, 55 per cent. This concentration of English-speaking people in the commercial cores undoubtedly reflected the concentration of commercial power. Of the six banks in Montréal, only one, the Banque du Peuple, was controlled by French Canadians. None of the city's fourteen assurance companies was French Canadian. Of forty-one wholesale drygoods merchants, two were French Canadian. The discrepancy was much less among retail merchants, but most of the retail merchants were small shopkeepers. In the central business district of Montréal, notaries were the only professional or business group in which there was a clear French-Canadian majority. Although slightly less extreme, the same situation prevailed in Québec.

Northeast of the central business district, Montréal was more than 60 per cent French Canadian and St-Roch, the large northern suburb of Québec, was almost 90 per cent French Canadian. These were predominantly working-class areas, the residences of laborers, artisans, and small shopkeepers. Although French Canadians provided labor for many waterfront tasks and for industry, particularly because of their skill as woodworkers in the shipyards, much of the heaviest manual labor appears to have been performed by the Irish. A surprising number of French Canadians were shoemakers, carpenters, joiners, or masons employing skills that were common in the villages of rural Québec. Most of this artisanal activity must have been supported by the wages of the regularly employed. As in the villages, poverty appears to have made artisans of several men when there was scarcely a comfortable

Québec in 1863. The great timber yards below the Plains of Abraham. The Public Archives of Canada.

living for one. Perhaps, indeed, the commercial character of the French-Canadian suburb and of the villages in rural Québec were not drastically different. Such a similarity would have eased the habitants' adjustment to urban life while delaying their adjustment to urban values.

In the 1840s, 20 per cent of the population of Montréal and 14 per cent of the population of Québec was Irish. The Irish were scattered through both cities, but tended to concentrate close to the waterfront to one side of the central business district. The immigrant sheds in Montréal, which were occupied almost entirely by Irish, stood near the mouth of the Lachine Canal, and for several blocks to the north the population was predominantly Irish. Most of the men were part-time laborers, and the area had the lowest per capita income and the poorest housing in the city. In Québec the waterfront strip below the Plains of Abraham and west of the lower town was almost 50 per cent Irish. Nearby was the principal booming ground of the St. Lawrence timber trade, and it is probable that the Irish, most of whom had come to Canada in the holds of timber ships, were employed to load timber.

Despite the large Irish proportion of the English-speaking sectors, in Montréal 32 per cent and in Québec 23 per cent of the population consisted of people born in England, Scotland, or Canada of English-speaking parents. These people spanned all income levels and were found in all wards of each city, but their highest percentage concentrations were in the central business district and in the adjacent upper-class residential areas. In Montréal, most of the rich lived northwest of the central business district within a few blocks of McGill University. Some were beginning to build their mansions on the flanks of Mount Royal where they had an imposing view of the city and were within easy carriage distance of an office on St. James Street. Factory owners frequently lived near their plants; the Molsons, for example, lived in the eastern ward of the city within a stone's throw of their brewery. In Québec the residences of the rich overlooked the lower town from a location that combined the security and the society of the garrison at their flank with a commanding view of the city and close access to the main business streets of the upper town. The principal criterion for entry to these areas was wealth; a few French-Canadian lawyers lived on the best streets in Québec, and a few years later such French Canadians as Jean Beaudry, president of the newly formed Banque Jacques Cartier and mayor of the city, had penetrated the English-speaking establishment in Montréal.

Much of this diversity of backgrounds and ways of life was reflected in the buildings. The Anglican cathedrals in Québec and Montréal were close copies of Saint Martins-in-the-Field in London, while some of the best residential streets in the upper town of Québec were examples of British terrace housing. The English neoclassical style of the bank offices on St. James Street, the customs house in Québec and many other official buildings made them conscious symbols of British, Protestant authority. Some of the mansions of the wealthy were Georgian, others incorporated the neoclassical and Italianate motifs of the early Victorian years in Canada, and the widespread use of cut granite reflected a Scottish influence. The general aspect of the main shopping streets was northeastern North American until they tailed off into areas where French Canadians predominated. There, fieldstone construction, massive chimneys and fire walls separating contiguous buildings, steeply pitched roofs punctured by dormers, and spare facades expressed an altogether different building tradition. The vernacular urban house of the French regime also was still built, now with a less steep roof, more dormers, and bits of neoclassical detail. The general aspect of a row of such buildings, each grafted to the next as if by accident rather than design and expressing the texture and feel of their materials, marked the final stage in Québec and Montréal of a medieval building tradition. In some Montréal parish churches, Gothic forms were being used, but these buildings were a calculated attempt to symbolize Frenchness and Catholicism; their architectural roots were in the Gothic revival rather than, as in the case of the vernacular house or some of the commercial buildings, in the depth of a folk tradition.

If an eighteenth-century traveler to Québec were to return a century later, he might at first have been astonished at the extent of landscape change. In the 1750s the forest still dominated the lowland, but in the mid-nineteenth century it often survived only in carefully tended sugar-maple groves at the rear of farms. The thin lines of settlement along the river had widened in places to fifteen or more rangs between the river and the Shield or the Appalachian highlands. The forest in the Shield fringe had been cut or burned, and had been replaced either by the bush of a young successional forest or by cleared farmland. There were sawmills and sawmill villages along many of the rivers in the Shield. In much of the Eastern Townships, where during the French regime the most important breaks in the forest were beaver meadows, there probably was less forested land than at present; and the farms and townscapes of northern New England were well established. Both Montréal and Québec had grown from small towns to cities. Many buildings from the French regime remained, but there was an infusion of new construction and styles in the older areas; and a great expansion, ranging from the cut-stone or brick mansions of the rich to the frame or fieldstone tenements of the poor, in the urban area.

Within an individual parish or seigneurie or, indeed, within an individual côte settled in the French regime, change was also apparent. Houses tended to be closer together, barns larger and higher. There may have been a village along the côte and perhaps a large sawmill. Farms and farmhouses were much less uniform in size than they had been a century earlier. Most fields were in meadow or pasture rather than arable. Wheat was not a major crop. Parish churches were larger and usually were part of a cluster of church buildings that included a presbytery and a school. Were there a manor house in the côte, it could be recognized easily by its size, and sometimes by its Georgian or neoclassical form.

And yet, after a time, the traveler probably would have decided that the landscape of the lower St. Lawrence was remarkably familiar. Change had been largely quantitative—more clearing, new areas of set- tlement—whereas the French-Canadian stamp on the land had changed little in one hundred years. Although villages had become common, the côte was still the basic unit of rural settlement. The roof and fenestra- tion of the vernacular house had changed, but the building's lineage was clear. Long-lot farms still dominated the lowland, and had been repro- duced with modifications throughout the French-Canadian settlements in the Shield and the Eastern Townships. While there had been an im- portant shift in crops, there had not been a corresponding change in agricultural techniques. French-Canadian fields looked as ragged and unkempt as they had during the French regime; the stock that grazed on them was not much better. Even the new parish church frequently evoked a feeling of the French regime. In a century which had seen a flood of immigration to North America and basic technological changes in agriculture, industry, and transportation, this stability was all the more remarkable.

During the century after the conquest French Canadians had become an inward-looking, defensive minority. The Constitutional Act, the de- cline of the fur trade, and the unfamiliar laws, language, and customs outside the province had shifted their view from the continent to Qué- bec. Even there, partly by force of circumstances, partly by conscious effort, French Canadians had cut themselves off as much as possible from an alien, English-speaking elite. In many rural areas the population was almost entirely French Canadian, most of them born and raised in the immediate area and tied to it by a web of blood relationships. Where a few Irishmen or Scots had settled among French Canadians, they had been absorbed into French-Canadian life and no longer contributed a distinctive point of view. Where sizable numbers of French- and Eng- lish-speaking people were settled in close proximity, as near the towns, in parts of the Shield fringe, and in the Eastern Townships, the two groups usually kept to themselves. Their landscapes and their social rounds were different and their prejudices deep and often antagonistic.

When French Canadians left their rural communities, they almost al- ways faced a contrast between their own poverty and the wealth and power of the English Canadians. In the Eastern Townships the prosper- ous farmers were English speaking; the factory or mill jobs were in Eng- lish firms with English-speaking foremen. In the Shield the French Ca- nadians encountered Irish immigrants who were in much the same plight as themselves, but also English-speaking foremen in the saw-mills, and English-speaking merchants to whom they quickly fell into debt. Nor was the situation different in the towns. Most French Canadians lived in lower-middle-class or slum areas. The better residential areas were overwhelmingly English. If a French Canadian took a laboring job, he was almost invariably hired by a non-French Canadian. Such repeated contact with English-speaking power had bred in the French Canadians a deep sense of their own inferiority. The colonization societies labored to convince French Canadians that they could be as successful as Anglo-Saxon farmers in the Eastern Townships. Some French-Canadian nationalists tried to strengthen French Canadians' pride in themselves, others to withdraw French Canada from a situation which they saw, with a measure of justification, to be the result of English patronage and disdain for a conquered, French-speaking, Catholic people. Out of all of this emerged an image of the French regime as a golden age when life along the lower St. Lawrence had flourished without the English. Out of it too came an attempt to pull back, to avoid as much as possible contact with the English-speaking population of Québec—the French Canadians' principal contact with the nineteenth-century world.

In folding inward in this way, French Canadians strengthened the institutions of their own rural community. The parish became more important than it had been during the French regime, and there is evidence that the kin group had strengthened as well. These institutions plus the rang and the nuclear family constituted the cement of the rural community, and held it together until long after the 1860s. Rapid population increase on a small amount of agricultural land meant, however, that the continuity of the rural system depended on emigration. The family farm supported one son, not four or five, and without a drastic change in the rural economy and society the others would leave. Emigration, then, was the price of continuity, and by the second decade of the nineteenth century this price was being paid. Few of those who left for Montréal, Québec, or New England returned to the rural area of their birth, but in many areas these few were the principal spearheads of agricultural or industrial change.

There was quite another landscape in mid-nineteenth century Québec, that in which English-speaking life took place. In this landscape the town loomed as much more important, particularly the central business district and the associated upper-class residential areas. But even in rural areas it contrasted sharply with the French Canadian. The architecture of houses and barns was different. Gardens were not landscaped and houses were not painted in the same way. English-speaking farmers created a highly dispersed pattern of settlement, whereas English-speaking artisanal and mercantile life tended to be highly agglomerated. The fields of English Canadians were tidier and better managed than those of the French Canadians; the stock on English-speaking farms was of superior quality. The distinction between the two landscapes was clearest in the Eastern Townships but was apparent in all areas settled by both French- and English-speaking people.

The landscape of the English in Québec stemmed partly from a different aesthetic tradition but much more from a different concept of the individual in society. The first substantial group of English-speaking residents in the colony had been merchants from New England who were soon joined by Scottish and English merchants. These were hard-working capable men, often ruthless competitors committed to the goal of commercial success. Their commitment, their contacts in Britain, their willingness to form partnerships, and a good deal of official patronage soon enabled the English-speaking merchants to drive most French-Canadian merchants out of business. In the first decades after the conquest, British officials in the colony were conservative and aristocratic, in some ways closer in temperament to the French-Canadian elite than to the merchants. In the longer run the liberal bourgeois view prevailed among the officials to the point that, by the end of the eighteenth century, merchant and official were often one and the same person. This same commercial individualism crossed the Atlantic with thousands of nineteenth-century British immigrants, people disrupted by enclosures or the beginnings of the factory system and aspiring to a better life in a new setting. For the destitute immigrant from Ulster just as for the merchant the values of community were subordinated to those of individual economic achievement. Probably it is misleading to argue, with the historian Louis Hartz, that liberal and feudal fragments of European society were contained in Québec, for French-Canadian society was only remotely feudal; but undoubtedly there was a stronger sense of community among the French Canadians than among the English. French Canadians looked inward, the English outward. The English adapted the architectural styles, the farm machinery, the transportation technology of the day. They sought to become as efficient as possible by settling in dispersed farmsteads or in villages as economic demands warranted. If successful, they built mansions on the flank of Mount Royal surrounded by extensive grounds and stone walls—symbols of individual success. In part the French-Canadian sense of community had developed in reaction to this strident individualism, but it also lay deep in the spirit of French customary law and in the medieval tradition from which New France had partly sprung. In the peculiar situation after the conquest this ethos had been nurtured into a fuller, longer life than it would have had if Québec had remained a colony of France.

Bibliography

In spite of the enormous importance of this period for an understanding of Québec and of Canada, the post-conquest century in Québec has only recently received substantial scholarly attention. As little enough of this work relates to many of the subjects discussed in this chapter, considerable sections of the chapter depend on our own somewhat provisional research.

For the period as a whole by far the most important work is Fernand Ouellet's *Histoire Economique et Sociale du Québec, 1760–1850* (Fides: Montréal and Paris, 1966). In this monumental book Ouellet attempts to relate economic, social, and political trends in a comprehensive overview of a changing Québec. In so doing he has written a type of history—common in France but rare in Canada—that has far more relevance for a historical geographer than the heavily political studies that are common in Canadian historiography. Ouellet's vigorously anti-nationalist interpretation of Québec has elicited a critical response from several French-Canadian historians. The book is indispensable reading for any student of the period because of the information and ideas it contains and because of its relationship to almost all subsequent literature on the period. An English translation will shortly be available in the Carleton Library series.

Some idea of a more nationalist interpretation can be obtained from several articles by Jean-Pierre Wallot, all of which are also relevant to issues discussed in this chapter. These include "Le régime seigneurial et son abolition au Canada," *Canadian Historical Review* 50 (Dec. 1969), 367–93; "Religion and French-Canadian Mores in the Early Nineteenth Century," *Canadian Historical Review* 52 (March 1971), 54-94; and, with Gilles Paquet, "La Liste Civile du Bas-Canada (1794–1812): Un Essai d'Economie Historique," *Revue d'Histoire de l'Amérique Française* 23 (Dec. 1969), 361–92; 23 (Sept. 1969), 209–30; 24 (June 1970),

3–43; 24 (Sept. 1970), 251–86. Wallot like Ouellet is more interested in French-Canadian society than in its individuals, and there is also an explicitly sociological literature on early French Canada that, although now somewhat dated, remains provocative. The articles by Phillippe Garigue, Léon Gérin, and Hubert Guindon in Marcel Rioux and Yves Martin (eds.), *French Canadian Society* (Carleton Library, no. 18) are an introduction to this literature.

On a number of specialized topics the following are also important. On settlement: G. F. McGuigan, "La concession des terres dans les cantons de l'Est du Bas Canada, 1763–1809," *Recherches sociographiques* (1963), 71–90; R. C. Harris, "Of Poverty and Helplessness in Petite-Nation," *Canadian Historical Review* 52 (March 1971), 23–50. On agriculture: Maurice Séguin, *La "nation canadienne" et l'agriculture, 1760–1850: Essai d'histoire économique* (Editions Boréal Express: Trois-Rivières, 1970); W. H. Parker, "A New Look at Unrest in Lower Canada in the 1830s," *Canadian Historical Review* 40 (1959), 209–18; and Fernand Ouellet and Jean Hamelin, "La crise agricole dans le Bas-Canada, 1802–1837," *Etudes rurales* (1962), 36–57. On timber trade: A. R. M. Lower, *The North American Assault on the Canadian Forest* (Toronto: Ryerson Press, 1938); and Louise Dechêne, "Les entreprises de William Price," *Histoire Sociale* 1 (April 1968), 16–52. On architecture: Alan Gowans, *Building Canada; an architectural history of Canadian life* (Toronto: Oxford University Press, 1966); and Georges Gauthier-Larouche, *L'évolution de la maison rurale Laurentienne* (Québec: Laval University Press, 1967).

4 ONTARIO

As late as 1780 the peninsula bounded by Lakes Huron, Erie, and Ontario and by the upper St. Lawrence River was still a densely forested tract broken only here and there by beaver meadows, by Indian campsites or, on some light and excessively drained soils, by prairies dotted with oaks. A bare handful of whites and not many more Indians lived in the entire area. A few forts either occupied or in ruins, Indian campsites and trails, and perhaps some young successional forests growing in the aftermath of Indian burning were the only obvious human imprints on the land. This had not always been so. Early in the French regime perhaps 20,000 to 25,000 Hurons and possibly even more Neutrals and Petuns had lived in the peninsula, but in the late 1640s and 1650s the Iroquois League invaded, destroying the palisaded, agricultural villages. For a time the conquerors themselves established similar villages north of Lake Ontario although, for reasons still unclear, these settlements had disappeared well before the last half of the eighteenth century. The fur trade too, had bypassed the peninsula. Early in the seventeenth century the Hurons were important middlemen, but as trade shifted westward, fur brigades only touched the base of the peninsula on the Ottawa River route to the upper lakes and beyond. In 1780 the hand of man rested more faintly on the peninsula than for centuries past. Yet its location just up-river from the rapidly increasing population of Québec and in the line of American westward advance might have suggested that this neglect would not last much longer.

By the 1860s more than one and a half million people lived in this peninsula—Upper Canada, as it was known in the early nineteenth century, or Southern Ontario, as it is known today. It had been organized since 1791 as a political territory, its forests had been largely cleared, and its agricultural settlement had spread north to the Shield fringe. Fields, fences, barns, and villages comprised a new landscape that eradicated the landscape of 1780. The peninsula had become a very different place, and it is this new place—its landscape, its patterns of human activity on the land—that this chapter attempts to describe and explain.

Unlike Québec, where there was only a trickle of immigration in the seventeenth and early eighteenth century, Southern Ontario was settled rapidly by several hundred thousand people moving in the midst of the technological, social, and ideological upheaval of the early and middle nineteenth century. The Loyalists (Tories), who had arrived first, were dislocated by the War of Independence. Following them came the northern fringe of the restless, moving van of American land seekers—Pennsylvanians, New Yorkers, or New Englanders who had heard that prospects were better farther west and who eventually, perhaps after several stops, found themselves in Southern Ontario. Then, and in larger numbers, came immigrants from the British Isles: Highland crofters, Glasgow weavers, Irish tenant farmers—all displaced in one way or another by agricultural, industrial, or demographic change. Some of them came out of tightly knit rural communities that had changed little over the years but far more frequently their roots in such communities were several generations back and quite forgotten. Most came to Southern Ontario as individuals or as members of nuclear families. A few, such as some of the Loyalists, had emigrated for political reasons; others, such as the Mennonites and Quakers, partly for religious reasons. But most came because they could not make an adequate living where they were. Often the more ambitious went directly to the United States or passed through Southern Ontario en route to the American Middle West. Those settling in Southern Ontario usually had been displaced by economic conditions in Britain and had nowhere else to go.

In settling in Southern Ontario, or indeed in almost any other area of nineteenth-century New World settlement, the immigrant had left one changing environment for another perhaps even more unstable. In the British Isles he had been confronted with new agricultural practices, with urbanization, with industrialization. In Southern Ontario he found a forest that was being cleared, simple log buildings that gave way in a generation or two to ample brick farmhouses, Indian trails that were re-

placed by pioneer roads or railways, barges and sailing vessels by steamboats, hamlets by towns. His neighbors changed several times as either
he or they, as likely as not, moved to new farm lots. His farm equipment changed with innovations and his ability to afford them. The immigrant had come to a place in motion, and in adapting to a new setting
he adapted to change itself. He came to expect new faces, new accents,
new clearings, new machines. He had little difficulty, as a clearing became a farm or a track a road, in coming to expect progress, which he
defined in material terms. His sense of time, weakened by the dislocation
that had led to immigration, by the pace of change in Southern Ontario,
and simply by his new setting, was not strong. Often his past tended to
become ceremonial. Protestant and Catholic Irish still brawled in Southern Ontario, particularly in Toronto and in parts of the Ottawa valley,
where numerically there was a near balance between the two groups.
But such cultural remnants, rather like the St. Patrick's Day parade in
New York, rarely interfered with an individual's economic life. His world
was the present, in which his basic task, which had led him to emigrate
in the first place, was to achieve a reasonable standard of living. Ontarians were far more sensitive to the market than, for example, most French-
Canadian habitants. As a whole they were little interested in conservation or the long-term management of land and sought to maximize
short-term profits. Within certain constraints, they were resolute individuals.

In stressing individual freedom before time and community, most
Ontarians held values that were liberal in the classic sense. In this,
they were but part of much of the North Atlantic world of the
nineteenth century. Similar values emerged in Jacksonian Democracy,
accompanied the growing power of the English bourgeoisie, and led to
a widespread weakening of social tradition. Nor were these distinctively
nineteenth-century values. Even their American roots lay not only in the
trans-Appalachian movement, but also in early Pennsylvania and New
York and in second- or third-generation New England. Yet the pace of
nineteenth-century technological change had strengthened the liberal
view, particularly in those New World areas where settlement was a
by-product of nineteenth-century dislocation, and where the human
landscape had emerged from the wilderness. Tradition and continuity
were weakened in such settings, as were value systems that did not emphasize individual initiative and freedom. For this reason groups of different background tended to merge in Ontario. In the few cases where

they did not, as in the clear separation between the French Canadians who settled near Windsor in the 1740s and the Americans, English, and Scots who later moved in around them, an older view of collective responsibility had somehow managed to survive. The habitant had been shielded from the nineteenth and even the eighteenth century, and he lived retrospectively in a strong community, little exposed to liberal ideology. He was not a product of the dislocation that had settled Ontario, but rather of a type of rural community that most emigrants to Ontario had left far behind, and of a value system that Ontarians who found a virtue in progress could easily mistake for indolence.

Yet the tone of early Ontario is not so easily summarized. In the 1790s John Graves Simcoe, the province's first lieutenant-governor, dreamed that the entire continental heartland might yet be retrieved for Britain. In Simcoe's mind was not simply a vision of empire but a concept of a stratified society capped by an aristocracy and a government that was paternalistic rather than democratic. Later governors held similar views, as did many of the Loyalists, the British officers retired on half pay, and most of the provincial establishment. At a political level the tory view dominated until approximately 1850, and among the social elite it lasted much longer, particularly among the predominantly Anglican establishment in the towns. Most Ontarians, too, were proud to be British subjects, proud to be part of the greatest empire on earth, proud of its symbols such as the Great Exhibition of 1851 in London. Many Ontarians admired the British parliamentary system and praised British liberties; in these terms liberals were as resolutely attached to empire as tories. Moreover, Ontarians accepted a larger and more paternalistic role for government than was common in the emerging states to the south, a government that laid out many towns, built major roads and canals, subsidized some railways, and withheld one-seventh of the land for the support of the established church.

Then too, the liberal values of most Ontarians were quite unconsciously tempered by the shortage of land in the province. Southern Ontario is a thin peninsula, nothing like the vast agricultural heartland of the American Middle West. At Toronto the Canadian Shield lies one hundred miles to the north; at Kingston it is only a few miles away. By American standards this is but a patch of agricultural land, and even within the patch much land is ill-suited for agriculture, including several limestone plains, broad morainic belts of steep slopes and thin soils, and, in the early nineteenth century, large areas of poorly drained land in southwestern Ontario. Most of the arable land in Southern Ontario was settled by the 1850s, more than thirty years before Ontarians began migrating in any number to the Canadian prairie. In this interval the government induced a few settlers to take up land in the Canadian Shield, but many times more Ontarians emigrated to the south. The expanding continental frontier had passed out of Ontario, drawing young Ontarians in its train. With them went a certain restiveness, while left behind was a society made more stable by their going.

But with these qualifications the predominant society of farm, village, and town in nineteenth-century Ontario was liberal. Tory values appeared here and there in the landscape—in the park lots intended for gentlemen's estates that were laid out around early Toronto, in the mixed farms of half-pay officers, in the heavy, British neoclassicism of many public buildings. The more subtle tory tempering of the essential liberalism of most Ontarians had few obvious expressions in the landscape. Settled Southern Ontario looked much like the rest of the Great Lakes region, but this would not have been so if the values of Ontarians and upstate New Yorkers or Ohioans had been fundamentally different.

Given the responsiveness of most Ontarians to technological change, it was particularly important that upstate New York and Ohio lay just across a river or a lake. The many practical innovations developed in these states were responses to much the same physical environment as that of Southern Ontario and depended on much the same economic context. The farm tools, the mill parts, even some of the economic institutions used in the Middle West tended to be more relevant to early Ontario than did their British counterparts. Agricultural innovations ranging from stumping machines to cheese factories and quarterly fairs reached Ontario from the south. Over and over again mills were established by Americans drawing on American experience and American capital. Travelers claimed that most gristmillers in the province were Americans. A New Yorker established the first foundry in Hamilton in 1836 and another American the second a few years later. Upper Canadians themselves were not particularly innovative. Less prosperous and much less numerous than the Americans south of the Great Lakes, and taking up land slightly later, it was far easier for them to borrow. Possibly the use of plank roads moved southward after the practice had found its way to Ontario from Russia; possibly the timber slide reached the United States from the Ottawa valley, where it had been introduced from Scandinavia in the late 1820s. Otherwise the direction of diffusion was the other way around, and the lag between American invention or improvement and Ontarian adoption often was remarkably short. In effect, location, an essentially Middle Western physical environment, and the frame of mind of the Ontarians very early had moved Southern Ontario within the technological empire of the United States.

The physical land of Southern Ontario and its small indigenous population were in many ways a neutral background for settlement, certainly far less important than the settlers' values and Ontario's location in shaping the human landscape. Indian lands were quickly acquired by treaty or purchase; and the few Indian skills that settlers did employ—snowshoeing, tapping sugar maples—had usually been learned from whites who were probably unaware of the Indian origin of these techniques. The Indian trails that influenced the earliest settlement patterns soon became roads. Pioneers were aware of the presence of Indians (occasionally white children disappeared and settlers often surmised that Indians had kidnapped them), and some good land was set aside in Indian reserves; but over-all the Indians neither impeded the white settlement of Southern Ontario nor contributed significantly to its character. For American settlers, the physical land was familiar. Coming from pioneer environments not far away, they knew its flora and fauna and found its winter little longer or colder than the one they had known. Half-pay officers and other English gentlemen—who almost invariably brought thermometers across the Atlantic with them—usually found the climate less rigorous than they had feared. January mean temperatures at Toronto (23° F) and in extreme southwestern Ontario (25° F) were only some fifteen degrees below the equivalent figures for most of the British Isles. In the Ottawa valley and along the escarpment near Georgian Bay temperatures were considerably lower, and the snow cover lasted some five months; yet in these, as in almost all other pioneer settings in Ontario, there was no shortage of firewood. Most settlers who wrote about the winter found it invigorating and healthy. Generally settlers found summer heat and fevers more trying than winter cold, although in Ontario, as throughout the American northeast, the forest rather than climate was the main environmental obstacle to settlement. A great many settlers, whatever their background, gave the better part of their lives to clearing. Once cleared, the land of Southern Ontario held neither exceptional challenges nor exceptional opportunities. Its soils tended to be better than those of the St. Lawrence lowland, but were not nearly as rich as the long-grass prairie soils of parts of the

American Middle West. Although Indian corn ripened only in the southwest, the growing season was generally long enough for wheat. Drought was rarely a problem. Southern Ontario, in short, was neither a garden nor a desert. The theme of many novels of Canadian prairie life centered around the elemental struggle between man and an inclement land; French Canadians came to see the St. Lawrence lowland as the cradle of a distinctive culture; but when the forest was cleared in Ontario the land almost dropped from sight.

Loyalist refugees from the American War of Independence began to arrive in Southern Ontario in the early 1780s, some coming up the St. Lawrence River from Montréal, others crossing the Niagara River, and a few entering British territory from Detroit. In all there were probably not more than 6000–10,000 of them in a few isolated settlements at the several points of entry (see Fig. 4-1). After them came another breed of Americans, men far more attracted by cheap land than by loyalty to Britain. Crown land was available for sixpence an acre plus survey costs and an oath of allegiance; at a time when settlers were moving into New York and spilling into the Ohio country, where land was selling on the average for two dollars an acre, cheap Southern Ontario land was a considerable attraction. Some of these Americans quickly returned, many others visited back and forth across the border, but few severed their American ties. In 1812 perhaps 100,000 people were in Southern Ontario, almost all of them living just across a river or a lake from the United States. Approximately 80 per cent of the population were of American origin, and at least three-quarters of this group were neither Loyalists nor their descendants. The fluid conditions of the expanding North American frontier had taken so little stock of the international border drawn through the Great Lakes in 1783 that the early settlement of Southern Ontario marked, essentially, the northern fringe of American westward advance.

After the War of 1812 the government decided to close the province to settlers from the south. Such a policy was not enforceable—speculators counted on immigration to augment the value of their land, and many of them courted Americans—but it did make it difficult for Americans to purchase crown land and, therefore, to establish themselves more cheaply than in the United States. As immigration from the British Isles increased to several thousand a year, the percentage of Upper Cana-

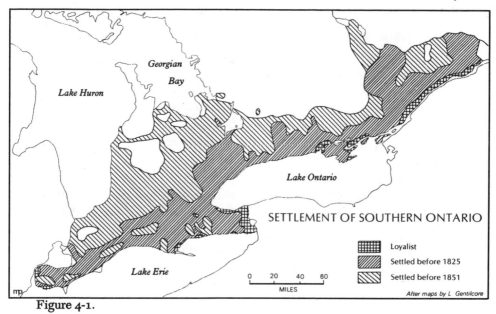

Figure 4-1.

dians of American background gradually declined. The government established demobilized soldiers at a few strategic locations and brought two large groups of poor to Upper Canada: in 1816 some 3000 Scottish weavers to the rocky uplands along the Rideau River south of Ottawa, and in 1825 a smaller group of Southern Irish to much better land near Peterborough. These proved to be expensive experiments, and most British immigrants were left to come as they could. Until the famine migration of the late 1840s, only a few of the immigrants to Ontario were indigent. Rather they were small farmers, artisans, or tradesmen—men of modest means who felt their position threatened and decided to move before they were reduced to poverty. They and the Americans mingled in Southern Ontario. Settlement spread along most of the Lake Erie shore and pushed slowly inland along a broad front (see Fig. 4-1). Yet in 1825 probably not more than 150,000 people lived in Southern Ontario. Most of the land, even within the areas marked as settled by 1825 on Figure 4-1, was still forested.

It was in the next forty years that the forest was cut, that settlement spread north to the Shield, and that the settled agricultural landscape of Southern Ontario emerged. Some 600,000 immigrants from the United Kingdom arrived in British North America between 1825 and 1846; in

1847 almost 90,000 people debarked at Québec alone. Many of these immigrants died in the immigrant sheds or en route up the St. Lawrence. Large numbers went on to the United States, but a great many settled in Upper Canada. In the years between 1825 and 1842 its population tripled to 450,000, and more than doubled again by 1851. Most of the newcomers were Irish. In 1829 it was estimated that English immigrants comprised 20 per cent of the arrivals at Québec, Scottish another 20 per cent, and Irish the remainder; and these proportions probably remained about the same for the next twenty-five years. Some of the Catholic Southern Irish stayed in the towns, and many moved on to the United States. A much higher proportion of Protestant Ulstermen (the Scotch-Irish) settled in Upper Canada. The great migration had settled Southern Ontario with Britons, but with Britons drawn principally from the northern and western peripheries of the British Isles.

At Confederation only about one-quarter of all Ontarians, including many descendants of Americans, claimed English origin. They tended to live in the older areas—along the Lake Ontario shore, particularly near Toronto, and in the Thames River valley and south to Lake Erie. On the northern fringes of settlement where pioneer farming was still underway, they were thinly represented. Scots, a fifth of the provincial population, were common throughout southwestern Ontario and predominated along much of the Lake Huron shore. The Scotch-Irish, three-eighths of Ontarians, were almost ubiquitous. In most of the Ottawa valley, in the uplands between Ottawa and Kingston, in newer areas of settlement north of Lake Ontario, and in most of western Ontario as well (except along the Erie shore and the lower Thames, which were predominantly English and the valley of the upper Grand River, which was German), they were the dominant group. It is not surprising that the small meeting hall of the Loyal Orange Lodge, a blatantly anti-Catholic society that had grown out of the Irish border tensions of the 1790s, had become a common sight in almost all parts of Ontario; that at Confederation there were four Presbyterians for every three Wesleyans and each Anglican in the province; and that dourness, attachment to empire, and fierce anti-Catholicism were characteristics frequently ascribed to Ontarians.

THE SPREAD OF SETTLEMENT

In a general way, as shown in Figure 4-1, settlement had spread from south to north, moving away from the lakes only as land along them was taken up. Yet it is misleading to picture a sharp line of advance separating a forested wilderness ahead from cleared farmland behind. Some areas in the interior were settled well before others near the lakes: one township would fill up early, another adjacent to it would remain unsettled for years. While it was generally true that settlement moved from south to north because immigrants had entered from the southeast and because trade flowed in that direction, many other factors affected patterns of settlement.

Of these factors, local accessibility, the settlers' appraisal of land quality, and the influence of land speculators were probably the most important. Immigrants had not come to Canada to settle into self-sufficiency. Men hoped to sell their labor or farm produce; to do the latter they had to have a farm connected by a passable road or by navigable water to the local village or gristmill. Nor were settlers indifferent to the quality of the land. Most of the Americans had prior experience in a similar environment and came with clear ideas about suitable land for settlement. Later arrivals from the British Isles were less competent judges of land quality, but by that time settlers' guides, district land agents, and earlier settlers were available—all with advice, some of it certainly contradictory, about land that was fit for settlement. Beyond this was the influence of land speculators. The government, with about a quarter of the land set aside in crown and clergy reserves, was the principal speculator, but a great many private individuals had received large land grants or had bought up land scrip at minimal prices. Some speculators, waiting for surrounding settlement to drive up the price, held their land for years, others were vigorous developers, but whatever their policy, their influence on the settlement pattern was considerable.

Although few roads were built in advance of settlement, accessibility in most parts of Southern Ontario away from the immediate lakefront depended on a road. Yonge Street, opened between Toronto (then York) and a point near Lake Simcoe in 1795, and Dundas Street, built west from the western end of Lake Ontario to the Grand River at about the same time, did precede settlement as did the colonization roads built to Georgian Bay in the 1840s and to the Shield in the 1850s and 1860s. All these roads attracted some settlers along them. As early as 1801, for example, more than two-thirds of the lots along Yonge Street were occupied, although settlement north of Toronto was also taking place well away from Yonge Street in areas connected to the outside by roads which the settlers themselves had opened.

First Home in Canada by William Armstrong. Probably few settlers' cabins had roofs of the massive log construction shown in this picture. Otherwise Armstrong's watercolor depicts a typical pioneer scene: stumps and logs in a small clearing, a small log house, the enveloping forest. Royal Ontario Museum, Toronto.

Many pioneer tales to the contrary, few settlers back-packed their own grain. Rather they relied on roads, but on roads of the lowest quality. Yonge Street, for example, was for many years a log- and stump-strewn swath through the woods. For an English traveler such a road was impassable; for the settler (who usually neglected the road duties stipulated in his land grant) it was an adequate connection to an export market. He could drive a sled over such a road in winter and, although with more difficulty, a wagon in midsummer. Some of the roads followed Indian trails, but even without a pre-existing trail, road-building was not an overwhelming task, given the pioneer's minimal road requirements. Evidence from York County north of Toronto suggests that settlers would build more than fifteen miles of such roads, that is, they were prepared to take up land more than fifteen miles away from an existing road and settlement. Farther north, where the colonization roads themselves were isolated, they may not have gone so far.

There are accounts of settlers cutting a road into a new area literally as they went. Perhaps accounts exaggerate, but there is no doubt that the "sled roads" required by settlers in early Ontario could be quickly built. Wherever settlers went, roads and land-clearing appeared simultaneously. In York County in 1834, 80 per cent of the cleared land was on lots touching a road; only 2 per cent of the cleared land was on lots more than two miles from a road. The settlers themselves had built most of the roads; occupance created roads, roads permitted settlers to develop lots and settle new ones, and these developments led to more roads. In general, then, the principal access routes had a marked bearing on the general pattern of settlement. In more detail the settlement pattern reveals the settlers' independence from the pre-existing road system, their independence stemming from their ability, up to a point, to build the essential road connection themselves.

Almost all settlers rejected swampland, and most of them rejected sandy morainic ridges. All of them required water at or very close to the surface. Within these limits soils with limestone under a few inches of topsoil, ill-drained clay loams, and light, sandy loams all were settled. Oak-opening parklands along the Lake Erie shore were preferred areas. One settler noted that these areas "are easily cleared or rather want no clearing at all for if you cut down any little underwood there may be and girdle, you can harrow up the surface." In these conditions a farm could be established quickly and cheaply, natural pasture was abundant, and wagons were easy to use. Most of the oak openings in the Lake Erie region tailed off into an oak–hickory association on light sand and silt loams, and settlers preferred this land to slightly less well-drained sites supporting a beech–maple–basswood association. The latter was a heavier forest that took longer to clear, and presumably many early settlers preferred lots in the oak–hickory association for this reason. In much of what are now Essex and Kent counties in southwestern Ontario, heavy, poorly drained soils were avoided for decades because of the expenses of clearing and drainage. When cleared and drained this land was often excellent, but the expense of putting it into production was a major consideration for most settlers. In Simcoe County, north of Toronto, some settlers with capital apparently selected heavy, wet soils, expecting large initial expense but eventually an excellent farm. Poorer settlers chose light land with a thinner forest, land that could be got into production quickly. If the soil were exhausted in a decade, the settler would have amassed the capital to make another start on better land.

But undoubtedly these patterns were extremely varied. There is no good evidence that different ethnic groups selected different kinds of sites.

The influence of land speculators on the spread of settlement was probably far greater. At various times the government gave important individuals 1000, 5000, or even more acres of land, a policy that rested partly on the intimacy of the establishment, partly on the need, when money was scarce, to repay officials for faithful service, but just as much on the tory view that a concentration of wealth among the elite was entirely fit and proper. Moreover, Loyalists and their descendants, including many land seekers who belatedly qualified as Loyalists, had been issued land scrip, much of which eventually collected in the hands of speculators. It was not unusual for a speculator to hold rights to ten or fifteen thousand acres, and when a new township was surveyed and opened for settlement, to claim a large block of it. An entire township could pass into private hands in hours or weeks, and in every district land speculators were at work. Wherever land of reasonable quality was not settled as quickly as land around, speculation was usually the cause. Viewed against such rampant speculation, the quarter of the land in crown and clergy reserves was not a major additional impediment to settlement. These lots, usually distributed throughout the townships in a regular pattern, were available for leasehold before 1826 and for purchase thereafter, and there is good evidence that they were developed almost as quickly as lots on either side of them. Occasionally private speculators were also developers. Colonel Talbot, who presided over more than 60,000 acres on the north shore of Lake Erie, directed and may have speeded their development; and the Canada Company, which had bought the crown reserves in 1826, opened up a large tract just east of Lake Huron. Over-all, the influence of land speculation, whether to hasten or retard settlement, was to increase the irregularity of the settlement pattern.

Of the influence of community on the spread of settlement we know very little. Undoubtedly a settler preferred to have neighbors on lots nearby and rarely struck out far on his own. Settlers who took up land ten or fifteen miles from a pre-existing road did so in small groups. Group settlement was often related to the accessibility and availability of lots, but also to the need for social contact and a local labor pool to contribute to clearing and building. A pioneer wife tied by her children to the vicinity of a tiny log cabin must have delighted in another family closer at hand than the next Sunday's church meeting. Often such ties were strengthened because a settler's neighbors were of his own national background. In some cases immigrants who had crossed the Atlantic together eventually settled together in the same Ontario township. In others an early arrival had written, perhaps sending money to relatives in the homeland. The immigrant agent in Québec reported in 1826 that many immigrants were coming to friends or relatives, and there is evidence of families from the same Scottish village trickling into the same Ontario township over fifteen years or more. Sociability was undoubtedly important, but it is not clear that it was important enough in a settler's eyes to direct him to a less accessible location, a poorer lot, or more expensive land. At the moment the best inference from thin evidence is that settlers took up land as close to neighbors, kin, or their own national groups as was possible without obvious economic sacrifice.

THE DETAILED SETTLEMENT PATTERN

In early Ontario a prior survey was a prerequisite to any land grant and, therefore, with the exception of occasional squatting, surveying preceded settlement. A township was the unit of survey. In 1789 the dimensions of townships along navigable waterways were set at nine by twelve miles, those in the interior at ten miles square, and throughout the pre-Confederation years these approximate dimensions were usually followed. Within the townships, road allowances and lot lines were laid out geometrically. There were many road and lot patterns, differences between them depending on the dimensions of the lots and the number of lots between the crossroads, but at Confederation at least 90 per cent of Ontario townships had been surveyed in one of three methods: the single-front system, the double-front system, and the 1000-acre-section system (see Fig. 4-2). The single-front system was common before 1818, the double-front system from 1818 to 1851, the 1000-acre-section system during the rest of the pre-Confederation years; and the distribution of each corresponded generally with the spread of settlement during each period. Lots in the single-front system were fairly long and thin (usually with a ratio of width to length of about 1 : 5), were 200 acres in size, and were arranged in single tiers of lots between concession-line roads. Although the lots were not as long, this survey resembled the single-*rang* system in Québec. In the double-front system the common unit of concession, the half-lot, was almost square and 100 acres in size. Each half of a 200-acre lot fronted on different concession-line roads. In the

PRINCIPAL SURVEY SYSTEMS AND SETTLEMENT PATTERNS
IN SOUTHERN ONTARIO

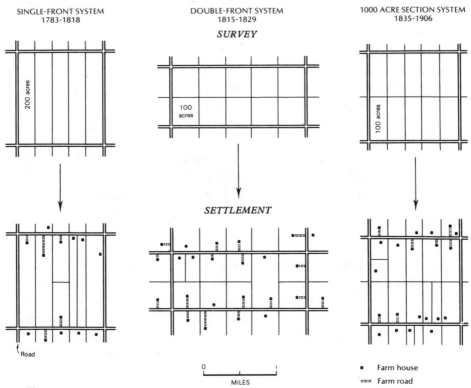

Figure 4-2.

1000-acre-section system, each 100-acre lot was two and a half times as long as it was wide; there were two tiers of lots between concession-line roads and five lots in each tier between crossroads. A block of ten lots made a 1000-acre-section. Each of these surveys imparted its own geometry to the landscape, affecting the layout of roads, the shape of fields, the location of woodlots and, to a substantial degree, the location of farmsteads.

Almost all Ontario farmers lived on their own lots. Often they built their first cabin close to an Indian trail or at a site with some obvious physical advantage—a spring or watercourse nearby, a former beach ridge giving better drainage, a south-facing slope giving protection from the winter wind. Sometimes the location of the first house became that of its successors, but as concession-line roads improved and off-the-farm travel increased, the location of the second house usually depended on the road. Unlike habitants in Québec, Ontarians did not often build at roadside, but they usually built the second house within 200 yards of a road. If a farmer's nearest neighbor was directly across the road, he might be no more than 200 yards away; if, as was rare, four farmers, two on each side of the road, settled near the common corner of their lots, there could be four families within perhaps 200 yards of each other; if lots in the single-front system were divided along their long axis, neighbors could be very close together. More commonly Ontario farmers were some 300 yards from their nearest neighbor, and wherever much of the land was swampy, in the hands of speculators, or in the process of being settled, they could be much more isolated. Figure 4-2 shows fairly characteristic settlement patterns associated with each of the three principal surveys. Settlement in the double-front system tended to be the most dispersed, whereas when single-front lots were well subdivided, farmers were no more isolated than the habitants along the lower St. Lawrence. Yet Ontarians had accepted a more dispersed pattern of rural settlement than had their counterparts in Québec.

In a sense, dispersed settlement had been imposed on the Ontarians. Yet while they railed against many aspects of governmental land policy, few of them complained about a survey system that made it virtually mandatory for a farmer to live on his own land and in isolation from his nearest neighbors. Of course most of the Americans in Ontario had known no other system, and only a small percentage of the settlers from the British Isles had once lived in compact, agricultural villages. But as other traditions were discarded in migration, dispersed settlement must have accorded with most Ontarians' economic and social objectives, and it should be understood in these terms.

Clearly, economic advantage lay on the side of dispersed settlement. Most settlers in rural Ontario farmed commercially within a few years of arriving on their lot, but required few commercial off-the-farm connections. In the years of wheat–fallow–wheat farming (see pp. 135–36) a man usually took his grain by sled to the local gristmill or to the Lake Erie or Lake Ontario shore, giving perhaps a week or two to the task. Several times a year he went to the nearest village for supplies. As wheat farming gave way to mixed farming, operations became more complex and required more off-the-farm connections although, with the exception of the Sunday drive to church, few farmers went as often as once a week to the nearest hamlet or village. To live in a village, therefore, would have increased his travel time enormously. Within the farm itself

Rural landscape, nineteenth-century Ontario. The achievement of a generation
of unremitting work, this was a landscape that must have given pioneer Ontarians enormous satisfaction. Although stumps remain in some fields, the forest
has been pushed back, the roads are much improved, and substantial farmhouses, barns, and a stone church are evident. Ontario Archives.

dispersed settlement allowed the farmer to save time and labor; the
long lot, for example, required more farm roads and considerably more
travel time each day than the shorter, broader lots that became common
in Ontario. Had Ontarians adopted a more agglomerated form of settlement they would have worked a longer day or have accepted a lower
standard of living.

On the other hand, dispersed settlement hindered certain types of social interaction. The tasks of clearing a forest and establishing a farm
involved seemingly interminable work in considerable isolation. At first
a man's clearing was surrounded by forest; many a work week must
have passed in which a pioneer saw none of his neighbors. In this situation pioneer Ontarians must have craved a release from work and isolation much as a logger in an isolated camp craves his Saturday night or
a spree in the city. Many of the logging, stumping, or barn-raising bees,
"noisy, riotous, drunken meetings," according to the English gentle-
woman Susanna Moodie, served this function. Men of different backgrounds, often complete strangers to each other, came from miles
around to a large bee. Usually enough work was done to justify the ex-

pense of holding a bee; but most of the men had come to drink, and farmers who disapproved of whisky and refused to provide it often had difficulty in raising a bee. A boisterous Saturday night at the local tavern could fill much the same role; and it has been averred that the exuberance of early Methodist or Baptist camp revivals were related as much to the isolation and hard work of frontier life as to the particular doctrines of revelation in these groups. Although few Ontarians saw themselves participating in bees or camp revivals because pioneering in Ontario had interfered with other forms of social interaction, this was probably the case.

Eventually less tumultuous forms of social interaction became more common. The concession-line road had filled up with settlers, a man's neighbors lived a little closer, and he had more time for them. Quilting, apple-paring, and pea-shelling bees were occasions for gossip and flirtation; a marriage in the neighborhood an excuse, if such activities were not frowned upon, for a dance. The gristmill, general store, and blacksmith shop in the local village or hamlet were social as well as economic meeting places. Local taverns became the scene of many a Saturday night dance. Some farmers joined the local agricultural society, which often served more as a social gathering than as a vehicle for agricultural improvement. Many more, not all of them Scotch-Irish, joined the Loyal Orange Lodge, attended its regular meetings and participated in its 12th of July parade. Others who were usually a little better off became Masons. Probably the church was the most important focus of social life. Most Ontarians attended church regularly; there they met many of their closest friends and exchanged the latest news. Dispersed settlement had not prevented strong social connections off the farm, but it had not forced them on the farmer; he could be socially involved or detached, and probably this was exactly as he wished it to be.

It is clear that in comparison with the habitants in rural Québec, most Ontario farmers lived in a much looser social context. For this there were many causes, not the least of them the great spatial mobility of the frontier. In several townships along the Lake Ontario shore near Port Hope, approximately 20 per cent of the initial settlers had moved within a year and 50 percent within five years. Subsequently the rate of turnover declined, but it remained far higher than among the nineteenth-century habitant population of lowland Québec. Moreover, the extended family or kin group was not a strong social institution in pre-Confederation Ontario. Here and there two brothers had taken up adjacent lots;

quite commonly 200-acre lots were subdivided between them. If a third son had acquired land in the vicinity and a daughter had married a local boy, a small, loosely knit kin group emerged. Such groupings were quite common by Confederation. They were, however, a far cry from the deeply interrelated rural communities that had grown up over many generations in lowland Québec. In Glengarry County, settled by Highland Scots at the end of the eighteenth century, there were more than 3000 Macdonells or Macdonalds, about one-fifth of the population in 1850. But even there consanguinous ties were not as close as in Québec, where settlers of a given name in a given parish almost invariably had common Canadian ancestors.

Equally disruptive was the mixture in rural Ontario of religious and national backgrounds. A Presbyterian Scot might have another Presbyterian Scot as nearest neighbor, but almost as likely an American Baptist or a Methodist. Along many concession roads denominational and national affiliations were mixed, along others quite homogeneous; in any area of township size, both types of settlement were likely. Wherever settlement was relatively homogeneous, social ties were undoubtedly strengthened. Gaelic was still spoken in Highland settlements at Confederation; some Germans still could not speak English. A group of Scots could preserve Old World social customs relating, for example, to meals or marriages; an isolated Scot was more likely to adopt the customs of his neighbors. But almost all Ontarians were exposed to people and ways of life that they had never encountered before, and the long-run effect of this exposure was to throw the individual back on himself and his immediate family.

Moreover, the immigrants had craved land. They had come, perhaps, from a few rocky acres; they associated land with economic security and social status, and a substantial house with the way of life of a successful farmer. The many promotional handbooks that depicted a one-room cabin in a stumpy clearing followed after perhaps two decades by a brick farmhouse and well-tended fields understood and played upon this basic yearning. Finally, the religious beliefs of most rural Ontarians emphasized a man's personal connection with God rather than the social responsibilities of the Christian ethic. Their Sundays tended to be days of long sermons and, ideally, of private reflection; even their temperance movements, while directed against drunkenness, struck hard at a common form of social interaction.

Undoubtedly Ontarians were proud of their farms. When in the 1870s

Canal Bank Farm, Carleton County. A plate from the *Carleton County Atlas* depicting progress and prosperity. The quality stock, the new farm machinery, the neat farmhouse and landscaped grounds, the railway, the steamboat, even the parliament buildings of the new Dominion of Canada suggest a bustling, changing, thriving place. Metropolitan Toronto Library Board.

they began publishing county atlases, they embellished their pages with engravings of the ample farmsteads of successful farmers: a sizable brick farmhouse, a barn and other farm buildings behind, a lawn in front, a small orchard to one side, a picket fence, all part of man's estate, all on his own land, all well set off from his neighbors. Such a picture was publicity for the county, an image of success that all could appreciate. Its popularity rested on the land hunger of immigrants, the materialism that had led most settlers to emigrate and that had been reinforced in the turbulent conditions of the frontier, and on the privatism of the Protestant tradition. Put most simply, it rested on the individualistic values that had been brought to and nurtured in Ontario. For the

Catholic Southern Irish who poured into Ontario in the late 1840s this ideology was as alien as the land system. The fifty-acre lots which many of them received near Georgian Bay or along the Shield fringe forced them into an isolation they had neither known nor admired. Powerless to change the land system, most of them moved to the towns, where, in the company of their fellows, the community values of Irish peasant life could more readily be preserved. For most other Ontarians the land system and their social ideology were completely compatible.

BUILDINGS

Most early nineteenth-century Ontarians built simple, functional houses reflecting the needs of pioneer life, but, because they had come recently and were responsive to the outside world, the prevailing architectural types influenced them. These styles, to be sure, were filtered through local builders, often appearing in the Ontario countryside ten or twenty years after their first vogue in Toronto; even so, two quite different architectural periods were reflected, sometimes in combination, in almost all Ontario houses. The first of these was eighteenth-century classical; the second was Victorian. The classical style, or Georgian as it was commonly called in the British Isles and in Ontario, was a somewhat austere, balanced, economical architecture; whereas the Victorian style employed classical, Gothic, and Italianate forms, often in combination, and became more extravagantly elaborate as the century wore on. The common Ontario farmhouse before Confederation may be thought of as a simple Georgian building with, by mid-century, more or less Victorian embellishment.

The shanty, the first building put up by many settlers, had none of these architectural pretentions (see Fig. 4-3). Two skilled workmen put up a shanty in a few days. Logs were left in the round and were cross-notched at the corners, the floor was usually dirt, the chimney, if built at all, was usually made of small green rounds chinked with clay, and the roof usually had but a single slope. As late as 1850 at least 3 per cent of the houses in the oldest townships were still shanties. After two or three years, however, most settlers had left their shanties for a more ample log building. These buildings were made of squared logs, frequently dovetailed at the corners. They had a plank floor with a root cellar underneath, two to three rooms on the ground floor, a half-attic above, and at least one stone or brick fireplace. With the door centrally

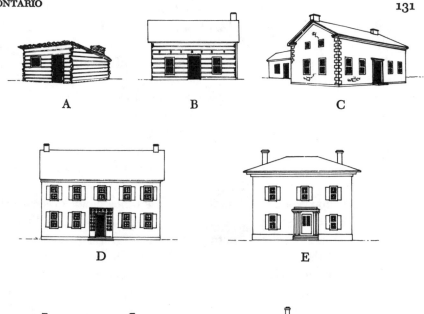

Figure 4 3. Ontario House Types

(A) Shanty and (B) Log house, which were common in pioneer areas before Confederation. (C) Georgian stone house (also of frame or brick construction) built, with minor modifications, from the late eighteenth to the mid-nineteenth century. (D) A larger Georgian or "Loyalist" house built, with changes in detail around door and eaves, until the 1850s and even later. (E) A substantial house, of a type built between 1825 and 1860, showing regency influences in the roof and chimneys and classical detail around the door. (F) Small board-and-batten house with Gothic window and fretwork trim. A very common Ontario house, whether of frame, brick, or stone construction, from approximately 1855 to the end of the century. (G) A substantial brick farmhouse of a type that was becoming common by Confederation and remained popular until the end of the century. (Drawings by Peter Ennals)

placed on a long side, with a single window on either side of the door, and the squared log work and flush corners de-emphasizing the construction materials as much as possible, they embodied in elemental form the basic classical principles of order and symmetry. This simple building, brought into Ontario from the south, was the most common farmhouse in the province throughout the pre-Confederation years, and shaped the vernacular style throughout the century. As late as the 1830s there were probably twice as many log farmhouses in the province as a whole as those of frame, brick, or stone construction; even in the 1860s log houses were still predominant in townships well away from the Lake Ontario or Lake Erie shores. Whatever their background most settlers lived for a time in such houses, their length of stay usually a measure of their economic position. Half-pay officers moved in a few years to a larger frame, stone, or brick building. On the other hand, descendants of the Irish settlers established near Peterborough in 1825 still lived in log houses at the end of the century. A group of Yorkshiremen settled nearby had left their log houses much earlier—not because they disliked them more than the Irish did—but because they were better off. For reasons discussed above farmhouses were always important status symbols in early Ontario, and, except for a handful of romantic Englishmen, log buildings marked a low status.

Eventually many settlers covered their log houses with boards or brick, and others built similar houses in these materials or in stone (see Fig. 4-3). Brick construction was more common than south of the border, and white clapboard walls were almost nonexistent. Other more prosperous settlers built full two-story buildings, often with five evenly spaced windows along the front of the second floor and two on either side of the central door. Usually there were a rectangular or fan transom, side lights, classical details around windows and eaves, and a chimney projecting above the roof-line at either end. Architecturally these were but larger versions of the small classical house, and they continued to be built, with minor variations in trim, until well into the 1850s and 1860s.

At the same time the early effects of the transition from Georgian to Victorian building were appearing in Ontario. This transition was expressed first by the American and British classical revivals, which began to influence Ontario building early in the century, and later by Italianate and Gothic revival buildings. Few houses were entirely faithful to either of these styles. Rather the Georgian house was gradually modified in detail and form until its Georgian quality disappeared entirely. Houses E and F in Figure 4-3 retain the symmetry of Georgian architecture, but their detail marks them as transitional between Georgian and high Victorian. The last house illustrated in Figure 4-3 is a considerable

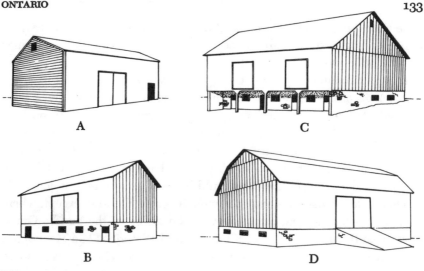

Figure 4-4. Ontario Barns
(A) Two-Bay Barn. (B) Raised Two-Bay Barn. (C) Pennsylvania Barn.
(D) Central Ontario Barn

departure from the classical principles of austerity, symmetry, and balance. Its asymmetry, elaborate fretwork, and porch mark it as a building of the middle Victorian years. Such houses had appeared here and there in rural Ontario before Confederation.

In Ontario, barns were always detached from the farmhouse, usually standing fifty to one hundred yards behind it or to one side. In the early nineteenth century there were two basic types of barn: the two-bay barn (see Fig. 4-4), and the Pennsylvania barn. By the 1850s and 1860s the increasing importance of livestock in the agricultural system had led to the evolution of the raised two-bay barn and a large, wide barn which, because of its present wide distribution in south-central Ontario, has been called simply the central Ontario barn.

The two-bay barn was a log or frame building of modest size, usually about thirty by sixty feet. A door large enough to take a wagon was located centrally in each long side. Inside there was a central drive-floor between the two doors, and on either side of it a bay, or storage area, suitable for grain, hay, or livestock. A similar barn was common in eighteenth-century New England, but the two-bay barn probably was introduced to Ontario from Pennsylvania and upstate New York, and perhaps also from England. Whatever its routes of diffusion it admirably suited the early Ontario farmers. Whether log or frame, it was easy to build, its narrow span easily roofed. Were more space required, a farmer usually built another barn, sometimes adding it to one end of the older building, sometimes creating L-shaped, U-shaped or even square arrangements around a barnyard. Generally, however, a single small barn sufficed. As long as the farmer depended on wheat rather than on livestock, as he did in early Ontario, he did not need a lot of storage space. One bay served as a granary, the other to store a few implements and, perhaps, to house a few stock. With both doors open on a windy day the drive-floor between the bays could be used as a threshing floor.

This style of barn became common in early Ontario except where Mennonites had settled, particularly in the valley of the middle Grand River near the present cities of Kitchener and Waterloo. The Mennonites brought a large, squarish barn with a stable area below, storage space above and an overhang (forebay or overshot) along one side of the barn, a type associated primarily with the Mennonites in Pennsylvania. Where possible this barn was built into a bank to give easy wagon access to the storage floor, the lower walls were usually stone, and several doors under the forebay led to stalls aligned across the long axis of the building. The superstructure was usually frame covered with vertical boards, and the interior timbering was massive and complex enough to support a roof over an area often sixty by one hundred feet or more. Pennsylvania barns probably appeared in Ontario early in the nineteenth century, but in an agricultural economy still dominated by wheat most of these buildings must have been small log versions of the large stone-and-frame barns that became common in Mennonite areas in the 1850s. In a province where distinctive traditions often were quickly blurred, the Pennsylvania barn, occasionally still built, has stood out as one of the most distinctive and long-lived landscape features of a particular ethnic group.

In the 1850s the wheat economy began to give way to a mixed commercial agriculture based on livestock, an agricultural system unsuited to the two-bay barn, which provided neither adequate storage nor stabling. Many farmers built another small barn, but it became increasingly common to place the older type of two-bay barn above a stone foundation story in which livestock were housed. Hay was stored above. As the threshing machine became more common it freed much of the drive-floor for additional storage space. In some cases existing two-bay barns were physically raised, in others new barns of the new style were built from scratch. Another solution to the need for more space was the central Ontario barn, which began to appear in the 1860s. Its dimensions were more nearly those of the Pennsylvania than of the two-bay barn, although it was without the forebay or the transverse alignment of stalls characteristic of the Pennsylvania type. Possibly the builders of central Ontario barns had borrowed from the Mennonites, but given the concentration of Pennsylvania barns and the relative ubiquity by the end of the nineteenth century of the central Ontario type, it is more likely that builders enlarged the raised two-bay barn to meet growing demands for space.

AGRICULTURE

Except where they happened on oak openings, Indian campsites, riverine marshes, or beaver meadows, settlers had to establish farms in the forest. For most of them the forest was unfamiliar and hostile, a barrier between themselves and a farm. Those who acquired land in the oak openings often girdled the trees and planted among them; elsewhere they cut the trees, used oxen or horses to haul them into piles, and burned the piles. Without constant attendance clearings in hardwood forest quickly became patches of fireweed, chokecherry, and hardwood suckers; those in pine lands often sprouted in wild raspberries and poplar. Although some promotional handbooks claimed that a settler could clear, fence, and put under crops ten acres of land a year, far more commonly he was fortunate to clear two to three acres annually. At this rate, clearing and the subsequent struggle against the recolonization of clearings by forest weeds could take most of his productive life. Out of this work developed an ingrained hostility to the forest and, eventually, a severe over-clearing of the land. English gentlemen visiting Upper Canada in the early and middle nineteenth century frequently contrasted their own sorrow with the settlers' exultation at the destruction of trees. For the one, trees were ingredients of a picturesque landscape; for the other, a severe economic liability.

Cleared land was fenced first with trunks piled around the edge of clearings, later with snake or patent-rail fences, and often in the 1850s, when stumping machines had spread into Upper Canada from upstate New York, with stumps set on edge around the boundaries of fields. In their first clearing most settlers planted potatoes, vegetables, and wheat for their families. A clearing of three acres could meet most of the food needs of a family of four. Cattle, hogs, and sheep browsed in the woods most of the year and survived in the dead of winter on branches the farmer piled in the yard. When three small fields had been fenced—perhaps only three to five years after the settler's arrival on his lot—the wheat–fallow–wheat farm, the most common agricultural system in early Ontario, had been established in its essentials. One field was planted in vegetables for the farm family and the others were in wheat or fallow. As clearing proceeded, farmers enlarged the wheat and fallow fields, but the agricultural system did not change. Animals still browsed in the woods, manure went uncollected, the fallow was plowed at least twice a year, and wheat was grown in a two-course rotation of wheat and fallow.

This agricultural system allowed settlers with little capital to emphasize the raising of produce for sale or barter within a few years of initial settlement; to devote much of their time to clearing; to combat with some success the recolonization of fields by forest species; and to produce the one crop for which there was a substantial market. In most pioneer areas agricultural produce could be sold to the incoming settlers, but the major market for wheat was in Toronto and other lakefront centers. Most farms necessarily depended on wheat as the principal cash crop, but some farmers felt that wheat on the same field in successive years exhausted the soil, and almost all found that successive wheat crops made it impossible to check the regrowth of forest species. In most farmers' eyes alternating wheat and fallow was sufficient to prevent soil exhaustion, while a bare fallow plowed at least twice was a satisfactory check on weeds. Such a farm required relatively little attention. Women and children tended the garden, and stock lived in the woods, rarely housed even in winter. The settler plowed, planted, harvested, and threshed, but most of his year was free for clearing. His capital investment was low: wheat seed, a few simple tools, a pair of oxen, and the labor of clearing were sufficient to bring his farm into production. It was sedentary agriculture pared to the bare essentials, producing one marketable commodity with little capital or labor. Most settlers saw no point in a complex rotation of unmarketable crops or in carefully tending livestock when there was so little demand for livestock products. In alternating wheat and fallow they made extensive use of land, but land was more abundant than any of the other essentials of the agricultural system.

A few gentlemen farmers who did not have to make their living from farming rejected this system. These men—many of them officers retired on half pay—were acquainted with the writings of the English agricultural improvers of their day, and they assumed that a rotation of wheat and fallow exhausted the soil. Thus they established mixed farms, and, because they had some capital or a regular pension, they were able to pursue a European agricultural ideal in the face of the physical and economic realities of early Ontario. Hence their elaborate crop rotations, their experimentation with new seeds and crops, their purebred stock. With little market for livestock products, most of their farms were unprofitable for years, but they did serve as models for the various forms of mixed farming that gradually replaced wheat–fallow–wheat farming from about 1840 to 1880. Not convinced by arguments about soil exhaustion or by references to European agricultural ways, farmers turned to mixed farming only as it became the more profitable system.

Wheat–fallow–wheat farming had relied on the British and American wheat markets; mixed farming on a more diversified market in the local towns, in the United States, and in Britain. Railway construction in upstate New York in the 1840s and in Upper Canada in the 1850s, and a reciprocity treaty with the United States in 1855 enabled Upper Canadian farmers to export larger quantities of wheat, barley, peas, hogs, cattle, sheep, wool, and butter to the United States. Although the treaty ended eleven years later, American demand for Canadian agricultural products continued, with the prices of many agricultural products higher in 1866 and 1867 than during any of the reciprocity years. Improvements in refrigeration in the 1870s allowed Ontario beef to enter the British market, and in the next decade Ontario cheese began to displace cheese from the United States in this market. Many Ontario farmers continued to grow some wheat, and a few still specialized in the crop, but in forty years the range of their market had widened to the point where, whether measured by the return per unit of land or of labor, wheat farming was rarely the most profitable of a farmer's options.

Often a farmer first modified wheat–fallow–wheat farming by reducing the fallow. With the weed problem largely solved by many years of bare fallow and with the market diversifying, he began to follow wheat with peas or oats, and eventually developed a rotation of several exhausting crops, such as wheat, oats, and barley followed by several years of recuperating crops, such as grasses, clovers, and peas. A bare fallow, if used, appeared only about every eight or ten years. Some farmers retained the biennial fallow but substituted a feed crop for part of their wheat acreage. These were still not mixed farms. Their low-quality animals were not raised for sale, manure was not collected, and the farm income depended almost entirely on the sale of wheat or barley to the grain merchants, or oats and hay to the lumber camps or the local mixed farmers. Closer to the mixed farm were those in which a quarter to a third of the cleared land was in wheat and the rest in field crops and pasture raised partly for the stock on the farm. Such farms often produced a surplus of wheat, feed, and animal products. On a full-fledged mixed farm even more of the land was in feed crops or pasture, with perhaps no more than one course of wheat on a given field in a decade. Livestock products were such a farm's principal commercial output. The earlier mixed farms emphasized sheep, cattle for beef, or occasionally hogs, but by the late 1860s and 1870s as cheese factories became common in many areas, dairying also became a common type of mixed farming.

Invariably there was a lag between the development of an external demand for a variety of agricultural products and the farmers' response to that demand. The change from wheat–fallow–wheat to mixed farming·depended on an adequate transportation system; on facilities for handling stock; on marketing agents in the local community; on an adequate supply of credit to permit farmers to purchase machinery; on better quality stock, improved seeds, feed, and fertilizer; and on suppliers who could provide these items. Some farmers, for example, could not respond to an American demand for beef because there were no agents in their vicinity to purchase and ship their cattle; others had stock of unacceptable quality and could not obtain credit to renew their herds. Such imbalance often continued for a decade or more. That the transition was as quick as it was reflected to some extent the presence of gentleman farmers, who had created much of the infrastructure on which a more general mixed agriculture could rest, and much more important, the proximity of the United States. American cattle buyers were common in many parts of Ontario, American farm journals circulated there, while the cheese factory, the agricultural fair, and most farm machinery had been introduced to Ontario from the United States. Moreover, the farm population in mid nineteenth-century Ontario was committed to a lively exchange economy, and as wheat–fallow–wheat became less profitable than the alternatives it was abandoned.

These farming systems were not uniformly distributed across Southern Ontario. When the market was predominantly for wheat, this crop was widely grown both on land to which it was little suited and by farmers who had had little previous experience with it. The only exceptions occurred where there were local or special markets for other agricultural produce: along parts of the north shore of the St. Lawrence River, where some farmers shipped butter to Boston and New York; in the Ottawa valley, where there was a market for oxen, pork, oats, hay, and potatoes in the timber camps; along the Lake Erie shore, where cattle were shipped across the lake to Ohio; and to a slight extent around the principal towns. These exceptions aside, early Ontario lay near the extensive margin of the agricultural hinterland of the British Isles. Virtually all of Ontario's agricultural produce other than wheat was excluded from the British market either because it was perishable or because it was not sufficiently valuable to support shipping costs. Although the cost of shipping wheat increased considerably from east to west, winter wheat, which could be grown in the milder climate of southwestern Ontario, brought a higher price that offset higher shipping costs. Hence the wide distribution of wheat in the early years.

The effect of developments such as the railways, the reciprocity treaty, and refrigeration was to reduce shipping costs and in so doing to bring the Ontario farmer closer to the market. In this situation he could market a number of different products, and with this choice could match, to some extent, his output to the particular qualities of his site. Eventually this process of regional differentiation led to the emergence of the Niagara fruit belt, to the tobacco region along the north shore of Lake Erie, and to a concentration of grain cultivation in the extreme southwest. At the same time, proximity to markets and rising population tended to increase land values and thereby to favor a more intensive utilization of land. This process was particularly marked around the towns, but throughout Ontario there was a positive correlation between land values and improvements in transportation. These two trends—an increasingly sensitive adjustment to the physical qualities of particular sites, and an equally sensitive adjustment to rising land values that in large part reflected shipping costs to market—came into play first in the belt of land near Lakes Erie and Ontario. Elsewhere the conditions that had favored wheat cultivation prevailed and—in some areas along the northern fringe of the agricultural ecumene—wheat cultivation was not displaced until the 1880s.

In 1851 wheat still occupied almost 40 per cent of the Ontario cropland and was an important crop in almost all areas (see Fig. 4-5). A

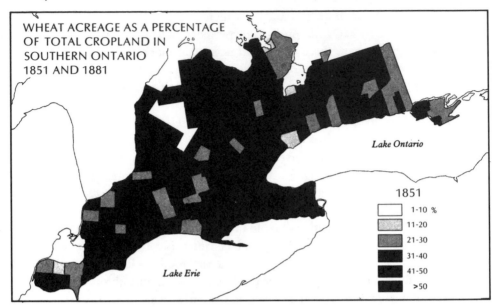

WHEAT ACREAGE AS A PERCENTAGE
OF TOTAL CROPLAND IN
SOUTHERN ONTARIO
1851 AND 1881

Lake Ontario

1851

☐	1-10 %
	11-20
	21-30
	31-40
	41-50
	>50

Lake Erie

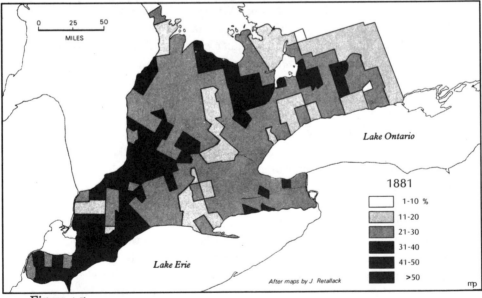

0   25   50
MILES

Lake Ontario

Lake Erie

After maps by J Retallack

1881

☐	1-10 %
	11-20
	21-30
	31-40
	41-50
	>50

Figure 4-5.

decade later the total wheat acreage had almost doubled, but as a result of rapid clearing the wheat acreage as a per cent of cropland had declined slightly. Around the lakes agriculture was clearly becoming more diversified. A broad belt of farmland north of Lake Erie made a specialty of livestock products for the American market. This long-standing market orientation had been strengthened by the reciprocity treaty and by the midge, a tiny, destructive fly that curtailed wheat yields along most of the Erie shore in the 1850s. Parts of the Niagara peninsula were already shipping fruits to Toronto, Buffalo, Montréal, and even to the British Isles. On the relatively valuable agricultural land around Toronto, truck gardening had expanded, and farther east along the Lake Ontario front, farmers were producing barley and livestock for the American market. In the next ten years the Ontario wheat acreage remained constant. Increases in the north were balanced by decreases along the lakes, but almost everywhere the wheat acreage as a percentage of total cropland declined sharply until in 1871 only 24 per cent of the Ontario cropland was in wheat. A great many farmers, responding to the diversification of the American market, to the widespread introduction of cheese factories and, in the late 1860s, to a succession of poor grain harvests, had converted to some form of mixed farming. A few years later there was a short-lived resurgence of wheat cultivation, but in total contrast to the earlier regional pattern, the crop had become most important in the extreme southwest (see Fig. 4-5), the area to which it was best suited climatically.

In conclusion it must be recognized that the drift from cereals toward mixed farming was part of a common trend in the North Atlantic world. In timing and in detail the agricultural systems varied from place to place, but the general movement was much the same. Ontarians operated within this context, depending heavily on external markets and on the general evolution of transport and agricultural technology. They were rarely innovative, borrowing from the British Isles and even more from the United States—particularly from upstate New York, the point of diffusion into Ontario of much of the agricultural technology of mixed farming. That Ontarians borrowed more than the Québec habitants is undeniable: Ontarians were rarely detached from the outside world by language or by the more intangible constraints of a protective code of civil law and a defensive nationalism. Equally clearly, Ontarians were not exemplary mixed farmers. They underemphasized root crops in favor of meadow and pasture; consequently they carried fewer stock and practised a more extensive agriculture than the better mixed farmers in Western Europe or in the eastern United States. This relatively sloppy agriculture probably reflected not only Ontario's distance from principal markets, which led to relatively lower land values and hence to more extensive agricultural practice, but also the careless approach to land that had developed in the years of wheat–fallow–wheat farming. In 1870 as in the pioneer years most Ontario farmers sought to make the most of their short-term returns, and arguments about soil exhaustion, long-term planning, or conservation fell on deaf ears.

MANUFACTURING

During the early years of settlement in Upper Canada most men farmed or worked in the timber trade. As late as 1861, 58 per cent of the total labor force was employed in the primary sector of the economy, and in some areas of recent settlement this percentage was still over 80. Simple manufacturing to supply settlers' basic needs had appeared, however, in the first pioneer years and became more important as time went on. Sales of wheat and timber attracted settlers and raised incomes which in turn encouraged manufacturing. The threshold at which a given item could be manufactured in the region more cheaply than it could be imported was more likely to be crossed as local purchasing power expanded. Most of this early manufacturing produced consumer goods—whisky, soap, shoes, brushes, and the like—for local settlers. Thresholds for the manufacture of producer goods such as agricultural implements, boilers, lathes, pumps, or even cigar boxes were crossed much later—partly because of the greater capital costs of some of these manufactures; partly because the simple technology of the wheat farm required little investment in producer goods; partly because initially, few manufacturers needed producer goods. As the production of consumer goods increased, markets emerged for more producer goods and, in the long term, their relative importance increased. In 1870, however, producer goods accounted for less than 30 per cent of the total value of manufacturing in Ontario and did not surpass the value of consumer goods until about 1910.

Manufacturing establishments in early Ontario were small, numerous, and scattered. Hardly a hamlet was without a blacksmith, and sawmills, gristmills, and distilleries were common. A dam across a stream or river,

Nappanee Village, Ontario. A gristmill, a sawmill, and an incipient village. Where waterpower was available, mills like these were often built. Later they became the nuclei of villages. Ontario Archives.

a millrace, and a stone or brick gristmill looking somewhat like a taller version of the early Ontario house became characteristic features of the landscape. Until the widespread use of steam power after mid-century, few villages or towns developed far from such a waterpower site. Tanneries, breweries, carriage works, and furniture plants were common but not ubiquitous, and many other manufacturing establishments were extremely small. The first distilleries were often adjuncts to gristmills, the first tanneries no more than sheds on a farmer's property. As late as 1871 the 105 breweries in Ontario employed just over 500 people; in the same year 38 soap- and candle-works employed some 150.

Most manufacturing establishments in early Southern Ontario produced consumer goods for a local rural or small town market which itself was scattered. Roads were poor and transfer costs high, while the value added by manufacturing to most goods was relatively low. Manufacturers attempting to sell to a large market would encounter exorbitant marketing costs. Moreover, production still depended heavily on crafts, and as long as it did there were not clear economies of scale in large, centralized operations. Many of the raw materials used in manufacturing—wheat, wood, barley, tanbark, hides, and clay, for example—

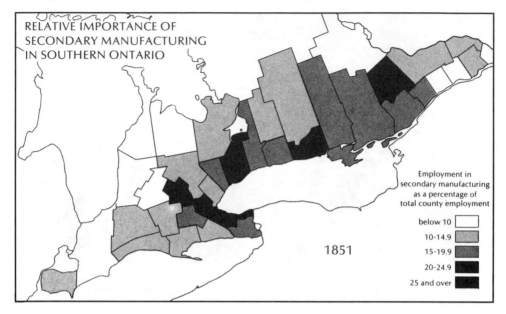

RELATIVE IMPORTANCE OF
SECONDARY MANUFACTURING
IN SOUTHERN ONTARIO

Employment in
secondary manufacturing
as a percentage of
total county employment

below 10

10-14.9

15-19.9

20-24.9

25 and over

1851

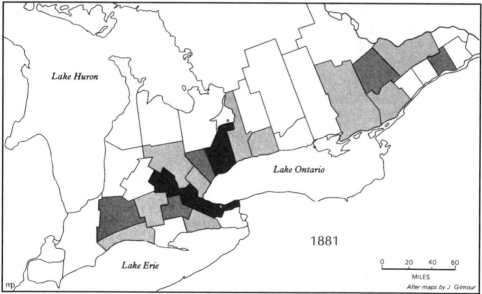

Lake Huron

Lake Ontario

1881

Lake Erie

0   20   40   60

MILES

After maps by J. Gilmour

Figure 4-6.

were widely distributed. Agglomeration of manufacturing depends on a concentrated market or on low transfer costs and on substantial economies of scale in production, none of which were conditions of manufacturing in early Ontario.

Figure 4-6 shows the relative importance of secondary manufacturing in Southern Ontario in 1851. A manufacturing belt extended along the north shore of Lake Ontario and west into the middle Grand valley, all of which was settled before 1815. Yet manufacturing was not important in all areas of early settlement, and even within the manufacturing belt its importance varied considerably. There was little manufacturing in the counties along the north shore of the St. Lawrence between Québec and Lake Ontario, although they were among the first settled in Southern Ontario. Conversely, a particular concentration of manufacturing had already emerged around the western end of Lake Ontario. In short only a fair correlation existed between length of settlement and extent of manufacturing.

Primary manufacturing did not conform to this general pattern. Sawmilling—without question the most important primary manufacture—depended on timber and could develop only where it was available. At first this led to a location in the Ottawa valley, along the lakes, or along a river in which logs could be floated to the lakes. Later, with the spread of settlement inland and the construction of railroads, it came to mean a location on the perimeter of the newest areas of settlement. In 1851 the most important concentration of sawmilling in Southern Ontario was along the northeastern shore of Lake Erie. By 1871 it had spread to a tier of counties along the fringe of the Shield.

Most consumer goods were produced within the manufacturing belt, but their importance in relation to other manufactures was greater in the newer area of settlement. Around Lake Ontario by 1851 consumer goods were relatively less important than they were toward Lake Huron and Georgian Bay and throughout the Shield fringe—all areas of more recent settlement. Again there were exceptions, such as the north shore of the St. Lawrence, an area of early settlement where because of the light development of producer-goods industries, consumer goods were relatively under-represented. Still there was a correlation between length of settlement and relative importance of consumer goods, the importance of these goods varying inversely with the length of settlement.

After mid-century this correlation virtually disappeared, that is, length of settlement ceased to be a dominant factor explaining the distribution of manufacturing activity. If the map showing the relative importance of secondary manufacturing in 1881 is compared with the map for 1851 (Fig. 4-6), the change is quite apparent. Secondary manufacturing was no longer simply spread out along the Lake Ontario shore; it was becoming concentrated in two areas: York County with Toronto its principal center, and a belt running along the southwestern shore of Lake Ontario through Hamilton to the middle Grand River valley. The tendency toward concentration was not new in Southern Ontario, but only after mid-century had the forces associated with it become the dominant influence on manufacturing location.

Concentration depended on declining shipping costs, on economies of scale in production, and on increasingly important linkages among manufacturers and between the manufacturing and service sectors. As long as transfer costs were high, the market area that could be supplied by a single manufacturer was limited; any reduction in shipping costs increased the potential market and hence the potential size of manufacturing establishments. In Southern Ontario, improvements in the network of concession-line roads as well as the planking or macadamizing of some trunk roads all tended to reduce shipping costs as, more dramatically, did the railway in the 1850s. At the same time, changes in production—the more widespread use of steam power and more expensive capital equipment, and the increasing division of labor—lowered the per-unit cost of manufacturing in larger establishments and made small operations steadily less competitive. Alone these developments explain the increasing size of manufacturing establishments but not their increasing proximity. The latter is usually explained by an initial market concentration, by the importance of linkages between the manufacturing and service sectors of the economy, and by linkages within the manufacturing sector itself. Essentially for these reasons small, widely distributed firms will tend to be replaced by large firms located in close proximity, and new firms entering the region will tend to locate within the greatest concentration of market, manufactures, and services. This snowballing process of concentration, which still dominates Ontario's spatial economy, had gained considerable momentum shortly after the middle of the nineteenth century.

The growing importance of the manufacturing belt (York County, including Toronto and the region extending along the north shore of the Niagara peninsula through Hamilton to the middle Grand River valley) is shown in Table 4-1.

Table 4-1. Percentage of provincial employment by category of manufacturing in the manufacturing belt, 1851 and 1891*

	1851	1891
Consumer goods	33.1%	42.9%
Finished producer goods	41.3	44.8
Unfinished producer goods	36.6	51.7
Producer goods	39.1	47.9
Secondary goods	34.9	44.8
Primary goods	25.5	13.4
Manufacturing	33.4	37.0

* After figures by James Gilmour, *Structural and Spatial Change in Manufacturing Industry: Southern Ontario, 1850–1880*, Ph.D. thesis, University of Toronto, 1970.

During a period of forty years when the manufacturing belt's share of the total population of Ontario remained almost constant, its share of secondary manufacturing increased from 34 to 44 per cent. Its increase in the proportion of producer goods was even greater. In 1891, before iron and steel were smelted in Hamilton, the manufacturing belt's share of unfinished producer goods amounted to more than half the provincial total. Only primary manufacturing had become more dispersed during these years—a reflection, largely, of the dispersion of sawmilling.

Considered at the level of individual industries, this process of concentration was far from uniform. In 1851 there were about 100 licensed distilleries in Upper Canada; twenty years later there were 17, the largest of them, Gooderham and Worts in Toronto, with a capacity of 7500 gallons of whisky a day. These distilleries were still widely distributed. The two located in Toronto employed 37 per cent of the provincial labor force in the industry—a slightly smaller percentage than had been employed in the city's distilleries two decades before in 1851. By 1891 Toronto accounted for more than half of the employment in the industry. In distilling, economies of scale in production were achieved first, concentration later. In 1851 there were 220 tanneries in Ontario, in 1871, 420, and the number of employees per factory had increased from about two to four. The industry remained extremely scattered, and it was not until the end of the century that there was a substantial increase in the size of tanneries, a sharp reduction in number, and a concentration in the manufacturing belt. The brewing industry showed signs of concentrating in Toronto and London by 1871, although there were still 70 brewing centers and just over 100 breweries in the province. In sum, however, the process of concentration was well under way by the 1850s, and the present manufacturing belt in Ontario could be identified before Confederation.

There is enormous inertia in urban systems. Places that are already large tend to grow larger, and small places usually remain small. Even in early nineteenth-century Southern Ontario, when an urban system was being created for the first time, initial population advantage could have a decisive bearing on the character of the developing system. A concentration of population tended to concentrate market and services and to focus transportation, developments which created the conditions for further urban growth. To be sure, the economic level as well as the number of people affect a center's capacity for growth. A rich man creates a larger market than a poor man and is likely to have more influential connections with key decision-makers. A capital city that also contains the head offices of banks, insurance firms, and shipping companies is more likely to grow than a place of similar size without these functions. A place combining a relatively large population with a central executive and administrative role is in an extremely strong competitive position.

At the same time, central places depend on their external connections. All central places in Ontario were connected to local service areas, some had larger ties across much of the province, and a few had direct international connections. Each of these connections was affected by improvements in transportation, but not necessarily by the same improvement. As a rule, canals, railways, or even the gradual improvement of the local road network had little impact on the villages and hamlets that grew up as rural service centers. Their role in rural life was not decisively altered until well into the twentieth century, when the automobile drastically changed the scale of individual mobility. Yet the automobile had little effect on the position of large cities in the urban system. In Ontario this position was more likely to have been worked out in an age of trunk roads, canals, and railways, when the changing pattern of regional and international trade associated with these transportation improvements bore heavily on the location of urban growth.

The earliest urban pattern in Southern Ontario depended directly upon John Graves Simcoe, the first lieutenant-governor. Shortly after his arrival in 1792 he laid plans to create a series of garrisons along the lakes,

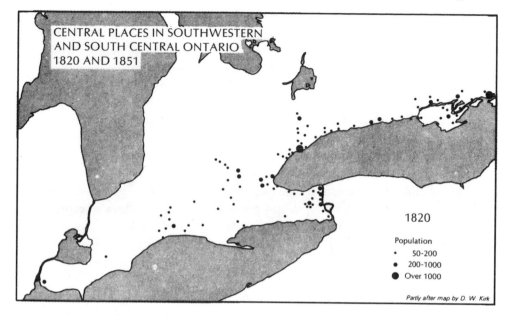

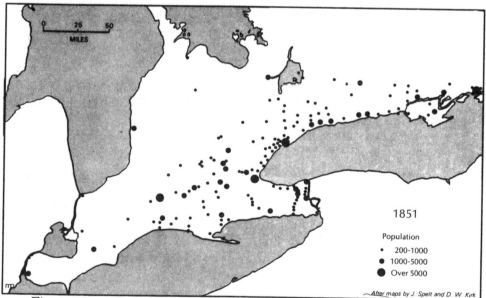

Figure 4-7.

with each garrison to be a focus of agricultural settlement. He also envisaged a string of towns in the interior. London, an interior town at the fork of the Thames River, would become the colonial capital. All settlements were to be linked by roads. Simcoe proposed two trunk roads: Yonge Street running north from Toronto (then York) to Lake Simcoe and on to Georgian Bay, and Dundas Street striking west from Toronto to the head of Lake Ontario and then westward along the route of the principal east-west Indian trail to London and Detroit. Although many of Simcoe's plans were not quickly realized, Yonge Street was cut through the woods to a point near Lake Simcoe, Dundas Street to the Grand River, and most of the proposed townsites were surveyed. At the insistence of Lord Dorchester, governor-in-chief in Canada, the capital was moved to Toronto. Dorchester judged London to be too remote, whereas Toronto had perhaps the best harbor on Lake Ontario, was some distance from the American border and located at the southern terminus of the overland route from Georgian Bay, a route whose importance in the fur trade colonial officials had much exaggerated. Still some roads had been cut, some townsites surveyed, and a few of them settled.

By 1820 the urban pattern had developed to the point shown in Figure 4-7. Many of Simcoe's townsites had become towns or villages, and new centers had emerged at other sites. Along Lake Ontario and Lake Erie there was a scattering of small ports; and west from the head of Lake Ontario a line of central places was beginning to emerge. Urban centers had not formed on a settled plain in which movement was equally possible in all directions, but along the corridors by which Southern Ontario was being penetrated and settled. The band of early settlement along the lakefronts and the importance of the lake ports as points of entry to the interior is clearly revealed in the urban map of 1820 (see Fig. 4-7). The most important route to the interior lay west of Lake Ontario along Dundas Street, where inland urban development was most marked. Villages and hamlets also appeared along Yonge Street and along several other roads extending inland from a port.

At this date Kingston, with 2300 inhabitants, was almost twice as large as Toronto. Earlier the town of Kingston had been primarily a fort and garrison, but well before 1820 it had become an important entrepôt, the point of trans-shipment between the bateaux and sailing boats of the upper St. Lawrence and the larger sailing ships of Lake Ontario. At this time the St. Lawrence entry supplied much of the American as well as the British fringe of the lakes, and Kingston's pre-eminence rested on its role in this larger trade. Toronto, on the other hand, controlled very little trade. Yet, because it was the capital, many of its citizens were prosperous and influential. They attracted a surprising number of retail and service activities, and they held political power. Although in 1817 both Kingston and Toronto petitioned for a bank of Upper Canada, the bank was established four years later in Toronto. The government appointed several of its directors and held one-quarter of the stock. A private bank of Upper Canada established in Kingston in the same year failed shortly thereafter.

Within thirty years of 1820 the population of Southern Ontario increased from perhaps 125,000 to almost a million. Settlement spread inland and new hamlets, villages, and towns emerged well north of the lakes. In these same years the orientation of Southern Ontario's external trade was changing. The Erie Canal had opened in 1825 and in 1828 a feeder canal was completed to Lake Ontario at Oswego; with these American canals Southern Ontario's dependence on Montréal and the St. Lawrence route began to decline. At the same time the American market was expanding for wheat, barley, lumber, and livestock. For several years in the 1830s Ontario merchants exported several times as much wheat across the lakes to the United States as they shipped to Montréal, and in 1845–46 the American Drawback Acts permitted Canadian goods bound for overseas markets to pass in bond duty free through New York. This challenge from the south led, belatedly, to the canalization of the rapids along the upper St. Lawrence, completed with the opening of an enlarged Lachine Canal at Montréal in 1848. By that time trade connections with the south were firmly established, the repeal of the British Corn Laws appeared to have undermined the British market, and the canalization of the St. Lawrence had little effect on the continental orientation of Southern Ontario's trade.

The declining importance of Montréal as an outlet of Ontario did much to undermine the position of Kingston at the head of the St. Lawrence, and to create a number of lake ports vying for commercial pre-eminence. Toronto, Kingston, and Hamilton were the largest ports, but there were at least six others along the northern Lake Ontario shore alone that competed vigorously in the export trade and saw themselves as potentially dominant metropolitan centers. Each controlled its own hinterland to which it was connected by a road and a string of villages and hamlets. Each published at least one newspaper. Each participated in the coastal trade, and each had direct connections with American ports across the lake.

The absence of a dominant city and the isolation of most interior centers from all but one port created strong local affiliations. Lord Durham described the situation well in 1839:

> The province has no great center with which all the separate parts are connected, and which they are accustomed to follow in sentiment and action; nor is there that habitual intercourse between the inhabitants of different parts of the country, which . . . makes a people one and united, in spite of extent of territory, and dispersion of population. Instead of this there are many petty local centers, the sentiments and interests . . . of which, are distinct, and perhaps opposed.

Because these local centers were not reinforced by distinctive national or cultural backgrounds or by fundamental value differences, regional isolation was less significant than otherwise it would have been. It did mean that most Ontarians perceived themselves within a relatively small world, one defined more by the nearest principal town than, as in this century, by the overpowering presence of Toronto. Imbued with notions of progress, most Ontarians adopted ideas far more readily than the French Canadians, but they knew a relatively small world. In this sense they too were a parochial people. At mid-century their local pride was being reflected in impressive city halls and other public buildings, and in the three-story brick façades, Italianate windows, and brick pilasters of many main streets. These were distinguished streets for distinguished places, and they reflected a localism that was already beginning to be undermined by the growing importance of Toronto.

The urban pattern in 1851 is shown in Figure 4-7. Toronto, with more than 30,000 people was now easily the largest city—more than twice as large as Hamilton and almost three times as large as Kingston. The villages in the Grand River valley had grown considerably since 1820, and what may be described loosely as an urban belt stretched west from Toronto through Hamilton to the Grand River. Farther west, London had become the largest city in southwestern Ontario. At different scales the pattern was strikingly linear. Over-all, it comprised a belt of centers along the north shore of Lake Ontario extending westward to the Grand River valley and on to London on the Thames. At a larger scale each of the towns along the north shore of Lake Ontario was connected to the interior by road, and along each of these roads were several villages or hamlets. The road between Hamilton and Niagara was also dotted with centers as was the west bank of the Niagara River, the Welland Canal, and the lower Grand River. Most of the small ports along the Lake Erie shore had at least a hamlet or two along the road behind. These, then, are the central features of the 1851 map: a concentration of urban development in a belt from Toronto to London and marked linearity everywhere.

The urban concentration by mid-century has no simple explanation. Settlement had begun relatively early in the urban belt, but not so early as along the north shore of the upper St. Lawrence, where there were few important towns; or in the Kingston area, which at mid-century was in relative decline. There were excellent waterpower sites within the urban belt along the Niagara escarpment and the middle Grand River, but other similarly endowed areas had not become urbanized. If early settlement and an abundance of waterpower sites were each necessary for the development of an urban belt, then it was true that few other parts of Upper Canada met both requirements so well. More important, probably, was the belt's central location in Upper Canada. It lay astride Dundas Street, the principal east-west road; in the heart of some of the best agricultural land in the peninsula; and, excluding the Ottawa valley, which depended on Montréal, the western corner of Lake Ontario was close to the center of gravity of Upper Canadian population. As the Erie Canal made the Hudson-Mohawk route an important commerical entry to Upper Canada, the importance of the Kingston entrepôt declined. Importers sought a central, well-connected destination for their goods; and both Toronto and Hamilton were admirably situated in this respect. Moreover, merchants in the urban belt were in a position to deal either with Montréal or New York, whereas those in Kingston were tied much more closely to the St. Lawrence.

Within the urban belt, Toronto was a special case. The city had grown more than twenty times between 1820 and 1850, the small capital of 1820 becoming a thriving commercial city. The value of Kingston's exports to the United States still slightly exceeded Toronto's, and five other ports along the north shore of Lake Ontario—Belleville, Port Hope, Whitby, Port Credit, and Oakville—each exported at least a third as much as Toronto. These ports drew on hinterlands that Toronto had yet to capture, while Kingston was still a point of trans-shipment for goods entering by the St. Lawrence and destined for the United States. On the other hand, imports from the United States were rapidly concentrating in

Toronto. Toronto imported more than twice as much as Kingston, and smaller cities with a substantial export trade to the south, such as Port Credit, had virtually no American imports. For the American exporter there was every reason to ship in quantity to one destination rather than in small lots to many, and Toronto appears to have captured this import trade for the following reasons: with the exception of Kingston, it had an early lead in population; it was centrally located in relation to the provincial population and the provincial road system; it offered a larger array of services than other centers, a reflection, initially, of its role as a capital; and it had an excellent harbor. By 1850 it was the main importing and wholesaling center of the colony.

The linear arrangement of central places in 1850 reflected, as in 1820, the principal corridors of regional penetration and trade. The towns along the north shore of Lake Ontario, along the Welland Canal, and along Dundas Street all lay along the principal corridor of east-west movement. Each port on Lake Ontario still served its own hinterland to the north, and secondary lines of central places developed at right angles to the lakefront along the roads from the ports to the interior. Settlers and supplies moved inland along these roads, grains, potash, and other pioneer products moved out, and villages and hamlets developed in response to the traffic. The largest center on these north-south roads was the port. In several cases the second center was located near the northern end of the road, with smaller villages and hamlets ranged between. In southwestern Ontario, where the principal centers lay inland along Dundas Street rather than along the Lake Erie shore, the ports were much smaller, and there was less urban development along north-south roads.

With the opening of the Northern Railway from Toronto to Bradford in 1853 and to Collingwood on Georgian Bay by 1855, the railway age came to Southern Ontario. At Confederation the lines shown on Figure 4-8 had been completed. The Grand Trunk, built from Montréal to Sarnia, was another attempt to maintain the importance of the St. Lawrence entry. The other lines, although often built by Canadian or British capital, were really northern or western extensions of American railways. Together with the Reciprocity Treaty of 1855, which permitted the free movement between Canada and the United States of agricultural and forest products, minerals, and fish, they enormously heightened the American orientation of Southern Ontario's trade. In 1856 exports to the United States were ten times the shipments along the St. Lawrence; in 1859 only 2 per cent of the large tonnage of wheat and flour shipped

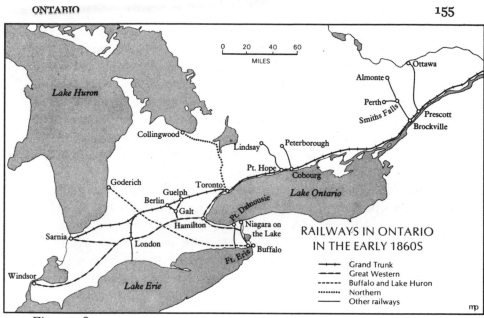

RAILWAYS IN ONTARIO
IN THE EARLY 1860S

- ―+― Grand Trunk
- ――― Great Western
- ------ Buffalo and Lake Huron
- .... Northern
- ――― Other railways

Figure 4-8.

from Toronto went to Montréal. Toronto and most of Southern Ontario moved more firmly than ever within the hinterland of New York.

The railways shifted lumbering abruptly northward, and centers such as Collingwood and Midland on Georgian Bay and others farther east near the fringe of the Canadian Shield expanded rapidly as a result. Their over-all effect, however, was to increase the concentration of urban development. Toronto was the first port to build a railway to the north, and by 1857 when a regular steamer service began operation out of Collingwood, timber and grain from Michigan began to move through Toronto. Moreover, the Northern Railway had opened up the timber stands around Georgian Bay, and the cut there soon became the largest in Ontario. Until a line from Hamilton reached Georgian Bay in 1878, almost all of it was tributary to Toronto. By 1856 Toronto had become the focus of a considerable railway system. The Grand Trunk connected it with Montréal, the Great Western with New York through Hamilton and Buffalo, and the Northern with the trade of the upper lakes. Ports close to Toronto such as Oakville, Port Credit, Whitby, and Oshawa which could not finance railways built at right angles to the lake lost almost all their export trade. Farther away from Toronto, both Port Hope and Cobourg had built railways to the north, although Cobourg eventually lost most of its hinterland to Port Hope when the causeway taking the tracks north from Cobourg across Rice Lake was irreparably damaged by ice. But even Port Hope was now far more accessible to Toronto, and goods that had passed directly through Port Hope before the railways were now being handled by Toronto middlemen. With the establishment in 1855 of the Toronto grain exchange, the forerunner of the Toronto stock exchange, Toronto's financial range was widening. Although still much smaller than Montréal, Toronto, with 45,000 people in 1861, was easily the metropolitan center of Ontario.

Well before this date—perhaps even as early as 1840—the contemporary urban pattern in Southern Ontario had been firmly set. Subsequently the relative importance of Toronto and of the entire urban belt has increased enormously, but there has been no striking change in the location of urban growth. In this respect the urban distribution led the distribution of manufacturing by perhaps two or three decades.

THE URBAN LANDSCAPE

Figure 4-9 shows the village of Waterdown, a bustling commercial center situated on the Niagara escarpment not far from Hamilton, as it was about 1845. Waterdown combined the advantages of excellent water-power sites along a stream that spilled over the Niagara escarpment with a location along Dundas Street, but it was not unlike many other small centers scattered across Southern Ontario. Over the years Waterdown had grown haphazardly as tradesmen saw commercial opportunity there, acquired lots from the local farmer, and set up their businesses. In 1845 there were five mills in the village and a number of shops and hostelries along Dundas Street; all the land not marked in village lots on Figure 4-9 still belonged to farmers. No one had ever considered an over-all plan for Waterdown, almost all its inhabitants lived there for commercial reasons, and its structure reflected an entirely individual response to commercial opportunity.

Waterdown was a small place, and most enterprise within it functioned at the scale of individual families, just as it did on the surrounding farms. The largest mill employed only two or three hands. One miller might keep the books, buy grain from farmers, and sell flour to farmers and merchants as well as actually mill the grain; and the blacksmith practised a variety of skills. In this intimacy and variety of individual enterprise, the many Waterdowns in Southern Ontario were brief and

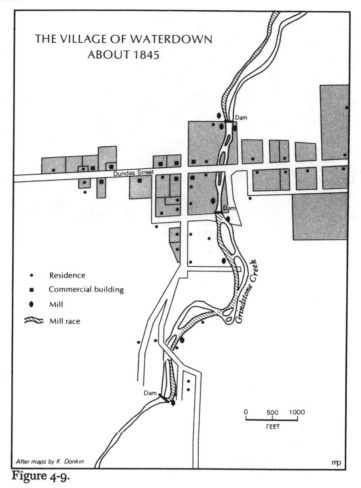

THE VILLAGE OF WATERDOWN
ABOUT 1845

Dam

Dundas Street

Dam

Grindstone Creek

• Residence
■ Commercial building
● Mill
〰 Mill race

Dam

0   500   1000
FEET

After maps by K. Donkin   mp

Figure 4-9.

extremely simple replications of an age-old craft and commercial tradition. To be sure, the rigidities of class, guild, and apprentice system had been largely undermined in the newness and smallness of Waterdown, but its scale of enterprise and the range of skills expected of many of its inhabitants had long been characteristics of the villages and small towns of Western Europe. Later in the century, indeed here and there as early as the 1840s, the scale of enterprise in Southern Ontario began to change as work became more specialized within larger units, and this change transformed the geography of urban life. The individualism that had shaped the early Waterdowns remained the ideology of the elite, who

Toronto in 1803. Royal Ontario Museum, Toronto.

depended on an enlarging scale of activity in which individuality counted for less and less.

A few places, admittedly, had their beginnings less in small-scale commercial individualism than in government planning. Land in such places was set aside for parks, schools, churches, and estates; and the provision of market squares implied at least some check on the freedom of commercial enterprise. Of these places, early Toronto was undoubtedly the most important. Its first plan, drawn up in 1788, described a town one mile square made up of 121 lots. Six lots—one in the center, four near each of the corners, and one in the middle of the lakefront side—were set aside for squares or public buildings; a strip of land about a quarter of a mile wide was held as reserve between the townsite and the lakeshore; and there was to be common land on the three remaining sides. Although this tidy geometry was not entirely adopted, the Toronto that developed before 1820 was strongly influenced by government planning. The land along the lakefront was reserved for a public park, the townsite was divided into a grid with land set aside for public buildings and a market. Northeast of the city a large tract was set aside as government reserve, or common, and west of this reserve thirty-two park lots of one hundred acres each intended for farms, summer houses, or country estates for the elite were also set aside. Such a layout reflected some concern for the public weal, a clear concept of class and social hierarchy, and a sense of the need for long-term planning.

But even in Toronto this conception of urban life quickly gave way to

Toronto in 1850, just before the coming of the railway. The change from the
village of 1803 could easily have been experienced in one lifetime. Note the
city's essentially Georgian architecture and the exaggerated activity in the
harbor, intended to suggest economic vitality. Lithograph by Edwin White-
field. Royal Ontario Museum, Toronto.

a more individual outlook that emphasized individual achievement in
the market place. One by one in the 1830s and 1840s the city's park lots,
created to be the landed estates of the privileged, were subdivided by
the original owners or their children. Planning had been replaced by
piecemeal development with the result that the streets laid out on one
park lot were often ill-fitted to those on the next, that little land was set
aside for public use, and that only a few far-seeing families—the Bald-
wins, who laid out the exceptionally wide Spadina Avenue, or the Robin-
sons, who created much of University Avenue and sold land to the Law
Society of Upper Canada for the building of Osgoode Hall—considered
the future of the city. Fortunes made from subdividing land consolidated
the position of the elite. In 1852 the Toronto businessman John G. Bowes
was elected mayor on the platform that railways and prosperity were
synonymous. His frame of mind was a far cry from the tory paternalism
of the earlier city, and he and many like him had made Toronto a larger
version of Waterdown.

    Out of the individualism, the small scale of enterprise, and the diffi-
culty of urban transportation emerged cities of relatively undifferen-
tiated structure. There were wharf and warehouse areas in the ports,
central business districts, and fashionable residential streets, but none of

these areas was as large, as homogeneous, or as sharply defined as they became later in the century. The mansions of the rich in one block might give way to the housing of the lower middle-class in the next; factory owners tended to live next to their factories, and their workers a little farther away; and many factories were scattered through the central business district. In general, the rich remained near the center of the city, there to manage its life and enjoy its benefits, while the poor tended to collect at the peripheries, where the inconvenience of transportation eliminated competition for land. Between these extremes of class and location, most of the city lived amid the confusion of shop and residence, occupation and class.

Yet it would be quite wrong to conclude from this that Torontonians or Hamiltonians at mid-century did not perceive clear differences in income and status. Quite clearly they did, but in the relative intimacy of the walking city these differences were expressed in a keen appreciation of fine locational variations. A location on one street might be associated with high status whereas another just around the corner was clearly lower class. The city was segregated socially and territorially, but not in the coarse grid that emerged later in the century. Probably segregation had gone as far as economic efficiency allowed. When foot, cart, or buggy were the principal means of travel, urban mobility was not great, and the workers, managers, services, and goods relevant to a single enterprise needed to be located in close proximity. Men of different ways of life came together but not as equals.

In Ontario during the last decades of the nineteenth century the widespread introduction of the factory system, the increasing size and specialization of commerce, and the advent of street railways transformed the earlier, finely grained city. Sizable urban areas emerged that were devoted almost entirely to manufacturing or to commerce, the rich moved to new residential suburbs well away from the noise and soot of the factories and the congestion of the central business district, and the poor took over deteriorating houses close to warehouses or factories. What had happened, of course, was that the increasing size and specialization of commerce and industry had led to an increasing specialization of human interaction. Whereas the owner of a small mill or shop had worked with his employees, such intimacy was lost in a large factory or warehouse. The gradual unionization of labor in the late nineteenth century and the increasing spatial differentiation of the city at the same time were parts of this same pervasive process of specialization. For the

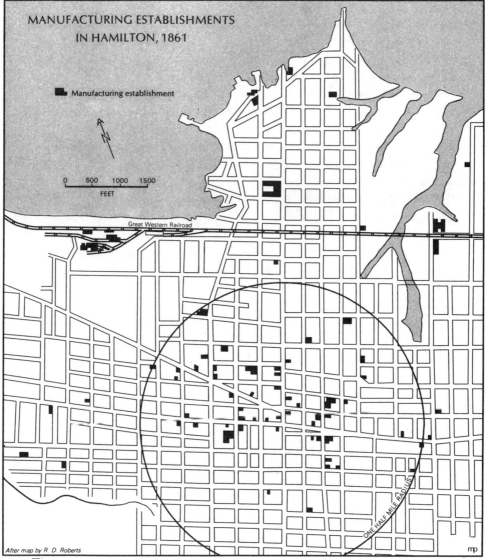

Figure 4-10.

most part its impact on Ontarians was felt after 1870, but in the larger cities—particularly in Toronto and Hamilton—it began a good deal earlier.

Take the distribution of manufacturing in Hamilton in the early 1860s (see Fig. 4-10). Most of the early manufacturing establishments had been located in the central business district, and even in 1861 some three-quarters of them were still within a half-mile of the busiest downtown intersection. But by this date a few larger plants—a felt-hat factory employing 150 men, an agricultural implements factory, a steam engine and boiler works, a locomotive construction and repair shop, and several others—had moved out of the inner city to a location on the railway. These plants, all built since 1850, accounted for only 10 per cent of Hamilton's manufacturing establishments, but for 21 per cent of its manufacturing employment. They depended on steam power; some of them required a sizable ground for the assembly of bulky raw materials or for the storage of finished products and direct rail connections with the railway; and most were too large, too noisy, or too dirty for a location in the central business district. A separate manufacturing area, well removed from the central business district, was beginning to emerge.

The commercial activities of the larger cities were also separating into clearer districts. Ranged along the Toronto waterfront in 1850 was a considerable mixture of trans-shipment, storage, wholesale, retail, and residential functions, and also some manufacturing in the east around the mouth of the Don River. Although wholesalers tended to concentrate near the wharves, there was not a recognizable district of large, uniform warehouses, but rather a hodgepodge of commercial activities in premises ranging from wooden sheds to substantial brick offices. A given commission merchant was likely to deal in many of the goods that passed through the port; a given wharf might contain a customs shed, an express office, a coal and wood merchant, a ship's outfitter, and several commission merchants. With the coming of the railway in the 1850s the volume of trade increased and was spread more evenly through the year. Merchants were able to become more specialized by drawing larger numbers of customers to their premises, and by employing traveling salesmen who took their wares to every railway stop. Warehouses tended to become larger, and the largest firms separated storage and showrooms in different buildings. At Confederation a warehouse district comprising three- to five-story brick and stone buildings had emerged, and even within it different types of wholesaling were becoming sharply segregated. Along the breadth of the Toronto waterfront, commercial land uses had totally taken over.

The case of the Toronto waterfront is particularly interesting because, from the earliest days of the city, much of it had been set aside as public land. Even at mid-century there was still a good swimming beach at the foot of Front Street lined by low, wave-cut cliffs and the residences of some of Toronto's wealthy citizens. At issue, then, was not only the most efficient economic use of this space, but also the more fundamental question of the priority of economic and non-economic objectives. At the beginning of the railway era early in the 1850s, there was no doubt in Torontonians' minds that the city should have its railways. It was clear too that the tracks should be connected to the lake, and that the city faced the problem of running tracks along the lakefront without entirely destroying its beauty and attractions. To this end a plan was presented for an esplanade on filled land south of Front Street, with access over the tracks to the waterfront and a walkway along the top of the bank and parallel to the tracks below. The *Globe* noted that this "Public Walk and Drive" would be "unparalleled . . . in America for extent and beauty of position," but also noted that the plan was expensive.

Businessmen on the city council argued that it was in the public interest to give the railways a free hand, to reduce the city debt, and to provide for maximum commercial growth. The few who were wont to argue for parks and other civic improvements—often men who were not in business and who came from the older, tory elite of the city—comprised a small minority. Moreover, the railway, with its simple, clearly defined goals and political power at the highest levels, was a formidable antagonist. When the city did take a stand against the total alienation of the waterfront to the railway, its position was over-ruled by the colonial government. The president of the Grand Trunk, the Honourable John Ross, was speaker of the legislative assembly of Canada, and several of the railway's important financial backers were members of parliament. Against this power and the euphoria of the early railway years, the older waterfront was doomed. In the end, under the threat that the Grand Trunk Railway would bypass the city to the north, the city adopted the Grand Trunk's own plan for the waterfront. The width of the esplanade was reduced and warehouses were built to the north of it; in effect, the waterfront was given over to the railway. By Confederation, tracks had replaced trees, warehouses and engine shops stood where beaches were before, and grain elevators competed with ships' masts and smokestacks along the whole length of the harbor.

Such changes were to be expected when the individualism that had underlain Waterdown and most of urban Ontario in the early nineteenth century was combined with the enlarged scale of enterprise of the later years of the century. The impact of the change in scale was felt first in the largest places, transforming them by the end of the century. Smaller places grew much more slowly, stagnated, or declined. Many of them survive today as incongruous relics in an age of massive technology and, perhaps, as reminders of a day recently past when the scale of human interaction was quite different.

In only three generations the whole peninsula of Southern Ontario was occupied by people of European descent. During this time the forest was cut; the geometry of roads, fence lines and fields was stamped across the land; and the prosperity achieved by many was reflected in ample brick farmhouses and in bustling towns. Everywhere the human landscape was new. In the most recent frontier regions settlers still lived in tiny log cabins on patches of cleared land; in the older areas there were still some stumpy fields and many people alive who had known the first pioneers. Whereas the human landscape of Western Europe often reflected centuries of human toil, this landscape reflected the recent arrival, the energy, and the apparent wastefulness of its creators. That Europeans had created the landscape there could be no doubt—the architectural forms, for example, were entirely of European origin. But although components of it existed in the British Isles, the human landscape of Southern Ontario could not be found anywhere in Europe. Nor did it resemble the settled land of the lower St. Lawrence. Not only the French but also the medieval heritage of habitant Québec set the two regions apart, for Ontario at Confederation was overwhelmingly a product of the nineteenth century. The area that did resemble Ontario lay just across the lake in western New York and Ohio. Although Ontario's vernacular architecture was often slightly different from that to the south, its institutional buildings usually derived from British neoclassical models, and less corn grew in its fields, still it looked to be what in so many ways it was—a part of the cultural region of the North American Middle West.

This interior heartland of North America had borne the full impact of the technical, social, and ideological upheaval of the nineteenth century. It had been settled by people dislocated by nineteenth-century change and was not affected by the inertia of an older, established society. Its settlers, coming as individuals out of different backgrounds, juxtaposed religious affiliations, customs, and social values that in Europe usually had been widely separated. The immigrants, with an increasingly powerful technology at their disposal, had transformed the land so rapidly that the very words "settler" and "settlement," with their connotations of fixity and permanence, are misleading. And unlike earlier immigration to colonial America or to Québec, this migration took place when the principles of laissez faire economics and of liberal democracy were becoming orthodox. For all these reasons the landscape of the Middle West reflected a weak sense of time and of community and an emphasis on individual achievement and material progress.

It was not, therefore, a landscape in which the distinctive material cultures of different immigrants, particularly those aspects that affected the pursuit of wealth, were likely to be preserved. The Mennonite settlements along the Grand River and the French-Canadian enclave in the extreme southwest stood somewhat apart because both groups had retained a relatively strong sense of community. But these were rare exceptions. A casual observer traveling through Peter Robinson's Irish settlement in the 1860s would most easily have identified its Irish antecedents by the gravestone inscriptions in the churchyard. And so it was with most immigrant traditions, except those that carried no economic impediments and could survive in ritualistic or ceremonial form. There were many clear regional differences visible in the landscape of Southern Ontario at Confederation—well-established farmland to the south, a pioneer fringe to the north, areas of mixed farming and others of wheat–fallow–wheat; pockets of orchard or market-gardening specialization; an urban and a manufacturing belt—but these regional differences can be explained in economic terms. Whether they lived on a pioneer farm on the Shield fringe or in a mansion on Jarvis Street in Toronto, the values of most Ontarians were essentially the same. Pioneer farmer and timber baron worked hard to achieve material success, were sensitive to economic pressures, and rarely considered the longer future.

What had been achieved was prosperity for many, more social mobility than in older societies, and the release of a great deal of human energy and practical ingenuity. The price of these achievements, partly paid before many of the immigrants had set foot in the Middle West, was a weakened regard for community matters or for the preservation of land. Yet such shifts in attitude are more relative than absolute; there were voices vigorously raised against the destruction of the forest or the presumed long-term effect on the soil of wheat–fallow–wheat farming. Although their hold on the individual had weakened, communities in town and countryside still existed. And there was the not-inconsiderable influence of the Christian church and sects. For all the dourness of much of the Protestant tradition, for all its accommodation to liberal values, it still spoke of brotherhood, and of the triviality of material belongings before the judgment of God. The Ontario novelist Charles Gordon thought that religion was "the biggest thing" in the lives of Scots of Glengarry County, and so it probably was with most Ontarians.

Nor, however much it resembled the Middle West in the United States, was Ontario exactly like that area. North of the border were more Presbyterians and far more Scots and Scotch-Irish; as a result life was probably a little more constrained. The strong conservative tradition of the early years—the conviction that people had fixed places in society, that government should be paternalistic, that land could be managed for long-term benefits—had had some moderating influence on more individualistic values as did the real attachment of almost all Ontarians to the British crown and empire. Well before the end of the century, southern American planters were building summer mansions in the smaller towns along the north shore of Lake Ontario, not only because they may have felt that summer breezes were a little cooler in Canada, but also because they found a society more congenial than that of the northern states. It may also be important that there was not nearly as much land as in the United States, that there was a close limit to settlement set by the lakes and the Shield. Southern Ontario had been settled by Confederation, the migration of young Ontarians to the Canadian prairie was still two decades away, and the attempts to settle the Canadian Shield had absorbed relatively few. The mineral deposits of the Shield had not been discovered and, unlike the image created by later rhetoric, the north was rarely viewed as a vast reservoir of untold wealth. In 1867 most Ontarians had an ignorant but inherently more realistic view. Many left for the south. Those who stayed coped with a more limited environment without an expanding western frontier, and this may have created a little more stability of land and life in early Ontario than in the rest of the Middle West.

Bibliography

There is now a considerable literature relevant to this chapter, but as much of it is in the form of unpublished M.A. or Ph.D. theses rather than books or journal articles, it is diffuse and often inaccessible.

Of general interest are articles by John Warkentin, "Southern Ontario; a view from the west," *Canadian Geographer* 10 (Fall 1966), 157–71;

and Jacob Spelt, "Southern Ontario," in John Warkentin, (ed.) *Canada: a Geographical Interpretation* (Agincourt, Ont.: Methuen Publications, 1968), pp. 334–95. A sound history of early Ontario, although weak in its treatment of social and economic issues, is G. M. Craig, *Upper Canada; the formative years, 1784–1841* (Toronto: McClelland and Stewart, 1963). The chapter on early Ontario in S. D. Clark, *The Social Development of Canada* (Toronto: University of Toronto Press, 1942), remains a provocative interpretation, if perhaps too strongly influenced by staple theory. The published documents and editorial comments by Michael Cross in *The Frontier Thesis and the Canadas: the debate on the impact of the Canadian environment* (Toronto: Copp Clark, 1970) comprise an excellent introduction to issues relating to the Ontario frontier.

Immigration to Ontario is treated in M. L. Hansen, *The Mingling of the Canadian and American Peoples* (New Haven: Yale University Press, 1940); while Fred Landon's study of *Western Ontario and the American Frontier* (first published in 1941 and republished in 1967 by McClelland and Stewart in the Carleton Library, no. 34) is a valuable introductory discussion of some of the implications for Ontario's development of the heavily American character of its earliest immigrants. The actual spread of settlement in much of southern Ontario is described in Jacob Spelt, *The Urban Development in South-Central Ontario* (Assen, 1955). The closely related matter of the emerging road network is treated in A. F. Burghardt, "The Origin and Development of the Road Network of the Niagara Peninsula, Ontario, 1770–1851," *Annals, Association of American Geographers* 59 (Sept. 1969), 417–40; and in more detail in Thomas F. McIlwraith, "The Adequacy of Rural Roads in the Era before Railways: An Illustration from Upper Canada," *Canadian Geographer* 14 (Winter 1970), 334–60. Articles by R. L. Gentilcore, "The Beginnings of Settlement in the Niagara Peninsula, 1782–1792," *Canadian Geographer* 7 (Summer 1963), 72–82; and "Lines on the Land," *Ontario History* 61 (June 1969), 57–73, discuss aspects of the early settlement of Ontario. For those who read German, this subject is treated more fully in Carl Schott, *Landnahme und Kolonisation in Kanada am Beispiel Sudontarios* (Kiel, 1936). An M.A. thesis by Colin Wood "Human Settlement of the Long Point Region, 1790–1825" (McMaster, 1966) includes an interesting discussion of settlers' perception of different environments. One of the few examinations of immigration in relation to social structure in nineteenth-century Ontario is K. Duncan, "Irish Famine Immigration and the Social Structure of Canada West," *The Canadian Review of Sociology and Anthropology* 2 (Feb. 1965), 19–41.

Vernacular architecture in Ontario is perhaps best treated in Alan Gowans, *Building Canada; an architectural history of Canadian life* (Toronto: Oxford University Press, 1966). *The Ancestral Roof; Domestic architecture in Upper Canada*, by Anthony Adamson and Marion MacRae (Toronto: Clark, Irwin & Co. 1963), although annoyingly precious, is also useful. V. B. Blake and Ralph Greenhill, *Rural Ontario* (Toronto: University of Toronto Press, 1969) contains an excellent set of photographs of the Ontario countryside and its buildings, and a helpful text. An M.A. thesis by Peter Ennals, "The Development of Farm Barn Types in Southern Ontario during the Nineteenth Century" (University of Toronto, 1968) is the only good treatment of its topic.

Robert L. Jones, *History of Agriculture in Ontario, 1613–1880* contains much important information that is not readily available elsewhere, but a more interpretive approach to the understanding of agriculture in early Ontario emerges in Kenneth Kelly, "Wheat Farming in Simcoe County in the Mid-Nineteenth Century," *Canadian Geographer* 15 (Summer 1971), 95–112; in his Ph.D. thesis, "The Agricultural Geography of Simcoe County, Ontario, 1820–1880," (University of Toronto, 1968); and in an M.A. thesis by Joan Retallack, "The Changing Distribution of Wheat in Southern Ontario, 1850–1890" (University of Toronto, 1966). The only worthwhile general discussion of the distribution of manufacturing in nineteenth-century Ontario is by James D. Gilmour, "Structural and Spatial Change in Manufacturing Industry: South Ontario, 1850–1880," (Ph.D. thesis, University of Toronto, 1970).

The emerging urban system in Ontario is discussed in Jacob Spelt, *The Urban Development in South Central Ontario* (Assen, 1955), and somewhat more theoretically in C. F. J. Whebell, "Corridors: A Theory of Urban Systems," *Annals, Association of American Geographers* 59 (March 1969), 1–26. Early Toronto is treated at some length in Donald Kerr and Jacob Spelt, *The Changing Face of Toronto*, (Ottawa: Queen's Printer, 1965). The changing residential pattern of the city in the late nineteenth century is analysed statistically and the results integrated with the more general urban literature by Peter Goheen in *Victorian Toronto* (Chicago: University of Chicago Publications in Geography, No. 171, 1971). Manufacturing in Hamilton is examined in R. D. Roberts, "The Changing Patterns in Distribution and Composition of Manufacturing Activity in Hamilton between 1861 and 1921," (M.A. thesis, McMaster University, 1964).

5 THE ATLANTIC REGION

The Atlantic region, comprising Newfoundland and the three traditional Maritime provinces of Prince Edward Island, Nova Scotia, and New Brunswick, has been variously regarded as the northeastern extension of the Appalachians, as an outpost of other regions in North America, and as a permeable curtain of islands and peninsulas lightly screening the eastern entrance to the population and economic heart of Canada. All of these views are quite appropriate, for the Atlantic region cannot be understood outside the context of its location between the north Atlantic Ocean and the immense continental territories to the west. One result of such sweeping continental and oceanic views is that all too often the internal qualities of the areas have been forgotten. Thomas Haliburton's complaint in the 1850s that Nova Scotia was little known in Britain is just one indication of the obscurity of the region within the perspective of the growth of North America in the nineteenth century. Yet the relatively long period of settlement and the great variety in people and in modes of resource development make the changing geography of the Atlantic region of compelling interest in its own right.

This is a very complex region. It has no unifying configuration of physical features, and even the surrounding sea provides a matrix rather than a focus. There is no centralization of economic activity or function, no rich heartland. If there is any unity, it is a unity of mutual problems arising from the attempt to wrest from modest resources a standard of living roughly equivalent to that of the rest of Canada and the United States.

The region has never controlled its own economic destiny, and since the mid-nineteenth century it has been affected ever more strongly by its hapless relationship with other parts of North America. In the eighteenth century it was a precarious border territory in the struggles between the French and the English in North America; in the early nineteenth century it achieved a strong trading role in the Atlantic based on its regional resources and strategic location. Yet as the century advanced the region was affected ever more strongly by the continent, even though it was outside the main thrust of North American industrial development. The discussion that follows attempts to bring out these changing relationships by concentrating on administrative decisions affecting geographical development, peopling, resource development, circulation, and urban growth.

The administrative framework within which an area develops has frequently been taken for granted in geographical studies. Yet in the Atlantic region, government decisions on the disposal of crown lands, immigration, and resource development were of crucial importance in establishing the outline of geographical growth. The population of the region does not form Canada's best-known ethnic mosaic, yet the mix is as complex as anywhere in the country. Many long-established cultural enclaves maintain their vitality to this day, holding their own in a society that has remained primarily resource-based and mercantile. As elsewhere in the New World, the economic development of the region took place in a mercantilist frame in which natural resources were exploited for overseas markets. No leading staple forced development in any one direction, and the dispersal of effort was considerable. Each staple industry was constrained by a limited resource base and chronically poor markets. Poverty was widespread. But it was not an entirely constricted society; an element of opportunity remained because of easy access to both the sea and the continent to the west.

More than anywhere else in British North America, towns with overseas connections had a vital role in opening avenues of economic opportunity, especially to the West Indies and the United States. Yet this sense of access also encouraged a colonial attachment to Britain. Towns and cities were actively fostering the development of their own hinterlands, but no one city was ever able to coordinate the life of the whole area. As a result the Atlantic region has an elusive duality composed of persistent sub-regional parochialism and simultaneous easy connections with the outside world. This chapter will encompass the geography of these colonies from 1749, when effective British settlement of the region began with the founding of Halifax, to 1871, the census date closest to Confederation and a time which marks a fundamental reorientation of interests in the Maritimes portion of the Atlantic region.

Establishing the basis for geographical development
CONFLICTS OF ADMINISTRATION

Administering the territories of the Atlantic region was complicated at first by the rivalry between the French and English. By the Peace of Utrecht in 1713, the French held Ile St-Jean (Prince Edward Island) and other islands of the Gulf of St. Lawrence, and Cape Breton Island. They also had retained the right to dry fish on the northwestern coast of Newfoundland. Nova Scotia and Newfoundland were British, and the former included present-day New Brunswick. After the Treaty of Paris in 1763, Nova Scotia was enlarged to include Cape Breton Island and the Island of St. John (Ile St-Jean); the French retained only the islands of St-Pierre and Miquelon and fishing rights on the coast of Newfoundland. In the American Revolution Nova Scotia and Newfoundland remained loyal to Britain—probably because it was in their economic interests to do so, but also because they would have been exposed to the formidable threat of British sea power had they become restive. By the Treaty of Versailles in 1783 the fish-processing rights of the French were extended along the west coast of Newfoundland (which came to be called the "French shore"); the Americans were granted similar landing privileges in 1818.

The British valued Newfoundland almost solely for its fisheries and its strategic location; when prodded by West Country merchants wishing to retain their monopoly over the cod fisheries, the government forbade Newfoundlanders to own property for any purpose other than the fishery. The same policy had been extended to Cape Breton, and in 1784 the island was separated from Nova Scotia to make it easier to impose special regulations, to encourage the fishery, and to prepare for the settlement of Loyalists. Gradually, grants of lands were made on Cape Breton, and in 1820 it was re-annexed to Nova Scotia to be administered from the capital, Halifax. In 1769 the Island of St. John (renamed Prince Edward Island in 1799) was separated from Nova Scotia for administrative convenience and made a separate colony. New Brunswick was chopped off from Nova Scotia in 1784 for similar reasons, mainly at the insistence of the Loyalists who had settled there.

For more than a century—from 1763 through the 1860s—economic relationships between the Atlantic colonies and the United States were
close, despite the American Revolution, the War of 1812 and various
trade and boundary disagreements. In 1854 a particularly beneficial trading association developed with the United States under the terms of the
Reciprocity Treaty. But after the treaty was abrogated in 1866, the mainland colonies of Nova Scotia and New Brunswick were ready to consider
seriously a union with Canada East and Canada West (after Confederation the provinces of Québec and Ontario), partly to counter possible
United States territorial expansion, partly because it appeared that the
Atlantic economy would benefit from the closer continental connection
that a railway to the St. Lawrence—one of the terms of union—would
bring. In 1867 Nova Scotia and New Brunswick joined the Canadian
Confederation, and Prince Edward Island followed in 1873. Newfoundland, which was least affected by continental ties, did not do so until
1949.

SETTLEMENT POLICY

The settlement of the Atlantic region in the later eighteenth and most of
the nineteenth century was part of an evolving British mercantile system, and policies concerning settlement, granting of land, and exploitation of resources were all worked out by the British government. Before
1749 only two significant groups of Europeans lived in the region. About
6000 people of British origin, largely from England's West Country and

Newfoundland. "The appearance of land off Great St. Lawrence Harbour, 1786." A. Ferryland Head; B. Cape Chapeau Rouge. From the logbook of H.M.S. *Pegasus*, 1786. The Public Archives of Canada.

Ireland, lived on the coast of Newfoundland and in Nova Scotia on the islands off Cape Canso, dependent upon the fisheries. Around the Bay of Fundy and in adjacent districts more than 10,000 Acadians lived on their farms, trading with the French garrison at Louisbourg and with coasting New Englanders. Most of the land was wilderness thinly occupied by Indians—meager development for an area known by Europeans for two and a half centuries and so conveniently located to Europe.

The main reason for the lag in development was that the Atlantic region had been prized more for its strategic value and its fisheries than for its potential for settlement. Colonization efforts were concentrated elsewhere while this area stood by. The French encouraged development of their lands on the St. Lawrence River and expended much energy on attempting to control the interior of the continent, and British migrants generally found the colonies south of present-day Maine much more attractive than the Atlantic colonies. Further, Britain's restrictive settlement policy, although generally ineffective, had had some impact in preventing settlement.

In mid-eighteenth century, British policy changed. Nova Scotia was not to remain an empty preserve, protected by naval forces operating from outside the region. In reply to the French fortress of Louisbourg a garrison would be established at Halifax, and an effort would be made to

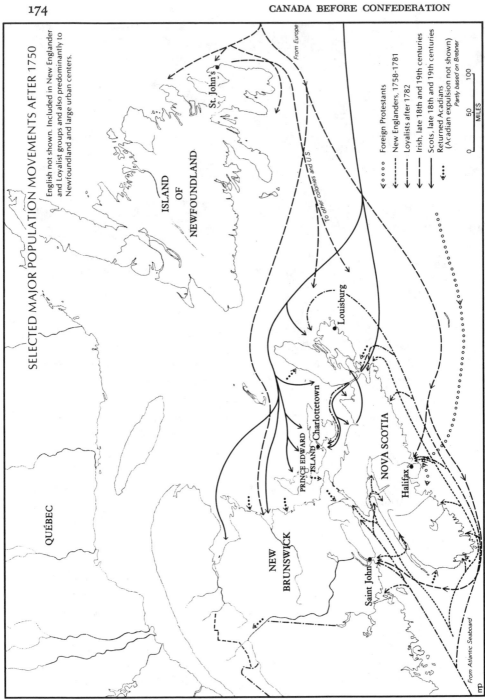

SELECTED MAJOR POPULATION MOVEMENTS AFTER 1750

English not shown. Included in New Englander and Loyalist groups and also predominantly to Newfoundland and large urban centers.

∘∘∘∘∘ Foreign Protestants
‑ ‑ ‑ ‑ New Englanders, 1758-1781
‑·‑·‑ Loyalists after 1782
—————— Irish, late 18th and 19th centuries
—————— Scots, late 18th and 19th centuries
•••• Returned Acadians
(Acadian expulsion not shown)
Partly based on Brebner

0   50   100
MILES

ISLAND
OF
NEWFOUNDLAND

St. John's

From Europe

To other colonies and US

Louisburg

Charlottetown

PRINCE EDWARD
ISLAND

QUÉBEC

NOVA SCOTIA

Halifax

NEW
BRUNSWICK

Saint John

From Atlantic Seaboard

Figure 5-1.

colonize the region and to develop its potential resources. The strategy was to recruit settlers from Europe and New England, subsidizing their transportation and allowing them government assistance while they established themselves. Even as these migrations were being planned, the Acadians were uprooted and many were expelled from Nova Scotia—accused of sympathizing with and assisting the French in Canada and Cape Breton Island. Following the American Revolution—less than a generation after the deportation of the Acadians—the Anglo-American Loyalists in their turn became refugees, and the British sent many of them to Nova Scotia. This was a continuation of migration into Nova Scotia already begun by New Englanders. Some of these diverse movements are shown in Figure 5-1. Thus out of the long-range strategy and short-range tactics of power politics and war there came a significant shifting of peoples in and out of the Atlantic region in the eighteenth century, much of it involuntary and under agonizing circumstances.

In the late eighteenth century the pattern of trans-Atlantic migration changed drastically. Thousands of persons crossed the ocean—usually as unsponsored individual migrants, and this remained the basis on which most people came until 1871. Figure 5-1 shows where some of these people went. In the Atlantic colonies official attitudes on migration were confused, and for many decades no comprehensive policies encouraging immigration existed. Land resources were scanty (except for the New Brunswick pineries) and there was no readily apparent need to bring in immigrants to develop the region. Many residents preferred to advance themselves by developing overseas trading rather than agriculture; indeed, the exploitation of regional resources was so poorly integrated that adding people might conceivably have led to local reductions in income per capita. Nevertheless immigrants did come, urged on by British policies designed to send poor people to the colonies and attracted by the alleged opportunities in the New World. Most of them, besides being very poor, lacked skills. They came to the Atlantic region because it was the part of North America that could be reached most cheaply—by securing passage on ships engaged in the fishing and timber trade. The colonies, particularly Nova Scotia, were very reluctant to receive these impoverished immigrants who could only add to existing economic problems. Nova Scotia went so far as to require masters of ships carrying immigrants to post bonds guaranteeing that settlers would not be indigent during their first year in the colony. New Brunswick, having much empty land along fertile river valleys and possessing large timber areas, was generally more receptive than Nova Scotia—at least when times were good. New Brunswick gave some assistance to immigrants, and in the 1820s immigration societies were formed in that colony. In the 1840s, however, jobs were few in New Brunswick and announcements were posted in Dublin stating that no immigrants would be received in the colony.

The attempts to guide immigration throughout much of the nineteenth century were generally feeble, consisting of little more than reacting to movements already underway. Even the policies for granting land operated inefficiently. Nor was there in the post-Loyalist era a sympathetic imperial government ready to support settlers during the grinding pioneer years.

ALIENATION OF RESOURCES

Government policies concerning the use of resources are vital factors in creating geographical patterns, directly affecting immigration, economic development and settlement. In the Atlantic region British mercantile forces, which attempted to manipulate colonial resources to their own benefit, were also important. Policies on resource use varied from colony to colony, but most of them involved the granting of favors to individuals rather than a consideration of the wisest long-term use of resources. Fortunately there were men in the colonies who began to fight the metropolitan officials—often for their personal benefit, but also in the interest of the colonies. In fact, the battle to gain control of revenue from crown lands was a vital part of the struggle for responsible government in Nova Scotia and New Brunswick.

Land policies. Newfoundland is a prime instance of an area where a resource policy was established to favor the center of Empire. The West Country's monopoly in the fishery would be threatened if permanent settlement was permitted in Newfoundland. Yet many fishermen ignored the firm regulations against settlement and stayed on to settle in outports. Indeed, a restricted form of private property was already recognized in the early eighteenth century—but with no right to inheritance or sale for the life of the individual who claimed it. Not until the second decade of the nineteenth century was owning property for purposes other than the fishery made legal. There was, however, little point in granting land for farms in Newfoundland. It was well known that the coastal lands were forbidding for agriculture; in 1822 W. E. Cormack made the first reconnaissance traverse of the island and confirmed that the interior, with a thin soil cover at best, was as hopeless for agriculture as was the periphery.

Prince Edward Island comprised the largest contiguous area of potential agricultural land in the entire region. In 1767 various political friends of the British government and naval and military officers, active and retired, were selected to participate in a lottery that disposed of the entire island in lots of roughly 20,000 acres. The new owners desired the land for speculation and had no intention to cultivate it themselves. In many areas freehold tenure was discouraged and the demand for rents frustrated development as late as Confederation.

Nova Scotia had another set of problems. The better timber suited for masts belonged to the crown for the use of the royal navy; because government authorities wished to control this timber, they were hesitant to grant large tracts of land. In mid-eighteenth century, policy changed and large land-grants were made to associations and individuals on condition that they bring in settlers—a policy that at least temporarily locked up much land in Nova Scotia, including some of the more favored parts of New Brunswick. From 1760–73, almost five and a half million acres (including much of the best land) were granted under this policy—at a time when no more than 13,000 people lived in the colony. In 1774 it was decided that all future grants would be disposed of by sale, but no one bought property, and free grants again became the policy the next year. Yet until the Loyalists arrived, there was no great popular demand for land for settlement beyond that given to the New Englanders.

The Loyalists were the first people to be affected by these land-locks, which were controlled by speculators. At the beginning of the Loyalist migration in 1783 the giving of huge grants ended, but much damage had already been done. Loyalist heads of families were to be given 100 acres and each additional family member an additional 50, with special grants to soldiers graduated up to 1000 acres, according to rank. In many places it was difficult to find land not already granted, though there might not be a soul living within miles. Considerable areas had been escheated for non-fulfillment of conditions, but frequently Loyalists were placed on land claimed by others, which prompted years of negotiating to clear titles. In the nineteenth century many farmers still lacked clear title to the land they had farmed for years.

In order to develop land more efficiently, increase revenues, and limit speculating, free grants again were cut off in 1790, the Colonial Office insisting on sales. But only New Brunswick was seriously affected because most of peninsular Nova Scotia and all of Prince Edward Island had long since been alienated. Immigration was hampered because few people who wished to emigrate had the money to buy land. Those who came either squatted or obtained licenses as actual occupying settlers, not property owners. In 1808 the granting of land commenced again, but the debate over free grants versus land sales continued, and in 1827 a system of selling land on a term basis was introduced by the Colonial Office over the opposition of the Atlantic colonies, who realized that their lands were not attractive to potential purchasers. In New Brunswick a policy of part-grants, part-sales, and shutting an eye to squatting continued until Confederation.

Reconnaissance explorations were undertaken in the nineteenth century in both Nova Scotia and New Brunswick to determine if there were additional agricultural lands. In Nova Scotia a pioneer ecologist and surveyor, Titus Smith, journeyed through the interior in 1800–01 appraising the soil and timber resources but reported only small pockets of land where farming could be tried. In 1849 J. F. W. Johnston, a British agricultural scientist, made what was probably the first agricultural land-capability survey in Canada using scientific procedures. He rated the land of New Brunswick on the basis of yields obtained and the inherent quality of the soil, dividing the land into five capability classes according to what it could produce. Johnston wrote a fairly optimistic report, emphasizing that improvements in agricultural practices could greatly increase productivity in New Brunswick. His estimate of the potential carrying capacity of the land—which suggested that food could be produced for more than five million people—was a gross error. Despite a few such absurdly optimistic evaluations, one is still left with the impression that the general limitations of the various districts for agriculture was fairly well known by mid-nineteenth century.

Timber regulations and conservation. The Atlantic region was admirably suited to the lumbering industry: fine forests covered much of the land and numerous rivers made the timber easily accessible. At first the only regulating policy was that of reserving trees for the use of the royal navy. Once settlement began, the regulations of crown timber lands became the responsibility of the lieutenant-governor and his agents. Yet in Nova Scotia and on Prince Edward Island there was little to administer because most of the land was privately owned. The woods could be and were ruthlessly exploited. In New Brunswick where the crown held most of the land a laissez faire attitude prevailed at first; as trade increased and rival lumbermen began to exploit the same territories, licenses were issued as a measure of control (1817). It was also realized that much-needed government revenues could be obtained from the woodlands: beginning in 1819 a charge of one shilling per ton was levied on timber taken from crown lands, and arrangements were made for leasing timber berths for single seasons. In 1836–37, after lengthy negotiations, the crown lands of the colony were transferred from the control of the lieutenant-governor and his appointees to the Legislative Assembly of New Brunswick in return for a guaranteed civil list protecting the salaries of various officials.

In the nineteenth century the exploitation of resources dominated, and there was little awareness of the need for conservation. The assault on timber resources was ruthless. Destruction proceeded blindly, occasionally hastened by disastrous fires such as the 1825 blaze on the Miramichi, which killed more than one hundred persons and destroyed 6000 square miles of forest. Soils fared little better. In characteristic North American fashion there was little concern for the soil once the land was cleared and cultivated. Indeed, once soils were depleted, land was often abandoned and new clearings were begun. The fisheries, however, were another matter; because the cod fisheries occasionally failed, the need for controls in the fishing industry began to be voiced by the mid-nineteenth century. There were complaints that capelin and herring (the food of the cod but a good fertilizer as well) were being depleted rapidly, and in Newfoundland a fisherman's society recommended that capelin no longer be used for agricultural purposes. In addition, the large-scale fishing operations introduced by the French were causing much concern. In Newfoundland in the 1850s and 1860s it was feared that cod were declining in the inshore waters because of the use of nets instead of hooks and lines, and by 1858 legislation had been passed prescribing that the size of mesh to be used in seines "shall not be less than 2⅜ inches from knot to knot." Yet few conservation measures could be implemented effectively at this stage of development. The basic policy for natural resources in the Atlantic region was to facilitate their exploitation for maximum short-term yields; careful regulation and husbandry of resources did not come until much later, even though there were blunt indications that such measures would be necessary.

Settlement

POPULATION GROWTH

In the 1840s Thomas Haliburton wrote an essay titled *The Seasons; or, Comers and Goers,* describing the movements of people in and out of Nova Scotia as seen in the life of a small town. In the coming and going of people he caught an essential element of life in the Atlantic region— the mobility of population that has existed from the beginning of settlement. Partly this mobility arises from the region's location on the great route for migrants from Europe to North America, the first stopping-off place for almost penniless immigrants. The region was also readily accessible to the United States, so that "going" was made easy. This mo-

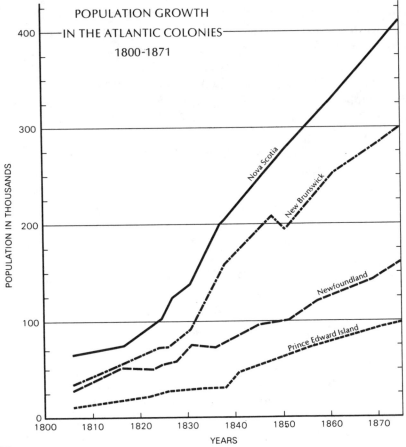

Figure 5-2.

bility and a relative poverty in certain natural resources during an era when primary activities were more important to economic growth than they are today made for a continual flux of population.

But the Atlantic region was by no means just a temporary accommodation point for migrants. On balance the population grew steadily throughout the nineteenth century, although Prince Edward Island and Newfoundland, lacking the diverse resources of Nova Scotia and New Brunswick, did not keep up with those colonies (see Fig. 5-2). The agricultural base of Prince Edward Island was good but limited, and by 1871 a population ceiling was being reached. Many people came to Newfoundland on European fishing vessels, but they quickly moved on to other colonies and to the United States. In Nova Scotia a diversified economy with more commerce and urbanization than in the other colonies supported the growing population; in New Brunswick the timber industry accounted for considerable growth. Although population was to continue to grow in the region throughout the century, the rate of increase was sharply reduced after Confederation by the steady flow of population west and south—particularly to the United States—from all of its parts.

One group of people, the Indians, did not increase in number. Probably about 5000 Indians lived in the region at the time of the British colonizations; as late as 1871 their numbers had not increased. In Newfoundland the Beothuks, weakened by introduced diseases, were harried and hunted down by French and English fishermen and by Indian groups from the mainland. By 1829 they had been completely exterminated, victims of completely cruel and brutal attitudes. Living on Prince Edward Island and in Nova Scotia and New Brunswick were 3000 to 4000 Micmacs, who had disliked the British but who had been friendly with the French—even intermarrying with them, and in the area of the Saint John River and adjacent Québec lived about 1000 Malecites who had also disliked the British. Disputes between the Micmacs and Malecites and the English over possession of land continued almost to 1780. As settlement advanced, the Indians were steadily forced to withdraw from the newly occupied areas, but they managed to continue their migratory life between the forest and the seashore and even began to turn to cultivation as a livelihood. The Micmacs and Malecites were an ignored people in the colonies and during the nineteenth century had almost as little impact on geographical development as the vanishing Beothuks.

EIGHTEENTH CENTURY COLONIZATION

In Newfoundland government policy was to permit no settlement, thus no attempt at group colonization was made. Yet many fishermen chose to stay on the island rather than return to Europe at the end of a fishing season, and by 1800 about 20,000 people resided on the island. The coves of the east coast were occupied first; then the other shores. Even parts of the "French shore" on the west were occupied by a few British fishermen. Settlement was accomplished by a steady trickle across the Atlantic of working fishermen—particularly men from Ireland and the West Country of England—who, seeing that they could make an immediate living by local fishing, were tempted to remain.

In the other colonies settlement was based more significantly on land resources, and official government policy could not be ignored so easily as in Newfoundland. In fact, as we have mentioned, the initial pattern of colonization in the mainland colonies was established by large, officially sponsored population movements (see Fig. 5-1). The three most important migrations were those of 2700 Foreign Protestants from Germany, France, and Switzerland in 1750–52; about 7000 New Englanders in 1760–76; and 35,000 Loyalists (including a few thousand blacks) after 1782. And, of course, there were the movements of the Acadians.

Knowledge of the resources of the Atlantic region was limited, and it was not easy to select suitable land for the first settlements. In Nova Scotia there was virtually an open choice of land because only the Acadian lands near the Bay of Fundy were occupied. The logical thing was to locate the new settlers near the garrison of Halifax, and this was done at Lunenburg: land was granted on a good harbor only fifty-five miles from Halifax, which made it feasible to protect the settlers from possible sustained Indian attack. The land was thought to be suited for agriculture, and it was hoped that the settlers could provide produce for the town.

New Englanders invited to settle in Nova Scotia after the expulsion of the Acadians were in a better position to know the character of the land because their countrymen had sailed the coastal waters for more than a century (Annapolis, for example, had been a New England outpost since 1710). They formed colonization associations and sent delegates to select land for settlement. The improved lands once farmed by the Acadians on the Bay of Fundy were favored locations as were the valley of the Saint John River, the area around Passamaquoddy Bay, and the small harbors along the south shore of Nova Scotia from Yarmouth to Canso. Few New Englanders settled on the shores of the Gulf of St. Lawrence because it faced away from New England. In the Pictou area, however, a large grant was made to a Pennsylvania land association which dispatched a number of Scots there in 1773–a portent of migrations to come.

The third large group to enter the region in the eighteenth century were the Loyalists, refugees from New England and the Middle Atlantic colonies. The poor quality of the land on which they settled revealed the hurried nature of their migration; distrustful of the Nova Scotian New Englanders, who had remained largely neutral in the Revolutionary War, the Loyalists attempted to settle apart from them, and all too often selected or were forced into miserable locations. On a number of occasions settlers had to relocate after a few years. The largest area of land suited for agricultural development was in New Brunswick. Many Loyalists were given grants there on the Saint John and Kennebecasis rivers, although in total an even larger number were placed in the areas of the Bay of Fundy and Northumberland Strait, on Cape Breton Island and the Island of St. John, and in widely scattered parts of Nova Scotia.

Only about 2000 immigrants came directly from Britain before 1775, a small number considering the great British migrations to the Thirteen Colonies before the Revolution. There were settlements of Yorkshire Methodists at Chignecto and Ulstermen at Truro, and some of the proprietors who owned land on Prince Edward Island brought out a few settlers, particularly Scottish Highlanders. The re-established Acadians settled in several places, especially in a township set aside for them on St. Mary's Bay (Nova Scotia), at Canso, on Prince Edward Island, and on the Baie de Chaleur. A few returned to the marshlands north of Chignecto Bay on lands not taken by New Englanders. The Acadian settlements in New Brunswick were particularly successful; in 1871 the Acadians comprised 16 per cent of the population of that province, a testimony to their rate of natural increase and the tenacity of their roots.

Almost all settlers had a difficult time establishing themselves. It was the usual story of the hazards of making a home in the forest, which was a frightening wilderness to Europeans. Indians raided homes and occasionally killed settlers, clearing required years of effort, forest fires caused havoc, drought and frost reduced yields, and the stock of animals grew slowly. Many settlers could not stand the test and took to the towns. Others turned to fishing or voyaging, worked for wages in the

Table 5-1. National origins: Nova Scotia and New Brunswick, 1871 and

	North American Indian		English and Welsh		Scots		Irish	
	Number	%	Number	%	Number	%	Number	%
Nova Scotia	1666	.4	113,520	29.2	130,741	33.7	62,851	16.4
New Brunswick	1403	.5	83,598	29.2	40,858	14.3	100,643	35.3
Prince Edward Island	281	.3	21,568	19.8	48,933	44.8	25,415	23.3

Source: Census of Canada.

woods, or left for the United States. Indeed, most men who stayed on the land had to supplement their incomes by off-the-farm activities.

The first large settlements in an area are of great significance in establishing its future character. Some groups are so successful in introducing their culture to a region that selected aspects of it are adopted widely. Yet other groups—usually small ones—may be successful for a limited length of time only in retaining their distinctive characteristics. Among the strongest cultural elements are the laws by which a land is administered. The military and government units established at Halifax after 1749 ensured that British institutions would prevail in the region, and the continuing migrations of New Englanders, Loyalists, and people from Britain stabilized the use of the English language and firmly established British customs, civil law, and methods of conducting commerce. Table 5-1 shows population by national groups in 1871 and reveals how the British remained dominant.

The Anglo-Americans transferred many facets of their culture to the Atlantic region, but they did not succeed in re-establishing all of their old ways. The New Englanders introduced townships as units of local administration; despite their vigorous protests, however, they were not allowed to introduce the local democratic procedures they had known, and the government remained centralized in Halifax. The Loyalists chose to stay under the crown, it is true, but most believed in individual liberty and as potential office holders demanded councils and assemblies in which they would have a powerful voice. They worked strongly to decentralize the government, and in separating New Brunswick from Nova Scotia they partially achieved this goal. A few decades later Loyalists joined the pre-Revolutionary New Englanders and other British immigrants, particularly the Scots, to work for responsible government. Among the many contributions that the Anglo-Americans made to the cultural landscape, vernacular architecture was the most conspicuous.

Prince Edward Island, 1881

French		German		Dutch		African		Swiss		Total population
Number	%	Number	%	Number	%	Number	%	Number	%	
32,833	8.5	31,942	8.2	2868	.7	6212	1.6	1775	.5	387,800
44,907	15.7	4478	1.6	6004	2.1	1701	.6	64	—	285,594
10,751	9.9	1076	1	292	.3					108,891

The New Englanders transferred their styles of building directly to Nova Scotia and through their associations in trade strongly influenced the Newfoundlanders, who adopted similar modes of construction. Although many Loyalists had strong Middle Atlantic roots, they tended to conform to the styles of New England.

Anglo-American influence was strong, but two groups—the Lunenburgers and the Acadians—managed to preserve their language and habits in their relatively isolated enclaves. (Table 5-1 shows their numbers in 1871 under the Swiss and French, respectively.) In Lunenburg the settlers had an admirable opportunity to establish a cultural island. No society, however, ever survives unchanged; if groups are small the changes normally come more quickly. The German language gave way to English by the nineteenth century, although German was still spoken in the 1870s and a German newspaper was still published. But by that time much of the cultural distinctiveness of the Lunenburgers had disappeared. The Acadians, however, created a stubbornly resistant community, speaking French and cherishing their Roman Catholic faith. They lived in scattered enclaves throughout the Maritimes with notable concentrations in eastern New Brunswick and in Clare Township, Nova Scotia. They learned the usefulness of speaking English but were in little danger of being absorbed by the British because the British had started to leave the region in large numbers in the 1850s. The Acadians, however, stayed on, becoming proportionately stronger in areas where they were already concentrated, particularly along the Gulf shore of New Brunswick. But they kept to themselves and had little to do with the wider affairs of the other colonies.

NINETEENTH CENTURY MIGRATIONS AND POPULATION PATTERNS

In the nineteenth century substantial migrations continued into the region, particularly from the British Isles. Figure 5-2 shows the population

growth of the colonies after 1800. Few of these migrations were sponsored; rather they were the movements of individuals and families often
fleeing from poverty, starvation, and hopelessness. An exception to the
individual pattern was a group migration to Prince Edward Island sponsored by Lord Selkirk, who in 1803 brought out some 800 settlers from
Scotland at his own expense.

The sequence of settlement is fairly straightforward. Large numbers
of Highlanders came to Nova Scotia, Cape Breton Island, and Prince Edward Island in the late eighteenth and early nineteenth century (see
Fig. 5-1). They settled in forested valleys running inland from the shore,
barely eking out a living. The difficulty of occupying the Nova Scotian
interior is demonstrated by the general failure of an attempt to settle
veterans of the War of 1812 along a projected road from Halifax to Annapolis. Most of interior Nova Scotia remained empty because it was a
wilderness comparable to the Laurentian Shield; the pleasant shores of
the interior lakes and bays of Cape Breton, however, were settled.

In a detailed study of immigration to and emigration from Nova
Scotia, J. S. Martell estimates that from 1815–38, 22,000 Scots, 13,000
Irish, and 2000 Englishmen came to the colony. In addition there were
1700 refugee blacks from the United States who came after the War of
1812 and settled in Halifax, joining an earlier black nucleus; 1400 other
immigrants from the United States, Québec, and New Brunswick; 1700
from Newfoundland, thought to be largely of Irish derivation; and 600
to 700 disbanded soldiers. Most of these people settled on lands near the
coast.

In New Brunswick immigration lagged badly until 1800; then the colony attracted settlers until the 1850s. The driving force of its economy
was timber, although dependence on this industry created special problems. For one thing, the industry flourished or stagnated depending on
international trade conditions and thus offered only sporadic employment. Also, the rowdy life in the lumber camps often led to small riots
on the Miramichi frontier. These conditions were not conducive to the
establishment of farm communities in a wooded area—a dull, back-
breaking task at best. Nevertheless, thousands of Irish found passage
aboard timber boats returning to New Brunswick. In the 1820s and
1830s the stream of immigrants was steady; in the 1840s the number
increased rapidly because of the great famine. In 1842, 8000 Irish migrated to New Brunswick; in 1846, 9000; and in 1847, 17,000. But in 1848
with diversions to the United States, Australia, and New Zealand the
number fell to 4000—much to the relief of the colonial authorities, who

had been desperately trying to control the inflow of indigents during the famine years. As a result of these migrations a distinct ethnic regionalization developed in New Brunswick, with the Irish and the Acadians concentrated in the northeast and English of largely Loyalist descent in the Saint John River valley and in the southeast (see Fig. 5-1).

All the colonies were ill-prepared for receiving immigrants. There were no large public-works projects such as canal building to provide work for the newcomers, and manufacturing was too primitive to generate many jobs. Farming, of course, was on far too small a scale to require hired labor. Thus the ports were always crowded with men looking for work, and disturbances were not uncommon. In the 1850s and 1860s it was thought that railway building would inject the necessary capital to provide jobs for some years, but railways did not advance quickly enough to spark a general change in the economy. In short, immigrants were usually left to fend for themselves. Some made a success of life, others moved on to lands of greater opportunity, still others remained poor—but all too often so did their descendants in this region of restricted resources.

These late eighteenth and early nineteenth century migrations of Scotsmen and Irishmen added significantly to the cultural complexity of the Atlantic region, their numbers even increasing to the point of breaking the cultural dominance of the English. Of the two groups the Scots had the most obvious impact. The Highlanders, who were strong in numbers in eastern Nova Scotia (particularly Cape Breton) and on Prince Edward Island, brought with them the Gaelic tongue and the last vestiges of the clan as a community unit. They had had little experience with productive agriculture on their Scottish crofts and were not so successful in farming as were the few settlers from the Lowlands, who tended to blend in with the settlers of colonial American origin. But they stuck to their land, their very tenacity and toughness giving character to the regions they had settled. Under the guidance of a few outstanding leaders they created settlements with vitality and spirit, exemplified in their dedication to improving education and their interest in literary and scientific pursuits. The Irish were widely dispersed, and in the ports or lumber camps of eastern New Brunswick where they congregated they had a reputation for being a peppery lot. As farmers they were not considered among the best. Their restlessness and edginess might be explained by their real goal: the "Boston States." New Brunswick had always been regarded as a second choice for most of them.

The main outflow of people from the region was to be after 1871 but

many left much earlier. The outward movement began, in fact, with the
Loyalists—many of whom, starting in the late 1780s, made their way
back to the United States. Those who left were generally dissatisfied:
pioneering was difficult, many had been involuntary émigrés, and differ-
ences in political systems no longer seemed of such vital importance.
Often Irishmen moved to the United States as quickly as they arrived.
The Scots did not move so readily, and the Acadians clung to their lands.
Nevertheless, after the 1840s the southward migration of established
Maritimers began to expand.

There were simply no great resources nor large urban centers to hold
the young, so they went. At first fishermen usually left to work for a season only; later they would move out permanently. This resulted in a
gradual but significant loss of skilled fishermen. Lumbermen moved
from the forests of New Brunswick to the United States when times
were bad. In the 1840s when the industry was in a depressed state along
the Atlantic coast, many lumbermen from the Maritimes joined the
migration from Maine to the Great Lakes region. With competition in
agriculture from the continental interior, farmers were even less prosperous, and many young farm people left for the United States. Similarly,
when commerce was depressed people would leave Saint John and Halifax; it was so easy to get a passage down to Boston and start a new
life. This was a fluctuating exodus. It slowed down in times of local prosperity and during the American Civil War, but the Maritimers were always aware of the many job opportunities in the burgeoning American
cities and factories and in building railways and participating in the development of the Middle West, and the drift continued through the middle decades of the century.

By 1871 the pattern of population (see Fig. 5-3) fit fairly well the pattern of resources in the Atlantic region. In Newfoundland the centers of
activity were on the coast and the interior was virtually empty. Most of
the people were in the Avalon Peninsula and along the northeastern
shore, with the population thinning westward. The south shore was occupied here and there at suitable harbors; on the west coast only spot
settlements had developed. In Nova Scotia the heaviest concentration of
people was on the Bay of Fundy and along the northern side of the peninsula, from Yarmouth in the west to Cape Breton Island. Interior Cape
Breton was also well-peopled. Settlement on the southern side of the
peninsula was sparse from Canso to Halifax, but along the coast west of
the capital the population was dense. Prince Edward Island was fully

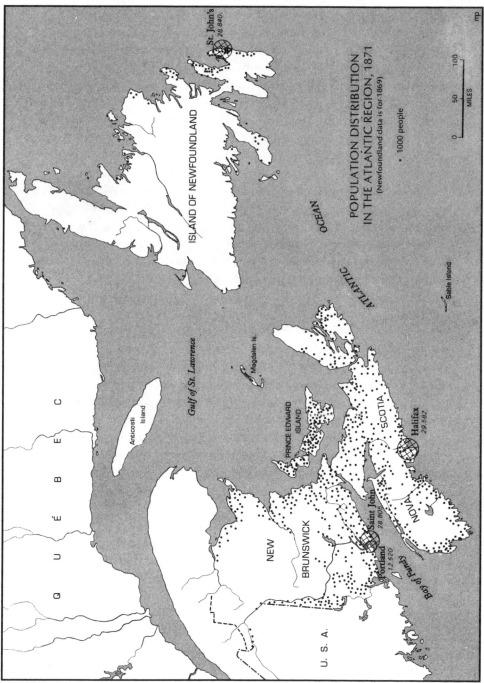

Figure 5-3.

settled although most of the eastern and western counties were of indifferent fertility. Only in New Brunswick did the question remain of
whether the limits of agricultural settlement had been reached. The
main river valleys in the south and west were densely occupied and provided connecting links through the body of the province. The east coast
and the north shore were settled, especially along the lower stretches of
the many rivers. In the north-central interior were vast forested areas;
other areas that were largely empty were the southeast highlands and
the plateau along the Bay of Fundy. Thus settlement in New Brunswick
comprised long slender linkages and finger-like penetrations inland.

After decades of settlement many areas in the Atlantic region had not
been intensively farmed or even agriculturally tested. It was too easy to
move to better lands and better economic opportunities in the United
States and elsewhere in Canada. Even so, there were almost 900,000 people living in the Atlantic region in 1871, although very unevenly distributed and dependent on diverse economic activities.

Economic development before 1800

Newcomers to the Atlantic region could make a living in a number of
ways: in the fishery, in the forest, as miners, or as farmers. The development of three of the area's resources—fish, timber, and minerals—depended largely upon foreign markets. Agriculture provided few staples
for export but supplied the base for settlement of much of the land. In
the years before 1800 the chief development in the economy was the beginning of the exploitation of the region's primary resources in the context of the North Atlantic mercantile system.

FISHING, FORESTRY, AND INTERNATIONAL TRADE

Fishing in the North Atlantic was an international enterprise involving
home ports in both Europe and North America and markets in Europe
and the Caribbean. Early in the eighteenth century the banks off Newfoundland (see Fig. 5-4) were fished primarily by ships based in Britain.
Cod, the main catch, was taken largely by hook and line. Catching the
fish was fairly easy, but preserving it was another matter, and the quality of the product depended upon how carefully this was done. Some of
the catch was heavily salted ("green fish") and carried back to Europe
where it had to be further processed for distribution. Increasingly, how-

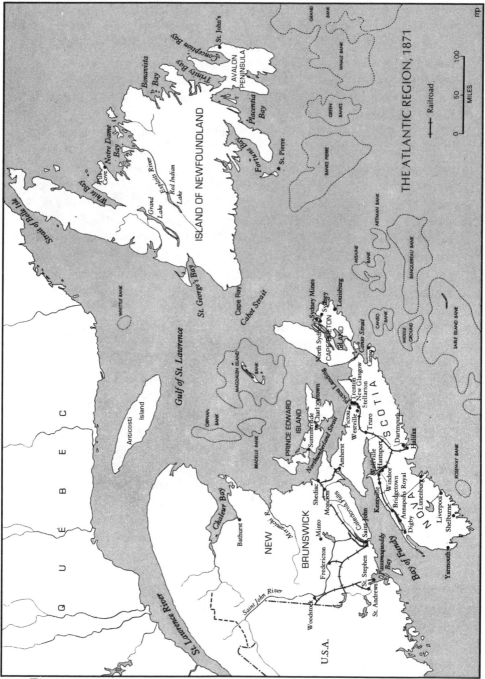

Figure 5-4.

ever, fish were prepared for market on the spot—cleaned, lightly salted, and dried on shore. Gradually a residential labor force was built up in Newfoundland. In 1713 the resident population was about 3000, and in the 1760s, of about 20,000 Britishers engaged in the fisheries, about 8000 were Newfoundlanders. By the early nineteenth century most of the fishing boats were based on the island and more and more of the fishery was locally controlled.

Much of the fishing in Newfoundland was close to shore, requiring less capital outlay for boats and allowing the fishermen's families to help in processing the cod for market. The resident fishermen disposed of their catch to enterprising floating merchants who took payment in supplies. Thus a truck, or barter, system evolved for handling the trade. Before the American Revolution much of the trade was in the hands of New Englanders, but in time Newfoundlanders developed their own entrepreneurial system. Merchants bought the fish, willingly advancing credit for future delivery, and dispatched the product to markets in southern Europe, the Caribbean, or elsewhere. A system of economic peonage slowly emerged with the fishermen kept in perpetual debt to the merchants—who often had financial difficulties of their own if they had to dispose of their product at a reduced price in Europe. The system stifled initiative, concentrated capital in a few hands, and left the fishermen in a life of endless toil. Unlike the farmer, who at least might see tangible improvement in his holdings through the years, who had the hope of leaving some equity to his family, the fisherman was on a treadmill, chained to it by debt and credit.

On Prince Edward Island and in the mainland colonies fishing was important too, but only part of wider economic interests. Canso had been an important fishing center in the early eighteenth century, and once settlement began, fishing boats sailed regularly from the many ports on the Bay of Fundy, the south coast of the Nova Scotia peninsula, Cape Breton, and the Gulf of St. Lawrence. The ports of Newfoundland, however, were much more conveniently situated to the largest and most productive deep-sea banks.

The international trade in fish in the North Atlantic was a complex system determined not only by supply and demand but by government policy as well. Trade with countries across the Atlantic was direct, but trade with the West Indies was complicated by changing political relationships with the United States after the American Revolution. Particularly affected were Nova Scotia and New Brunswick, whose ships were engaged in a broader trade than merely conveying fish. The Atlantic colonies were rich in fish and lumber but deficient in beef, flour, and other staples required in the Caribbean; thus they were not fully competitive with New England and the Middle Atlantic colonies. When the British barred American ships from West Indian ports, however, captains from Nova Scotia and New Brunswick took over much of the trade with the tropical islands, carrying fish and lumber products from their home ports and agricultural goods picked up in American harbors or illegally imported from the United States. The New Englanders, of course, entered the trade again, but these early ventures to the Caribbean helped to establish a future profitable carrying trade for the Maritime colonies.

When the Atlantic region was first settled, its vast forests were not considered a valuable commercial resource; nevertheless, a small trade in timber was soon established with Europe. During the French regime the French navy obtained masts and spars from Acadia; as early as 1772 Britain obtained masts from Nova Scotia; in the 1780s New Brunswick became an important supplier for the British fleet. Britain's more ordinary timber requirements, however, were supplied by the Baltic forests. After the American Revolution an important market for lumber developed in the West Indies when ship captains from Nova Scotia and New Brunswick opened trade in that area.

Prince Edward Island and Nova Scotia exported timber as early as the 1770s, although in Nova Scotia by the 1790s woodsmen had to go far back from the coastal settlements to procure logs. Water-driven sawmills were functioning in both Nova Scotia and New Brunswick at this time. The great timber era, however, was to come in the next century.

AGRICULTURE

Before 1871 the Atlantic region produced no agricultural product in sufficient quantities to provide a major export staple. In fact, although individual areas produced surpluses, the region as a whole remained a net importer of agricultural goods. Climate was not basically at fault. Precipitation is abundant and grasses grow well. The growing season everywhere is long enough to permit the cultivation of most common middle-latitude crops. The late spring, however, is a handicap, and the proximity of the sea depresses summer temperatures sufficiently so that wheat does not mature to the highest quality. Terrain imposes a more severe restraint than climate. On Prince Edward Island, most of the gently sloping lands can be farmed. Most of Nova Scotia, New Brunswick, and Newfoundland, however, do not lend themselves to farming—either because of thin soil cover over bedrock or because surface materials are sandy and gravelly. In 1871, 73 per cent of Prince Edward Island was occupied farmland; but only 37 per cent of Nova Scotia, 20 per cent of New Brunswick, and less than 1 per cent of Newfoundland were in farms.

The settlers made determined efforts to till the land; but a poor land base, lack of capital, competition from other areas, poor farming techniques, and the absence of an effective marketing system all greatly hindered agricultural development. Indeed, except for tree fruits, hay, oats, potatoes, and turnips, few crops could be produced competitively in the North American agricultural context.

Immigrants did not come to the Atlantic region with a view to establishing a particular kind of farming and producing a specific staple for export as they did later in other parts of Canada. Their hopes were somewhat different, both more and less ambitious. Some favored men obtained large land grants in the hope of establishing family estates on the British pattern, but even where suitable land was to be had, such enterprises required capital and cheap, docile farm labor, neither of which was usually available. Therefore, the task of making a farm reverted to the North American epic of the individual man hacking out a clearing in the forest or draining the marshes, turning the land into an economic unit that provided much of the subsistence for himself and his family. The better districts soon yielded local surpluses of livestock, hay, oats, potatoes, eggs, and even wheat for sale or barter.

When settlers arrived the land was often not surveyed, but in time property lines were measured and holdings legally defined. Except in Prince Edward Island there were no extensive uniform surveys covering an entire colony; even there such surveys were not carried down to the level of the individual holding. Normally the land was laid out only after the settlers had moved into an area. This casual, unsystematic practice proved a hindrance to settlement in various ways. All too often no evaluation had been made of the agricultural suitability of the land. Settlers were often widely scattered. Connecting roads could not easily be provided and close-knit communities failed to emerge. Highly commercial farming, in which large-scale agricultural production is required from the aggregate of many farms located close to one another, was difficult to achieve under these conditions.

Land varied greatly in quality—even within those districts surveyed and generally considered suited for settlement. There was much contemporary comment about different categories of agricultural land, and three very different kinds were recognized—diked land, intervale, and upland.

After the Acadians were expelled, the diked lands in the tidal basins at the head of the Bay of Fundy were taken over mainly by New Englanders. Skill was required to utilize these lands, and the New Englanders would not have been able to cope with them as well as they did if they had not been assisted by the returning Acadians. The lands had been reclaimed by building earthen dikes up to eight feet high and fifteen feet wide at the base. Sluice gates at the creeks, called aboîteaux, allowed fresh water to escape but prevented tidal flooding. Usually three years of fresh-water leaching were required to reduce the salt content of newly reclaimed soil to levels tolerated by pasture, grasses, and grain crops. The diked land was used mostly for growing hay, although wheat, oats, and barley were also sown. After about seven years of cropping, some farmers opened the gates to the tides, which carried mud containing plant nutrients. After every rejuvenation, which lasted for an entire season, the land had to be left idle for one or two years to allow the salt to leach out. This process was probably no easier than clearing forests, but the farmland thus created could be fertilized more effectively than forest soils, which lost their fertility quickly.

A similar process of fertilization occurred naturally in intervales (or intervals), the floodplains along the large rivers. Intervales are often covered with floodwater in the spring, but make fine farmland once the rivers subside. Such land was very important along the Saint John and Kennebecasis rivers in New Brunswick and along some streams in Nova Scotia.

Most farming, however, took place on the less productive uplands. The 1861 census of Nova Scotia recorded 35,487 acres of diked lands, 77,102 acres of cultivated intervale, and 894,714 acres of cultivated upland. There was probably an equivalent area of diked land in New Brunswick, and even more intervale.

Covering the uplands were the characteristic podzol or forest soils of humid eastern North America. In Nova Scotia and New Brunswick the land is largely sloping and the soils are normally thin, considerably leached, and of limited fertility. On Prince Edward Island the soils developed on friable sandstones are considerably better, but they must be treated with care if they are to remain productive. After a few years of settlement, differences in agricultural success from one area to another became apparent in the uplands. People stayed on the land if the soil was at all suited to farming, but in the haphazard search for land, districts hopeless for sustained agriculture were occasionally settled, such as the north shore of the Bay of Fundy. Today such areas are almost totally abandoned.

It is not easy to assess the agricultural practices of the pioneers. Once we allow that immigrants brought with them some skills in planting, harvesting, and raising animals it is easy to overstress the connection with old cultures—if for no other reason than that no society is static or exists by itself. Important factors in determining the nature of farming in a new environment are the agricultural system into which immigrants move and the associations they establish. That is, in functional if not in sentimental terms, the new forward connections quickly assume more importance than links to the past. If pioneers form limited associations with the prevailing commercial agricultural economy, or, indeed, if a commercial agricultural infrastructure does not exist, then they may well continue their old farming habits. In the Atlantic region some settlers quickly adopted new techniques; others continued most of their traditional ways, barely advancing. Examples of the former are New Englanders who moved into the diked lands on the Bay of Fundy; of the latter, the Highlanders who settled in eastern Nova Scotia.

Few early statistics are available on the development of agriculture. There was a good market for cattle, sheep, and pigs in the ports and the emphasis appears to have been on preparing land for pasture and keeping livestock. In the 1770s Halifax had a weekly market partly supplying a large demand for ship's provisions. Animals were secured from a wide area; for instance, butchers went across the peninsula to farmers in Cornwallis, bought animals, and drove them back to Halifax for slaughtering. Contemporary descriptions mention the low proportion of land under tillage in comparison with hay and pasture. Grain was grown, but mainly for home use, and in early accounts of the region, it was considered worth noting if a district was self-sufficient in breadstuffs.

PROCESSING AND MANUFACTURING

Fishing, forestry, and farming were supplemented before 1800 by rudimentary industrial activity. In countless places on the coasts fish were processed for shipment overseas, and at many small, water-driven saw-mills lumber was produced for local use and export. Gristmills were found in districts where grain was grown. Commerce was already important on the south shore of Nova Scotia and in the Bay of Fundy towns, and the demand for ocean-going ships was considerable. The first craft built in Halifax was completed in 1751; in 1760 three vessels were built at Liverpool; in 1770 the first at Saint John. By 1758 a dock-yard had been established at Halifax. The relatively unskilled labor required for constructing wooden ships was readily available, wood was at hand, and iron gear was easily imported from Britain. The critical need was for master shipwrights, and fortunately a few arrived from both England and New England early in the eighteenth century. This industry was soon widespread, and each year practically every harbor had one or two vessels on the stocks.

Economic development in the nineteenth century

Between 1800 and 1871 the population of the Atlantic region increased approximately from 100,000 to 900,000. The main sectors of economic development continued to be in primary industries and shipbuilding, with the region supplying timber products, fish, minerals, and wooden ships to the North Atlantic market. The colonies remained closely tied to economic developments in Europe and the Caribbean. The relationship between the Atlantic region and Lower and Upper Canada was not close; the region looked more to the embracing ocean and the lands bordering it than to the colonies on the St. Lawrence River and the Great Lakes.

FORESTRY

Forestry, the leading growth industry in the nineteenth century, attracted many immigrants to the region, supported other activities such as farming, and supplied raw materials for shipbuilding. The timber trade was stimulated in 1807 when the Napoleonic wars cut off Britain's supplies of Baltic timber. New Brunswick especially shipped large quantities of timber across the Atlantic; and the development of forest resources became fundamental to its growth.

The variable market for timber frustrated New Brunswick's economic development on occasion. There was particular concern in the late 1840s when the British lowered duties on foreign timber and abolished the Navigation Laws, which had given preference to British shipping. New markets developed, however, as the forests in New England states were depleted. The Reciprocity Treaty and the American Civil War further stimulated demand. Meanwhile, shipments of lumber and staves to the West Indies continued. There was a small local market for lumber for houses, piers, and shipbuilding but that demand was not large enough to even-out fluctuation in the foreign markets. So timber exploitation remained a boom-or-bust affair, affecting all aspects of life in New Brunswick. Repercussions were felt in the economies of Nova Scotia and Prince Edward Island not so much in the timber trade itself as in the lost job opportunities in New Brunswick and in markets for horses and agricultural produce. Squared timber dominated the export trade at first, but by the mid-nineteenth century, sawmill products, planks, boards, and scantlings were of greater importance—which meant more value-added in the region. Throughout this period Great Britain remained the chief market for New Brunswick, and the British West Indies for Nova Scotia. In 1868–70 New Brunswick sent 77 per cent of its forest products to Britain and 13 per cent to the United States; whereas Nova Scotia, which exported only about one-third as much by value as New Brunswick at that time, shipped 36 per cent of its timber exports to the British West Indies, 25 per cent to the United States, and 18 per cent to Britain. The comparative importance of the timber trade to New Brunswick is evident: in 1865 forest products comprised 66 per cent of New Brunswick's total exports by value, but only 9 per cent of Nova Scotia's and 8 per cent of Prince Edward Island's exports.

The lumber entrepreneurs were mainly from Britain. They sent agents to the colonies who arranged with local merchants or farmers to organize timber gangs to work in the woods. In the early years, when a great deal of hand labor was required in squaring pines, it was tempting for local men to earn money by supplying timber to an entrepreneur on contract. The gangs worked in the wilderness from November to April or May, hauling the lumber to the frozen rivers; then floating it downstream in spring. At the mouths of the rivers the logs were hewn into squared timbers or sawed into planks and loaded into ships for dispatch to Britain or elsewhere. The whole operation was simply administered, requiring little effort of the entrepreneurs, who stood to gain the greatest profit. The small operators who worked in the bush usually suffered financially when the market dropped. The resulting local disasters—such as foreclosure on mortgaged farms on which money had been borrowed in expectation of winter earnings in the pineries—gave the industry a bad name. The colony received limited revenue from the timber lands, and the residents built up little capital. Thus the lumber industry became a classic example of *raubwirtschaft*, a ruthless exploitation of resources for the benefit of distant metropolitan areas.

Within New Brunswick the location of forest exploitation shifted considerably during this period. At first large timbers were sent overseas from the Saint John River area. Later the many rivers flowing into the Bay of Fundy were used to turn the waterwheels at the sawmills. On the Gulf shore, however, few streams were suited for this purpose, and after about 1812 that area became the major producer of squared timber for the British market. The timber trade was a vital factor in shaping the geography of the Gulf shore because many immigrants—Irishmen in particular—found their way there in returning cargo ships. In addition many men from Prince Edward Island and Nova Scotia were attracted to work in the woods. When steam-powered mills were introduced in the 1820s milling became significant along the Gulf shore as well. The great rivers—the Saint John, the Miramichi, and the Restigouche—reaching far back into the hinterland were the axes along which the chain of forest destruction moved in the interior. Few parts of the colony were spared. In the 1850s and 1860s, when the large pines were almost depleted, much of the piecework in squaring timber also went. As the proprietors turned to processing spruce, operations were integrated and sawmilling was consolidated into fewer and larger mills. The day of the small sub-contractor who had so often lost his shirt was gone.

Many persons were critical of the timber trade. Lumbering was not considered a frontier of development and settlement in its own right, but a hindrance to stable agricultural growth. The attitude that the cutting of trees was merely a stage in converting an area into farmland possibly encouraged the rapid and ruthless exploitation of the forests and allowed people to forget that forests are a renewable resource requiring careful stewardship.

There is little doubt that lumbering retarded the development of an ordered agricultural society, but one should be careful in attaching too much blame to the industry. Many farmers had settled in areas where farming was difficult, and lumbering offered an additional means of income in the off-season. If conditions for farming had been better, the lumber camps would have been less attractive. As it was, wages earned in the woods supplied most of the cash income without which agriculture would have been impossible for many farmers. Moreover, the timber trade offered a market for agricultural produce. Nor can we ignore the fact that many who migrated to New Brunswick to work in the woods stayed to add to the population of that colony. The timber trade thus was not entirely inimical to the balanced growth of the region.

AGRICULTURE

The development of a prosperous agricultural economy in the Maritimes was hindered not only by severe natural limitations but by competition from foodstuffs from other areas. In addition there were always ready opportunities for farmers to follow alternative ways of making a living. In the Atlantic region "progressive" agriculture as practised on some British farms and estates was a conscious goal for a few, but the aims of most farmers were more modest: they simply wished to wrest a living from the land.

Perhaps no economic endeavor is so susceptible to gratuitous and well-meaning advice as is agriculture. Yet it is difficult to change the ways of hundreds of individual farmers—as is exemplified in the Atlantic region. As early as 1789 the "Society for Promoting Agriculture in Nova Scotia" was founded under the aegis of John Inglis, Bishop of Nova Scotia, but little was accomplished. In the early nineteenth century, livestock raising was emphasized because of a lucrative market created by the Napoleonic wars and the War of 1812. Crops—especially wheat— were neglected. To counter this trend, John Young, a lawyer in Halifax, began to send anonymous letters over the signature "Agricola" to the *Acadian Recorder,* expounding the conventional agricultural wisdom of Britain—such as the growing of wheat and crop rotation. But such advice had little effect on farmers. It was much simpler to clear a few more acres, reaping the benefits of virgin soil, than it was to maintain fertility. After Agricola's campaign, agricultural societies began to spring up in Nova Scotia and New Brunswick, but in general, strictures on farming continued. In New Brunswick in 1850 J. F. W. Johnston reported on the quite inadequate and "lazy" agricultural practices and the absence of market facilities. His remarks could have held for Nova Scotia and Prince Edward Island as well. Despite these cries for reform, local fragmented markets continued to exist, and enthusiasm for change was usually short-lived: the people who gave the advice forgot that this was a new world of small farmers where relative costs of land and labor were far different than those in Europe.

Even if many of the ideals recommended were not attained, agriculture did, in fact, advance. The greatest progress in improving farmland was made on Prince Edward Island, where 43 per cent of the occupied land was improved in 1871, compared with 32 per cent in Nova Scotia and 31 per cent in New Brunswick. Figure 5-5 shows these proportions in greater detail by county. In 1871 Prince Edward Island had 445,103 acres under cultivation, Nova Scotia 1,627,091, and New Brunswick 1,171,157. Much of this land was improved pasture. By 1871 most of the land on Prince Edward Island and the more fertile valleys in Nova Scotia were occupied. In New Brunswick the Saint John and Kennebecasis river valleys were well settled, as were the lands at the head of Chignecto Bay and along the rivers flowing into the Gulf of St. Lawrence, but areas near the headwaters of streams were largely unoccupied and the breaking of new land continued into this century.

Agriculture was the leading economic activity in each colony, based on the number of people dependent on it. In 1871 more than 46,000 persons in Nova Scotia, 31,000 in New Brunswick, and 11,000 on Prince Edward Island reported to the census enumerators that farming was their principal occupation. Farms did not vary greatly in size from colony to colony, and they varied even less in improved acreage per farm. The average size of a farm was 123 acres in New Brunswick, 108 acres in Nova Scotia, and 90 acres on Prince Edward Island. Acres improved per farm were 38, 35, and 39 respectively.

Farming throughout the region remained an unspecialized combination of crops and livestock (see Fig. 5-5). No detailed long-run statistics are available, but the evidence is consistent that the largest acreages were in pasture, hay crops, and oats. Much of the hay was used as winter livestock feed, but some went to the markets in towns such as Halifax and Saint John and to the lumber camps. Oats were fed to farm animals, sold to timber operators, or milled for human consumption. Most farms had horses, oxen, cattle, pigs, and chickens. Sheep, although not ubiquitous, remained important throughout the period. The quality of livestock was generally of a low grade, but improved as efforts were made to introduce better stock. Apparently there were no herds with good blood lines; thus the area was dependent on outside breeders for animals to upgrade livestock.

Wheat never became a dominant crop in the Maritimes, and the fail-

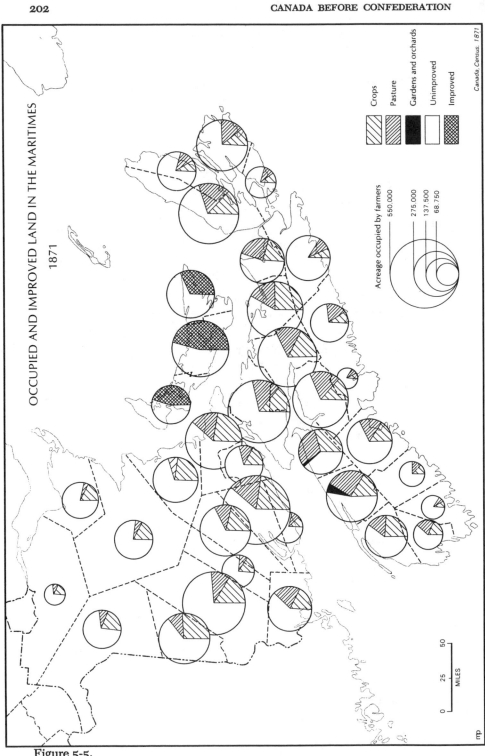

OCCUPIED AND IMPROVED LAND IN THE MARITIMES
1871

Crops
Pasture
Gardens and orchards
Unimproved
Improved

Canada, Census, 1871

Acreage occupied by farmers
550,000
275,000
137,500
68,750

0   25   50
MILES

Figure 5-5.

ure of farmers to produce enough of the grain to make the colonies self-sufficient was frustrating to many observers. Yet wheat acreage gradually increased—perhaps through the encouragement of the agricultural societies—and a few districts, such as Pictou, even produced a surplus for export. The main growing districts were in Prince Edward Island and along the Gulf coasts of Nova Scotia and New Brunswick. The wants of the region were not met for many reasons, among them a widespread belief that successful local varieties made poorer flour than imported wheat, destruction caused by the wheat midge scourge of 1840, and a lack of coordinated marketing. But perhaps of greatest importance, vast wheat-producing areas were opening up in Upper Canada and on the American prairies—areas with which the Maritimes could not compete.

Some specialization in farming did emerge. Diked lands on the Bay of Fundy were ideal for growing hay, and farmers owning such land often became cattle-raisers. Usually a farm consisted of both diked land and upland fields; on diked lands yields averaged two-and-one-third to three tons of hay per acre compared to one-and-one-half tons on typical upland fields. After the hay had been harvested in the fall, animals were permitted to graze freely over the land.

Apple orchards had been in existence in the Annapolis–Cornwallis valley since the French era, but commercial orcharding did not evolve until the nineteenth century. New varieties of apples were introduced from England and the United States, often by grafting on existing stock. Early in the nineteenth century, exports had already begun on a small scale. Before 1825 Nova Scotia was shipping apples to the West Indies as well as to New Brunswick and Newfoundland; in 1849 the first shipment was made to Liverpool and in 1856 the first one to Boston. By the 1860s the valley's apples were well known in British markets. The Nova Scotia Fruit Growers Association, formed in 1863, did much to foster orchard development. Most of its activities were concentrated in the Annapolis–Cornwallis valley; through its efforts small orchards began to appear in all parts of the Maritimes. It is estimated that in 1870, 50,000 barrels of apples were produced in Nova Scotia, of which 12,000 were exported, chiefly to England.

Since no major agricultural staples were exported, no comprehensive marketing organizations developed in the Atlantic region. In the main only a local barter market existed for agricultural goods. Often farmers shipped their produce to market themselves in homemade boats. On the Saint John River a farmer might fill his boat with potatoes, top it up

Saint John's River, New Brunswick. Track boats were used to carry goods between Fredericton and Woodstock before the railroad came. C. Mercer, watercolor, 1840. The Public Archives of Canada.

with a load of hay, and take it to town where he would stay until he had peddled or bartered the entire cargo. From the Northumberland Strait area, boats carried produce to the Miramichi lumber camps, and Prince Edward Island farmers sent livestock, potatoes, and oats to Newfoundland. The market in Halifax received produce from scattered places along the coast and animals from Pictou, Truro, and Windsor. Merchants in Halifax and Saint John bought livestock and potatoes for ships' stores and for sale to Newfoundland and even to the United States and Great Britain. From Prince Edward Island agricultural products were exported directly. Oats were shipped both to the United States and Britain with the latter becoming a more important market after the end of the Reciprocity Treaty in 1866.

Only Prince Edward Island produced a general surplus of agricultural goods. In 1865 agricultural products, mainly oats, comprised 73 per cent of the island's total exports as compared with 18 per cent in Nova Scotia and 7 per cent in New Brunswick. Imports of agricultural products to Nova Scotia and New Brunswick always greatly exceeded exports: in 1865 the two colonies imported foodstuffs worth approximately $2 mil-

lion dollars from the United States, their major supplier, while export-
ing to that country produce valued at less than half that amount. Prince
Edward Island alone showed a favorable trade balance in food: in 1865
it exported $373,000 worth of goods while importing $247,000 worth.
The agricultural situation of the Atlantic region could not change significantly because the limits of good farming had been practically
reached everywhere. And as an integral part of the larger North American economy, it was not worthwhile for the region to attempt to become self-sufficient in foodstuffs.

FISHING

The international export trade continued to dominate the fishing industry after 1800, becoming the basis of the economic growth of Newfoundland and parts of the other colonies. Fluctuating trade relations with the
Caribbean were stabilized when the British government gave bounties to
ship owners from the Atlantic colonies who were sending fish to the West
Indies. Thus, instead of bartering with the New Englanders in Passamaquoddy Bay, the Maritimers sailed directly to the Indies with their fish,
and after 1807 when the Americans placed an embargo on shipping in
American bottoms to British areas, Nova Scotia and New Brunswick took
over even more of the trade to the West Indies. These events helped to
promote the development of Saint John, Halifax, and other centers where
cargoes were assembled for shipment to the south. By the 1830s trade between Britain and the United States had become more normal, but the
effective connection between the Maritimes and the West Indies had
been firmly established. In Newfoundland a few firms also engaged in the
West Indies trade, even extending their markets for cod southward to
Brazil. Most of the cod from Newfoundland, however, still went to the
Mediterranean, where the colony's high-grade product was much in
demand.

After mid-century, changing market demands began to affect the
Nova Scotia fishery. In the United States a market for fresh fish packed
in ice was growing, and Nova Scotia was better able than Newfoundland
to supply that market. By the 1850s a fish cannery had been established
in Nova Scotia, but in 1871 the major export product was still dried cod
for the Mediterranean, South American, and Caribbean markets.

In Newfoundland the carrying trade in fish was dominated by St.
John's in both the inshore and offshore fisheries. In the inshore fishery

St. John's merchants had controlled only the Avalon Peninsula, but in the 1850s, as steamboats came into wider use, merchandising of the fish became concentrated ever more strongly in that city. Merchant-agents in major fishing ports collected the fish and forwarded it to merchants in St. John's who controlled a credit system that kept both fishermen and merchant-agents perpetually in debt.

Deep-sea fishing continued to be carried out from ports in Newfoundland against competition from the English, French, and Americans and from the other colonies. Newfoundlanders fished for cod off Labrador, in the Gulf of St. Lawrence, and over the continental shelf, marketing the fish through St. John's. Much of the cleaning and drying took place on shore, although the fish could be processed on board ship if the vessel was large enough. Thus the French continued to value their long-time landing rights along the south and west coasts of Newfoundland. During the Reciprocity years (1854–66) the Americans made use of similar privileges in the Gulf, to the profit of Prince Edward Island farmers in particular, who sold provisions to the fishermen. Both the French and the Americans used trawl-lines, which require large quantities of herring and capelin for bait. As demands for these fish increased, many fishermen from the south coast of Newfoundland left the cod fishery and turned to fishing for bait.

Off the north coast of Newfoundland, sealing was an important activity. Sealing from ships had begun late in the eighteenth century, gaining importance as merchants began organized annual spring hunts to the ice floes. In the 1860s, as steamboats came into use for sealing, the industry began to concentrate in fewer hands, eventually centering in St. John's—although other places, such as ports in Conception Bay, still remained important.

The international demand for fish supported a growing number of fishermen in all the colonies. Newfoundland especially was dependent on the fishery: in the 1850s there were more than 600 outports with nearly the entire population (just over 100,000) earning its living directly or indirectly from the sea. By 1871 approximately 37,000 persons worked in the fisheries in Newfoundland; 17,000 in Nova Scotia, 5000 in New Brunswick, and 2000 on Prince Edward Island. These figures alone do not show the relative importance of the fisheries in Newfoundland. The other colonies had important sectors in their economy that Newfoundland did not have.

An outport—particularly in Newfoundland—might consist of half a dozen to a dozen families located on a cove or a tiny harbor. In some large bays the harbors were so close together that a considerable population might be concentrated in one bay. Houses were built close to the shore and the wharf where the fish were cleaned. Some areas had enough soil for growing potatoes, cabbages, and turnips. All other provisions, such as salt, flour, rum, fishing gear, and clothing, were advanced by the merchants against codfish and cod liver oil. Many fishermen were contented with their life, but the economic peonage that the industry had generated was enervating. Further, the merchants' claims were so extensive that most fishermen could not leave their villages and their way of life whether they liked it or not.

In the Maritimes many fishermen earned additional money through working a farm or through winter employment in the woods or shipyards. Fish were also marketed there through merchants; the truck system prevailed as in Newfoundland but generally was not so oppressive because there were alternative ways of making a living. In some isolated areas, however, as along the Gulf shore of New Brunswick, the fishermen were badly exploited by English merchants, who held much the same position as the St. John's entrepreneurs. Moses Perley, a commissioner investigating the fishing industry in the 1850s, said that the settlers on the Gulf shore were in a state of serfdom worse than that of the southern slaves.

MINING

In Nova Scotia mineral resources were controlled from 1826 until 1858 by a company called The General Mining Association. It has been suggested that the company's monopoly position greatly retarded mineral development, but a lack of markets for mineral products at the time and evidence that the Association spent considerable sums on developing the mines suggest otherwise. Coal, the most important mineral, was mined in Pictou County beginning in 1815 and, until it was surpassed by Cape Breton, Pictou remained the leading coal mining area in Atlantic Canada. In 1870 there were six mines near Pictou employing 937 men, and fifteen mines in Cape Breton with 1448 employees. Until the late 1860s, about two-thirds of the coal produced was exported to the United States, but with changes in American tariffs after the Civil War there was a change in trade, and by 1871 more than half of the production was consumed in Canada. Coal was also mined at Minto, New Brunswick, but the deposits there were much less important than those of Nova Scotia.

Many small iron-ore bodies had been located in the region, and numerous efforts had been made to mine the ore for local smelting. Furnaces were established at Annapolis, Stellarton, Digby, Colchester, and other places in Nova Scotia; and near Woodstock in New Brunswick. Charcoal, made locally, was at first the only medium for smelting; thus iron ore and nearby woodland were the major locational factors. Smelting establishments were small and usually operated for only a few years —closing down when the initial supply of capital was consumed, the local sources of iron ore or charcoal ran out, or the competition from imported iron products became too severe. No large iron industry emerged in the region at the time, although there were 220 men employed at the iron works in Colchester County in 1871.

Extracting metals from igneous and metamorphic ores was difficult given the technology of the time. Yet the general interest in metallurgy was increasing, and in 1837 a 50-year lease was given to a mining company that wanted to exploit the metallic ores at Bathurst in New Brunswick. Only manganese was found in significant amounts. In the 1860s copper was mined at Tilt Cove on Notre Dame Bay in Newfoundland; during the same decade a small gold rush started when gold was found in several places in Nova Scotia. Sedimentary rocks, much easier to exploit than crystalline rocks, were used locally for building material. Gypsum from the Windsor area in Nova Scotia and Hillsborough in New Brunswick was shipped in huge quantities to the United States for use in making plaster and as fertilizer. Grindstones made from a local gritstone in Chignecto Bay found a ready market in the United States as well.

The many and varied rock formations of the region were challenging to amateur scientists and prospectors alike, and there was considerable activity in mapping formations and in prospecting for ore bodies. As early as the 1820s a rudimentary geological map of Nova Scotia was published; in 1841 Charles Lyell, the eminent geologist, visited Nova Scotia; and in the decade of the 1840s the colonies of Nova Scotia, New Brunswick, and Newfoundland all supported geological surveys in the hope that significant mineral discoveries would be made. But the hope was largely unrealized.

MANUFACTURING

Even before the end of the eighteenth century the resource industries of the region had stimulated a limited amount of processing or other manu-

Dorchester, Nova Scotia. Shipbuilding was still carried on in the fields near Dorchester in 1880. The Public Archives of Canada.

facturing. Developments continued in the next century, but generally on a modest scale. In countless places fish were prepared for shipment overseas, timber was cut into deals or lumber, wheat and oats were ground into flour and meal. A few iron-ore smelting furnaces were built, but most of them were short-lived. All of these enterprises were technically unsophisticated and operated on a small scale, as the following statistics taken from the *Census of Canada* indicate: in 1861 there were 689 sawmills in New Brunswick and 1401 in Nova Scotia. But centralization was under way: ten years later New Brunswick had 565 sawmills employing 7434 hands; and Nova Scotia had 1144, employing 2858 hands.

The manufacturing activity for which the region was best known was the building of wooden vessels. Shipbuilding had maintained its importance because of a continuing local demand for vessels and an increasing overseas market. With the decline of shipbuilding in New England in the early 1800s, many American shipwrights and carpenters migrated to the Maritimes, bringing their skills and knowledge to the fledgling industry. Before 1840 the quality of the ships was often not high, but by the 1850s ships with a reputation for seaworthiness and speed came off the stocks to find a wide market. The introduction of iron hulls and steam power foreshadowed a decline in the building of wooden ships; yet the industry continued to increase in volume, peaking in the mid-1860s with about half the ships built for export. In 1871 there were still seventy-eight shipyards in New Brunswick employing 1344 hands and producing ships valued at $1,086,714; in Nova Scotia there were 112 yards with 2058 hands producing $1,634,920 worth of ships. Not only did the shipyards employ many people, they also stimulated employment in the forests and sawmills and created a cash market for farmers. Further, because locally built ships were the foundation of the carrying trade of Halifax, Liverpool, Yarmouth, Saint John, and many smaller ports, they contributed to much urban growth in the region.

At the time of Confederation, manufacturing in Atlantic Canada had an inadequate base for future growth. Craftsmanship and creativity in wooden shipbuilding masked mediocre development in the secondary industries based on iron and steel. The region did not even have the small manufacturing establishments producing agricultural implements that characterized Ontario at the time. There was no rich agricultural hinterland to provide a strong consumer market, and there were few experienced, aggressive entrepreneurs in manufacturing. After Confederation a large iron and steel company was founded on Cape Breton Island, but apart from that, manufacturing in the Atlantic region increasingly lagged behind the rest of the country. As the area came under the influence of metropolitan central Canada and the national tariff, all of the economic weaknesses of the Maritimes were cruelly exposed.

SHIPPING AND TRADE

Three main types of shipping and trade developed in the Atlantic region. Local coastwise trading in sloops and schooners sailing from dozens of ports throughout the region was one form of commercial activity. A second form involved supplying overseas markets with fish and timber in a regular seasonal trade to England, the Mediterranean, the Caribbean, and South America; and in a third, sailing vessels from the region became common international carriers to many parts of the world. These carriers were particularly active whenever special situations, such as the Australian gold rush or the Crimean War, created a demand for sailing ships. The welfare of the colonies was at the mercy of extra-regional demands, but even with ups and downs a great deal of money was earned in world trade—partly compensating for money spent on imported foodstuffs and manufactured goods.

Trade was conducted by ships' masters and their backers as a speculative venture; in Newfoundland it was also conducted as an integral
part of the enterprises of the merchant barons. A few small shipping
firms operated out of the larger ports, but no large passenger and cargo
fleets were built up in the region. A native of Halifax established the
largest passenger-cargo line on the North Atlantic, the Cunard Line,
but he operated his firm from Britain. Within the region, regular shipping services connected major centers; such enterprises, however, were
often dependent on mail contracts and government subsidies. Worldwide
trade as conducted from the region depended on picking up cargoes at
any world port where they could be found. In a way the famous Maritime captains and sailors could be compared to the voyageurs of the
continental fur trade, more footloose and carrying on a more varied
trade it is true, but just as susceptible to disaster as technological
changes came about.

Little more success was achieved in establishing home-controlled
firms for exploiting regional resources than was attained in establishing
large companies in the world carrying-trade. An exception was the
highly centralized fish trade, which was controlled largely by family
firms in the colonies, although British firms were also involved. It has
been described as a feudally run enterprise, but the callous lack of concern for the welfare of either sub-agents or fishermen hardly suggests a
paternalistic attitude. The timber trade was capitalized and controlled
largely by family firms based in Britain, where the profits went. No integrated marketing system where farmers could sell their products on
a regular basis existed. Agricultural trade was mainly at the village- and
town-market stage, although individual merchants bought produce from
farmers and disposed of it overseas.

Urbanization and internal organization

In the eighteenth century, towns in the Atlantic region were but outposts
of European imperial and commercial interests, including garrisons such
as Louisburg and Halifax and mercantile centers such as St. John's.
Since the region's major markets were overseas and since the local hinterlands were almost always reached by boat, good harbors and orientation to the Atlantic were of prime importance. Some of the centers were
spurred on to further growth because they were located on rivers dominating a well-defined hinterland; others because they added to their
commercial functions administrative activities. Thus a relatively ad-

vanced mercantile society existed almost from the beginning of European contact.

Nearly all towns were on the sea; the few exceptions were located on navigable streams or near a mineral deposit. The accessibility conferred by a salt-water location gave a certain freedom to the growth of villages and towns, allowing them through trade to escape the confines of the immediate hinterland and encouraging the growth of sub-regional centers. On the other hand, ease of access may have been responsible for the relatively small number of towns in Atlantic Canada. Thomas Haliburton, writing in the 1820s, suggested that few towns existed in Nova Scotia because local farmers had eliminated the need for local merchants by sending their produce to market from their own landings.

Judging from the proportion of people living in large towns, the Atlantic region was not highly urbanized. Mercantile centers grew with the region rather than ahead of it. Population figures for the eighteenth century are sketchy; for the nineteenth century, however, the Census of Canada provides reliable statistics: in 1824, 11.5 per cent of New Brunswick's population lived in Saint John; in 1871, 10 per cent. In Nova Scotia 7 per cent of the population lived in Halifax in 1838; in 1871 the figure was 7.4 per cent. These towns assumed their roles as commercial and administrative centers at an early stage but did not experience the thrusting growth brought on by large-scale manufacturing and metropolitan functions.

The rivalries between towns in the Atlantic region were strong, growing out of vigorous attempts to organize and extend individual hinterlands effectively. Halifax, on a magnificent harbor, had received at its founding in 1749 the greatest external impetus of any of the cities through its function as a great naval base and a colonial administrative center. It continued to flourish not because of the resources of its *umland,* which is rocky and unsuited for agriculture, but because of Britain's strategic needs and the development taking place elsewhere in the region. Its situation in the center of the southern coast of Nova Scotia near fertile pockets of land on Minas Basin and not far from the isthmus connecting Nova Scotia to New Brunswick was an inherent advantage, but one only fully realized in the railway era.

The significance of Halifax is made apparent by comparing it to Shelburne, a small port located near the southern end of the peninsula. Established in 1783 as a Loyalist center, Shelburne within a year had grown to 10,000 people. By 1820, however, fewer than 500 remained.

Although it too has a splendid harbor, Shelburne has an *umland* as unproductive as that of Halifax. Since Halifax already was an outpost of Empire as well as the administrative and trading center of Nova Scotia, Shelburne quickly withered and remained a modest outport.

Halifax had hoped to become the administrative center for the entire Maritime region, but with the establishment of New Brunswick in 1784, Saint John became the new colony's dominant port and commercial nucleus, and Fredericton became its capital. On Prince Edward Island Charlottetown (the capital) had too small a base to compete effectively with Halifax or Saint John, as did Sydney when Cape Breton Island was separated from Nova Scotia. And in Newfoundland, St. John's was not even a competitor since that colony was largely administered from London.

In the eighteenth and nineteenth centuries many small ports throughout the region carried on a widespread oceanic trade, especially in the days of sailing ships. With steamships this ubiquity disappeared and the increasing dominance of the major centers over their coastal hinterlands became evident. In the 1820s steamships enabled Saint John to bring towns such as Digby, Annapolis, and even Windsor on Minas Basin under its influence since land communications between these centers and Halifax were extremely poor. In turn Halifax brought Prince Edward Island, Cape Breton Island, and the Miramichi country of eastern New Brunswick increasingly under its control. Each city also sought to enlarge its back country and to capture that of rival centers by promoting canals. As early as 1800 Saint John was strongly behind the Chignecto Canal (which was to connect the Bay of Fundy with Northumberland Strait), and in the 1820s Halifax was promoting the Shubenacadie Canal (to connect Halifax with Minas Basin), hoping to bring the Bay of Fundy into *its* orbit. Only the Shubenacadie was completed, but it was so small and inadequate that it could not be used.

The town of St. John's in Newfoundland had no effective rivals, although there were a few competing merchants established in other ports on the Avalon Peninsula. In the 1850s the first steamships from St. John's began to visit the outports beyond the peninsula, integrating them more closely than ever into the commercial life of the Newfoundland metropolis.

Roads were also used as a means of extending hinterlands in Nova Scotia and New Brunswick. In New Brunswick a number of valleys—those of the Saint John, Kennebecasis, Petitcodiac, and Miramichi, for example—were important links with the interior. As settlement moved inland, rough trails were chopped through the woods along the streams, and by the 1830s Saint John was connected by stage to Amherst on the east and the Miramichi country to the north. In Nova Scotia a road was begun between Lunenburg and Halifax in 1767, and much effort was devoted to constructing a cross-peninsula road from Halifax to the Bay of Fundy—a badly needed connection. By 1815 two main roads, called "Great Roads," crossed central Nova Scotia. One connected Halifax to Windsor and Hantsport, the other connected Halifax to Truro with an extension to Pictou. In 1816 stages began to operate on these roads; from Halifax it took nine hours to travel the forty-five miles to Windsor, and about two days to Pictou. Despite considerable efforts the roads in New Brunswick and Nova Scotia were not adequate to serve the general needs of the inhabitants or to support the metropolitan ambitions of Halifax and Saint John. A new means of communication, the railway, would be much more effective.

Railways were attractive for a number of reasons. They could, for example, be a means of recasting the role of the Atlantic region within the context of the North American continent. It was proposed that railways from Canada and the United States—such as the Intercolonial and the Europe and North American—carry passengers and goods as far eastward as possible on the mainland. Cape Breton Island or Newfoundland, reached by ferry, would then become the jumping-off points for Europe. The region would also benefit from increased trade with the United States and Canada, and Saint John and Halifax would have the added advantage of improved connections with their own hinterlands. These schemes of the mid-nineteenth century were largely abortive because the Canadian, American, and British investors and politicians did not see the same advantages the Maritimers did. The construction of one trunk line, however, the Intercolonial, did begin in the 1860s. It raised many questions of locational strategy within the region, especially that of a terminus. In the end Halifax won that role over Saint John, but as compensation Saint John was linked to the line near Moncton. The Intercolonial was finally completed in 1876, its route following the Gulf shore of New Brunswick and the Isthmus of Chignecto into Nova Scotia.

The major towns were anxious to build railways inland in order to enlarge their hinterlands. Lines from Halifax to Truro and to Windsor were completed in 1858; the Truro line extended to Pictou Landing in 1867 and the Windsor line to Annapolis in 1869. In New Brunswick a line from Saint John to Shediac was operating in 1860 and one to Fredericton in 1870. Another railway from St. Andrews to Woodstock was completed in 1868—a venture that indicated the ambitions of a much lesser center. In 1871 even Prince Edward Island, which would not be left behind, started a line. Newfoundland, however, did not start railways building until more than a decade later.

Despite the introduction of steamships and railways, no one city fully dominated the region. Equal avenues to the outside world and slow, insufficient growth of both the economy and population prevented the metropolitan dominance of one center—although Halifax continued to aspire to leadership. Saint John (New Brunswick) and St. John's (Newfoundland) were too strong in their own regions to allow Halifax to eclipse them; direct access to Boston or London enabled them to bypass Halifax as an intervening center. Neither control of the primary economies nor wholesaling and finance were centralized. Small-town merchants secured their supplies by visiting central jobbers, usually in Halifax and Saint John, but no tightly organized and centralized wholesale distribution system existed. The ease of setting up independent financial facilities and the importance of individual initiative is demonstrated by the fact that the first bank in Halifax was not established until 1832—twelve years after one had been set up in Saint John.

It is difficult to define the relationships of metropolitan centers outside the Atlantic region to Halifax, Saint John, and St. John's, the three leading cities. Relations with Québec City and Montréal were never close or effective, although both land and sea communications had been long established between the colonies. London and Liverpool had close commercial relationships with all three cities, and London also served as the political administrative center before 1867 for all the colonies. Boston was a significant focus in trade and higher education for New Brunswick, Nova Scotia, and even Prince Edward Island. Clearly the New England metropolis was the gateway to opportunities in the United States for many Maritimers; this close association was emphasized by the contrasting poor communications with Canada before Confederation. It is doubtful, however, that even the combined commercial and cultural influences of London and Boston could account for the failure of a dominant regional metropolitan center to emerge in the Atlantic region in the nineteenth century. That failure more likely stemmed from the internal conditions of land configuration and resource development and from the existence of four separate colonies in the region.

In 1871 there were many towns and villages along the periphery of Nova Scotia, with a few gaps east of Halifax and on the shores of Cape Breton Island (see Fig. 5-4). Halifax (the capital) and Dartmouth together had 31,773 people—only 8.2 per cent of the total population of the province. Halifax was engaged in the Caribbean trade and heavily involved in world commerce, and it was the banking, judicial, and intellectual center of the province. Yet, because the town had no great entrepreneurs or new industries to propel it forward, it remained small and complacent—less enterprising in commercial matters than its earlier struggle for regional dominance might have led one to believe, but comfortable in its role as the administrative heart of Nova Scotia. It had good access to other parts of the province and beyond, with weekly sailings to Charlottetown, Pictou, and Yarmouth and railway connections to Windsor, Truro, and Pictou.

In northern Nova Scotia three separate urban agglomerations had developed at resource sites. In the coal-mining area of Sydney Harbour (Cape Breton Island) there were 4000 people in 1871 in the three towns of Sydney, North Sydney, and Sydney Mines. In Pictou County more than 8000 people lived in five centers in and around Pictou Harbour, the largest urban complex in Nova Scotia outside of Halifax. Pictou, the service town and shipping point for a flourishing agricultral area, was also the cultural center for the many Scots in the district. Growth in the surrounding places—New Glasgow, Stellarton, Trenton, and West-ville—had recently been stimulated by the development of the coal fields and the coming of the railway. The development of the third group of closely spaced centers, located along the west side of Minas Basin, was more fully based on agriculture and shipping, and the towns were not so functionally related as at Sydney or Pictou. Windsor, Hantsport, Wolfville, and Kentville, spaced over a distance of about fourteen miles, together had a population of 6500. These were old, well-established settlements in the "garden" of Nova Scotia. Kentville was a farm service-center for Cornwallis Valley; Wolfville, a farm service-center and college town as well; Hantsport, a shipping point; and Windsor, an old county seat and an export depot for gypsum.

Along the south shore of Nova Scotia were many urban centers dependent on fishing and commercial shipping. Yarmouth, with 4696 people in 1871 was the second largest city in the province and a good example of what could be accomplished by enterprising mariners in a place without a productive back country. It was a jumping-off point for

Saint John, New Brunswick. Harbor and city in 1866. The Public Archives of Canada.

Boston, but it was also heavily involved in ocean shipping. But as wooden sailing vessels began to become obsolete, Yarmouth and similar places (Shelburne, Lunenburg, Liverpool) suffered greatly, becoming increasingly dependent upon fishing as their role in commerce waned.

The central places of New Brunswick were in marked contrast to those of Nova Scotia. Saint John and its suburb Portland had a combined population of 41,325—14 per cent of the population of the province and the largest urban cluster in the Atlantic region. Saint John had grown rapidly, serving two rich agricultural areas extending up the Saint John and Kennebecasis rivers. By the 1820s its influence had extended as far as the Digby–Annapolis and Minas Basin districts across the Bay of Fundy. (As Halifax improved its rail connections across the Nova Scotia peninsula, however, it cut into Saint John's hinterland, recovering much of the commerce the steamship had taken away.) Saint John was a more specialized work-a-day town than Halifax, benefitting directly from the great timber stands of the interior. It was a timber-shipping port and an important shipbuilding locality besides being an importer of goods for redistribution to its hinterland. In 1871 there were weekly sailings to Boston, four-times weekly connections to Annapolis, and daily service to Fredericton.

Fredericton was the quiet capital city and center of higher education of New Brunswick—out of the mainstream of commercial development, but still a local service center and lumbering town. Woodstock, with a population of about 3000 people, had a similar service role. The other leading towns in New Brunswick were closely tied to the timber trade, although some were also local farm or fishing centers. No places had grown much beyond 2000 people. To towns such as Bathurst, Chatham, Richibucto, Milltown, and St. Stephen, the forest frontier was all-important. They existed to organize timber cutting and sawing and to arrange for shipment of wood products overseas. In some places ship-building was noteworthy too, but towns in New Brunswick did not have the additional support of a diversified shipping trade as did towns in Nova Scotia. On Prince Edward Island, Charlottetown (the capital and chief market center) had a population of about 8000 and Summerside just over 2000 in 1871, out of a total population of approximately 100,000.

St. John's, Newfoundland (population about 29,000 in 1870), contained about 20 per cent of the people on the island. Newfoundland was almost entirely oriented to the sea—but to the fishing banks and the shore fishery, not to world shipping. St. John's had achieved what Halifax and Saint John had not achieved; it had brought the outlying centers of its hinterland under very close control. Other towns had difficulty in

Charlottetown, Prince Edward Island in the 1860s. On Richmond Street, identifiable storefronts had begun to appear. The Public Archives of Canada.

growing under an arrangement where all commercial affairs were conducted in St. John's. Some of the harbors in Conception Bay, however,
had large agglomerations: in 1874, 6600 people lived in Harbour Grace
and 4400 in Carbonear, yet these were little more than extensive, straggling villages. From St. John's there was fortnightly steamboat service
to Cape Ray and to Tilt Cove on Notre Dame Bay, and a fortnightly
mail service to Halifax. Newfoundland was much more closely related to
Britain, however, than to the urban centers of the mainland.

Around the Gulf of St. Lawrence there was an urban lacuna—an in-
ward-facing crescent in which a separate arena of interests evolved—
reflected in the existence of Prince Edward Island as a separate colony,
in the short life of Cape Breton Island as a colony, and in the alienation
of northeast New Brunswick from Saint John. This alienation went so
far that in the 1860s the lieutenant-governor of New Brunswick stated
that there was no real unity of interest in New Brunswick; the different
parts, he said, looked to Québec and Nova Scotia; some sections even
had interests of their own.

The easily navigated seas certainly had not contributed to the unifica-
tion of the region; the physical and psychological orientations—outward
to the North Atlantic and inward to the Gulf and Canada—were simply
too numerous. Railways might have helped to overcome disintegration
within the region, but by 1871 it was not yet clear whether Halifax and
Saint John would continue to cancel out one another's efforts to extend
their hinterlands. Nor was it clear what relationship the new town of
Moncton, strategically located on the Intercolonial at the hinge point of
the two mainland provinces, would have with the two leading centers.
The presence of competitive regional growth-centers had resulted in un-
coordinated development and too often the rivalry of cities or sections
had nullified innovations and ideas for growth within the region. Consequently an effective scale of urban growth, entrepreneurial initiative, and
flow of capital into the region had not been generated by 1871. This
proved to be a major deficiency when massive economic development began to take place in the rest of the continent, and the Atlantic region had
to fight for economic parity. It did not have a strong and recognized
metropolitan base to carry on the struggle in competitive terms.

Culture, landscape, and regionalism

Life in the Atlantic region was largely rural and small-town in nature.
The administrative and professional establishments in the capitals, how-

Table 5-2. Principal religious denominations in 1871.

	Baptist		Catholic		Church of England	
	Number	%	Number	%	Number	%
Newfoundland*			61,040	41.6	55,184	37.6
Prince Edward Island	4371	4.7	40,442	43	7220	7.7
Nova Scotia	73,430	18.9	102,001	26.3	55,124	14.2
New Brunswick	70,597	24.7	96,016	33.6	45,481	15.9

* Figures for Newfoundland 1869.

ever, were vital elements in setting the style of cultural development. These establishments tended to be cautious and not too innovative, placing great value on property and the revenues to be derived from it. This predilection provided a mature and ordered social structure, but one so conservative that it tended toward stagnation. Community life varied substantially from one section to another because of differences in economic activities and the absence of an integrated communications system. In this era before radio, television, and the wide distribution of daily newspapers communities could still remain distinctive within the framework of a larger society.

Throughout most of the Atlantic region a stable agrarian life based on freehold tenure was generally regarded as the ideal rural society. This ideal was approached in parts of Nova Scotia and southern New Brunswick and in much of Prince Edward Island, where a diversified economy and a closer spacing of hamlets and villages contributed to the development of close-knit, sedate, and comfortable communities. Yet the very diversification of resources had made it possible for many of the inhabitants of such communities to establish a distinctive approach to making a living. They turned from farm to bush camp and back again, easily diverted from the "prudent" aim of developing one's own property. Indeed, if a man chose to stay in this region of limited economic development, it often made sense to diversify. At a time when the market for agricultural produce was uncertain, it was possible to obtain a job in the woods, sawmills, or shipyards, or to supplement income through fishing; thus there was less attraction in agrarian values based on developing a commercial farm property. Furthermore, the attitudes of the times did not rate specialization for the working man as highly as our much more closed industrial society has tended to do; this flexibility in the Atlantic region was possible because in the main no rigid exploitative economic infrastructure under the control of large business firms dominated the

| Congregational | | Lutheran | | Methodist | | Presbyterian | | Total |
Number	%	Number	%	Number	%	Number	%	population
338	.2			28,990	19.8	974	.7	146,536
				11,070	11.8	29,579	31.5	94,021
2538	.7	4958	1.3	40,871	10.5	103,539	26.7	387,800
1193	.4	82	—	29,856	10.4	38,852	13.6	285,594

Source: Census of Canada and Newfoundland.

colonies—except in Newfoundland and parts of lands facing the Gulf from Cape Breton to Baie Chaleur.

The mariner's life, too, was an integral part of the economy of the Atlantic region—an accepted and even respected way to fortune. Privateers, captains and seamen found their frontier in the oceans of the world; for all young men in the Maritimes the quays were an open door to adventure and fortune. On the other hand many people were genuinely perplexed at the kind of turbulent society that developed in the woods of New Brunswick; a miniature frontier in the Turnerian sense, a life considered disruptive to the agrarian ideals of the time.

Religion played an important part in the lives of the people. The churches, which were often more effective in transcending differences between town and country than other social institutions, were a strong force in the establishment of a stable society. There were strong rivalries among denominations and active evangelical movements, but they did not nullify the role of churches in providing a framework for everyday life. (Table 5-2 shows the composition of the main religious groups in 1869 and in 1871.)

Schooling was valued highly in the Atlantic region, both in its own right as knowledge and as a means of improving the economy and the life of the region. When the Loyalists arrived, the many Anglicans among them re-enforced the military and administrative group and together they managed to establish their own churches and associated colleges as state-supported institutions. They retained such special privileges for only a few years, however, because other religious groups were also strongly represented in the community. Many denominations supported institutions of higher learning from the beginning of settlement and even before the community was really ready for them. In Newfoundland the schools were under the control of the churches, but in the other colonies they were largely state-supported. Many children received little or no schooling—particularly in Newfoundland—but a full range of facilities was available for those with means throughout most of the region.

Many men were able to see that progress in an area of restricted resources could be made by broadening the skills of the people: John Young's (Agricola) goal was to improve agriculture; that of Thomas McCulloch and J. W. Dawson to improve the school system of Nova Scotia. James Robb worked to establish an athenaeum in New Brunswick, and writer T. C. Haliburton in his histories and essays urged his fellow colonists to become as enterprising as the New Englanders.

Artistic and scholarly endeavors were not neglected in the region. A few visiting topographers and watercolor artists left a good record of the landscape in some areas, but no outstanding artist emerged in the region in this period. Poetry, novels, and histories were written; T. C. Haliburton, especially, provided an acute insight into the character of Nova Scotia in his writings.

It is characteristic of colonial societies that budding literary and artistic talent is strongly affected by what is in vogue in the metropolitan centers. This is revealed in the Maritimes by the characterizations of Haliburton, or by the British influences on the genre in which lawyers, teachers, and clergymen wrote. Such larger influences are even more clearly evident in scientific work. W. E. Cormack, a native of Newfoundland who made early mineralogical observations on that island, was Edinburgh-trained, and the first geological investigations in Nova Scotia were made by two Bostonians. The world-renowned British geologist, Charles Lyell, and the chemist and agriculturist J. F. W. Johnston both visited the region in mid-nineteenth century. Lyell's visit greatly influenced a Pictou man, J. W. Dawson, who embodied this international-intellectual exchange, visiting museums in Boston, obtaining his formal training in Edinburgh, doing field work in Nova Scotia, and ultimately writing the classic geology of the region. James Robb, a Scot also trained in Edinburgh, carried out similar work in New Brunswick. These were impressive intellectual achievements, ranking with work in geology in Europe and elsewhere in North America at the time. Interest in natural history was not confined to the work of these few individuals, however. Literary and scientific societies were founded in Halifax, Pictou, and Yarmouth in the 1830s. Such intellectual activity showed that outside contacts were not merely commercial or sentimental ties with other parts of the world.

Halifax in August 1842. C. Mercer's watercolor of the city's closely built-up central area. The scene is from a window on the first floor of the Halifax Hotel.

In the 1870s ethnic cultural diversity was clearly evident in the life of the region. The English and Scots were dominant in government, education, and commerce, comprising the host society to which other groups gradually tended to conform. But the customs and attitudes and even the languages of the Old World (greatly modified after a century or more in the region) lingered on among the minority groups. These traits persisted most likely because the settlements of Germans, Acadians, Gaelic-speaking Highlanders, and others were often discrete enclaves. In addition Anglo-conformity was not so pervasive as it tends to be today. In the larger ethnic communities language might even remain distinctive, standing against the dominant use of English. Even English was spoken in different ways, as in Newfoundland, where sharply distinctive accents persisted. This cultural heritage is still apparent in many localities, alive in the memories of people, a part of their oral history. In the Acadian parts of the Atlantic region cultural identity is not just a matter of sentimentally nurturing valued cultural traits of the past, but of establishing rights as Francophones in a bilingual country.

The cultural landscape was influenced by the settlers' inclinations to re-establish building styles familiar to their homelands and by variations in the natural-resource base. In Newfoundland the building style tended toward the rectangular gable-roofed structures characteristic of the Atlantic seaboard, but the villages had none of the serene, composed unity of those in New England. Building was helter-skelter, over and around rocky outcrops next to the sea. The Irish also brought over many aspects of their material culture. In Nova Scotia the settlers managed to make more of an impress on a greater proportion of the land. The trading ports were well-laid out villages with wooden buildings of New England style—not so rich and spacious as those of New England but not so austere as those of Newfoundland, either. In the well-ordered agricultural districts of Nova Scotia—the Windsor, Annapolis–Cornwallis, and Lunenburg areas—buildings were substantial and took on a more decorative look. In Antigonish and Cape Breton Island simple wooden houses were the rule, but in Pictou the Scots had put up solid structures of local stone. Stone buildings were most commonly found in Halifax and Saint John, whose residents had built many substantial homes and business places. But the general aspect of those towns was somewhat snaggletoothed, with high and low buildings, empty lots, and wretched roadways—as is true in any developing city.

In New Brunswick the contrasts of wilderness and settlement were great. Settlement, often confined to woodlands, extended along trails and trees crowded in on the farmed plots. Along the Saint John River, farms were open and spacious, although the view was still restricted by long slopes of hills; along the Kennebecasis, farms lined the valley sides. On the wooded plain of the Gulf shore a narrow strip of settlement followed the coast. The settlers, of course, had cleared many trees—too many, they later found when cold winds from the Gulf blew over their exposed farms. As in other districts there was a great contrast of buildings ranging from the comfortable houses of the earlier settlers to the shanties and cabins of the new arrivals. On Prince Edward Island a true agrarian landscape had emerged on the gently rolling terrain, with well-laid out, if often very modest, farmsteads.

Urban planning—when it existed at all—was unimaginative. The surveyors who laid out villages and towns usually did not think beyond the simple rectangular grid (an approach, however, which had intrinsic appeal in the classicist era when many of the plans were prepared). Out

Figure 5-6.

of necessity surveyors took into account the shorelines of a harbor, but they did not create plans for entire sites. The gridiron layouts of Halifax (see Fig. 5-6) and Saint John are a prime example of planning ill-adapted to a sloping site. In Saint John, however, a large square which became the crossroads of the city was laid out. And in Charlottetown a central square provides a focus for the small provincial capital. Another exception to the stereotype—in intention if not execution—is Sydney on Cape Breton Island; there Governor Des Barre's plans of 1785 envisaged a cluster of four towns four to seven miles apart, each laid out in circular fashion and joined by axial roads along which lots were to be arranged. The lots were to become progressively larger outward from the town. Such coordination of town and country planning unfortunately only demonstrates what might have been, for few settlers came to Sydney and the plan was abandoned. Most villages and towns owed their aesthetic qualities, if any, to their beautiful settings and to the sound, unpretentious quality of their buildings.

The Atlantic region was a pleasant country in which to live in the 1870s, except perhaps in the harshest of the outports where shelter from wind and storms was provided by cliffs, not trees. As yet there was no well-defined line between farmland and wilderness. Even residents of Halifax and Saint John could easily escape to the streams, rocks, and trees of the countryside. This made for a satisfying life in most communities; no lengthy traveling was necessary to find restful riverside places or woodlands suited for walking and hunting.

In the 1860s most inhabitants of the Atlantic region identified strongly with their local areas. Much of this feeling could be attributed to parochialism, although often a recognition of a somewhat wider community existed as well. D. C. Harvey argued that in Nova Scotia a sense of wider regionalism had emerged, including a feeling of common purpose in the colony as a whole. This was not true of New Brunswick, where the difference between Saint John and the Gulf shore was marked; where no larger entity had developed. Prince Edward Island, too, was a discernible unit, involved in its own problems; and Newfoundland was even more a region unto itself. Such internal regional identities were so strong that there was little awareness of the wider Atlantic region as a functional unit; as an area closely related to the other colonies in British North America.

Convincing the different colonies to join Confederation was no easy matter, and the debates on this issue were vigorous. Yet Nova Scotia and

New Brunswick both joined Confederation in 1867, hoping that their coal, iron ore, and small manufacturing enterprises could be parlayed into a modern industrial enterprise and that the promised Intercolonial railway would not only establish the essential links for trade, but that it would make the region the winter outlet for all of Canada. Prince Edward Island, temporarily secure in its farm economy and not yet bankrupted by its railway-building, waited until 1873 to join Confederation; and Newfoundland, seeing that its market for fish lay in the Caribbean and across the Atlantic, not in the United States and Canada, delayed joining for more than eighty years.

For a time hope in the advantages of Confederation remained high. In 1789 Sir Samuel Tilley, speaking in the House of Commons, still envisaged that "the day is not far distant when the population in the Western country will be greater than in Canada, and when the Maritime Provinces with their coal, iron, and water power will be the manufacturing center for this vast Dominion. . . ." But he did not reckon on the dynamism, the immensity of resources, and the power of the entrepreneurial organizations of the interior, or on policies such as the protective tariff; further, he overlooked the essential weaknesses of a primary resource-based economy in which resources are limited and the working force lacks a reservoir of special skills—not stopping to consider that talent and effective entrepreneurship seek fortune where the scale of operations and the rewards are largest. Moreover, the labor force shared much of this mobility. Once the industrial economy of the continent came to life, the Atlantic region could not keep pace, and large numbers of people in search of better opportunities, left their farms and villages and a "make-do" society behind them. The odds against catching up with the rest of Anglo-French America became steadily worse; finally, in the twentieth century the Canadian government began to mount development programs in an attempt to redress the balance and to compensate for an excessive labor force in the primary industries inherited from the previous century. For much of that bygone age, however, resources and technology had been appropriate, and the contrasts with the crowding, noise, and pollution of a century later have left many in the Atlantic region with a keen nostalgia for what seem—at least in retrospect—to have been the halcyon years of Canada's provinces by the sea.

Bibliography

W. S. MacNutt, *The Atlantic Provinces; the Emergence of Colonial Society, 1712–1857* (Toronto: McClelland and Stewart, 1965) provides a firm historical background, emphasizing political development and settlement; and G. A. Rawlyk's compilation, *Historical Essays on the Atlantic Provinces* (Toronto: McClelland and Stewart, 1967, Carleton Library no. 35), includes some provocative interpretations of the role of the colonies within North America. MacNutt has written *New Brunswick, A History: 1784–1867* (Toronto: Macmillan Co. of Canada, 1963), but there are no comparable histories on the other provinces.

Andrew H. Clark's *Acadia; The Geography of Early Nova Scotia to 1760* (Madison: University of Wisconsin Press, 1968) is an essential source on the early settlement geography of this region; and Helen I. Cowan, *British Emigration to British North America, the First Hundred Years* (Toronto: University of Toronto Press, 1961), and Norman Macdonald, *Canada, 1763–1841: Immigration and Settlement; The Administration of the Imperial Land Regulations* (London: Longmans, Green, 1939) and *Canada: Immigration and Colonization 1841–1903* (Toronto: Macmillan Co. of Canada, 1966), provide basic documentation on immigration policy and the peopling of the area. J. B. Brebner, *The Neutral Yankees of Nova Scotia; A Marginal Colony During The Revolutionary Years* (New York: Columbia University Press, 1937; reprinted 1969, Carleton Library no. 45), and M. L. Hansen and J. B. Brebner, *The Mingling of The Canadian and American Peoples* (New Haven: Yale University Press, 1940) give a fine sweeping view of the cross currents of migration and the economic and social conditions under which these movements took place. Books and articles on general patterns of settlement and development are scarce, but some research exists, such as William Ganong's study of the spread of settlement in New Brunswick, "A Monograph of the Origins of Settlements in the Province of New Brunswick," in *Transactions of the Royal Society of Canada* Section II (1904), 3–185; the outstanding work by Winthrop Bell, *The 'Foreign Protestants' and the Settlement of Nova Scotia; The History of a Piece of Arrested British Colonial Policy in the Eighteenth Century* (Toronto: University of Toronto Press, 1961); and meticulous studies by J. S. Martell, *Immigration to and Emigration From Nova Scotia 1815–1838* (Halifax: The Public Archives of Nova Scotia, 1942), and R. L. Gentilcore, "The Agricultural Background of Settlement in Eastern Nova Scotia,"

Annals of the Association of American Geographers 46 (1956), 378–404.
A. H. Clark, "Titus Smith, Junior, and the Geography of Nova Scotia in
1801 and 1802," *Annals of the Association of American Geographers* 44
(1954), 292–314 discusses an early resource survey of Nova Scotia, and
O. F. G. Sitwell "Land Use and Settlement Patterns in Pictou County,
Nova Scotia" (Ph.D. thesis, University of Toronto, 1968) provides useful information on agricultural change in part of Nova Scotia.

Harold Innis, *The Cod Fisheries; The History of an International
Economy* (New Haven: Yale University Press, 1940) when carefully
searched provides obscure information on the economy besides stimulating the reader with its wide-ranging interpretations on North Atlantic
trade. S. A. Saunders in *Studies in the Economy of the Maritime Provinces* (Toronto: Macmillan Co. of Canada, 1939) has brought together
data on the mid-nineteenth century economy of the region, and a look
at the riches of H. A. Innis and A. R. M. Lower, *Select Documents in
Canadian Economic History 1783–1885* (Toronto: University of Toronto Press, 1933) reminds us how little thorough work has been done
in analyzing the materials they collected. A. R. M. Lower, *The North
American Assault on the Canadian Forest, A History of the Lumber
Trade Between Canada and the United States* (Toronto: Ryerson Press,
1938) provides a good background on the forest industries of the Maritime provinces and some of the figures used in this chapter are derived
from it. W. J. A. Donald, *The Canadian Iron and Steel Industry* (Boston: Houghton Mifflin Co., 1915), supplies early information on industrial activity; and A. H. Clark in *Three Centuries and the Island; a
Historical Geography of Settlement and Agriculture in Prince Edward Island, Canada* (Toronto: University of Toronto Press, 1959) shows the
fine geographical results that can be obtained by an assiduous study of
all available data on one of the provinces. J. S. Martell has two fine articles on official encouragement of agriculture in Nova Scotia, "The
Achievements of Agricola and the Agricultural Societies 1818–25," *Bulletin of the Public Archives of Nova Scotia* vol. 2, no. 2 (1840), and
"From Central Board to Secretary of Agriculture 1826–1885," *Bulletin of
the Public Archives of Nova Scotia* vol. 2, no. 3 (1840). F. G. J. Comeau
prepared an account of the orchards of Nova Scotia, "The Origin and
History of the Apple Industry in Nova Scotia," *Collections of the Nova
Scotia Historical Society* vol. 23 (1936), 15–40. Much can be learned on
early transportation in Nova Scotia from R. D. Evans, "Stage Coaches
in Nova Scotia, 1815 to 1867," *Collections of the Nova Scotia Historical*

Society vol. 24 (1938), 107–34. *Tackabury's Atlas of the Dominion of Canada* (Toronto, 1875) contains statistical information on the Maritimes and the maps are useful. Contemporary books catching some of the character of the economic geography of the time include Abraham Gesner, *New Brunswick; With Notes for Emigrants* (London: Simmonds & Ward, 1847); J. F. W. Johnston, *Report On the Agricultural Capabilities of the Province of New Brunswick* (Fredericton: J. Simpson, printer, 1850); and M. H. Perley, *Report On the Sea and River Fisheries of New Brunswick, Within the Gulf of Saint Lawrence and Bay of Chaleur* (Fredericton: J. Simpson, printer, 1850).

Older works which reveal some of the scientific and the cultural attainments and also supply vignettes of life in the region include W. E. Cormack, *Narrative of a Journey Across the Island of Newfoundland in 1822* (London: Longmans, Green and Co., Ltd., 1928), J. W. Dawson, *Acadian Geology. An Account of the Geological Structure and Mineral Resources of Nova Scotia, and Portions of the Neighbouring Provinces of British America* (Edinburgh: Oliver and Boyd, 1855), and T. C. Haliburton, *A General Description of Nova Scotia* (Halifax: C. H. Belcher, 1825) and *The Old Judge; Or Life in a Colony* (London, H. Colburn, 1849; reprinted in 1968 by Clarke, Irwin, Toronto). *The Old Judge* contains "The Seasons, or, Comers and Goers." J. M. S. Careless opened new ground in studying the early urban development of the region in his essay "Aspects of Metropolitanism in Atlantic Canada" in Mason Wade, (ed.) *Regionalism in the Canadian Community, 1867–1967* (Toronto: University of Toronto Press, 1969); D. C. Harvey's and A. G. Bailey's essays "The Intellectual Awakening of Nova Scotia" (1933) and "Creative Moments in the Culture of the Maritime Provinces" (1949), both reprinted in Rawlyk, *Historical Essays on the Atlantic Provinces* cast light on the culture of the region, and the chapters on Maritime literature in Carl F. Klinck, *Literary History of Canada, Canadian Literature in English* (Toronto: University of Toronto Press, 1965) are valuable in this regard. For architecture one can turn to the start made by Michael Hugo-Brunt, "The Origin of Colonial Settlements in the Maritimes," *Plan* 1, 2 (1960), 78–114, "Two Worlds Meet: A Survey of Newfoundland Settlement, Part 1—the Great Fishery and Early Settlement," *Plan* 5, 1 (1964), 22–36, and "Part 2—Development in the 19th and 20th Centuries," *Plan* 5, 2 (1964), 59–83, and the work of Alan Gowans *Building Canada: An Architectural History of Canadian Life* (Toronto: Oxford University Press, 1966) is helpful. John Mannion's "Irish Imprints on the Landscape of Eastern Canada in the Nineteenth Century: A Study in. Cultural Transfer and Adaptation" (Ph.D. thesis, University of Toronto, 1971) points the way to new work in cultural geography. Sir Leonard Tilley's statement on Maritime development is quoted in a voluminous compendium of statistical information on the Maritimes, *The Maritime Provinces in their Relation to the National Economy of Canada* (Canada: Department of Trade and Commerce, Ottawa, 1948).

6 THE WESTERN INTERIOR:

1800-1870

We have already seen how fur traders from Hudson Bay and the St. Lawrence River met in the western interior of British North America, that part of Rupert's Land extending from Lake Superior and Hudson Bay to the Rocky Mountains. In 1821 the Hudson's Bay Company absorbed the Northwest Company and continued to administer Rupert's Land under crown charter until 1870, when the entire area was transferred to Canada.

This chapter will center neither on geopolitics nor on the continental and global strategists who proposed to develop the region. Until 1870 the western interior remained effectively protected by distance from the surge of North American settlement and, before the pace of change could be hurried along by the railway, a distinctive set of human relationships was being worked out as Indians, traders, mixed-bloods (persons of Indian and European parentage), farmers, missionaries, and adventurers mingled in the area. For most of the century the western interior saw little progress in the nineteenth-century sense; thus this chapter will emphasize the life and activity of the region rather than sequential geographical development.

The varied perceptions of nature and resources

The western interior has few pronounced breaks in relief as it rises from sea level at Hudson Bay to 5000 feet at the Rockies over a distance of 1000 miles. There are, however, significant contrasts in many other aspects of physical geography (see Fig. 6-1), based mainly on differences in bedrock, climate, and vegetation.

Central to an understanding of the geography of the interior is the existence of two contrasting natural realms, grasslands and forest, and the transition zone between them of aspen groves and prairie meadows— a belt of parkland up to one hundred miles wide. The Indians and the mixed-bloods had a different appreciation of the land and its resources than did the newly arrived fur traders and farmers, who brought with them the biases and aspirations of another world. For all groups this could be an area of hazard, where a careful assessment of resources and flexibility in their exploitation were essential for survival.

Both the plains and the woodlands Indians led a nomadic life. On the grasslands thousands of bison—commonly called buffalo—provided a splendid resource for the plains Indians, especially in summer. The Indians were well aware of the hazards of the open grasslands in winter and the need to seek shelter in wooded river valleys, in bluffs of trees, and in the foothills of the Rockies. The bordering parklands were another distinctive environment to the plains Indians. When in 1802 fur trader Peter Fidler sketched a map of the plains based on the ideas of a Blackfoot chief,[1] he drew a line along the rim of the map and called it "Woods Edge." The boundary evokes a feeling of a new world lying beyond just as do the lines marking the edge of the known world on ancient maps. Clumps of trees, hills, and the great rivers were drawn on the map as if to serve as guide posts for Indians crossing otherwise unmarked plains.

In the forested uplands, rivers and lakes were the avenues of movement, to be traversed by canoe in summer and by foot in winter. Indian maps indicate the many interlinking rivers and lakes that served as the lines of reference in their world. The intricacies of the water systems were so great that the uninitiated were as likely to get lost there as on the plains. Numerous fur-bearing animals such as beaver, marten, and muskrat, and large game animals such as moose, caribou, wood bison, and deer populated the forest, but the huge herds of bison that made the plains so unique were not to be found.

In the parkland, which combined the advantages of both areas, the woodlands and plains Indians converged each season. This zone of transition was in fact the central axis of human activity in the interior— not only because it was crossed by one of the main channels of the fur trade (the North Saskatchewan River), but because it was a core area

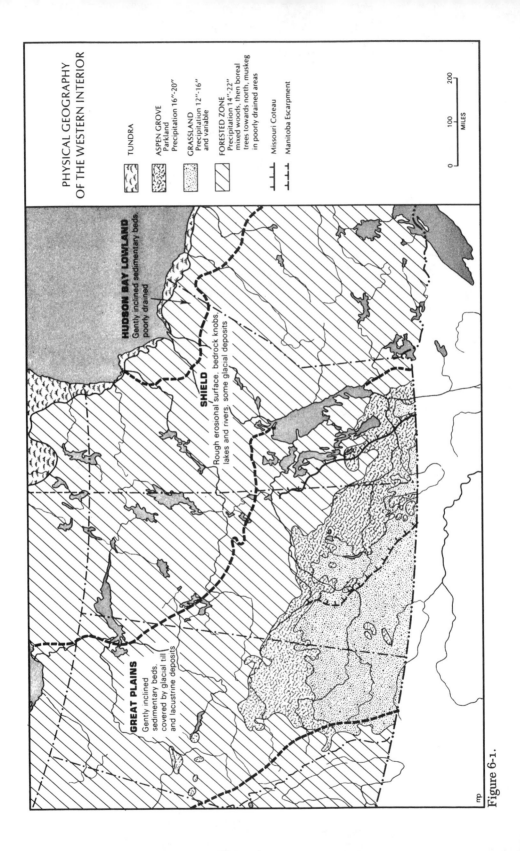

PHYSICAL GEOGRAPHY
OF THE WESTERN INTERIOR

TUNDRA

ASPEN GROVE
Parkland
Precipitation 16″-20″

GRASSLAND
Precipitation 12″-16″
and variable

FORESTED ZONE
Precipitation 14″-22″
mixed woods, then boreal
trees towards north, muskeg
in poorly drained areas

Missouri Coteau

Manitoba Escarpment

0   100   200
MILES

HUDSON BAY LOWLAND
Gently inclined sedimentary beds,
poorly drained

SHIELD
Rough erosional surface, bedrock knobs,
lakes and rivers, some glacial deposits

GREAT PLAINS
Gently inclined
sedimentary beds,
covered by glacial till
and lacustrine deposits

mp

Figure 6-1.

in the cultural life of many Indian groups, as has been demonstrated by some scholars.

Traders from Montréal traveled across hundreds of miles of Shield before reaching the meadows near Lake Winnipeg and a change in landscape. But men from Britain posted to Rupert's Land and traveling by ship to York Factory had a much more abrupt and rude introduction to the interior. In their journals they complained of the depressingly cold and long winters near Hudson Bay, commenting on the bleak, treeless landscape of the tundra, especially north of Churchill, which became known as the "barren ground." But to these men as to the Montréal traders, the starkest change in landscape was from woodlands to grasslands. Henry Kelsey, the first European to reach the interior, noted this change in the early 1690s, as did many traders who followed him. In the 1770s and 1780s Alexander Henry and Peter Pond drew maps on which they marked boundary lines between the forest and grasslands. One of the best indications of the way in which the interior was perceived is shown on a map of the region as viewed from Carlton House (see Fig. 6-2).[2] Probably the earliest map of the interior to show the transition from woodlands to grasslands as more than a line, it even conveys the impression of a belt of parkland, indicating "Woody Country," then "woods and Small plains," then "Patches of small woods," then "Last tuft of woods," and finally, "Wide Plains."

The parkland was well known to traders and other travelers and was often described. The ever-changing arrangements of meadows and trees were considered picturesque, reminding some of landscapes on large English estates. Many also noted that the zone was changing. The subtler underlying climatic controls, involving balances of precipitation and evaporation were, of course, not known to the traders, but the agency of fire in expanding the grasslands northward was often mentioned. By the 1780s the land along the North Saskatchewan was known as the "Fire Country."[3] Fires were often set by man, both accidentally and deliberately, although lightning also was a cause of prairie blazes.

The grasslands were not a zone of great activity for the fur traders despite the several fur posts located on the Qu'Appelle River. Traders did travel south, however, to visit the Mandan Indians on the Missouri River. In the early nineteenth century two forays by Hudson's Bay Company traders up the South Saskatchewan approached the watershed of the Missouri and the American traders' territory, but no permanent bases were established. From the time of Kelsey the grasslands had been called

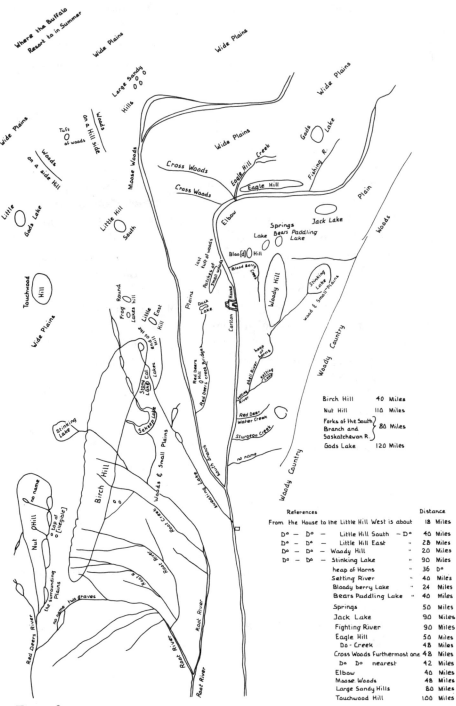

Figure 6-2.

Red River carts stopped at the elbow of the North Saskatchewan River, September 1871. Metropolitan Toronto Library Board.

"barrens," just as had the tundra northwest of Churchill. "Barren" likely meant bare of trees, although the term also implied a lack of resources and cast doubts on the potential for agriculture. Yet the plains were anything but a wasteland to the traders, who depended upon the abundant bison for food. Other terms less ambiguous than "barrens," such as "prairies," "meadows," and "plains," were also used by the traders to designate the grasslands. In the early nineteenth century there were indications that some traders considered the southern plains not nearly so fertile as those on the North Saskatchewan[4]—a hint at future evaluations of scientific explorers. Clearly, however, it was not a region known at first hand to the traders. By and large they left it to the Indians and mixed-bloods, knowing that these inhabitants would come to them at their posts on the edges of the plains to trade.

By contrast, the traders had a direct knowledge of the forested land between Hudson Bay, Lake Superior, Lake Winnipeg, and the Saskatche-

Fig. 6-2. Carlton District About 1815
Redrawn by Hania Guzewska, York University, from Map G. 1/27, Hudson's Bay Company Archives, and printed by permission of the Hudson's Bay Company.

wan River. Few of their reports described the landscape apart from mentioning kinds of trees, enumerating rivers and streams, or commenting on the permanently frozen ground near Hudson Bay. Generalizations were difficult to make, although the explorer Alexander Mackenzie did suggest that Lake Winnipeg was at the boundary between what we designate today as the sedimentary rocks of the plains and the crystalline rocks of the Shield. Most traders said little about the details of the forest landscape, but the rare perspicacious observer did exist, such as the trader who reported on the country east of Lake Winnipeg. Commenting on the special qualities of the terrain, he used words that seem to describe muskeg:

> Those places where from the wetness of the soil the trees are of dwarfish or stunted growth, are called swamps, a definition which includes large tracts of ground baring [sic] few perhaps of the characters comprehended under that term in England. Much of this kind of ground has so little of a swampy nature, that it may be traversed with perfect safety at any time of the year & even frequently without getting wet: besides the stunted trees already mentioned it produces vast quantities of moss, covering the ground in some places [what follows is illegible] to two or three feet in depth.[5]

The same man alluded to the ancient lake deposits of glacial Lake Agassiz eight years before the American scientific observer W. H. Keating made similar observations in the Red River plain:

> About Berens River the soil is a whitish argillaceous earth containing a considerable quantity of sand in a state of intimate division, with only a very small portion of vegetable matter. It also contains lime but no considerable quantities. As it very much resembles the mud at present deposited at the bottom of the Lake [Winnipeg], it is probably a deposition from the waters, made during an inundation, or when the level of the lake was permanently different from what it is at present.[6]

In the early nineteenth century when the first agricultural colony was established in the region, resource appraisals varied widely. The Indians kept gardens on the Missouri, the lower Red River, and elsewhere; and the traders usually had kitchen gardens at their posts, but such cultivation made at best only a tiny contribution to the total food requirements of the area's inhabitants. Lord Selkirk thought it possible to sustain an agricultural colony on the prairies of the Red River and demonstrated his faith by establishing there a settlement called the Red River colony

(Assiniboia) to exist in association with the fur trade. The colony proved that cropping and livestock raising were possible at Red River; nevertheless, their experiments did not indicate whether farming was possible in the more arid country to the west.

Meanwhile nomadic mixed bloods spanned forest, parkland, and plains in their activities. Some were based at the fur posts, others at Red River, and in time a number even wintered in the poplar bluffs and wooded valleys of the plains—mainly living off the buffalo, but also fishing and trapping. They demonstrated that with appropriate techniques, the whole interior—whether grassland or forest—could be utilized by man.

Many outsiders had formed still other views of the resources based upon perceptions imported from other parts of the mid-continent. Among the first to make comparisons were well-informed fur traders such as Peter Pond, Alexander Henry the Elder, Alexander Mackenzie, and David Thompson, each of whom had remarked that the plains extended all the way to the Gulf of Mexico. After the expeditions of American explorers Zebulon Pike and Stephen H. Long early in the nineteenth century, large portions of the interior American plains were called "The Great American Desert." The inhabitants of Rupert's Land, whether Indians, Métis, or the colonists at Red River, did not think of the British North American Plains as a desert, but in the late 1850s expeditions from Great Britain and Canada led by Captain John Palliser and Professor H. Y. Hind in association with others were sent out to make reconnaissance resource surveys of the interior. One result of their investigations was that the drier plains of the South Saskatchewan River were designated an extension of the Great American Desert (see Fig. 6-3). These explorers also identified the parkland as a rich area for farming, Hind naming it the "Fertile Belt" (see Fig. 6-3). The local inhabitants were well aware of the differences between the regions on which these images of good and bad land were based, but they had a much wider view of the drier grasslands of the southern plains than of its potential for agriculture alone. There they trapped animals for furs and hunted buffalo for provisions and skins; the area was no desert to them.

Even during the day of the fur trade, the distribution of animals was affected drastically by the onslaught of man in both woodlands and grasslands. Fur-bearing animals such as beaver, marten, fox, and muskrat were so reduced in many districts that trading had to be abandoned until the areas had been nursed back to production. Larger animals such as moose and deer were also depleted; in many districts they were almost

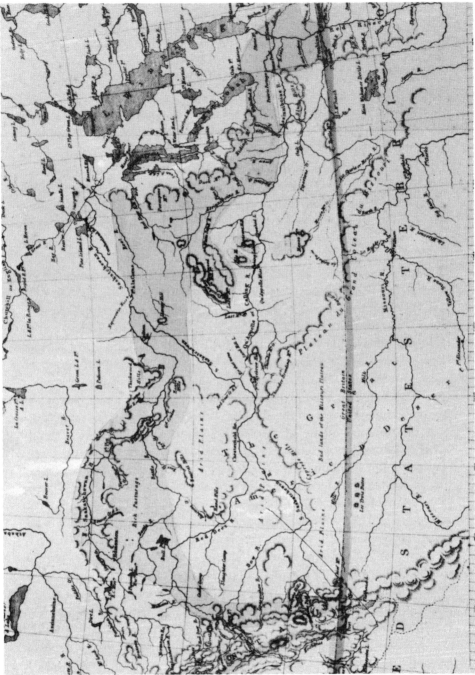

Figure 6-3.

eliminated. On the grasslands the buffalo herds survived the fur trade only to fall prey to the hunters; in the early nineteenth century huge herds roamed as far north as Lake Manitoba and beyond the North Saskatchewan River. By the 1820s the retreat was under way; and by the 1860s the herds were staying well south of Edmonton, not moving much north or east of Turtle Mountain. In the 1870s and early 1880s the free-roving herds were eliminated from the Great Plains, making way for a new civilization that viewed the land in a very different way and tackled it with very different techniques. When change came in the 1870s it was explosive, creating an entirely new geographic structure.

The people

THE INDIANS

In the interior the tribes of three language groups met and fought for territory; Algonkian-speaking Cree and Ojibwa from the northeastern forests, Siouan-speaking Assiniboine from the Great Lakes area, and Athapaska-speaking Indians (such as the Chipewyan and Beaver) who may have come from the east just ahead of the Algonkian-speaking tribes (see Fig. 6-4). On the plains lived the Blackfoot groups, also of Algonkian speech. Traders, in order to communicate effectively with the Indian inhabitants, had to know one or more of the Algonkian and Athapaskan dialects.

In historic times there was a general movement of Indians into the interior, especially from the eastern forests into the parklands and grass-lands. The Indian sense of territoriality was not so strong as that of the Europeans, and territory was not so effectively defended. On the plains, tribes claimed large areas as home territories, although bands moved far beyond these areas to follow buffalo or to go trading or raiding. The strength of warriors established the right to an area, and weaker groups hesitated to hunt where strong opposing parties were likely to be camped. Among the woodlands tribes, territorial claims were slightly stronger. Bands had a fairly firm right to their hunting grounds, although members of other bands could hunt on those grounds as long as they did

Fig. 6-3. "The Fertile Belt" According to H. Y. Hind (shaded area)
From H. Y. Hind, "Report of Progress Together with a Preliminary and General Report, on the Assiniboine and Saskatchewan Exploring Expeditions," London, 1860.

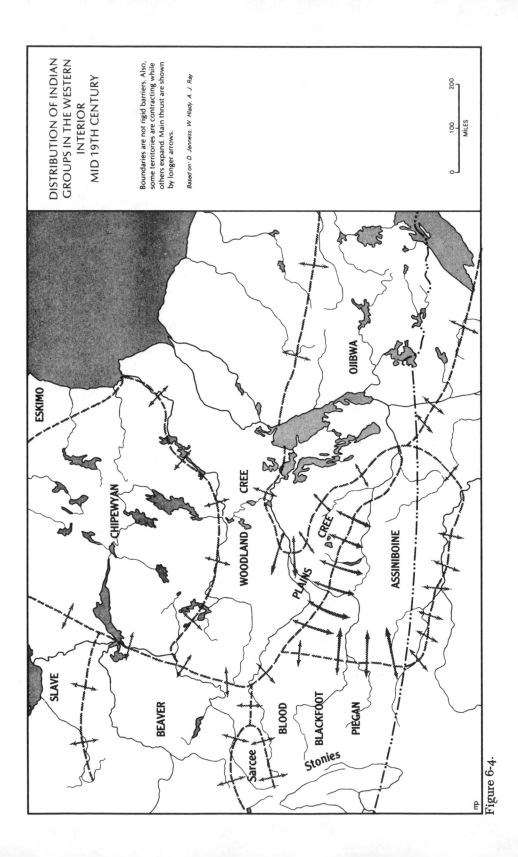

DISTRIBUTION OF INDIAN
GROUPS IN THE WESTERN
INTERIOR
MID 19TH CENTURY

Boundaries are not rigid barriers. Also,
some territories are contracting while
others expand. Main thrust are shown
by longer arrows.

Based on: D. Jenness, W. Hlady, A. J. Ray

0   100   200
         MILES

ESKIMO

CHIPEWYAN

SLAVE

BEAVER

WOODLAND

CREE

Sarcee

BLOOD

BLACKFOOT

PIEGAN

Stonies

PLAINS

CREE

ASSINIBOINE

OJIBWA

Figure 6-4.

not stay too long or kill out the fur-bearing animals. The woodlands Indians also respected cultivated plots and maple sugar groves.[7]

Tribes were constantly shifting. As in all migrations, both propelling and attracting forces were at work: the push of aggressive tribes, the lure of better hunting grounds, the possibility of taking over an attractive area where the inhabitants had been weakened by disease. Shifts within the woodlands or the plains required no cultural adaptation, but if movements were from one area to the other, the adjustments to be made were considerable. Accommodations to new environments were made during the time that the tribes spanned the parklands and adjacent areas; there they spent part of the year in the woods trapping and part on the plains hunting buffalo, gaining the advantages of both areas.

The most significant population shifts occurred in the nineteenth century. Large numbers of woodlands Indians in particular moved westward, away from the depleted eastern hunting grounds. The missions in the Red River colony and the mission stations established after 1840 also affected population patterns; many Indians gravitated toward them in search of a more stable life. The missions in existence in 1856 are shown in Figure 6-5. Traders were antagonistic to them, thinking they would lower fur production.

It is difficult to estimate the size of native populations because comprehensive accurate records were not kept by the Hudson's Bay Company. In any event, numbers in any given area were subject to sharp changes due to disease, warfare, and migration. The population carrying capacity of the woodlands was low. Estimates by George Simpson (governor of Rupert's Land), Hind, and Palliser suggest that in the 1850s only about 18,000 Indians lived there. Normally there was abundant food on plains, supporting larger concentrations of Indians; yet taking into account the size of the area, total numbers also seem low. Estimates vary widely: one placed the numbers at 23,000 plains Indians in 1843; another at about 20,000 in the 1850s.[8] Limiting numbers more than poor nutrition, however, were warfare and disease. In 1825 it was stated that more than 400 Indians had been killed in native battles in the previous year.[9] Diseases such as smallpox and measles could and did wipe out entire bands of Indians in a few months. Figure 6-6 attempts to show the relative location of the population of the Interior, but the distribution is based on limited evidence. Other than the population at Red River and near Edmonton most of the people were Indians.

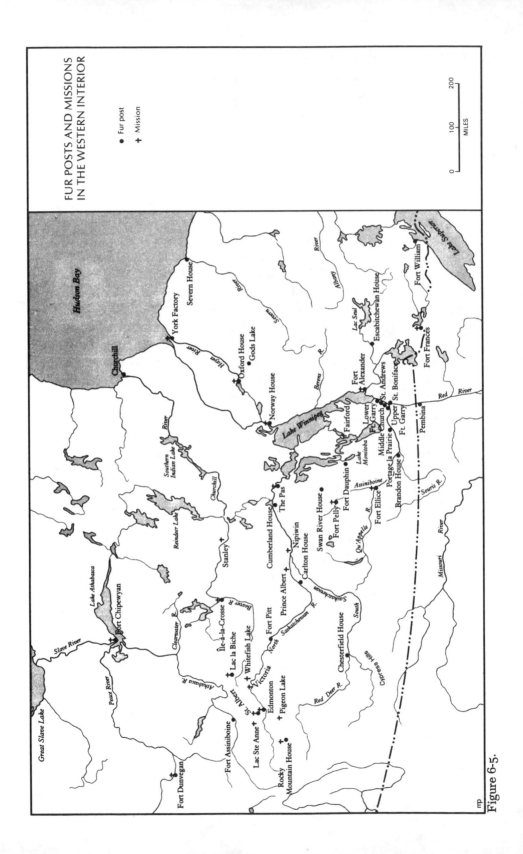

FUR POSTS AND MISSIONS
IN THE WESTERN INTERIOR

● Fur post
✝ Mission

0   100   200
MILES

Figure 6-5.

THE FUR TRADERS

The fur traders imposed a robber economy on the region, with both animal and human resources relentlessly exploited by the Northwest and the Hudson's Bay Company men for their own ends. Relatively few men were required to conduct trade with the Indians, who did the actual trapping, and to convey the pelts to markets thousands of miles away.

In the early nineteenth century the Northwest Company employed approximately 2000 men west of Lake Superior. Most of the controlling partners were of English or Scottish origin, from Britain or the old British colonial areas of North America, lineal descendants of the men who had taken over the fur trade from the French after the Conquest. The proprietors did not put roots down in the interior; on retiring they returned to their homelands. Yet by far the greater proportion of the personnel engaged in carrying goods and furs and working at the posts were of Canadien (French Canadian) ancestry. If they survived the hard and often dangerous life, they, like the proprietors, might eventually return to the shore of the St. Lawrence where they had been recruited.

After the Hudson's Bay Company absorbed the Nor'Westers in 1821, the total number of men engaged in the fur trade was from 2000 to 3000. In 1857 Governor Simpson reported 16 chief factors, 29 chief traders, 5 surgeons, 87 clerks, 67 post masters, 1200 regular servants, and about 500 tripmen and others hired for short-term tasks.[10] Scotland, especially the Orkney Islands, was a major recruiting ground for prospective employees. Often in their mid-teens, the young men signed on as servants, but it was possible to advance: some even became factors in charge of several posts, sharing in a very limited way the profits of the Company.

The men were stationed at posts throughout the Northwest where furs were abundant or at important transfer points (see Fig. 6-5). Edmonton, one of the most strategic posts, in 1862 was staffed by fifty men, five of whom were officers. In the same year there were twenty-seven (three officers) at Carlton, and six (one officer) at Lac la Biche, a lesser post.[11]

During the seventeenth century most of the Hudson's Bay Company traders retired to Britain, but by the early 1800s a few men who had married Indian women expressed a desire for a settlement where they could live in retirement with their families. The Red River colony served this purpose once it was established. Thus traders originally

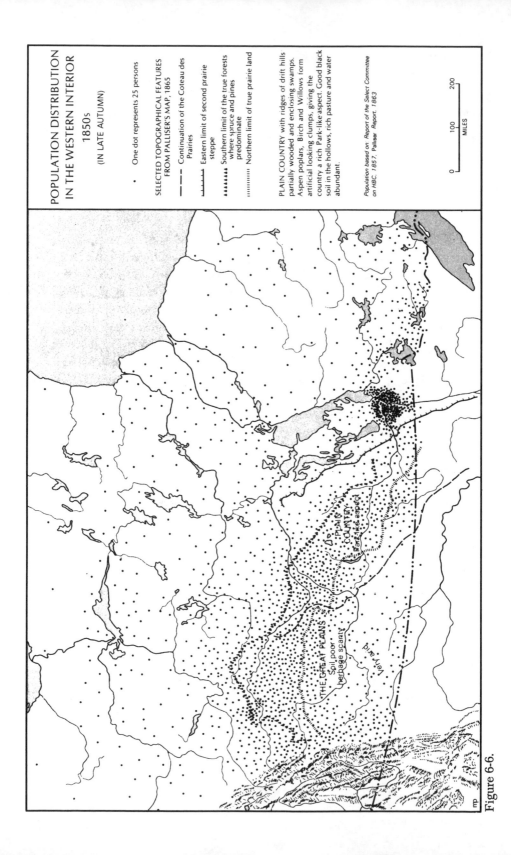

POPULATION DISTRIBUTION
IN THE WESTERN INTERIOR
1850s
(IN LATE AUTUMN)

• One dot represents 25 persons

SELECTED TOPOGRAPHICAL FEATURES
FROM PALLISER'S MAP, 1865

— — — Continuation of the Coteau des
Prairies

┴┴┴┴ Eastern limit of second prairie
steppe

▲▲▲▲▲ Southern limit of the true forests
where spruce and pines
predominate

············ Northern limit of true prairie land

PLAIN COUNTRY with ridges of drift hills
partially wooded and enclosing swamps.
Aspen poplars, Birch and Willows form
artificial looking clumps, giving the
country a rich Park-like aspect. Good black
soil in the hollows, rich pasture and water
abundant.

Population based on: Report of the Select Committee
on HBC, 1857. Palliser Report, 1863

```
0          100          200
└──────────┴──────────┘
        MILES
```

rp

Figure 6-6.

from Europe finally began to establish homes in the land where they had spent their working lives, and slowly a sense of commitment to the country began to take root among these people and their descendants.

THE RED RIVER COLONY, MÉTIS, AND MIGRATIONS

A major new element in the geography of the interior was the agricultural settlement at Red River. Founding a colony in the interior at this time was an extremely risky venture, and only the vision, will, and large fortune of one man, the Earl of Selkirk, made the Red River colony possible. Selkirk had sponsored two settlements early in the century, one in Prince Edward Island and another in Upper Canada. He envisioned a third in Rupert's Land, and to achieve this purpose acquired a substantial interest in the Hudson's Bay Company. Once the main reason for establishing a colony is accepted, other purposes can be discerned which lend substance to the enterprise. The Company needed an agricultural provisioning base and a place where servants could retire. A local labor force could be gradually built up. In fact even before Lord Selkirk came forward with his scheme, the Company's directors had given thought to setting aside a tract of land either on the Saskatchewan River or on the Red River for a colony of its own.

It is all very well for a starry-eyed philanthropist to propose transporting people into the wilderness, but what motivates the people themselves? Many of Lord Selkirk's colonists were from Scotland and Ireland. Poverty and the promise of land where they could become independent farmers likely drove them to this hazardous adventure. Even so, recruiting settlers was no easy task in Britain, especially given the opposition of the Nor'Westers, who campaigned strongly against the colony. As a result Selkirk's agents were forced to recruit in Switzerland as well.

In the first three years of colonization (1812–15) about 280 settlers arrived from Scotland and Ireland via York Factory, including more than eighty from Kildonan parish in Sutherland County, Scotland. The first Swiss came in 1816; most of them had been members of a disbanded regiment engaged by Lord Selkirk for the struggle against the Nor' Westers. Two years later about forty French Canadians arrived from Montréal by the Great Lakes route; in 1821, in the last and largest overseas migration 170 Swiss were brought out via Hudson Bay. Thus the first colonization of the interior lasted less than a decade.

In the 1830s thirteen English families arrived to work on a Company farm, and in 1848 and 1850 a number of British army pensioneers brought over with their families to help defend the colony stayed to settle. The two groups added about 200 people to the colony. Until the 1870s when the Canadian government began to bring in immigrants there were no more significant migrations directly from Europe.

By the mid-1820s many of the early migrants had left Red River for Upper Canada or the United States. They left for many reasons: isolation, intimidation by the Nor'Westers, natural hazards such as grasshoppers and floods. The Hudson's Bay Company actually encouraged many to leave when it became apparent that they were not suited for pioneering. By 1826 the continental Europeans had all departed, leaving Scottish Highlanders as the dominant colonists from overseas.

From within the region came a significant addition of people as former officers and servants of the fur trade retired to the colony: Orcadians (Orkneymen), other Scots, Englishmen, French Canadians, and mixed-bloods. In 1822 there were 1281 people in Assiniboia; in 1832, 2751; in 1856, 6691; and in 1871, 11,963 (see Fig. 6-6).[12] As the original colonists died, the population became increasingly composed of mixed-bloods, especially since there was no large European immigration from the outside. Of Red River's total population in 1871, 5754 were of French mixed-blood descent and 4083 of British mixed-blood origin.[13]

The French mixed-bloods became a separate cultural group, the Métis. The creation of this small indigenous society—a group that was to have a profound impact on the development of Canada—is unique in Canadian history. They had attained an early separate identity while associated with the Northwest Company, and by the time of the union between the two companies had become a distinctive group. They were Catholic and French speaking, and although most of them made their home base at Red River or at posts and missions in the parkland, they preserved a mobility characteristic of the Indians—represented in its extreme form by the *hivernants*, Métis who wintered on the plains. A distinctive ethos emerged, and once the Métis developed their own leaders, they were a redoubtable group with a sense of purpose and direction, truly a "New Nation" neither Indian nor European.

The mixed-bloods of British descent were generally not a strong element of the Métis "nation," although Cuthbert Grant, who became the first Métis leader, was a striking exception. The Scots mixed-bloods were identifiable at Red River and at settlements such as the Anglican mission at Prince Albert on the Saskatchewan and Methodist mission stations at Victoria and Whitefish Lake, but they were not a recognizable action group as were the Métis. They tended to blend in with the Métis and the Scots and even with their Indian relatives, never forming a separate society.

In 1857 Governor Simpson estimated that about 8000 mixed-bloods lived east of the Rockies, approximately 5000 in Assiniboia, and the rest at scattered locations throughout the interior.[14] Some had settled at Catholic mission stations such as Lac Ste-Anne, Lac la Biche, and St. Albert (see Fig. 6-5). St. Albert had a population of 700 Métis in 1870; the other two about 3000 each. The English-speaking Protestant mixed-blood communities at Prince Albert, Victoria, and Whitefish Lake were smaller, with perhaps 150 people each in 1870 (see Fig. 6-5). In the 1860s there was a migration to the plains and parklands from Red River, and by 1870 probably 4000 mixed-bloods lived between the colony and the Rockies.

Other migrations occurred closer to Red River, movements by people whose main interest was agriculture. In 1861, under the leadership of the Reverend William Cochran, a settlement at Portage la Prairie was founded by farmers from Middle Church who could no longer find satisfactory land on which to expand. A few score Canadians arrived there in the 1860s, and by 1870 almost 1000 people lived in the Portage la Prairie area.

Migrations in and out of the region continued as well. In the 1840s and 1850s the Hudson's Bay Company sponsored two notable migrations totaling more than 200 settlers from Red River to the Oregon Country in an effort to hold that territory against the Americans. During the same period many people moved to the United States as a result of a growing trade with Saint Paul. In their turn a number of Americans came to Red River as the American frontier settlement expanded into Minnesota. Eventually people began to view the plains as a possible area for agricultural development, and in the late 1850s a small number of Canadian fortune seekers made their way to Red River, followed by a few farmers in the 1860s who took up land near Portage la Prairie. The 1870 census of Assiniboia recorded that 118 people were born in Ontario, 111 in Québec, and 166 in the United States.

The colony at Red River, however, was not founded in an auspicious period for migration to the interior. Agricultural development had to mark time until railways were built and competitive free lands elsewhere were filled. Only then did large numbers of immigrants enter the plains.

The Indians and the fur trade

INDIAN LIFE

By the nineteenth century, Indian life had already been drastically affected by association with European traders; many aspects of that life, however, continued essentially unmodified since they did not conflict with the European's desires to exploit the Indians as fur trappers.

The Indians of the forest zone included the woodlands Cree, the Ojibwa, the Chipewyan, the Beaver, and the Rocky Mountain Stonies (see Fig. 6-4). They lived in small groups of two to three families in order to hunt more effectively but still maintained close links with the rest of the band. When times were good, a group might consist of as many as ten families; when food was scarce, some groups were reduced to a single family. Moose, deer, caribou, bear, and small game and fish provided subsistence. Rarely would a group stay longer than two weeks in any place except in summer: they were restless, always moving on in search of better hunting grounds.

A hunter family of Cree Indians at York Fort about 1821. Watercolor by Peter Rindisbacher. The Public Archives of Canada.

Life was even more difficult in the barrens. Before the Europeans came, the Chipewyans had lived south of the Churchill River, but the Cree, armed with guns supplied by the fur traders, had driven the Chipewyans toward the tundra. There they lived on deer, caribou, and fowl. Travel was difficult: they were forced to pack their possessions over the terrain because birch bark large enough for making canoes simply was not available.

The grassland was the home of the plains Cree, the Assiniboine, and the Blackfoot with their federated tribes, the Blood, Piegan, and Sarcees (see Fig. 6-4). By the mid-eighteenth century the Blackfoot had horses; within a few decades their use was widespread in both hunting and warfare. The plains Indians traveled long distances to trade. In 1826, for instance, the Cree of the Carlton area traded with Americans at the Mandan villages,[15] 500 miles distant. Canoes were not used; when camp was moved most of the effects were carried on the *travois*, a carrying device made from two poles with cross pieces. Women, dogs, or horses pulled it with the pole-ends dragging along the ground. The relative abundance of bison made it possible to support large camps, and a stronger sense of tribal unity evolved among the plains Indians than did among the woodlands groups. It was acknowledged that the chiefs' primary leadership role was to lead tribes in war: in contrast to life in woodland areas, conflicts on the plains were frequent.

Shelters were extremely simple. The woodlands Indians fashioned oblong and round wigwams of birch bark and skins. Some of the oblong structures measured 14 × 30 feet and could hold four or five families. On the plains the Indians built conical tipis of buffalo hides, in which they lived both winter and summer. Usually twelve to twenty skins were used for one tipi, but the Blackfoot sometimes used forty or fifty skins. All these shelters—wigwams and tipis—were portable. Techniques of construction were occasionally transferred from one group to another; for example, Peter Fidler reported seeing in 1820 an Indian house built in the European manner; and the Ojibwa, moving from the woodland of Lac la Pluie to Red River, ultimately adopted the skins tents of the Cree, although for a time they also retained birch-bark shelters.[16]

"COMPANY" INDIANS

Once contact was made with Europeans, the Indians began to barter pelts for goods such as guns, blankets, knives, and metalware, which soon became essential to their existence. Not all Indians hunted fur-bearing animals. The Cree, for instance, who controlled the waterways between Hudson Bay and the plains, at first acted as middlemen, bartering with more distant tribes for furs and carrying them to tidewater. This self-assumed role was eliminated once Hudson's Bay Company posts were established in the interior, beginning in the 1770s, although some exchange of furs between Indians continued.

The dependence of woodlands Indians on trade goods turned them, with few exceptions, into "Company" Indians, free in day-to-day activities but constrained in the long run to secure pelts for the Hudson's Bay Company. In most places a wary but workable symbiotic relationship existed between Indians and traders. Because in the fall many Indians arrived at the posts virtually naked, they were given a "debt" (credit) toward the furs they were to bring in during the winter. In 1825 a basic allowance at Lac la Pluie consisted of a coat, blanket, leggings, cap, ax, file, spear, ammunition, and sometimes a gun.[17] Debts were calculated in the equivalent of beaver skins, called "Made Beaver" (MB). Tariffs varied through the years. In 1823 Lieutenant John Franklin reported that one knife cost 1 MB; a fowling piece, 15 MB. In 1826–27 eight musquash (muskrats) were worth 1 MB in the Winnipeg District, and a three-point blanket, 6 MB; that is, forty-eight muskrat skins.[18] The debt system attached Indians to particular posts. Before the union of the fur companies in 1821, each company tried to induce the Indians to hunt exclusively for it, and credit was given much more freely than in later years. Also each company employed runners to urge the Indians on in their work and to ensure that the furs were delivered to the right post.

Hunters varied greatly in their skills, and the kill varied enormously from season to season, depending on how prolific the animals were. Each woodlands post kept a careful record of the hunting accomplishments of the Indians attached to it, and on this basis "debt" was given. It appears that most of the pelts were brought in by a few good men; at Indian Lake in 1818–19 the better hunters brought in thirty-five and forty-five beaver skins and the best hunter brought in fifty-eight.[19] Hunting territories varied in size; in some districts the Indian hunters would go no farther than four days' travel from a post.

The plains Indians were neither part of the loosely controlled trading system described above nor were they attached to particular establishments by the debt system. They arrived at the posts in such large numbers that identification of individual hunters was impossible. Fur resources on the plains were restricted and spatially concentrated, most fur-bearing animals being found only in the woodlands along the larger rivers, the slopes of the Rockies, and on higher features of the terrain, such as the Cypress Hills. Furthermore, the large Indian bands concentrated far too much killing power over limited areas and rapidly depleted the animal resources. This did not matter at first in hunting buffalo because the herds were so large. Thus instead of a source of furs, the grasslands became a provisioning base for the traders: Indians supplied "prairie produce"—dried meat, fat and pemmican, besides buffalo robes and hides, and wolf and fox skins. The Indians were well aware of the value of the provisioning trade and tried to monopolize it, even allegedly driving the buffalo away from the vicinity of the posts in order to retain control of the provisions. Production of provisions fluctuated. If the winter was mild the buffalo stayed out on the plains and the Indians drifted with them. Occasionally grassland fires drove buffalo so far out on the plains that it was impossible to supply the posts efficiently, and seasons of deep snow hampered horse travel so much that the Indians were unable to reach the posts at all. At times, when the buffalo herds could not be located, the Indians literally starved to death. The occurrence of such tragedies on the grasslands serves to remind us that it has always been a difficult country to exploit, demanding foresight and discretion from its inhabitants.

CONSERVATION AND FOOD SUPPLY

Conserving fur-bearing animals, particularly beaver, became a problem early in the nineteenth century. In some areas disease had killed many beaver in 1795, 1805, and 1812, and this combined with ruthless exploitation, caused disaster in those areas. Conserving beaver thus became a matter of the highest importance to the Hudson's Bay Company. In the 1820s it began to nurse depleted districts into higher productivity and in the 1840s established firm regulations to enforce the conservation of beaver in designated areas. Traders were directed to barter fewer pelts in the hope that Indians would stop killing the animals. In some districts Indians began to see the need for conservation and left a few animals for breeding in every beaver lodge they demolished. Yet neighboring bands often took advantage of this, raiding beaver that had deliberately been spared. Many Indians simply could not practise conservation because they had debts to pay or, more important, because they needed food. Indeed, the worst food shortages were in the very districts where the beaver most needed protection. One factor, located in an area with only one tribe, actually purchased the safety of the beaver lodges by giving "debt" to the Indians for leaving them alone. He also intended to grow more food in his garden for the tribe's families so that they would not have to kill beaver for provisions.[20] In some districts pressure on beaver resources was reduced when the Indians voluntarily moved out to allow the animal population to recover. Once the district was rejuvenated the Indians could return.

It is to the credit of the Hudson's Bay Company that it did not regard conservation merely a matter of abandoning the posts in a depleted area but that it generally tried to manage a district back into productivity. The traders had established close relationships with the Indians and often felt a responsibility to remain in an area and to revive it as a whole—beaver, game animals, and Indian occupants. One can be cynical and say that in the long run this was in the Company's best interest—and this is true—but a more humane purpose frequently shines through the traders' reports. Many of these men had a genuine concern for the welfare of the Indians and earnestly desired to help them in what often was a miserable existence.

A continuing problem was how the Indian hunters were to obtain food for themselves and their families while trapping animals for pelts. Provisions had to be obtained on the side, and this was often incompatible with efficient production of furs. In the nineteenth century this problem was most acute in the area from Lake Superior to Reindeer Lake where moose and deer—the basic sources of food—had been practically exterminated. Even beaver were sometimes killed for food; the Indians' reply to any protests was "feed us & it shall not take place."[21] The Company urged them to hunt marten, but they were reluctant to do so because the animal supplied little meat for the effort. At Fort William lack of food often forced the Indian to stay at the post during the winter —the very season when they should have been out hunting.[22] Wild rice was available at Lac la Pluie, but elsewhere Indians often had to fish for subsistence, which left them little time to hunt or trap. In the Saskatchewan District they were occasionally forced to leave the trapping districts in the woodlands and to head for the plains in search of food. The Company was aware of this and in 1822 established outposts in the woods to prevent the Indians from deserting productive areas in winter, but to little avail.[23] As early as 1815 such difficulties led the chief factor at York Factory to suggest that Indians should be settled at lakes and gardens started so that the hunters would be free to pitch about for furs, no longer wasting time hunting animals for meat.[24] In many districts, Indians were becoming increasingly dependent on the fur posts for food during the winter; by the 1860s even posts in the once buffalo-rich parkland were supplying food to them.

Persistent shortages of food and a wish to establish a more reliable source of supplies induced a few Indians to try cultivating gardens. Tiny plots of corn and potatoes were planted at Netley Creek near the Red River delta, and starting in 1805 corn grown on Plantation Island in Lake of the Woods was sold to traders during and after the period of competition between the Nor'Westers and the Hudson's Bay Company. William Brown, a Hudson's Bay Company trader, reported in 1820 that he had seen an Indian garden cultivated in common on an island at the north end of Lake Manitoba,[25] and Peter Fidler noted in 1821 that other groups had gardens on Whitemud River near the south shore of the lake.[26] The Indians in these districts were probably influenced in their endeavors by contacts with the Mandan on the Missouri River and the fur traders. Corn seed was traded among the Indian groups, but potato seeds likely were obtained from the traders.

Indians in the exhausted area east of Lake Winnipeg started gardens to augment their dwindling food supplies in the early nineteenth century. The master at Fort Alexander reported in 1823 that he had distributed seeds and hoes among the local Indians and had tried to teach them how to cultivate.[27] Other post masters had done the same. At Escabitchewan the Indians successfully grew corn, beans, and potatoes for some years before 1816; in 1827 they were clearing land at Lac Seul.[28] On occasion Indian gardens in the Lac la Pluie area provided food for the traders; elsewhere they provided the seeds for the traders' gardens. In sum, however, little of permanent value was achieved.

Early Indian gardening was concentrated in districts where big game was scarce, but in later years agriculture was introduced to mission stations at Norway house and on the Qu'Appelle, Saskatchewan, and Churchill rivers. In the 1860s, for instance, a missionary started a farm on the Qu'Appelle River at the request of Indians who were short of food in the once-productive buffalo country.[29] But generally the missionaries had no greater success in establishing sustained agriculture among the Indians than had the fur traders.

IMPACT OF EUROPEANS ON THE INDIANS

Some aspects of the lives of the Indians were drastically modified by the Europeans. The woodlands Indians were tied much more closely to the posts than were the plains Indians, but the need of the latter for guns, powder, and shot induced them to trade at the fur posts as well. Traffic in guns with the plains Indians was a mixed blessing: the weapons were of little use in the buffalo hunt (spears and bows and arrows had long been more efficient); on the other hand, guns enabled the warriors to form strong fighting groups—a force that the traders could not possibly control. It is fortunate that no general holocaust ever engulfed the British North American plains.

There was constant tension at Edmonton, Fort Pitt, and Carlton over the possibility of attack; and several bad encounters—even killings of Europeans—took place close to these parkland posts. But the blind clash of different peoples and civilizations bent on mutual annihilation—as happened so often in the United States—was avoided. We can only guess at some of the reasons. The continued presence of a long-established commercial firm that traded methodically and fairly must have had a considerable stabilizing effect on the Indians. The Hudson's Bay Company maintained sizable garrisons in the parkland posts but always were aware of the need to use caution in dealing with the plains tribes. Disease and internecine warfare also diminished the Indians' militancy. Further, as Irene Spry and E. J. Dosman have suggested, the Métis, "mediating between the aborigines and the first settlers, constituted a bridge across the 'gulf of ignorance, misunderstanding, fear, and clashing interest that created the havoc of Indian Wars south of the border'."

Before the union of the fur companies, liquor was freely used everywhere, debauching Indians in what quickly became a tragic and destructive human environment. After 1821 the Hudson's Bay Company largely prohibited the use of liquor, permitting trading only at posts where the Company faced competition from free traders and American rivals. At Lac la Pluie, however, the Indians effected an early trading boycott by refusing to supply vital rice without receiving liquor in payment; in that instance the Company lifted its restrictions. In mid-century it was clearly the free traders and not the Company that fostered the liquor traffic.

Various solutions for helping the Indians achieve a more stable existence were proposed in the 1850s by members of exploring expeditions from Canada and Great Britain. H. Y. Hind advocated more mission work—especially the introduction of mission schools—in the hope that education would lead to the adoption of agriculture and shift the Indians away from their hunting economy. Dr. James Hector of Palliser's party, impatient of inadequate missionary efforts, suggested that only massive support from the government in helping the Indians to adjust to advancing civilization would avert an annihilating war or their genocidal elimination. This might or might not have worked, but one part of his plan was sound: that Indians should be seen as citizens with rights and privileges, not as captives to be exploited and then left to fend for themselves. A century after the end of our period of study the problem remains unsolved.

Fur trade operations

COLLECTING FURS

After 1821 the mode of the fur trade varied little for half a century. The Hudson's Bay Company was divided into two large administrative units, the Northern Department and the Southern Department. The Northern Department, which was supervised by Governor George Simpson from 1821 to 1860, covered the western interior and was divided into the districts shown in Figure 6-7, each under a chief factor or a trader. Administrative arrangements were very simple. Each June, frequently at Norway House, Simpson met with the chief factors of the Department to lay plans for the following year. The number of men assigned to each post, routes to be followed, wages to be paid, whom to advance and whom to retire, posts to be opened and those to be closed were all decided at these meetings.

The location of posts was determined by the productivity of the fur-producing districts and the need to face competitors. Many of the older districts, such as the country between Lake Superior and Reindeer Lake had been badly depleted by the nineteenth century. Conservation measures were not always successful, and starting in the late eighteenth century the search for virgin territory began with the traders moving north and west into the Athabaska country, the Mackenzie District, and the Pacific slope.

Even while it was expanding the territory of its operations, the Hudson's Bay Company had to face increasing competition. By purchasing

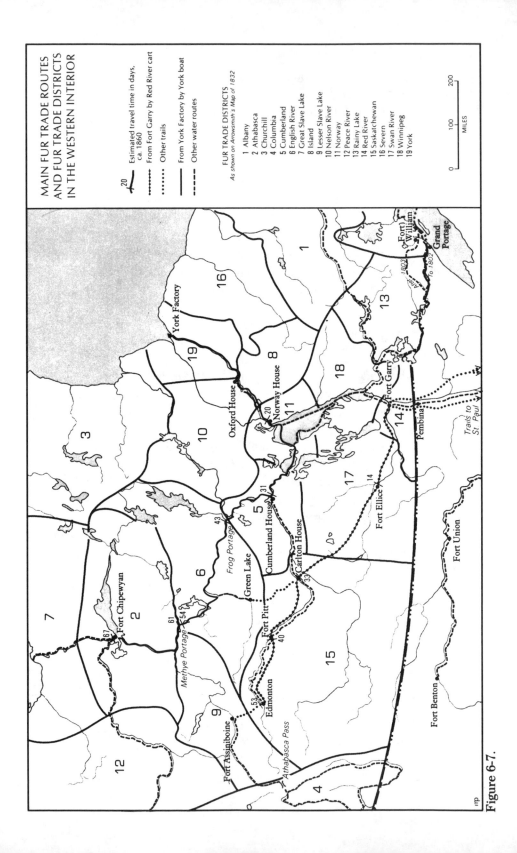

MAIN FUR TRADE ROUTES AND FUR TRADE DISTRICTS IN THE WESTERN INTERIOR

20 Estimated travel time in days, ca. 1860

┼┼┼┼ From Fort Garry by Red River cart

∙∙∙∙∙∙ Other trails

——— From York Factory by York boat

– – – Other water routes

FUR TRADE DISTRICTS
As shown on Arrowsmith's Map of 1832

1 Albany
2 Athabasca
3 Churchill
4 Columbia
5 Cumberland
6 English River
7 Great Slave Lake
8 Island
9 Lesser Slave Lake
10 Nelson River
11 Norway
12 Peace River
13 Rainy Lake
14 Red River
15 Saskatchewan
16 Severn
17 Swan River
18 Winnipeg
19 York

MILES

0   100   200

Figure 6-7.

furs from the free traders it was able to control at least part of this competition, but many of the traders and Indians as well disposed of their furs to American companies operating south of the 49th parallel. In 1827–28 Brandon House was reopened especially to help combat the southward flow of furs, and in 1831 Fort Ellice was established to hold the trade of the Assiniboine country. Certain private traders were authorized to trade along the international boundary from Pembina to Turtle Mountain in order to intercept Indians heading south with their furs. It was even hinted that the border area might be deliberately over-trapped (turning it into a non-producing wasteland) but such a plan never materialized, at least not as intentional policy of extermination.[30] But these attempts at controlling free trade met with little success. In 1849 a free trader at Red River was tried for smuggling and pronounced guilty; local opinion, however, would not allow him to be punished. The trade in effect had become free, although the Company nominally retained its monopoly. As free traders became more numerous they gradually expanded their range to the Swan River and Saskatchewan districts, by the 1850s even penetrating the area northwest of Lake Winnipeg as far as Methye Portage. Nevertheless, the Company still had its own preserve: the best pelts came from the distant Athabaska and Mackenzie districts, which required the logistical resources of a large operation to bring them to market.

Most of the fur posts were simple structures consisting of a few log buildings for housing and storage space for food and furs. If there was danger of Indian attack or if the post was to exist for a number of years, it was enclosed by a stockade. Carlton House (see Fig. 6-8) shows some of these features. The main factor considered in selecting a site was the potential productivity of the district but beyond that, accessibility to a river or lake, availability of wood, proximity to a fishery, and a site for a garden were taken into account. Wood was essential: the fuel consumption of one fireplace was about half a cord a day in winter—and each post had several fireplaces. The Qu'Appelle post was even moved two or three times through the years to remain close to sources of firewood.

The size of a post was determined by local trading requirements. The post Peter Fidler built at Dauphin in 1820 to house ten to fifteen men measured 19 × 56 feet and was divided into four parts along the length of the building. The first fifteen feet of space was for the master and his family; then came twelve feet for the kitchen; thirteen for the trading

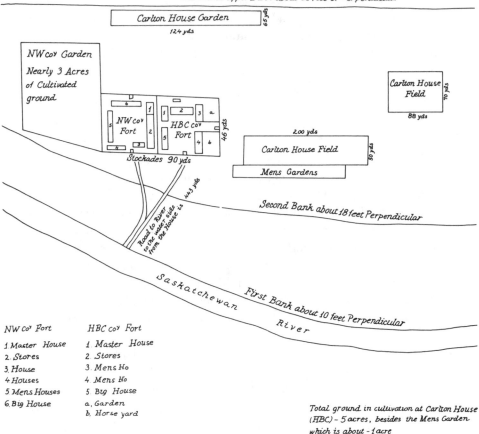

Figure 6-8. Carleton House About 1815
Redrawn by Anna Parker, York University, from Map G. 1/76, Hudson's Bay
Company Archives, and printed by permission of the Hudson's Bay Company.

room and sixteen for the men. Each room was the full width of the
building.[31]

The round of life began in fall. Credit arrangements were made with
the Indians for furs to be brought in, and preparations for the cold
weather were started: firewood was gathered, fish procured, and pemmican processed if it was a southern post. During the winter when the
pace slowed, the traders occasionally visited auxiliary outposts to collect
furs. In spring activity renewed: more pemmican was made, furs were
packed into ninety-pound "pieces," (bundles) for shipping, and canoes
and boats were readied for the summer voyaging. After breakup of ice

on the rivers and lakes, the pieces were transported in canoes or York boats to Norway House and then on to the Bay for shipment overseas.

In 1856, according to Governor Simpson, the exports of furs were the largest to that time. Nearly £237,000 worth of furs from east of the Rocky Mountains were shipped that year; the governor listed some sample returns:[32]

	No. of Skins	Price	Amount
Beaver	52,899	9/-	£23,804/-11/-
Marten	139,154	15/-	£104,356/-10/-
Mink	39,223	9/-	£17,650/- 7/-
Musquash (muskrat)	269,100	6ᵈ	£6727/-10/-
Buffalo Tongue	4629	2/2	£501/- 9/6
Buffalo Robes	18,000	20/-	£18,000/- /-

He stated that returns from west of the mountains were £45,000 on the average, and those from Canada £15,000. By mid-century, beaver, once the staple of the trade, had declined in importance because the demand had dropped but also because beaver had been killed out in many districts. Muskrat production fluctuated wildly from year to year depending on changes in water level in the rivers.

FOOD SUPPLIES FOR THE FUR TRADE

Provisioning the posts was a severe problem. At many locations the supply of large game animals (moose and deer) was not enough to supply a post for an entire year; thus the people found themselves depending largely on fish. Governor Simpson reckoned three-fourths of the food consumed in the Hudson's Bay Company territory was fish.[33] In some areas, however, there were other sources of food. York Factory and Churchill were mainly provisioned by wild fowl such as the Canada goose, of which Dr. John Richardson wrote:

> One goose, which, when fat, weighs about nine pounds, is the daily ration for one of the Company's servants during the season, and is reckoned equivalent to two snow geese, or three ducks, or eight pounds of buffalo and moose meat, or two pounds of pemmican, or a pint of maize and four ounces of suet.[34]

At Lac la Pluie wild rice was the principal item of subsistence; at posts on the edge of buffalo country, hunters brought in fresh buffalo meat.

But even the buffalo was unpredictable, and Edmonton, after experiencing a shortage of provisions, established a fishery to avert such occurrences.

As a whole, scarcity of food was not the main difficulty in provisioning in the interior; rather it was local deficiencies and a lack of adequate transportation links. It was not uncommon to find one area in plenty and a neighboring one starving.

In an attempt to diversify diets and to ensure a more regular food supply many post masters planted gardens. Figure 6-8 shows the gardens at Carlton. The Hudson's Bay Company encouraged agricultural pursuits but provided no constructive long-term planning or assistance; thus this aspect of provisioning remained very haphazard, depending on the initiative of the individual masters.

A few traders thought of agriculture as an important prop for the fur trade. In 1827 the chief factor at God's Lake strongly supported the development of agriculture in his annual district report, suggesting that since game and plains provisions were no longer readily available (the latter due to the hostility of the Indians) that farming should be encouraged.[35] He suggested that extra men be assigned to posts in summer to tend the gardens; further, he argued that the Peace River area might serve as the agricultural provisioning center for the northern posts. Other factors also supported agriculture strongly, suggesting that experienced farmers be assigned to the posts.

Seed could be obtained from the Company, but often it was of such poor quality that it would not germinate; thus the traders brought their own seed or obtained it in trade from the Indians. Usually the traders disclaimed a knowledge of agriculture, but many took good care of their gardens. In the forested zone the soil was so sandy and infertile that at some posts, plots were moved every three or four years. Manuring was common in places where cattle were kept; the presence of cattle at Churchill made gardening possible even though the climate and soil virtually prohibited it. At York Factory the garden was actually planted in night soil.[36] Systematic crop sequences were followed at a few posts; in some instances they were regular enough to be called crop rotations, and one factor attributed not having to manure his plots to his method of rotation.[37]

The acreage in crops varied greatly. The Nor'Westers had operated large farms at Fort William (120 acres) and Lac la Pluie, but the Hudson's Bay Company farms were much smaller, ranging in size from a few square yards to twelve and a half acres at Carlton in 1827 and twenty to thirty acres at Fort William in 1828.[38] The total acreage cultivated at the posts was probably no more than a few hundred acres in any given year. Limitations were imposed by the difficulty of farming and operating a fur post at the same time: in spring before the voyaging began, there would be enough manpower on hand for planting, but in the summer often there would be no one left. If men did stay behind, they usually were too busy fishing, obtaining provisions from the Indians, cutting firewood, or making hay to be able to tend the crops. As a result the gardens were often little more than weed patches. To add to the problem, the Indians wantonly damaged the crops if they were not watched closely.

There were returns of up to 1000 bushels of potatoes and several thousand heads of cabbage—in many places an adequate yearly supply for the post. Fur traders experienced most of the cropping hazards that later were to confront farmers of the interior, ranging from drought and frost to grasshoppers, grubs, and ground squirrels. In the northern posts the short growing season and poor soils were identified as limitations. At places such as Edmonton and Carlton the length of the growing season was generally adequate, but June and August frosts could damage the crops. Even more important, at Carlton early summer droughts had caused crop failures.[39]

Cattle were kept at many posts from Fort William and Churchill to Ile-à-la Crosse and Edmonton, but most of them were of poor quality. Hogs are not often mentioned in the district reports but some were kept at Churchill and other posts. The main food supply still remained fish and meat obtained from the hunt rather than from domestic animals.

Each post had to manage its food supply almost entirely on its own, but provisioning was well organized and coordinated for the tightly scheduled fur brigades. Because the men had no time to live off the country as they traveled they carried with them light, highly concentrated food such as pemmican. Pemmican was usually prepared from buffalo meat: thin strips were dried in the sun or over a slow fire, pounded between two stones into small bits, and thoroughly mixed with melted fat. Berries were occasionally added to improve the flavor. The concoction was then poured into buffalo-hide bags (care was taken to exclude air) to form ninety-pound packages. Eighty to one hundred pounds of dried provisions could be made from one buffalo cow. Some of the far northern posts made pemmican from caribou meat; thus even

the barrens became a minor provisioning base! The area south of the Assiniboine and the North Saskatchewan rivers, however, was the major
reservoir of provisions. The early important provisioning posts were Pembina and Brandon House and, in later years, Forts Ellice, Pelly, Carlton,
Pitt, and Edmonton. Prairie produce became one of the main trading
items of the plains Indians, and in time the Métis competed with them.
Pemmican was prepared and traded in the fall, winter, and early spring
and carried to points on the fur trade routes for distribution to the brigades. Before 1821 the Nor'Westers picked up their supplies at Bas de la
Rivière Winnipeg (later Fort Alexander) and at Cumberland House; in
succeeding years the Hudson's Bay Company men obtained provisions
at Norway House, Cumberland House, and Ile-à-la-Crosse.

Red River produce—corned beef, butter, eggs, ham, flour, and corn—
began to fit into the scheme of supply in the 1830s; for instance, flour was
sent to Norway House whence it was dispatched to western and northern posts or even to York Factory. In this way the colony on the Red
River began to play a role in the geography of supply of the interior.

COMMUNICATIONS

There was continual movement in the interior: the Indians and Métis
wandered everywhere, leaving no part of the region untouched, and
traders moved along the established routes of the fur trade in a steady
stream. Three water passages provided the great corridors to the interior: Lake Superior (the central route), Hudson Bay (the northern
route), and the upper Mississippi and Missouri rivers (the southern
route).

The famous 1500-mile "main line" Lake Superior canoe route used by
the Nor'Westers extended from Montréal to Lake Winnipeg (see Fig.
6-7). After 1821 it was abandoned as a fur route but was still occasionally
used by persons coming from Canada. In the late 1850s Canadians
showed interest in re-establishing connection to Red River by this middle corridor. The British and Canadian scientific exploring expeditions
explored the route in 1857, with S. J. Dawson of the Canadian party
carrying out surveys to determine the feasibility of a road and a railway.
His conclusion was that a combination steamboat and wagon-road route
could be operated from Fort William to Fort Garry; Captain John Palliser, however, recommended against linking Canada with Fort Garry.
In 1858 the Northwest Transportation and Navigation and Railway

York Factory, 1880. Arrival of the Ship. The Public Archives of Canada.

Company was organized in Toronto to connect Canada West to Red River by the middle route. The venture proved an expensive failure; nevertheless, it revealed the nature of things to come.

York Factory was the major trans-shipment point for the Hudson's Bay Company on the northern route. The supply ship, which made the once-yearly voyage from Great Britain to York in six to eight weeks, brought trading goods and new recruits. Times of arrival and departure varied, but the ship usually arrived at York in early August, picked up bundles of furs, and coasted to James Bay, leaving in late August or early September. Part of the trade goods were distributed immediately to the brigades that had come to collect them, and part were stored for shipment inland the following year. In addition a one-year supply of goods was always kept for emergency use.

The route to the interior from York Factory followed the Hayes River —mainly because it had fewer rapids than the strong-flowing Nelson. Clinker-built York boats replaced canoes after 1800 because it was reckoned that the savings in carrying costs amounted to one-third. A freighting canoe carried approximately one and a half tons (25–30 ninety-pound "pieces") and a crew of five or six men, where the York boat carried three to four tons, about seventy-five pieces and nine men. The advantage of the York boat was that it required fewer men per ton of goods than the canoe, was sturdier, and not so prone to accident. It also freed the Company from dependence on the rapidly diminishing supply of the large birch needed for canoes. The river trip from the Bay across the Shield to Lake Winnipeg was difficult and back-breaking, and as

Upper Fort Garry about 1870. The steamboat *Dakota* unloading at a warehouse on the Assiniboine River. The Public Archives of Canada.

early as 1814 thought was given to constructing a winter road linking Red River to York Factory. Work was actually begun in 1828, but the project was abandoned after a few stretches were tested.

An all-season connection, however, was established in the 1840s between Saint Paul and Red River. By about 1850 organized brigades were making the 550-mile journey in about three weeks. Once the Hudson's Bay Company started shipping supplies by cart (1858) and steamboat service began on the river (1859), the success of the route was assured. By the 1860s about 1500 cart journeys were made annually, some 500 carts usually making two round trips each year, with each cart carrying 600–800 pounds of goods. The first brigade made the trip in early summer when the sloughs could be crossed, and the second left Red River in late August and returned in early October. Furs were still sent to York Factory for shipment to Britain, but the Saint Paul route gradually replaced the entrepôt on the Bay because it was quicker and less expensive to ship goods through the United States. In winter dog-drawn carrioles were used for rapid communication between Red River and Saint Paul.

Within the region the York boat brigades, manned by workers recruited in Red River, supplied a transportation service each summer from Fort Garry to Methye Portage, Lake Winnipeg, York Factory and back to Red River, starting in the first week of June and returning in early October. To facilitate the constant movement of goods between Norway House and Red River, two vessels were built in 1831–32 for use on Lake Winnipeg. Each carrying over thirteen tons, they were particularly useful for hauling Red River agricultural produce to Norway House for further distribution. Private freighters from Red River also carried goods to and from York Factory—particularly the goods settlers ordered from Britain—before the Saint Paul route became dominant.

Most of the men who worked the York boats were Métis, although many were Indians from the missions. The only men who could stand the grueling labor were tough, unruly, and often hard to control—and as it became more and more difficult to find satisfactory employees, overland cart trails began to replace the York boats, especially in the Assiniboine and Saskatchewan river areas. In the 1860s thought was even given to conveying supplies north of the Saskatchewan by cart along the Green Lake route (see Fig. 6-7).

The most important long-distance cart road was the Carlton Trail from Fort Garry to Forts Ellice and Carlton, with a much less frequently used extension to Edmonton (see Fig. 6-7). The Carlton Trail is said to have developed after Governor Simpson journeyed across the prairies in 1825, showing that it was possible to travel overland, but the eastern parts of the trail were in use well before that time. In 1860 the first freight was carried along the route for the Hudson's Bay Company. For a few years about one hundred men in charge of 300 carts made one trip a season from Red River, carrying trading goods outbound and furs inbound, the journey taking sixty to eighty days return to Carlton. But this method of conveying goods was short-lived; the use of trails began to be affected in the 1870s by steamboats on the Saskatchewan River and even more drastically in the 1880s by the railway.

Figure 6-7 shows the length of time required to carry goods from York Factory into the interior by boat and from Red River to Edmonton by Red River cart. The data can only be aproximate because no brigade on water or land could keep to a schedule if delayed by winds on Lake Winnipeg or by poor fords across rivers. The map, however, gives some idea of the time spent in covering the vast distances of the western interior.

In winter the Hudson's Bay Company empire was kept together by the winter packet, a delivery service using dog teams, which carried orders and private letters from one post to another. The teams traveled quickly and could cover forty miles in a day. Carlton was the redistribution center; runners coming from as far as Fort Garry and the Mackenzie District converged, exchanged packets, and then returned to their own posts. Goods and furs also were conveyed by dog team in winter, but normally only for short distances because food for the dogs had to be carried on the sleighs, reducing the payloads as journeys lengthened.

Despite sustained efforts to improve and coordinate communications more effectively, the western interior remained well beyond the frontier of regular and easy transportation services until the railway between Winnipeg and St. Paul came into operation in 1879. If it was difficult for the Company to maintain effective communications with the outside world, it was even more so for the settlers. Yet it was this isolation that allowed the buffalo hunt and the associated Métis culture to flourish in the west for a crucial fifty years during the nineteenth century.

The relative isolation of Rupert's Land before 1870 becomes very apparent when we compare it with the corresponding plains area of the United States. Despite Indian wars and other hazards of travel many immigrants on their way to Utah and the Pacific coast crossed the American plains. It is true that some gold seekers crossed the British North American plains in 1859 and 1862 heading for the Fraser River, but they were exceptions. Scientific exploring expeditions and adventurers such as the Earl of Southesk, Lord Milton and Dr. Cheadle, and Dr. John Rae came to the region, but they accepted the existing way of life during their brief stays. No major transcontinental avenues of commerce crossed the plains before 1870, apart from those that were an integral part of the existing economic life of the region.

Colonization at Red River

LAYING OUT THE LAND

Lord Selkirk was astonishingly sanguine about establishing an agricultural colony in the western interior. The site, along the Red River on

Fig. 6-9. River Lots on the Red River near Lower Fort Garry surveyed in the early 1870s (lower map), and Park Lots (dark shading) in the adjacent "Outer Two Mile" lots. The Park Lots were occupied well before the river lot survey was extended over them in the late 1870s. The maps vary in scale, so the lots as depicted do not quite match. Redrawn from manuscript maps of St. Andrews and St. Clements Parishes in the Surveys Branch, Manitoba Department of Mines and Natural Resources.

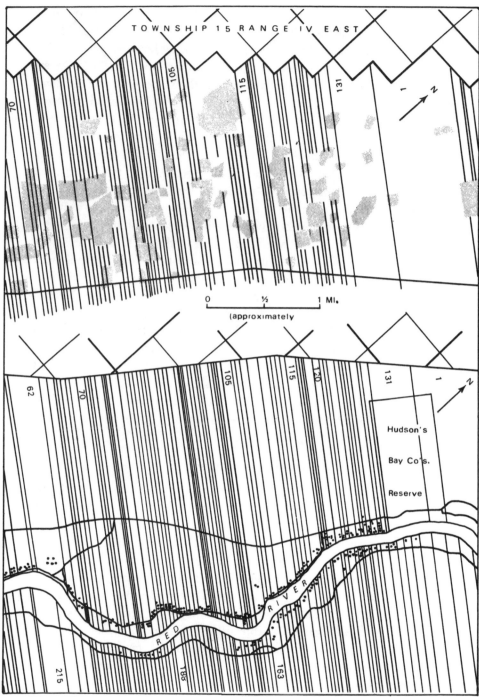

TOWNSHIP 15 RANGE IV EAST

0   ½   1 MI.

(approximately)

Hudson's

Bay Co's.

Reserve

RED   RIVER

Figure 6-9.

deep soils near a belt of woods and close to the buffalo grounds and fishing areas, was believed to be good, and it was thought that supplying provisions for the fur trade would provide a market for some years.

The river set the general pattern of settlement (see Fig. 6-9). Governor Miles MacDonell, who was in charge of the settlement, took his lead in laying out the land from the French-Canadian cadastral patterns along the St. Lawrence. In 1813 Peter Fidler surveyed rectangular river lots that extended deeply back from the river but about one-third again as wide as in Canada. The depth was not specified, but in time it was accepted that a settler was entitled to a holding extending two miles back from the river, and a hay-cutting "privilege" that extended for two more miles. Figure 6-9 shows the survey system near Lower Fort Garry as it was in 1874. The river lots, which gave every farmer ease of access to water supply and communication, were important in the early days of settlement. They provided an equitable allocation of the narrow belt of trees bordering the river; they were adapted to an efficient pioneer road pattern; and, by concentrating settlement, they nurtured a strong sense of community. Moreover, the best-drained land was on the natural levees close to the river; farther back were swamps or flats which dried slowly in spring. These wetlands offered their own advantages for haying, but they were unsuitable sites for homesteads. The long-lot system was followed for some sixty years, even when the area along the lower Red River became crowded. The advantages of compact linear settlement were evident to all, and there were no strong pressures before 1870 to change it.

ESTABLISHING THE AGRICULTURAL SETTLEMENT

Most of the early farmers at Red River were a pitiful lot. In Scotland, Northwest Company propaganda against the settlement had had its impact; skilled farmers were not willing to go to the new land. Some colonists, however, such as the Kildonan settlers, displayed the perseverance necessary for success, and the fur traders who came to retire at Red River made a contribution as well. The traders were not proved agriculturalists, but they were generally intelligent, knew the country, and helped to create a more stable society within which good farmers could work and advance. Progress was difficult. Natural hazards; the procuring of implements, seed, and animals; the creation of a market for agricultural goods; and a pessimistic attitude toward the future of farming in an isolated colony were formidable problems.

Precipitation in the area averages twenty inches annually. There were occasional drought years (1836–46 and 1862–68), but no agricultural adaptations had to be made for low precipitation. Floods on the Red River plain were a recurring hazard and in the early years drove some farmers away from the colony. In 1826, 1852, and 1861 the floods were the worst and there was great destruction of property. Length of growing season was of grave concern to farmers because frost could readily ruin a late-maturing crop or one planted too early. The frost-free period was 110 days, just enough to allow the wheat first used in the colony to ripen. Grasshoppers did much damage in the early years, setting people to wondering whether farming ever would be possible. Fortunately, like the floods, the grasshopper plagues were intermittent, and Red River did not suffer seriously from grasshoppers again until the 1870s, although there were occasional smaller infestations in the late 1850s and in the 1860s.

Securing wood for fuel and building was a problem that did not fade; indeed, it became worse as time passed. In 1859 the Council of Assiniboia at the request of almost 200 residents along the Assiniboine River forbade cutting wood on unoccupied land on the stream—a convincing demonstration of the need for conserving timber. Thus one of the main problems of settling open prairie was already pressing in on the people.

Tools, seed, and stock all had to be brought to the colony. The first settlers broke the land with spades and hoes; plows were not made at Red River until 1823, although they had been made earlier at some of the fur posts. Other implements, however, such as scythes, were available by then.

More critical was the need for good animals and seed. Sheep sent out by Lord Selkirk in 1812 did not thrive; others driven from Kentucky in 1833 were more successful. A cow and a bull from the Hudson's Bay Company and cattle brought out from Scotland did not provide good foundation stock either, but in the early 1820s, cattle driven from Missouri and even farther in some extraordinary drives provided the colony its first basic stock and its first trading connection with the United States. Horses were procured from fur posts and from Indians. Rude stables were usually provided for the animals, but they could survive outside during the cold winters if sheltering trees were present.

The immigrants brought with them wheat, barley, and many other kinds of seed. Occasionally early wheat crops failed or—during the conflict between the Hudson's Bay Company and the Nor'Westers—enemies of the colony deliberately destroyed them. Seed was then obtained from Prairie du Chien (Wisconsin) and fur trading posts. The Prairie du Chien wheat was not a carefully selected variety, but it remained the basic wheat sown. In 1846 Black Sea wheat was introduced from England and Canada.

Lord Selkirk and later the Hudson's Bay Company were concerned about the quality of agriculture and attempted to improve it by sponsoring in the 1830s "master farmers," whose operations were grandly called "experimental farms." Better quality horses, cows, and sheep were imported, but the experimental farms failed, partly because they were geared to providing staples for export, which proved unfeasible. As so often happens, the ordinary farmers living in the area developed practices suited to the area more quickly than the alleged experimental farmers, whose farms ended as ignominious failures. Indirectly, however, the Red River farmers were helped because better breeding stock was introduced by the Company—although lack of controlled breeding dissipated much of the potential benefit.

Farming moved beyond the tentative stage following a succession of good years after 1827. With more than 2000 acres under cultivation in 1831, the colony contributed substantially to local subsistence although farmers rarely profited from sales of agricultural produce. Yet the farmers produced enough wheat to provision part of the Bay Company's operations. Alternative sources of food such as pemmican weakened the position of farming in the colony. In addition, farming was just one of many possible economic activities in the interior. The Scots-Orcadians and the other British farmers concentrated on agriculture but the Métis generally did not; a concerted community focus on agriculture did not develop before 1870, nor probably, in view of the limited market, could it have developed.

FARMING AND EXPANSION OF FARMING AREAS

Farming operations were very simple and changed little from basic patterns established in the first decade of settlement. The main crops were wheat, barley, potatoes, and oats. Wheat was ground into flour in the many gristmills, some driven by wind (the first was built in 1825) and others by water. A steam-driven mill was erected in 1863. Corn was desired by the Hudson's Bay Company for provisioning the fur trade, but the available varieties could not be safely grown because of the frost hazard. The largest farms in the 1850s and 1860s had perhaps fifty acres in crops; but a more common figure was about twenty acres, and many a man had just a mistreated acre or two. Mixed farming characterized Red River agriculture. Cattle, swine, horses, and occasionally sheep were an important part of every farm, with thirty to forty head of cattle comprising a good-sized herd.

Farm practices in Assiniboia are difficult to describe, since little exact data exists. It has been reported that farmers practised no crop rotation until 1850. Rotation then consisted of four or five years of wheat followed by barley and a year of fallow, but likely only a few farmers adopted it. There was little manuring, and by the 1860s weeds had become a serious problem because of casual cultivation practices. All grain was sown by hand, although a number of reaping, threshing, and winnowing machines were in use by 1870. These implements proved a boon to the few larger farmers because of local labor shortages.

Haying, an important aspect of Red River farming, was closely regulated. Cattle were pastured in summer and fed wild hay in winter. It was reckoned that winter feeding required ten cart-loads of hay for a horse, five for an ox. Farmers were permitted to cut the grass at the back of their lots (the hay "privilege") only after a designated date in July. Later in the season, usually on September first, farmers could cut hay wherever they wished. Occasionally they would travel twenty miles or more to find suitable hay meadows. Nothing so well demonstrates the rudimentary, expansive nature of farming in the colony as this dependence on widely scattered natural meadows beyond the farms.

From 1830 to 1850 the increase in acreage improved was remarkably slow; in 1831, 2152 acres were under the plow; in 1840, 4041; and in 1856, 8371.[40] There are no figures for 1870, but the increase in improved acreage after 1856 does not appear to have accelerated. Farming along the Red River had spread only from present Selkirk to about five miles south of the Forks; along the Assiniboine from the Forks to Sturgeon Creek; and but a few miles up the Seine River. A small separate settlement had developed at Portage la Prairie (see Fig. 6-5). Most of the farmed land along the rivers was only one-quarter to one-half mile in depth, with few farms extending beyond those limits.

A desire on the part of the farmers to secure additional cultivated land but at the same time to remain close to the established farming area may have led to a distinctive feature of Red River agriculture, the cultivation of "parks," small fields scattered throughout the hay privileges (see Fig.

6-9). This practice appears to have begun in the late 1850s. Since lot lines were not clearly defined, the parks commonly straddled property boundaries and were quite irregular in outline. Farmers avoided clearing land if possible; instead they sought out patches of prairie in the bush or dry sites beyond the back swamps, and this may partly account for the dispersion of the lots and their odd shapes. Occasionally they built outbuildings, but as a rule they lived on the parks in the summer only, tending animals and preparing dairy products. The use of these fields may have been restricted because it was thought that wells could not be sunk on the heavy clays of the Red River plain. Often plowed, cropped, and then abandoned after only a few years, the parks as agricultural enterprises had a somewhat fugitive quality.

Barry Kaye, a student of the Red River colony, has suggested that there was no general expansion of farming back of the rivers because of prairie fires, lack of water, difficulty in breaking prairie sod, and poor drainage. Flooding followed by slow drainage was a general problem in the colony, and works designed to prevent flooding were started as early as 1844. In subsequent years a little public money was allocated to draining land and comprehensive drainage schemes were advocated, but not much was accomplished. For most of the Red River settlement, drainage remained a severe constraint on expansion of cultivation; it was easier to avoid the problem by moving to drier lands than attempting to solve it by digging drains.

Settlement could easily have expanded up the Red River toward the 49th parallel, but when expansion actually started in the 1850s, it was on the Assiniboine River at Portage la Prairie, where conditions were considered more favorable. There the settlers found dry land, light soil (for easy breaking), a mixture of prairie and wood, and access to hay and water. Portage la Prairie was the westernmost point to which agriculture directly associated with Red River had extended by 1870.

THE AGRICULTURAL ECONOMY

Markets for the produce of the colony were limited. There was a small surplus of wheat as early as 1824, but in many years not enough grain was harvested to make any available for sale. Since practically everyone farmed, hunted, or fished, there was little local market for food; beginning in the 1820s, however, the colony began to supply some of the provisions for the Hudson's Bay Company, helping to maintain the Company's one-year reserve of flour at Red River. Each year the Council of the Northern Department requisitioned from the colony supplies needed for the next year. The following items were to be purchased for 1844: 60 firkins butter, 56 lbs. each; 240 lbs. cheese; 600 cwt. best dried flour, first and second quality; 200 cwt. best dried flour, first quality; 10 assortments garden seeds; 15 kegs eggs; 4 bushels of onions; 2 kegs of salt cabbages; 2000 bushels of wheat, and so forth. The Company even closed a number of "meat" posts on the Assiniboine River in anticipation that Red River would supply provisions. The market was little better for livestock than for grain, although some horses and cattle were exported to Saint Paul beginning in 1839. In any event, there was never much food for sale. When in 1847 there was an unexpected need for grain because of the presence of troops and a poor harvest caused by drought, flour had to be imported from Saint Paul. And when in 1868–69 drought and grasshoppers ruined the crops, there once again was a shortage of food— this after the district had been farmed for half a century.

The uneven production of farm produce was disconcerting to both the farmers and the Company. When there was a surplus, farmers complained about low prices, even forming combinations to raise them. In reply the Company in the 1850s tried to ensure its supplies by establishing two wheat farms at Lower Fort Garry and White Horse Plains, the latter located on the lower Assiniboine River.[41] A cattle herd intended for droving to Fort Garry was assembled by the Company at Fort Pelly, but this endeavor was a failure.[42] The relationship of producer and purchaser was not a happy one, exacerbated by the cramping scale of operations and by natural hazards which could wipe out any surplus.

Under the energetic Governor Simpson, a search for alternate products to widen the economic base of the colony was made, but without success. In the end, farmers settled into a simple life of producing a little grain and keeping a few cattle. Isolated and ineffective on their tiny farms in the center of the continent, the Red River colonists were heirs to a land whose potential was only to be released by the larger strategies of commercial development in North America.

SETTLEMENT FACILITIES AND LIFE IN THE COLONY

Despite the constraints described above, many a settler attained a fairly comfortable level of living, which was reflected in his house. The earliest houses were primitive shelters built with the assistance of the Hudson's

Assiniboia in the 1850s. W. G. R. Hind painted this scene of the Red River plain. The settler's house is of Red River frame construction; a Red River cart is in the foreground. The Public Archives of Canada.

Bay Company men, who even taught the newcomers how to cut timbers. By the 1840s more substantial log-gable structures were being built, generally in what was locally called "Red River frame" construction (vertical logs provide a frame for horizontal logs forming the walls). In this essentially modular form of construction, short logs could be used to make a large house. Such structures remained the basic style of building for many of the settlers.

The typical Hudson's Bay Company building in the larger posts was a simple rectangular structure with a central doorway and evenly spaced windows under a hip or pavilion roof. This design was adopted by the more prosperous settlers of Red River after mid-century, particularly by the retired fur traders. By the 1860s buildings were larger, straw or sod roofs were giving way to shingles and, nearer to Fort Garry where limestone was available, stone houses were occasionally built. The first attempts at brick construction were made late in the 1860s.

The first evidence of the North American trading-town atmosphere in Assiniboia could just be discerned in the early 1860s. In those years a separate settlement began to develop just north of Upper Fort Garry, where the trails along the Red and the Assiniboine intersected. Specialty trades were established as the farmer-artisan-storekeeper began to disappear. This together with the formation of a Board of Trade in 1864 indicated that a business group was emerging in the community and that a town would soon develop. In the fall of 1865 the colony's newspaper, the *Nor'Wester*, was published (according to the heading) in the "Town of Winnipeg RRS [Red River Settlement]," and by then it was evident that the present intersection of Portage Avenue and Main Street in Winnipeg was the nucleus of a town. The civilization of eastern North America—to the extent that it is based on trading centers—was coming to Red River.

Cultural institutions and business and agricultural services remained widely separated within the colony: the fur trade and the Council of Assiniboia were at Upper Fort Garry; the new commercial nucleus of saloon, store, and newspaper office was at Winnipeg; and agricultural services such as gristmills were spread throughout the settlement close to the farms they served. Churches—particularly Anglican churches—were well scattered. Red River was still a very dispersed community with no sharply defined trading centers except for the emerging Winnipeg.

Hunters, voyageurs, farmers, retired fur traders, laborers, military men, Hudson's Bay Company administrators, missionaries and other churchmen comprised the society. Few trained persons from the outside came to the colony to stay in the early decades of its existence because it was so remote; thus the settlement was fairly closed and inward looking. The significant link with the outside world—apart from the commercial connections through the fur trade and some individual associations—was the church. Two Roman Catholic priests arrived in the colony in 1818, the Church of England began its ministry in 1820 through the Church Missionary Society, the Methodists sent four missionaries in 1840, and a Presbyterian minister arrived in 1851. These men, steadily augmented in number through the years, did missionary work among the Indians and helped to provide a stable social base for the colonists. They were also among the first to introduce schools to Red River.

Despite the colony's straggling appearance and its distance from other centers of population, the inhabitants possessed a remarkably wide range of interests. Many men took a responsible attitude toward participating in local affairs and providing leadership in cultural matters. This meant not only serving on the Council Assiniboia, organizing the maintenance of roads, endeavoring to establish an agricultural improvement society, and helping to administer justice, but also assisting in education and promoting scientific investigation. There was, for instance, considerable interest in natural history. Many of the retired fur traders were excellent observers of nature. Donald Gunn sent meteorological data to the Smithsonian Institution and A. G. B. Bannatyne collected natural history specimens for Louis Agassiz. In 1862 the Institute of Rupert's Land was formed under the presidency of the Bishop of Rupert's Land to encourage this scientific work, although its ambition outreached any accomplishments. There were even writers in the colony who recorded its economic and social history. All these interests speak of a society where it was possible to acquire some learning, where the pace of life permitted contemplating the wonders of nature and the vagaries of human behavior. Even though Red River was situated far beyond the North American agricultural frontier, it was a self-reliant, civilized, and orderly settlement—a remarkable achievement for a frontier community.

The Métis Economy

The Métis, born into a society in which trapping, buffalo hunting, fishing, and snaring small game were important, held a very different view of the resources of the land than did the colonists from Britain or many of the retired traders. Only after 1820 did the Métis start to practise farming, and even then it was makeshift. In summer they could work for the Hudson's Bay Company and the Red River merchants, hauling goods to the Bay, the Saskatchewan District, the Athabaska country, or Saint Paul. Many were freemen, trading with the Indians or hunting buffalo and selling provisions and robes to the Company or other buyers. To the "New Nation," as the Métis considered themselves, the region offered many alternatives for making a living; only rarely did they share the aspirations of a European or Canadian immigrant to own a farm and spend his life improving it.

Even though most of the Métis were willing to establish a home base, they were subjected to deprecatory comments about their casual attitude to the land as early as the 1820s[43]—criticism that remained tediously the same for the next fifty years. Their main source of food had always been the buffalo, but after about 1820, with buffalo becoming more and more scarce in the southern part of the Red River plain, the Métis were occasionally forced to travel as far as the South Saskatchewan River or even to the Missouri and the Yellowstone in search of the animal.

In the organization of the buffalo hunt the Métis modified the horse culture of the plains Indians, changing it to a well-administered field operation on the plains in summer and fall. Had the Métis been exposed to the Spanish manner of herding semi-domesticated cattle, it is possible they might have adopted a similar way of life; they were a free-living people who probably would have enjoyed the activity of herding and perhaps could have built it into a lasting agricultural enterprise. As it is, they placed their dependence on chasing a wild animal, using hunting strategies that were as well coordinated as the communications operations of the Hudson's Bay Company itself.

The large-scale hunting expeditions that began in the years 1818–21 were very carefully arranged—both because of the large numbers of people involved (more than 1500 on some hunts) and the danger from Indian attack on the plains west and south of the Assiniboine. The summer hunt took place from mid-June to September. A para-military organization ran the entire hunt, deciding on camping sites and when to run (attack) the buffalo. The buffalo that were hunted in summer provided dried meat, tongues, and skins for tents, moccasins, and straps. The fall hunt provided supplies for people who had been unsuccessful in the summer, and thicker pelts for buffalo robes. The Métis from Red River tended to go to the South Saskatchewan country, those from Grantown to the Missouri. In the 1860s smaller hunts left from Edmonton, St. Albert, and Lac Ste. Anne.

In the late 1860s the number of buffalo began to dwindle as a result of unscrupulous killing of the animals by professional hunters in the United States; in the following decade the last great hunts by the Métis took place. The slaughter by the Métis and the Indians had been great, but F. G. Roe, a student of the buffalo, does not think that the hunting of these groups brought an end to the buffalo herds.

On returning from a good hunt, the Métis settled into their houses, simple mud-plastered log cabins in clearings on the banks of the Red, Assiniboine, and Seine rivers. These were crude dwellings, often consisting of only one large room with a clay floor. Their food supply came from the hunt, and they had some credit from selling meat to the Hudson's Bay Company and the colonists, and buffalo robes to the Company and the free traders. Many also earned part of their livelihood in summer by working on the Company brigades, signing up by mid-winter for the next year's tripping. They received advances on which to live; thus they frequently found themselves obligated to serve the Company, caught in a system like that of the "debt" of the fur trade itself, or the truck system of the Newfoundland fishery.

Before 1870 Métis life was essentially a life of movement. Differences gradually appeared between those who lived at the settlements for part of the year and those whose life was spent almost entirely on the plains— the *hivernants*, who visited the trading posts or missions only occasionally. But for more than seventy years the Métis comprised a special society in Rupert's Land, intimately associated with a resource that was on the road to extinction, dependent upon freighting work that would vanish when steam power arrived, regarding a region larger than many kingdoms as their home. Shortly after 1870, in a change so drastic as to be a revolution, the land over which they roamed would be subdivided into thousands of farms. It is no wonder that the Métis have been a misunderstood people. The standards that were to predominate—stability of income, sanctity of property, and rigid concepts of territoriality—were foreign to them and their way of life. They could live their distinctive ways in association with the modest farming colony at Red River, but when they were confronted with the introduction into their midst of a traditionally structured agrarian culture from humid areas, that was another matter—ultimately producing a clash in which their society could not survive. Given time and opportunity they might have come to terms with the disappearance of the buffalo and the appearance of the farmer. But there was barely a transition period, and by the 1850s it was becoming apparent that the meeting with the new culture could not be long delayed.

Scientific reconnaissance and outsiders' perceptions of the region

In the 1850s, as agricultural settlement in Canada West pressed against the borders of the Shield, the southern part of Rupert's Land was perceived more and more as a promised land in Canada, even though it was not surely known if the plains were suited for settlement. Apparently Hudson's Bay Company officers were genuinely skeptical about the possibilities for agriculture in the interior because of its remoteness, limitations of climate, and absence of trees;[44] but few residents of the region thought of the southern plains as a wasteland. In the United States, on the other hand, the idea that the plains just east of the Rocky Mountains were a great desert still held at mid-century.

At this time the views of an American climatologist on the potential resources of the interior had a significant impact in Canada. Lorin Blodget's climatic enquiries revealed that in the northwestern part of the interior, temperatures were higher during the critical summer growing months than in the same latitudes farther east. Others had already pointed this out, but Blodget's vital contribution was the conclusion that middle-latitude crops could be grown successfully in these high latitudes. His work was referred to in the report of the Canadian Department of Crown Lands for 1856, and in May 1857 the Toronto *Globe* printed an extensive quotation from Blodget. His words were persuasive, but still quite inadequate to convey an understanding of the agricultural potential of the interior.

In the late 1850s British and Canadian scientific exploring expeditions to the northwest began to supply more information. The British spent three field seasons in the interior, the Canadians two. Both expeditions amassed a great deal of field data, particularly the British party under Captain John Palliser, which covered the ground from Lake Superior to the Rockies and beyond. The Canadian expedition under H. Y. Hind reached the South Saskatchewan River. In their reports the explorers made some provocative generalizations on natural resource distributions and prepared maps of the interior showing districts thought to be good for agriculture and others thought to be ill-suited. Generalizing widely, the parklands were considered good and the dryer grasslands, poor. The Palliser expedition did much of the resource mapping, but it was II. Y. Hind who first stated that the arid grasslands zone was a northward extension of the "Great American Desert," and that the area of good agricultural land bounding it should be termed the "Fertile Belt" (see Fig. 6-3).[45] The synoptic view that resulted had the virtues and defects of a caricature; it contrasted in vivid image major areas of good and bad land, distinctions which had not been conceived of so sharply before. Others soon took up these ideas. Visionaries extolled the virtues of the land for agriculture, particularly the "Fertile Belt," which was sanctified as early as 1866 as an "ordained garden" and later as a "Paradise of Fertility."[46]

The ideas of Blodget, Palliser, and Hind did not significantly affect the way in which the residents of the interior perceived their own land; indeed, the local inhabitants hardly seem to have been aware of the two exploring expeditions and their appraisals. But the explorers' reports immediately provided a better appreciation in Canada of the potential of the southern part of Rupert's Land as a future home for Canadians—even though the images of good land and bad land did not have a direct effect on migration and railroad building until the 1870s.

In the 1860s economic reality was still the fur trade. No new transcontinental avenues of commerce crossed the plains, but scientific expeditions had "confirmed" that parts of the area could be settled, making it increasingly desirable for Canadians to take an interest in the area—particularly because the American frontier was moving into northern Minnesota and the danger that the United States might have territorial ambitions was increasing. Changes were soon to come.

New forces

By mid-nineteenth century, the Hudson's Bay Company control of Rupert's Land was not only disputed by free traders, it was questioned by the government of Canada, Canadian immigrants, and advocates of colonization in Great Britain. The Company knew that large numbers of settlers would be detrimental to its fur-trading operations and looked with alarm at the encroaching frontier of settlement. Nevertheless, its senior officers realized that a change in the administration of Rupert's Land was inevitable.

In 1862 there was a very real possibility that the Company would be faced with maintaining law and order in a gold rush to the upper Saskatchewan. The rush did not occur, but the possibility had raised concern. Indian warfare in the United States brought dangerous jurisdictional problems as Indians fled to Rupert's Land; fortunately, however, there were no serious territorial violations by U.S. troops. Various internal administrative pressures were also building in the areas beyond Assiniboia. In 1864 a meeting was held at Edmonton to discuss the form local government should take, with the few Americans panning for gold in the North Saskatchewan River expressing a desire for a republican government.[47] At Portage la Prairie there was an attempt to turn the local council into a representative colonial government within the British Empire. On the plains the Indians were relatively peaceable, yet in 1867 there was dangerous pillaging by Indians at Fort Pitt, and it was evident that this could easily happen elsewhere.

More and more it became apparent that the Company's administration of Rupert's Land was inadequate and ineffectual; even the officers realized that they governed by sufferance at Assiniboia and had no effective jurisdiction in the plains. By the 1860s the administrative procedures for governing the region had evolved little beyond those established in the early years of the Red River colony, and it was doubtful whether the Hudson's Bay Company was capable of introducing effective administrative innovations so far beyond the frontier of settlement.

An entire way of life in Assiniboia and the plains was threatened by the invasion of the middle-class farming structure and values of the humid east. In Canada West, property was important, steady income and steady employment were held in high esteem, and the "Protestant Ethic" toward work prevailed. Similar traits had not developed in Assiniboia. With few exceptions an individual entrepreneur—farmer or otherwise—could not progress. The movement of Canadians and Americans into the area after 1850 was significant not only as the first probing from the frontier of farm settlement but, more ominously, as the vanguard of a new link with the competitive metropolitan economy of eastern North America, which could only be in direct conflict with the monopolistic Hudson's Bay Company. These settlers represented a connection with the world market that could make commercial farming possible; without that, freedom of settlement and availability of land meant nothing to farmers.

Wide differences among the people of the interior resulted in contrasting attitudes to this new civilization. The Indians and Métis wanted their life to remain largely as it was, although the Métis hoped to throw off the administrative control of the Hudson's Bay Company. On the other hand, the colonists and a few Métis interested in farming really hoped for a change. They needed a stronger market in order to enlarge their farm operations; this meant establishing a transportation system and becoming part of a national and international trading system in staples such as cereals and meat. The Canadians in Assiniboia were most anxious to promote such changes.

In any changes that might occur it was apparent that the Indians, the Métis, and the fur trade would be crushed or, at the least, bypassed and ignored by the newcomers. The proponents of the new civilization eventually would have to come to terms with the physical environment, but in their view an accommodation with the existing cultures on the plain was not necessary.

It was under such circumstances that the Colonial Office had to decide how the region was to be administered in the future. The question was whether Rupert's Land should be annexed by Canada, made a separate colony, or combined with the new colony of British Columbia. It was urged that there was a need to act quickly to prevent the United States from taking over the domain. These were important matters, and in the sweep of such considerations the wishes of the Indians, the Métis, and the colonists were given no place when it was finally decided in 1869 to transfer Rupert's Land to Canada.

The various communities of the interior were fragile creations quickly broken by the events of the Riel Resistance of 1869–70 (the Métis resistance under Louis Riel to the transfer of Rupert's Land to Canada), the agricultural occupation beginning after 1870, and the Riel Rebellion of 1885. In the woodlands the structure of the fur trade was maintained, but the Indians of the plains were placed on reservations, their way of life completely altered. Many Métis barely eked out an existence on the margins of the new civilization; and the colony at Red River was subsumed in the new agricultural and urban developments. Elsewhere in Canada a closer link with metropolitan markets had strengthened the local economy by providing outlets for timber and wheat. This new connection, more powerful in its effects than the metropolitan link associated with the fur trade, was to quickly destroy the mutual tolerance of different social groups and the delicate equilibrium between trapping and fur trading and farming, hunting, and fishing that had evolved over two centuries in the western interior.

Bibliography

An indispensable source on the geography of the western interior are the documents in the Archives of the Hudson's Bay Company, London, England. This material is constantly being reworked by scholars from different disciplines, not only for information on the fur trade but for data on physical geography, way of life of Indians, and the interaction of fur traders and Indians over many decades. The published volumes of the Hudson's Bay Record Society are helping to make some of this information available to a wider public.

A. S. Morton, *A History of the Canadian West to 1870–71* (Toronto: T. Nelson, 1939) stands out as a basic source for its comprehensive treatment of the west. W. L. Morton's many books and articles are all relevant to a study of the interior, but only three will be singled out here: *Manitoba: A History* (Toronto: University of Toronto Press, 1957); Introduction to *London Correspondence Inward From Eden Colville* edited by E. E. Rich (London: Hudson's Bay Record Society, 1956); and "Agriculture in the Red River Colony," *Canadian Historical Review* 30 (1949), 305–21). H. A. Innis, *The Fur Trade in Canada; an Introduction to Canadian Economic History* (New Haven: Yale University Press, 1930, reprinted in 1956 by the University of Toronto Press) and Marcel Giràud, *Le Métis Canadien: son rôle dans l'histoire des provinces de l'ouest* (Paris: Institut d'Ethnologie, 1945) are both classic studies. E. E. Rich, *The History of the Hudson's Bay Company 1670–1870*, 2 vols. (London: Hudson's Bay Record Society, 1958–59) contains many important details on the functioning of the fur trade. Rich's *The Fur Trade and the Northwest to 1857* (Toronto: McClelland and Stewart, 1967) treats the west more generally. Geographers have recently been turning their attention to the historical geography of the interior, and valuable studies are being produced. Eric Ross, *Beyond the River and the Bay* (Toronto: University of Toronto Press, 1970) is a fine account of the patterns of activity in the interior in 1811, and A. R. Ray discusses the vital role of the park belt in the geographical development of the interior before 1821 in "Indian Adaptations to the Forest–Grassland Boundary of Manitoba and Saskatchewan, 1650–1821: Some Implications for Interregional Migration," *The Canadian Geographer* (Summer 1972), 103–18). Two M.A. theses at the University of Manitoba are John Clarke's "Population and Economic Activity: A Geographical and Historical Analysis Based Upon Selected Censuses of the Red River Valley in the Period 1832 to 1856" (1967) and Barry Kaye's "Some Aspects of the Historical Geography of the Red River Settlement from 1812 to 1870" (1967).

Some splendid contemporary accounts of the interior are available. David Thompson's account of his experiences in the west, *David Thompson's Narrative of his Explorations in North America* edited by J. B. Tyrrell (Toronto: The Champlain Society, 1916), and reprinted with added material by the Society in 1962 as *David Thompson's Narrative, 1784–1812* under the editorship of Richard Glover, is a fine example of early Canadian regional writing, and Alexander Ross, *The Red River Settlement: Its Rise, Progress and Present State. With Some Account of the Native Races, and Its General History, To the Present Day* (London: Smith, Elder and Co., 1856, reprinted by Ross and Haines, Inc. in 1957) is an intimate account of the development of the Selkirk Settlement. H. Y. Hind, *Narrative of the Canadian Red River Exploring Expedition of 1857 and of the Assiniboine and Saskatchewan Exploring*

Expedition of 1858, 2 vols. (London: Longman, Green, Longman, and Roberts, 1860, reprinted by M. G. Hurtig Ltd. in 1972) and John Palliser, *The Journals, Detailed Reports, and Observations* . . . (London: Parliamentary Papers, 1863, and most readily available in Irene Spry's edition for the Champlain Society, *The Papers of the Palliser Expedition 1857–1860,* 1970) show how men from humid areas struggled with the task of trying to grasp the agricultural potential of the prairies. The beautiful Palliser map of 1865 included with the Champlain Society volume is worth long study in its own right to obtain a picture of the Canadian west before agricultural settlement.

1. Unnamed map of the plains east of the Rocky Mountains. Drawn by Ki oo cus— or the Little Bear, a Blackfoot Chief, 1802. In Peter Fidler's Journals in the Hudson's Bay Company Archives, London, England (hereafter referred to as "H.B.C. Archives") E.3/2, pp. 206–7.
2. Sketch of Carlton District, H.B.C. Archives, Map G.1/27.
3. John Kipling, "The Abstracts From Mr. Kipling's Journal." Entry of August 3, 1786. "Albany Letters Inward." H.B.C. Archives, A.11/5, fol. 43r.
Governor and Committee to Edward Jarvis, Chief at Albany House, 23 May 1783. H.B.C. Archives, A.5/2, fol. 161v.
4. James Bird, "A Short Account of Edmonton District 1815." H.B.C. Archives, B.60/e/1, fol. 1v.
5. "Reports on the Eastern Coast of Lake Winnipeg 1815." This report is unsigned, but it was likely written by James Sutherland. H.B.C. Archives, B.16/e/1, fol. 2v.
6. *Ibid.*
7. Peter Fidler, "General Report of the Manetoba District for 1820 by Peter Fidler." H.B.C. Archives, B.51/e/1, p. 34.
8. J. H. Lefroy, "On the Probable Number of the Native Indian Population of British America," *Canadian Journal,* 2 (1853), 193–98. Great Britain, Parliament, *Report From the Select Committee on the Hudson's Bay Company, 1857* (London, 1857), pp. 365–66.
H. Y. Hind, *Narrative of the Canadian Red River Exploring Expedition of 1857 and the Assiniboine and Saskatchewan Expedition of 1858* (London, 1860), 2 vols. vol. II, pp. 145–46.
John Palliser, *The Journals, Detailed Reports, and Observations* (London, 1863), pp. 200–201.
9. John Rowand, "Saskatchewan Report For 1824 & 25 per John Rowand." H.B.C. Archives, B.60/e/8, fol. 1r.
10. Great Britain, Parliament, *Report From the Select Committee on the Hudson's Bay Company.* Evidence of Governor G. Simpson, p. 57.
11. Wm. Christie, "Memoranda regarding the Saskatchewan District," December 28, 1862. H.B.C. Archives, B.60/e/10, fol. 1r.
12. Based on the censuses of the Red River Colony and the first official map of Manitoba, Map of the Province of Manitoba, compiled by A. L. Russell, February, 1871. This map is in the Public Archives of Canada.
13. Map of the Province of Manitoba, by A. L. Russell.

14. Governor Simpson, "Notes on Trade and Territory of H.B.C. drawn by Sir George Simpson." 1857. H.B.C. Archives, E.18/8, fol. 44r.

15. J. P. Pruden, "Carlton Reports 31st May 1827." H.B.C. Archives, B.27/e/4, fol. 1r.

16. Fidler, "General Report o fthe Manetoba District for 1820." pp. 32, 36.

17. J. D. Cameron, "Rainy Lake Report for Years 1825/6." H.B.C. Archives, B.105/e/6, fol. 8r.

18. D. Mackenzie, "Report on the H. Hudson's Bay Company's affairs in Red River District Year 1825/7." H.B.C. Archives, B.235/e/3, fol. 5r.

19. J. Charles. "New Churchill Department Report 1818/19." H.B.C. Archives, B.91/e/1, fol. 1r.

20. "Report of Island Lake District 1827." This report probably is by Colin Robertson. H.B.C. Archives, B.283/e/1, fols. 4v, 7v.

21. J. Huldane, "Report on the State of the Country, & Indians in Lake Superior Department, 1824." H.B.C. Archives. B.231/e/1, fol. 4r.

22. Ibid.

23. F. Heron to Governor George Simpson, 14 March 1822. H.B.C. Archives, D.4/116, p. 33.

24. W. H. Cook, "Report of York Old Factory Department by Wm. H. Cook, 1815." H.B.C. Archives, B.239/e/1, fols. 6–9.

25. William Brown, "Report of the Manitoba District by William Brown for 1818 & 19." H.B.C. Archives, B.122/e/1, fols. 8r, v.

26. Peter Fidler, "Report of the Manetoba District by Peter Fidler 1821." H.B.C. Archives, B.51/e/2, p. 5.

27. Roderick Mackenzie, Jr., "Report For Winnipeg District 1822/3." H.B.C. Archives, B.4/e/1, fol. 3r.

28. John Davis, "Reports on Osnaburgh District 1816." H.B.C. Archives, B.155/e/3, fol. 7v. Charles Mackenzie, "General Report of Lac Seul Trading Post & the out Posts For 1827." H.B.C. Archives, B.107/e/3, fol. 1v.

29. Thomas Cook, "Journal Fort Ellice Jan. 1st. 1863," Entry of April 6, 1863. Archives of the Society for the Propagation of the Gospel in Foreign Parts, London, E.14, p. 1460.

30. Francis Heron, "Report on the Business of Brandon House, Outfit 1828." H.B.C. Archives, B.22/e/3, fol. 4v.

31. Fidler, "General Report of the Manetoba District for 1820." p. 26.

32. The figures in this paragraph are from Simpson, "Notes on Trade and Territory," 1857. fol. 46r.

33. Simpson, "Notes on Trade and Territory," 1857. fol. 38v.

34. William Swainson and John Richardson, Fauna Boreali-Americana; or the Zoology of the Northern Parts of British America (London, 1831), p. 468.

35. "Report of Island Lake District 1827." H.B.C. Archives, B.283/e/1, fols. 7v. 8v.

36. W. H. Cook, "Report of York Old Factory Department by Wm. H. Cook 1815." H.B.C. Archives, B.239/e/1, fol. 5r.

37. J. Bird, "A Short Account of Edmonton District 1815." H.B.C. Archives, B.60/e/1, fol. 3r.

38. John P. Pruden, "Carlton Reports 31st May 1827." H.B.C. Archives, B.27/e/4, fol. 2v.
R. Mackenzie, "Report for Fort William District," 1828. H.B.C. Archives. B.231/e/5, fol. 1v.

39. J. P. Pruden, "Report of Carlton District from the 27th of May 1818 to May 1819." H.B.C. Archives, B.27/e/2, fol. 1v.

40. Figures from Red River censuses.

41. Governor G. Simpson to Governor and Committee, 21 June 1859. H.B.C. Archives, A.12/10, fol. 163v.

42. Governor G. Simpson to W. G. Smith, Sect., 9 November 1857. H.B.C. Archives, A.12/8, fol. 603r.

Governor G. Simpson to Governor and Committee, 24 June 1858, H.B.C. Archives, A.12/9, fol. 151v.

43. D. Mackenzie, "Report on the H. Hudson's Bay Company's affairs in Red River District Years 1826/27." H.B.C. Archives, B.235/e/3, fol., 6r.

44. For instance, see Governor G. Simpson to Governor Shepherd, 26th January 1857. H.B.C. Archives, A.12/8, fols. 375–409.

45. The term "Fertile Belt" first appeared on a map, "Map of the Country From Lake Superior to the Pacific Ocean, showing the Western Boundary of Canada & the Eastern Boundary of British Columbia, also the Fertile Belt stretching from the Lake of the Woods to the Rocky Mountains," in H. Y. Hind, *British North America. Reports of Progress, Together With a Preliminary and General Report, on the Assiniboine and Saskatchewan Exploring Expedition* (London, 1860). See also Hind, *Narrative*, 1860, vol. I, pp. v–vii; Vol. II, pp. 222–36.

46. Thomas Rawlings. *What Shall We Do With the Hudson's Bay Territory? Colonize the "Fertile Belt," which Contains Forty Million Acres* (London, 1866), p. 7.

Alfred Waddington. *Overland Route Through British North America; or, the Shortest and Speediest Road to the East* (London, 1868), p. 13.

47. *The Nor'Wester*, March 17, 1864.

7 BRITISH COLUMBIA

The far northwestern coast of North America, almost halfway around
the world from Europe and more than 10,000 sea miles from New York
or Montréal, was not explored in any detail until the late 1770s (by Captain Cook); and for years only high-value, low-bulk goods such as sea
otter or beaver pelts and gold attracted Europeans to the area. Late in
the eighteenth century it was as remote from the centers of European
civilization as any mid-latitude coast on earth, and this remoteness was
compounded by the inaccuracy of the European's or even the eastern
North American's perception of the area. For traders coming overland
from Montréal just as for explorers coming by sea, the cordillera and its
inhabitants were exceedingly unfamiliar. Yet their arrival connected the
area, however thinly at first, to the main currents of the North Atlantic
world. The trade in land furs tied it to Montréal or Hudson Bay and on
across the Atlantic to the British Isles. As the fur trade dwindled, the
British connection—and to some degree the connection with British
colonies to the east—was maintained by colonial administrators or by
entrepreneurs who were beginning to exploit the area's forests and fish.
There were also connections to the south with California, source of
many settlers, capital, and skills, and a market for some products. Moreover, as whites spread into the northern cordillera, the values of the
nineteenth century spread with them. Hudson's Bay Company men, employees of the largest private North American monopoly of the day and
representatives of British imperialism throughout the North American
north and northwest, tended to believe in a managed, stable, socially

stratified society, a view running counter to the individualistic outlook of the miners who poured into the area from California in 1858. In the isolation of the far northwest, these values acquired a certain momentum of their own, so that even today in British Columbia there is both a retrospective Britishness and something of the heady exuberance of a gold rush.

The first problem for the Montréal traders (the Nor'westers) was to move about in the cordillera. Alexander Mackenzie, who made the first northern continental crossing in 1793, never found a practical route for a fur brigade through the cordillera. Simon Fraser, who reached the mouth of the Fraser in 1808, discovered that the wild river he had descended was not the Columbia, as he had thought, and that its canyon was an impossible canoe route. Moreover, canoes damaged in the turbulent rivers often could not be repaired for want of local birch. Along the Peace River and parts of the upper Fraser, the Montréal traders found forests similar to the dense tangles of spruce, tamarack, aspen, and birch of the Shield; but to the south and in the immediate lee of the coast mountains, the dominant riverbank vegetation was bunch grass and sage with patches of poplar in the moister gullies. The transportation system developed in the Shield and used there for more than 200 years was simply unsuited to the conditions of the cordillera.

The Montréal traders were more unsettled, however, by the high Indian population densities and their repeated failure to conclude binding trade agreements with the Indians. There may have been more than 60,000 native people along the coast of what is now British Columbia and in the Alaska panhandle, and some 30,000 to 40,000 in the interior of British Columbia. The Coast Salish along the Strait of Georgia were the most numerous linguistic family, but there were at least 8000 Haida on the Queen Charlotte Islands, several thousand Tsimshian along the Skeena and lower Nass rivers, more than 7000 Nootka on the west coast of Vancouver Island, and some 15,000 Interior Salish along the middle Fraser River and its tributaries. Except among the Kootenay Indians of the southeastern corner of British Columbia, whose culture was of plains origin, there were no political organizations with which traders could deal. The winter village, the basic unit of settlement along the coast as well as in the southern interior, comprised several extended family groups—each internally stratified, but only loosely connected to one another by marriage, potlatch obligations, and the few village activities such as winter dances. Most tasks were performed by individuals, households, or extended family groups, and even such common activities as brawling and raiding were usually organized at this scale. The many languages and dialects sharply limited the range of oral communications— even within linguistic families—and had the effect of further atomizing Indian life. For these reasons the Nor'westers could find few Indians who spoke for their fellows. The men they took for chiefs were heads of extended families, and the agreements they concluded with them never meant to the Indians what the traders intended them to mean. Furthermore, the Indians were primarily salmon fishermen, not hunters, and were not easily persuaded to trap furs in winter.

The Nor'westers never fully adjusted to these conditions. They rarely used the coast Indians' cedar dugout canoe, and at least once sent birch bark from Montréal to London for shipment to the Columbia River. By 1814 they were beginning to transport goods by pack horses but made much less use of these animals than did the Hudson's Bay Company a few years later. Because of their failure to conclude binding agreements they introduced a new method of obtaining furs. Rather than trading furs with the Indians, as had been the practice since the earliest days of the Canadian fur trade, they organized brigades made up largely of eastern Indians which moved slowly about the mountain valleys, trapping as they went. The local Indians resented incursions of other Indians into their territory, and for safety the brigades comprised twenty-five to fifty or more men when five or six might have taken more furs. Often, too, the eastern Indians traded independently with the local Indians and on occasion incited them to raid the Nor'westers. Along the upper Fraser, where physical conditions and the Indian population were more familiar to them, the Montréal traders conducted a profitable trade. Their trade in the Columbia basin, however, was a heavy financial drain throughout the Company's final years.

The Northwest Company's cordilleran operation lay more than 3000 canoe-miles from Montréal. Alexander Mackenzie had hoped to reduce transportation costs by supplying the entire area from the sea and shipping its furs to the Orient, but such a plan depended on the discovery of a practical route to the coast, which neither he nor Simon Fraser had made. By 1811 David Thompson had established that much of the Columbia River system was navigable, and for several years thereafter the Nor'westers hunted for a water connection between the upper Fraser and the Columbia. Not finding it, they divided the cordilleran trade into two districts (see Fig. 7-1). One was the most westerly extension of the

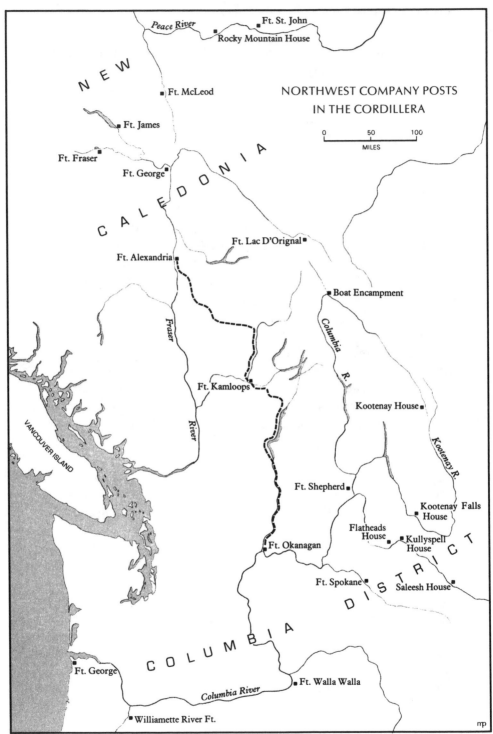

Ft. St. John
Peace River
Rocky Mountain House

N E W

Ft. McLeod

NORTHWEST COMPANY POSTS
IN THE CORDILLERA

0   50   100
MILES

Ft. James

Ft. Fraser

Ft. George

C A L E D O N I A

Ft. Lac D'Orignal

Ft. Alexandria

Boat Encampment

Fraser

Columbia R.

River

Ft. Kamloops

Kootenay House

VANCOUVER ISLAND

Kootenay R.

Ft. Shepherd

Kootenay Falls
House

Flatheads
House   Kullyspell
House

Ft. Okanagan

Ft. Spokane   Saleesh House

C O L U M B I A   D I S T R I C T

Ft. George

Columbia River   Ft. Walla Walla

Williamette River Ft.

mp

Figure 7-1.

canoe trade in Montréal; the other was supplied by sea. New Caledonia, the trading area of the upper Fraser and western Peace rivers, was supplied overland from the northeast, and its furs were sent down the Peace to Fort Chipewayan on Lake Athabaska where they joined the brigade for Montréal. The Columbia district—essentially the drainage basin of the Columbia River but extending north to Fort Kamloops on the Thompson River—focused on Fort George on the lower Columbia where interior traders deposited furs and took on the year's supplies. By 1814 some supplies for New Caledonia were taken by pack horse along an overland route between the two districts (see Fig. 7-1), and a few furs from New Caledonia came south for shipment to China.

In 1821 the Hudson's Bay Company absorbed the Northwest Company and within a few years George Simpson, governor of the Company in Canada, had planned to reorganize the trade of the Pacific slope. The Company would grow more food at the posts, would enter the coastal fur trade to forestall American competition, and would supply all the cordilleran trade from the Pacific rather than from Hudson Bay. In the area that is now northeastern California and southeastern Oregon, the Company hoped to discourage American encroachments by trapping out the furs. Elsewhere, recognizing that furs were an exhaustible resource and that there was no longer territory for expansion, it began a policy of conservation. Until 1828 when he worked his way down the Fraser canyon by canoe, Simpson had hoped that the Fraser River could become the main route inland, but having seen the canyon for himself, he turned instead to improving the overland route that the Nor'westers had pioneered between the Fraser and the Columbia. Before long most of the supplies for, and the furs from, the upper Fraser country traveled by pack horse between Fort Okanagan at the confluence of the Columbia and Okanagan rivers, and Fort Alexandria above the rapids on the Fraser (see Fig. 7-1). The cordilleran trade was no longer connected directly to the east, and had been organized along the north-south grain of the topography.

In 1846 the boundary between British and American territory was extended along the forty-ninth parallel to the Pacific, cutting the Company's main supply line to the northern interior and leaving it without a practical route to the coast. The fur trade and all subsequent settlement in southern British Columbia was forced to adapt to the presence of an international border cutting across the topographic axis. Initially there were two adjustments. In anticipation of the boundary agreement that the influx of American settlers in Oregon was making more and more probable, the Company had established Fort Victoria as a likely main Pacific base in 1843. On the mainland it attempted to connect the interior pack trail with the lower Fraser valley, and by 1848 it had cut a brigade trail from the lower Fraser to the Thompson River, the first of many attempts to enlarge the economic hinterland of the lower Fraser valley by breaking through its mountainous rim.

BRITISH COLUMBIA IN 1855 ON THE EVE OF THE GOLD RUSHES

After more than half a century of fur trading, the northwestern cordillera was still isolated from the outside world. Furs were the only product that withstood shipping costs, and the number of men required to manage the fur trade was small. In all the British cordillera there were not more than 1000 whites, most of whom lived on the southeastern corner of Vancouver Island near Victoria. Perhaps 200 were scattered in the various trading posts on the mainland (see Fig. 7-2). The slight European penetration of the northern cordillera had not undermined the Indian way of life. In spite of several smallpox epidemics which had reduced their number by perhaps a third, Indians outnumbered whites by more than fifty to one. Their distribution (see Fig. 7-2) was broadly that of the immediate pre-contact period. The Indians incorporated goods such as rifles, iron pots, or beads into their cultural patterns; the increased time devoted to hunting and trapping had changed the emphasis but not the nature of Indian activity.

The European life of the northern cordillera still revolved around the Hudson's Bay Company. Company goods were shipped by water from Victoria to Fort Langley on the lower Fraser, the western terminus of the pack-horse trail to the interior. At Fort Kamloops the Company built stockades for 300–400 animals; thereafter the post supplied most of the pack horses for the area. All forts had kitchen gardens, usually tended by hired Indian women, and near Victoria and Fort Langley there were several large Company farms. When the Hudson's Bay Company leased the southern Alaskan shore from the Russian America Company in 1839, it had contracted to supply foodstuffs to the Russians' remaining North American posts. These large farms produced largely for the Russian American market, accounting for the bulk of more than 1000 cattle, 6000 sheep, 4700 bushels of wheat, 6000 bushels of potatoes, and 4500 pounds of butter listed in the Vancouver Island census of 1855. The

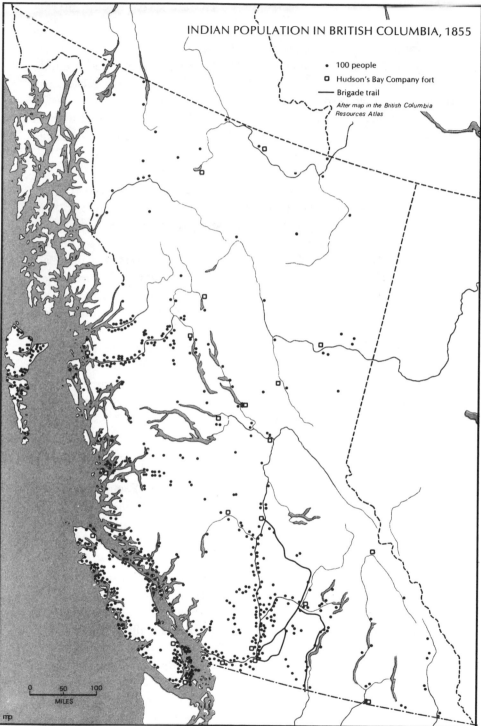

INDIAN POPULATION IN BRITISH COLUMBIA, 1855

• 100 people
□ Hudson's Bay Company fort
— Brigade trail

*After map in the British Columbia
Resources Atlas*

MILES
0   50   100

mp

Figure 7-2.

establishment of individual private farms on Vancouver Island had been discouraged by the abundance of fertile land in Oregon, the relatively high price the Company charged for land (£1 per acre), and the obligation the Company placed on land purchasers to bring out settlers. On the eve of the gold rush private farming was virtually absent.

On the lower Fraser at Fort Langley the Company operated a small salmon fishery where more than 2000 barrels of salted fish were packed annually. Yet the market did not warrant the further expansion of this trade. Lumbering had begun on a more individual basis. In the 1840s one entrepreneur had cut a few masts near the northern end of Vancouver Island. The best were "116 feet long to the first branch, without a knot, 30 inches square at the root to 20 inches at the head," but their very size and the length of the voyage to London kept these timbers from the British market. The California gold fields created a more accessible market, and in 1853 eighteen ships loaded with timber left Vancouver Island for San Francisco. Two years later there were six small sawmills—several of them owned by independent operators—near Victoria.

Yet in 1855 the northwest was still a corner of a far-flung fur trading empire, a place where Indians lived much as they had for generations and where a handful of whites, isolated from the main currents of North American social and intellectual change, added a measure of rough gentility to the routine of the Hudson's Bay Company.

THE GOLD RUSHES

In comparison with the other gold rushes along the Pacific rim in the nineteenth century, the one that brought the sequestered life of the northwest fur trade to an abrupt end in 1858 was a small affair. Eighty thousand people had come to California in 1849, even more in 1850, when at least 100,000 men were actually working in the California mines; but only 25,000 came to the lower Fraser in 1858, most of whom left again in weeks or months. In 1863, at the height of another rush to the central Fraser (the Cariboo), not more than 7000 whites came to the diggings. The annual gold production in British Columbia reached a maximum value of some $4 million, whereas California produced ten times as much each year for more than a decade. Five years after the first rush to the lower Fraser, Victoria was a city of 6000 people; San Francisco in 1854 was a city of 40,000. Yet the Fraser River rushes transformed the northwest, giving the region a stamp that is still apparent. They also exhibited the general characteristics of all the nineteenth-century rushes and, indeed, in quintessential form, of much of North American settlement.

The miners who worked on the bars and gravels of the Fraser had arrived as individuals rather than as members of families or of larger groups. In part, their individuality reflected the speed of the rushes, the miners' driving conviction that gold was the prize of those who got there first rather than of those with capital—impetus enough to pry men loose from many different backgrounds and social bonds. The rushes brought a population of adult men, and the initial dislocation was perpetuated in the drifting life of the miners and in the belated appearance of families. Equally important, the rushes were intensely competitive. Gold was the lure, few men had an initial advantage, any miner might find the mother lode. Sometimes miners banded together for prospecting or to build a road or a flume, but the common collapse of these partnerships when gold was actually discovered and claims staked is a measure of their superficiality. And because the rushes developed rapidly in remote areas and at a time when laissez faire thinking prevailed, there was little governmental structure to check their inherently individualistic, competitive nature.

For those reasons intense, reckless energy was characteristic of all the rushes. Miners had responded to rumor in embarking for the gold fields and continued to do so at the diggings as reports circulated of finds on this or that stream. Settlements appeared in days and sometimes disappeared almost as quickly, prospectors scoured the country, and the most accessible gold was discovered and removed in a short time. As a rush progressed, capital costs rose as rockers were replaced by sluices and then by large-scale hydraulic operations. Faced with such organization ordinary miners either left or became day laborers. In British Columbia, where most of the early miners had come from the California diggings and were well acquainted with the techniques of placer mining, this process was particularly rapid. With it came a sharp decline in population and a waning of the restless drive that had dominated the heyday of the rush. A handful of those who left took away small fortunes, but most left only with shattered expectations; many died along the difficult route to the diggings or perhaps in collapsed shafts sunk in Cariboo gravels.

Along the Fraser, as in the other gold fields, the concentrated energy of men bent on making their fortunes in a season or two scarred the dig-

TWO VIEWS OF BARKERVILLE

Barkerville in its setting. Note the traces of placer mining and the scatter of miners' shacks.
The main street.
The Public Archives of Canada

ging sites beyond recognition. Freshly eroded gullies, flumes, shaft heads, gravel heaps, and miners' shacks were jumbled for miles along the richest creeks. In the Cariboo the forest had been cut bare near the diggings to provide material for buildings, flumes, cribs, and pit props, and a good deal more of it had been merely burned off to facilitate prospecting or mining. The towns at the diggings, too, revealed in their appearance the haste, the uncertainty, and the social disorganization of this type of mining. Barkerville, Cameronton, Richfield, Van Winkle—the mining towns in the Cariboo—each resembled collections of closely grouped miners' shacks, and even the rectangular false front appeared only after larger placer operations gave the diggings a certain air of permanence.

Much of the character of the rushes is also revealed in their effect on the Indians. Here and there along the Fraser the Indians had resisted the miners but, lacking an over-all political structure, they could not coordinate and sustain their opposition. The miners employed some Indians to backpack and to work at the diggings, but more often their only connection with the local Indians was in taking their potatoes and their women, and in leaving disease. During the decade after 1858 the Indian population of British Columbia declined by some 50 per cent. In an oral, family tradition, cultural loss is an almost inevitable effect of sudden population decline, and the abrupt drop in population coupled with the missionaries' attack on the potlatch and medicine men had largely undermined the Indian way of life.

From the miners' point of view most of this destruction was entirely accidental. They had come for a specific purpose, and the changes they had wrought during their short stay—the new landscapes created by the diggings or by the forest fires intentionally set—were simply a means to an end. In a remote part of a remote corner of a vast continent there was no reason to do otherwise. Moreover, most of the miners had no intention of staying. They dreamed of a fortune they would spend elsewhere, on liquor and women in San Francisco, on a mansion in an eastern city. Most of those who stayed did so by accident—the shopkeeper whose business trickled away but who had some capital tied up in the place and could not make up his mind to leave, the miner who had made and lost some money and had convinced himself that he could strike it rich again. Almost no one came with the thought that his effect on an out-of-the-way place was of any consequence, simply because he did not expect to be there long.

The gold-seekers did not become different men as they approached the diggings. They and the gold rushes were very much products of their time; individualism, competitiveness, productive energy, and destructiveness were characteristic of much of North American settlement, particularly in the nineteenth century. In many ways they may be thought of as rough models of much of North American settlement, although in one respect they were different. Where, after some initial movement in the early pioneer years, men usually settled down to farm, some held the belief that the encounter with the wilderness marked a fresh start, the beginning of a new and better society. Almost inevitably this belief was tied in one way or another to Christianity. It provided a collective view that contrasted with and sometimes diluted the strong individualism and competitiveness of the frontier, giving rise to much of North American idealism. In the gold rushes such a view was almost entirely absent.

Quite apart from these considerations, the discovery of gold along the Fraser had a decisive bearing on the particular development of British Columbia. Although Vancouver Island had become a crown colony in 1849, the mainland had remained Hudson's Bay Company territory. Shortly after news of the gold rush to the lower Fraser reached London, the mainland was withdrawn from direct control by the Company, designated a crown colony, and placed under the governorship of James Douglas, chief factor of the Hudson's Bay Company in the northwest and governor of Vancouver Island. But the hasty creation of another colony did not, in itself, solve the political problem the gold rush had created. The areas along the middle and upper Fraser in which much of the gold was eventually found had been connected to the sea until the mid-1840s by the Montréal traders' route from the upper Fraser to the Okanagan, on to the Columbia, and thence to the Pacific and after 1846 by fur brigade trails from the lower Fraser valley. These trails, which were blocked by snow in the higher passes for eight months of the year, were a roundabout route to the Cariboo and totally inadequate for the heavy traffic of a gold rush.

Most of the first miners were Americans and almost all of them were from California. Whatever the area's legal status, the rush could conceivably put British sovereignty of the northwest into question, particularly if the principal route to the diggings passed through American territory and depended on an American port. Largely with this fear in mind, Douglas ordered all miners to purchase a license in Victoria; even so some 8000 of them in the spring of 1858 crossed the border in the Okanogan valley, although the importance of this entry eventually dwindled.

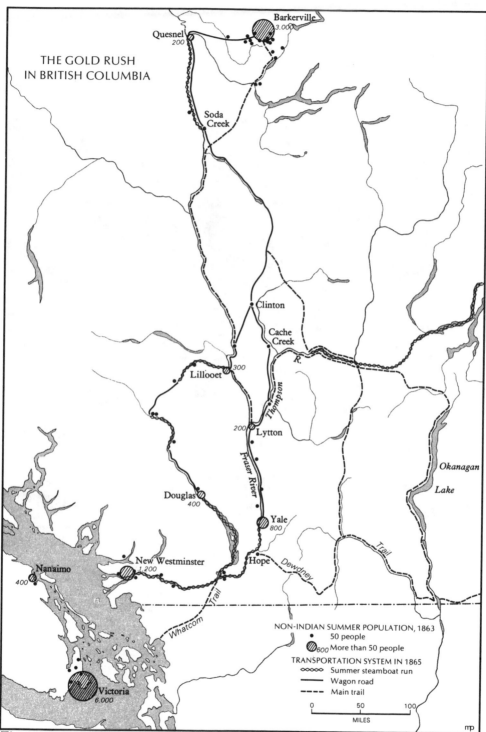

Figure 7-3.

In July 1858, American steamboats reached Yale, a point more than one hundred miles up the Fraser River, and in the next two months, miners had cut mule trails from Yale to Lytton and from Fort Douglas to Lillooet (see Fig. 7-3). Although a British official likened these routes

VIEWS ALONG THE CARIBOO ROAD, 1867-68

Above: The Cariboo road through the Fraser Canyon.
Opposite, above: Clinton, a typical stagecoach and wagon stop.
Opposite, below: Soda Creek, junction of road and steamboat line.
The Public Archives of Canada

to goat tracks, the Fraser canyon became a commercial artery that summer. An American attempt to deflect trade from the lower Fraser along the Whatcom trail to an American port (see Fig. 7-3), was undertaken privately on too small a scale to be successful. In 1861 a detachment of Royal Engineers began replacing mule trails with wagon roads along the Douglas-Lillooet route and, in 1863 through the most difficult sections of the Fraser canyon. By 1865 a wagon road extended from Yale to Barkerville in the heart of the Cariboo, and, with regular steamboat service on the lower and middle Fraser, an efficient transportation system to the interior had been laid out entirely within British territory and along the river that the fur trade had largely ignored. The expense of such a system would have been unthinkable in fur trading days, but the gold rushes provided the economic justification and the political necessity to elicit an energetic official response. The Fraser wagon road and the Canadian Pacific Railway (built twenty years later), together constituted the physical basis for a continuing British presence in northwestern North America, and without the impetus of the gold rushes neither would have been built so soon.

The gold rushes also created a new pattern of non-Indian settlement (compare the distribution of fur posts in Fig. 7-2 with the distribution of non-Indian population in Fig. 7-4) that was not altered substantially until the building of the Canadian Pacific Railway and the mining boom in the Kootenays in the 1890s. Although many of the settlements near the diggings were short-lived, most of the small transportation centers had a considerably longer life, some as points of trans-shipment from wagon to steamboat, others as stagecoach stops. New Westminster, a port on the mouth of the Fraser where goods were trans-shipped from ocean to river steamers, was replaced in importance by Vancouver only when the railway displaced the steamboat. As before the gold rushes, Victoria remained the principal center north of the border, a position it had maintained by its status as a free port, by the licensing requirements mentioned above, and because of the hazards of navigating the shoals and bars of the lower Fraser. In the summer of 1858 Victoria's population rose to 3000, and 200 commercial buildings went up. There were eight wharves, a shipyard, a Chinatown, and several paved and lighted streets by the end of the year. At the height of the Cariboo rush in 1863 some 175 firms advertised regularly in the local newspaper.

For the group of Hudson's Bay Company employees and colonial officials at the helm of government in British Columbia, the extreme individualism of a gold rush jeopardized the concept of law and order on

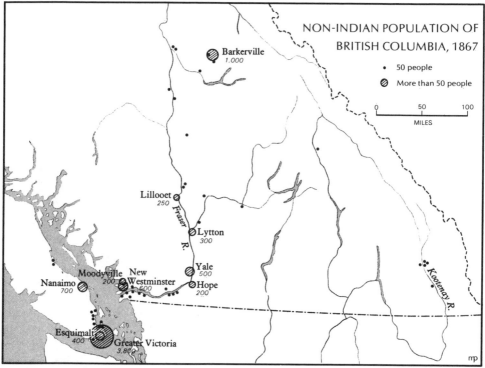

Figure 7-4.

which, they felt, any civilized society must rest. From the earliest weeks of the rush they attempted to bring the miners within the rule of law, and one aspect of this policy was the creation of a body of law relating to the alienation of crown (public) land. Stockmen and farmers, attracted by the high food prices at the diggings, and almost as transient as the miners themselves, were an early part of the Fraser River rush. No agricultural land law had existed on the mainland before 1858; now, suddenly there was a need for a comprehensive land policy. Most Americans, and soon colonial officials as well, favored a pre-emptive system, that is, the right to settle on and improve ungranted crown land and eventually to purchase it at a fixed, low price. Early in 1860 a Pre-emption Act came into effect, its provisions based largely on an American act of 1841. With few trained surveyors in British Columbia, no certainty where surveying was most needed, but vigorous demands for the right of land ownership, pre-emption was probably the only feasible policy. That such a law was in effect within two years after the beginning of the rushes reflects the efficiency of the colonial administration. Officials did not consider pre-emption an ideal policy, and thought of the Pre-emption Act as a provisional measure (although it remained in the books, with modifications, until 1874). They were realistic enough to recognize that in the middle of a gold rush more regulation could not be achieved.

Pastoral law presented more intricate problems: essentially the relationship between cattlemen and farmers and the protection of the range from overgrazing. In the first summers of the rush to the Cariboo, cattlemen and farmers clashed sharply; although one British magistrate described the interior grasslands as "clothed with every description of herb and plant that could possibly be desired by the stock farmer," and another likened them to "a vast park attached to a nobleman's mansion in England—nothing but grass and ornamental clumps of trees," it was apparent by the mid-1860s that bunch grass was being replaced by sage under the pressure of overgrazing. In 1865 the colonial government started to charge up to seven cents an acre per year for grazing cattle on crown land and set a range-carrying capacity of ten acres a head. A fence ordinance in 1869 stipulated that any area in the colony could be designated a "fence district" if so requested by two-thirds of the landowners. Within these districts farmers could not claim damage for animal trespass. These policies reveal an early attempt to conserve range land—just as before the rush the Hudson's Bay Company had conserved beaver—and to strike a balance between conflicting agricultural interests. As such, they were years ahead of similar legislation in the United States. The example of land law was but one instance of the speed with which the rule of law was imposed on the gold rushes to the Fraser River, with the result that there was less violence and more management of society and land than in California.

What had happened, of course, was that at the level of official policy the view of the Hudson's Bay Company and its ideological and administrative successors in the colonial administration had asserted itself strongly. The more popular view was individualistic, especially in the first years of the rush when almost all the miners were Americans. But many of the Americans drifted back across the line, and as the population of British Columbia became predominantly British and Canadian and the effectiveness of some aspects of official policy became apparent, the popular view contained both strands.

BRITISH COLUMBIA IN 1867

By 1867 British Columbia was entering a post-gold rush slump. Its resources were much better known than before 1858, but the problem of an isolated location far from world markets was as acute as ever. A technology suited to its forests and fishery was only beginning to evolve. Although the discovery of gold had broken the hold of the fur trade over the northern cordillera, it became apparent as the rushes waned that neither furs nor gold could form the economic base of the area, but it was equally apparent that there was no obvious alternative to them. Yet by this date some 12,000 non-Indian people lived in British Columbia, more than half of them in the southeastern corner of Vancouver Island, from 1000 to 2000 in the lower Fraser valley, and the remainder at the mine sites and along the routes to the sites or at the remaining fur posts (see Fig. 7-4). The population was still predominantly male and of varied national background. Since most Americans had returned south, at least three-quarters were British or Canadians. There were also more than 1000 Chinese from California who had stayed at the diggings after other miners had moved on. Although several gold rush towns were now deserted, 2000 miners—a third of them Chinese—worked in the Cariboo. With meat and flour produced locally a man could live on fifty cents a day and hope to earn two or three dollars at the diggings. Chinese had taken over most of the claims in the Kootenays where there had been minor rushes in 1864 and 1865. The Dewdney trail (see Fig. 7-3), built in 1865 to open a route through British territory to the Kootenays, had never been much used. Even in 1867 it was reverting to bush, and the small population of the Kootenays depended entirely on supplies from across the border.

Victoria was still easily the largest city in the colony although its population had declined by almost half since 1863, and a corresponding decrease had taken place in the number of shipping companies, realtors, saloons, boardinghouses, tobacconists, and gentlemen's outfitters. Cricket was to be seen on a Sunday afternoon, and something of the city's pre-gold rush character had re-emerged, although in 1867 many of its businesses were owned in San Francisco, and some were simply branches of San Francisco firms. These same firms advertised in the New Westminster and Cariboo papers. To some extent Victoria remained as it had been in the early days of the gold rushes—the channel through which commercial interests in San Francisco penetrated the Fraser River settlements. But there were also British or Canadian firms in Victoria, and former employees of the Hudson's Bay Company who operated successfully in both Victoria and San Francisco. In 1862 the London-financed Bank of British Columbia had opened in Victoria, and five years later had several branches in California, its branch in San Francisco quickly becoming the second bank in that city. Victoria was not simply a dependent of San Francisco; rather, both cities participated in a triangular pattern of trade and finance dominated, in many ways, by London.

There was still some farming in the Cariboo, on the high terraces along the middle Fraser, and in the lower Fraser valley where by 1867, 1000 acres of the massive coastal forest had been cleared and more than 200 men were farming. Wheat was the principal crop along the middle Fraser, barley and oats in the Cariboo, where the growing season was shorter, and almost all farmers—many of whom were Chinese—grew potatoes and raised swine. In the lower Fraser valley some 4000 cattle grazed on the natural meadows along the river. Dairy farming was beginning here, and a little butter was shipped to the Cariboo. Most of this farming had begun almost as hurriedly as the diggings. Farm buildings resembled miners' shacks, and farmers did not plan for sustained yields. With a lucrative local market during the peak years of a rush and, as the rush declined, with a meager market that might disappear altogether, farmers had little incentive to plan ahead.

Later in the century the economic vacuum created by the waning of the rushes would be filled by silver and lead mining in the Kootenays, the salmon fishery, and the lumber trade, but in 1867 these developments lay ahead or were barely taking shape. As in 1855, salmon continued to be salted and barreled on the lower Fraser, and in 1867 the first cannery, modeled on canneries in Scotland and New Brunswick, began operation near New Westminster. Most of the canning and even the manufacture of cans from imported tinplate was done by hand. Fishing techniques were those of the salt fishery: open boats twenty-six feet long with a two-man crew, one to row and the other to handle the net. Many of the fishermen were Indians, for fishing was familiar to them, and the irregularity of daily and seasonal work accorded well with their traditional routine. Crude as the techniques were, the cannery did begin to provide a non-perishable commodity with some export potential.

In Burrard Inlet, the harbor of the present city of Vancouver a few miles north of the mouth of the Fraser River, there were two steam saw-

Road near New Westminister, British Columbia. In distorting the relative size of man and trees, this sketch by the Marquis of Lorne gives a vivid impression of what must have been a common reaction of European visitors to the towering west coast forest. The Public Archives of Canada mills, and in the forests nearby the distinctive technology of west-coast logging was beginning to appear. A large cedar or Douglas fir of the coastal forest, perhaps ten or twelve feet in diameter at the butt, was usually felled only by the labor of several men over a day or more. First, notches were cut in the trunks above the underbrush (cedars, however, were notched above the flaring of the trunk, the diameter of which could double in the last few feet from the ground) and split planks were driven into the notches. A man could then undercut the trees while standing several feet off the ground. Sawing required crosscut saws that were usually nine but occasionally as much as eighteen feet long. When felled, these large trees were even more difficult to move, and, until the introduction of short logging railways near the end of the century, logging stayed close to tidewater. Skids were built of smaller logs; ideal sites for skidding had a continuous slope to the beach. Oxen could haul small logs on level ground. In these terms the Burrard Inlet site had several advantages: a deepwater port, some of the finest Douglas fir and cedar along the coast, and steady grades to the waterfront. Together with an earlier mill on the west coast of Vancouver Island, the two mills on Burrard Inlet marked the beginning of the large-scale commercial exploitation of the coastal forest.

Here were the beginnings of another economy, but in the decline of the gold rushes, there were no substantial markets for British Columbia's products. A little coal mined on Vancouver Island and a little lumber were shipped to California, but for the most part the California market was closed to British Columbia by tariffs and by competitors in Washington and Oregon. Markets in Montréal, Toronto, or Halifax were on the other side of the continent. London was farther away. British Columbia's lumber was used to build cities around the Pacific rim, but the volume of this trade was small. Most of the possible connections had been explored; none was well developed. Yet a society that was not American had been established in the northern cordillera, and this was somewhat remarkable, given that only twenty years before, the entire cordillera from northern California to Alaska had been managed as a single unit and that in 1858 thousands of miners from California had rushed to the lower Fraser. The conservative British hand of the Hudson's Bay Company and the Colonial office had drawn back but had maintained a hold on a segment of the cordillera, there to fashion a society and a settled place that were not simply a northern replication of California.

Bibliography

The nineteenth-century geography of British Columbia remains to be written, and for the historical geographer as well as for the historian, the best general sources on the area and period are F. W. Howay, W. N. Sage, and H. F. Angus, *British Columbia and the United States; the North Pacific Slope from Fur Trade to Aviation* (Ryerson Press, 1942); and Margaret A. Ormsby, *British Columbia: A History* (Macmillan, 1958). A useful short discussion of the early cordilleran fur trade is Frederick Merk's *Fur Trade and Empire; George Simpson's Journal* (Cambridge: Harvard University Press, 1931). S. B. Jones's article "The Cordilleran Section of the Canada–U.S. Borderland," *Geographical Journal* 89 (1937), 439–50, contains a good discussion of the influence of the boundary settlement of 1846 on the pattern of cordilleran trade. Two recent articles in the *Journal of B.C. Studies,* one by Keith Ralston, "Patterns of Trade and Investment on the Pacific Coast, 1867–1892: The Case of the British Columbia Salmon Canning Industry," *B.C. Studies* No. 1 (Winter 1968–69), 37–45; and the other by J. M. S. Careless, "The Lowe Brothers, 1852–70: A Study in Business Relations on the North Pacific Coast," *B.C. Studies* No. 2 (Summer 1969), 1–18, do much to correct the widespread assumption that developments in British Columbia immediately after the gold rushes were directed from San Francisco. Beyond these studies, the volumes of the *British Columbia Historical Quarterly* contain many useful articles and reminiscences. The following M.A. theses in history at the University of British Columbia contain information not readily available elsewhere: Phyllis Mikkelsen, "Land Settlement Policy on the Mainland of British Columbia, 1858–1874" (1950); Sylvia L. Thrupp, "A History of the Cranbrook District in East Kootenay" (1929); Helen B. Akrigg, "History and Economic Development of the Shuswap Area" (1964); John E. Gibbard, "Early History of the Fraser Valley, 1808–1885" (1937); and J. C. Lawrence, "Markets and Capital; A History of the Lumber Industry of British Columbia, 1778–1952" (1957).

8 CONCLUSION

After the end of the fifteenth century the European consciousness gradually came to include most of the territory that is now called Canada. The process begun by Cabot continued with Cartier, Champlain, Hudson, La Vérendrye, Henday, Mackenzie, Thompson, and others until, early in the nineteenth century, the outline of Canada could be mapped with considerable accuracy. Except in parts of the Arctic the coastline was known; so too were the major rivers, lakes, mountain ranges, and plains. Although there were still gaps in the map, the shape and the major contents of the northern half of a continent had come into focus. Moreover, European influences had spread throughout the area. In parts of the far north and northwest, European trade goods and diseases had reached peoples European traders had not seen; across the breadth of the southern Shield and northern plains and cordillera the fur traders had established posts; and by Confederation many people of European background had settled in the St. Lawrence–Great Lakes lowland and in parts of the Maritimes.

The significance of the European extension into Canada depends on the side of the Atlantic and the latitude in North America from which it is viewed. The archeologic record at most Indian sites has been transformed by the appearance of European goods; while a pollen profile of a Southern Ontario bog reveals a sharper break in the vegetative record early in the nineteenth century than at any time since deglaciation. The history of Canada, as written by Canadian historians, is a history of people of European origin. But in histories of France, of England, or even

of the United States, Canada has figured little more prominently than
has a minor border war or a defeated presidential candidate.

Although the exploration of Canada was a part of the great age of
geographical and scientific discovery, Canada had contributed none of
the notable discoveries. Columbus had apparently discovered Asia or a
terrestrial paradise—he himself believed that the Orinoco River flowed
out of heaven—but John Cabot had sailed to a forbidding, rocky coast,
and for this modest discovery received a ten-pound gift and a twenty-
pound annuity from Henry VII. The Caribbean sugar plantations, Cor-
tez, and Pizarro have no Canadian counterparts; in their place was the
cod fishery. Codfish fed many European stomachs but inspired neither
poets nor kings. In the sixteenth century the land beyond the eastern
shores of Newfoundland intrigued Europeans only so long as they could
believe that it was something it was not. After Cartier and Roberval
they left it alone for two-thirds of a century. Subsequently exploration
revealed an ice-clogged Arctic shoreline, an inland sea blocked by ice
for most of the year, treeless barrens, a vast boreal forest dotted with
lakes and rock outcrops and thinly occupied by nomadic Indians; and a
few pockets of land with demonstrated or potential agricultural significance. These discoveries interested a few merchants, brought some
settlers in their train, and considerably altered the European price of
some goods, but had little effect on the pattern of European thought or
the reach of European imagination.

In terms of their own experience Europeans had come to an inhospi-
table land. To sail west from La Rochelle or Bristol was to leave the
warm waters of the Gulf Stream for the cold waters of the Labrador current; a moderate marine climate for a severe continental climate; a land
suited to arable and pastoral farming for another which, in most of its
extent, had no agricultural potential whatever. Faced with this contrast,
Europeans came to conceive of Canada as a sullen, forbidding wilderness. Only a handful of Cartier's men survived the horror of a winter at
Québec in 1535–36. An account of Martin Frobisher's voyage described
his little ships at "the mercy of the merciless yce," and in the next century the *Jesuit Relations* reported not only the glory of bringing God to
the savages, but also massacres, tortures, and martyrdoms. There were
gentler, happier reports such as Marc Lescarbot's description of Acadia
but, in sum, Canada emerged on the European consciousness as bleak
and uninviting. With little evidence to the contrary, this image lingered
on. At the close of the Seven Years War the British seriously thought of

exchanging Canada for the sugar island of Martinique. In the nineteenth century Charlotte Bronté considered a "Canadian temperature" to be one that "froze the very blood," while settlers' guides and many a letter back home sought to convince Europeans that Canada was fit for settlement.

Of course, the idea of wilderness was not necessarily unattractive, but its hold on the Western mind largely depended on the contrast between the wilderness and the civilized or romantic landscape of the garden. The Canadian wilderness, however, was so unremittingly vast, there was so little prospect of a garden deeper in the forest or of ever tempering granite, spruce, or cold, that in the European mind Canada became synonymous with wilderness. It was only farther south, where the climate was less severe and the land inherently richer that the images of wilderness and garden could find a comfortable coexistence. Fundamentally this was the reason for Canada's weak hold on the European imagination and, by contrast, much of the reason for the Europeans' almost endless fascination with the United States. A member of Sir Walter Raleigh's expedition described Virginia in 1584 as neither explorer nor the most enthusiastic settlers' guide ever described Canada. The soil, he said, was "the most plentiful, sweete and fruitful, and wholesome in all the worlde," the land so bountiful that "I thinke in all the worlde a like abundance is not to be found." Even the natives were "most gentle, loving and faithful, voide of all guile and treason, and such as live after the manner of a golden age." Some years later William Bradford, settler and historian of the Plymouth Colony, wrote that he had come to a "hideous and desolate wilderness, full of willd beasts and willd men." Virginia, as many of its settlers discovered, was not an unqualified garden; whereas, as the Puritans cleared land in Massachusetts, a garden was gradually hewn from the wilderness. The land that became the United States evoked symbols that not only influenced the European conception of America, but that eventually became part of the Americans' conception of themselves. Above all, the wilderness and the garden together suggested boundless possibilities. They were the symbolic geography of Edenic myth and of the wanderings of the children of Israel. "In the beginning," said the philosopher John Locke, "all the world was America." America, indeed, was born as much out of hope for a New World beginning as Canada was born out of the fur trade. The one was a place for dreams and settlement; the other a source of raw materials.

The failure of Canada to excite the European imagination meant not only that fewer people would come to Canada but also that the people

Hunting on snowshoes, from André Thevet's *Les Singularitéz de la France Antartique, autrement nommé Amerique*, Paris, 1558. An attempt to depict a New World garden within a snowy wilderness of which Europeans still had the most meager knowledge.

who settled Canada and the United States would be somewhat different. Most of the 10,000 immigrants who came to Canada during the French regime were unemployed men rounded up in ports and sent to Canada as *engagés;* or were soldiers, girls from Paris poorhouses, or petty criminals sent by French officials. Canadian settlement was essentially the result of decisions by the French government to counter the military and economic power of European rivals rather than by individuals to emigrate to an attractive colony. In the English colonies to the south were Puritans who had come to build a City of God; people of varied language, church, and sect who had been attracted by William Penn's claim that his colony was "the best poor man's country in the world"; and a few English gentlemen who had come to make their fortunes on a plantation. The seaboard colonies contained a great many immigrants who had crossed the Atlantic with no more individual purpose than most of the immigrants to Canada before 1760, but many others had been drawn by the allure of a new land. In the nineteenth century most of Southern Ontario and the Maritimes were settled by poor from the British Isles, by men and families dislocated by demographic and technological change. Many of them came to Canada because they could obtain the cheapest Atlantic passage in the hold of a timber ship. Most came because economic conditions at home had become unbearable, not because Canada held any particular appeal. For many Canada was the only place to go, a place where, if fortune smiled, they might maintain or improve their standard of living. The more ambitious immigrants usually went to the United States, although some who strongly preferred to remain in the British Empire emigrated to Canada for this reason. Earlier many of the Loyalists had come because Canada was the most accessible British territory. Having fought on the losing side of the American Revolution, the Loyalists found Canada a haven from persecution; for a few of them, it was also a haven for a retrospective Britishness that was rooted in a conception of a functioning Old World society rather than in the possibilities of a New World beginning.

Here lies much of the basis of what Northrop Frye has called the inductive quality of Canadian life. Failing to excite the European imagination, Canada rarely became the playground of European ideals. For this reason it attracted few utopian immigrant communities. Rather, it was the territory of fishermen, of lumbermen, and of poor Scotch-Irish or Highland Scots who struggled to make a living on a farm lot in Southern Ontario or in the stony Nova Scotian uplands. Its leaders tended to be competent administrators and merchants, men with more practical interest in achieving prosperity in an ordered society than vision of the future. The statement of principle in the American constitution, Thomas Jefferson's pastoral ideal and de Tocqueville's analysis of American democracy were replaced in Canada by Lord Durham's report.

The area that had registered so little on the European imagination has remained thinly occupied to the present. Dominating it is the rocky arc of the Canadian Shield, land which by the end of the sixteenth century was appreciated for its valuable fur-bearing animals and by the early nineteenth century for its timber. By the middle of the nineteenth century farmers had settled here and there on the Shield, which had never been attractive for settlement. Most of its soils are thin, bouldery, and acidic; its climate, even along the southern rim, marginal for cereals. That at Confederation any of the Shield was farmed is a measure of the pressure of man on land in lowland Québec and in Ireland. For the most part, early agricultural settlement in Canada was on patches of arable land between the Shield and the American border. Whereas granite or growing season fixed the northern limit of Canadian agriculture, the southern limit was a political boundary. It had been determined in each major section when the dominant activity to the north was the fur trade, when the agricultural potential of the northern continent was largely unknown and unconsidered, and when American agricultural settlers were pushing vigorously westward. As a result the border between Canada and the United States crosses the North American agricultural ecumene near and in some places beyond its northern limit.

Of the arable patches the largest are the St. Lawrence–Great Lakes lowland and the western plains. By Confederation the former was the home of some two and a half million people; the latter, but for a small colony along the Red River, was still the territory of a few thousand Métis and Indians. In the Maritimes there were fragments of agricultural land close to the fishing ports and more extensive clearings in the river valleys and uplands, but no contiguous area of agricultural settlement larger than Prince Edward Island. In the far west a few thousand people of European background lived near the southern tip of Vancouver Island and along the Fraser River. This at Confederation was the outline of British North America (see Fig. 8-1): just over three million people scattered in a discontinuous, unbalanced line across a continent; and to the north a few fur posts, a few Indians and Eskimos, and a landscape that had hardly changed since the time of John Cabot.

Nor were the patches of settlement well connected to each other. Before 1821 brigades of men and supplies regularly headed west from Montréal, but with the merger of the Northwest Company and the Hudson Bay Company in 1821 most of this traffic stopped. In 1867 regular travel through British territory between the western plains and the St. Lawrence lowland was more difficult than it had been fifty years before, and the people at Red River relied on connections with Hudson Bay or St. Paul. In 1862 two young Englishmen, Lord Milton and his able doctor-companion Cheadle, making what they described as the first tourist trip across British North America to the Pacific, took many months to reach the Cariboo gold fields after leaving the Red River settlement. The many settled patches in the Maritimes were not part of an integrated system of transport and commerce. No primate city had emerged in the Maritimes; rather, the Newfoundland outports fed into St. John's,

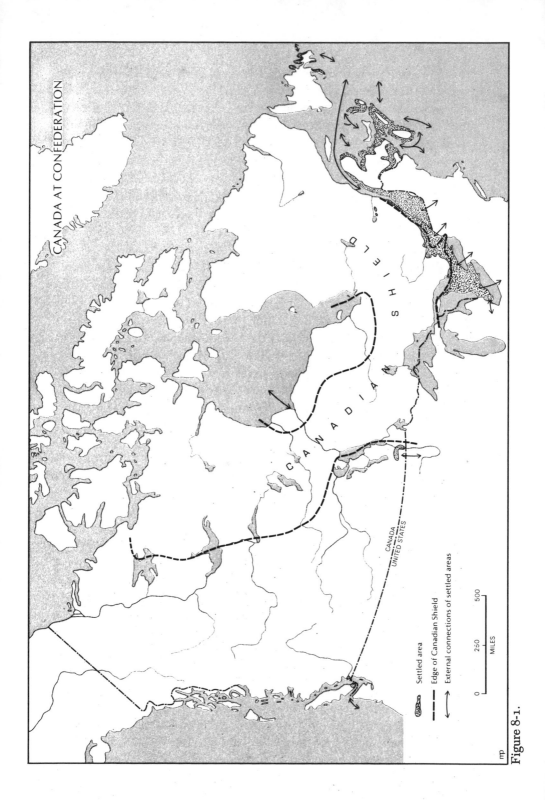

CANADA AT CONFEDERATION

SHIELD

CANADIAN

CANADA
UNITED STATES

Settled area
Edge of Canadian Shield
External connections of settled areas

0   250   500
MILES

rrp

Figure 8-1.

most Nova Scotian settlements fed into Halifax, and the Saint John valley into Saint John. These centers, in turn, were tied independently across the Atlantic to London. The whole Maritime region stood well apart from the St. Lawrence lowland. In 1840 there was no wagon road from the St. Lawrence lowland into New Brunswick; at Confederation there was only one such road, no railway, and little shipping between Montréal and any port in the Maritimes.

Commercial unity existed only within the St. Lawrence–Great Lakes lowland. Canals bypassed rapids on the upper St. Lawrence and the Grand Trunk Railway ran from Montréal to the southwestern corner of Southern Ontario; to a considerable extent Montréal's commercial vitality depended on these westward connections. To be sure, most of the export trade of the Great Lakes basin flowed through New York—it was largely for that reason that New York was a much larger city than Montréal—and even Southern Ontario's exports drained heavily southward. Still, agents of Montréal firms operated in Toronto, Kingston, and Hamilton. Montréal banks had a large share of Ontario's financial business and most Ontario farmers bought or sold some goods which passed through Montréal. However strongly it was connected to the south, here was a considerable commercial network. Anchored in London, England, it funneled through the central business district and better residential areas of Montréal, influencing in one way or another almost all the inhabitants of the St. Lawrence–Great Lakes lowland.

But within the commercial empire of the St. Lawrence were two dominant languages, two dominant religious affiliations, two sets of broadly different historical experiences. The French Canadians, who supplied a good deal of the labor force and a little of the agricultural produce for the St. Lawrence trading system, had a different attachment to place, different views of the relationship of an individual to society, and different conceptions of government and of themselves in the world than had the English-speaking businessmen in Montréal and the English-speaking farmers in Ontario. Although many French-Canadian girls had married demobilized British soldiers or Catholic Irish immigrants, and the lines of some families straddled different cultures through several generations, the cultural distance between French- and English-speaking people living side by side in the St. Lawrence lowland was usually enormous.

During the French regime insouciance, bravado, and considerable disdain for authority were dominant characteristics of the life of the habitants. They lived boisterously, spending their small incomes, enjoying the independence and moderate prosperity of their lives in the côtes and perhaps too the Indian girls along the upper Ottawa. In the century after the conquest much of this zest remained—French Canadians still spent rather than hoarded, spun tales, sang, drank, and raced their horses to mass—but their lives were gradually contained in the tight frame of the local rural community. With English dominance in commerce and government, French Canadians became a minority in Québec and Montréal; with the loss of the fur trade to Hudson Bay and with English-speaking settlement in Ontario, the west dropped out of French-Canadian life; with the filling up of the seigneurial lowlands, habitants could no longer move easily from one seigneurie to another. The remote world of the North Atlantic reached the habitant, if at all, through the filtering eyes of English-speaking merchants, colonial administrators, or parish priests. His outlook was overwhelmingly local, built around immediate family, kin, côte, and parish, the community and place in which he had been born and in which, unless forced away by population pressure, he would spend his life. Only a few French Canadians were in contact with the thought of the nineteenth-century world, and the energies of the most vigorous of these few were expended in a defensive nationalism. Thus the outlook of even the French-Canadian elite was essentially retrospective and exceedingly conservative. For some, as for example many of the seigneurs who argued in the 1840s and 1850s for the maintenance of the seigneurial system, conservatism was rooted in self-interest; for others, in the poverty and helplessness of the French-Canadian minority in British territory, where power and patronage were not in French-Canadian hands. In this situation French-Canadian society as a whole clung as tightly as possible to the institutions, the memories, and the myths of an earlier era.

The English-speaking people who settled among and to the west of the French Canadians had come out of the nineteenth century. Today, we probably would say that the values of most of these newcomers were liberal. They tended to value individual freedom and achievement above the constraints of community, believed in the necessity and inevitability of progress, and occupied themselves with the task of building a prosperous life in a new place. Most of them were Britons, products of the early Victorian years; Scots and Ulstermen, however, outnumbered the English, and this strongly tinged their outlook with an earlier Calvinism. Even in the 1860s settlers in the broad belt of Scotch-Irish settlement that ran most of the length of Southern Ontario were reminded in their newspapers and probably more frequently in their sermons that work was a fundamental law of God, and this ethic undoubtedly bore upon both the methods and the goals of a people engaged in clearing land, building towns, and achieving commercial prosperity. There were other elements in the English-speaking population of the St. Lawrence–Great Lakes lowland—poor Catholic Irish, who often had more in common with the habitants than with other English-speaking immigrants, and Anglican gentry, whose belief in a stratified society capped by a cultured elite had some parallels in the values of the seigneurial class in Québec— but on the whole there were basic value differences between English- and French-speaking people within the St. Lawrence–Great Lakes lowland.

These differences, coupled with the power that lay behind the English-speaking elite, meant that the central business districts and better residential areas of Montréal and Québec were overwhelmingly English-speaking; that the New Englanders in the Eastern Townships were prosperous whereas the habitants in the St. Lawrence lowland were poor; and that Southern Ontario and the Eastern Townships were alive with the bustle of new mills, hamlets, and towns whereas there was little sign of commercial vitality in rural French Canada. The main street of a French-Canadian village was a straggling collection of small white-washed farmhouses dominated by a church; that of a Southern Ontario village was a shorter, contiguous line of two- or three-story brick store facades. The one grew retrospectively out of the countryside, while the other grew out of urban aspiration. The Ontario farmhouse was an amalgam of the architectural modes of the late eighteenth and nineteenth century whereas French-Canadian vernacular building was rooted in the French regime and, ultimately, in medieval France. The rang reflected the gregariousness of French-Canadian rural life; the isolated farmhouses of Southern Ontario and the Eastern Townships, the subordination of the rural community to commercial achievement. Wherever French- and English-speaking people came together in the St. Lawrence– Great Lakes lowland the break in the cultural landscape was as sharp as anywhere in eastern North America.

There were even deeper cultural discontinuities such as those between white and Indian or between white and Métis, but involving fewer, more scattered, and less organized people who could more easily be ignored or pushed aside. But even the English-speaking settlements in British

North America were not larger or smaller versions of each other. No-where in Southern Ontario were there the crisp white and green settle-ments that marked the extension of New England into parts of Québec, Nova Scotia and New Brunswick. The retired fur traders, descendants of Lord Selkirk's crofters, French Canadians, half-breeds, Americans, and Ontarians who comprised the Red River settlement were not a western extension of Ontario; nor were the miners along the Fraser River or the merchants and colonial officials in Victoria. In the Maritimes and New-foundland the fragmentation of terrain and coastline and the isolation of local economies created conditions in which the cultural variety of immi-grants often could be perpetuated for generations. At Confederation many scots on Cape Breton Island and Acadians in many parts of the Maritimes spoke no English, German was still a household language among the Lunenburgers, and the culture of the Irish farmer-fishermen around the Avalon peninsula included many ancient Irish folkways that were rapidly disappearing in Ireland. Haligonians considered that New Brunswickers were another people; the settled rural communities on Prince Edward Island had little in common with the boisterous logging camps along the Miramichi and the Restigouche. Few Maritimers knew enough about Ontario to have any idea what its remote population was like.

Further fragmenting British North America at Confederation was the extremely local scale within which much of ordinary life was still organ-ized. In the nineteenth century ancient craft traditions in the British Isles were being replaced by the massive scale of the machine age, with the result that local communities were weakening, cities were en-larging, and the exercise of power over more people and wider areas was becoming easier. Although not themselves industrialized, Southern On-tario and most of the Maritimes never really partook of the pre-industrial age. The wave of disconnected people who largely settled these areas was itself a by-product of industrialization, and in the rush of nineteenth-century technological change there was not time, except in a few pockets in the Maritimes, to recreate a pre-industrial society. Still, elements of the pre-industrial structure survived for a time. Most gristmills were still family operations that served the surrounding farmers. Blacksmiths, coo-pers, wheelwrights, tinsmiths and many other artisans practised their trades much as they had been practised for centuries, making many rural areas highly subsistent in the basic needs of farm and household. Local marketing centers were still important, and these villages or small towns were the largest places that many rural people ever visited. This decentralization was threatened by railways, the growth of specialized wholesaling and merchandising, and the introduction of the factory system; but as late as the 1860s pre-industrial methods of production and distribution still fostered a strong localism in British North American life. Even in Southern Ontario there were many important regional centers. Toronto was far from the overwhelmingly pre-eminent city it subsequently became, and a great many people had little sense of the larger world beyond their farm, the local village, and the nearest town. In the Maritimes where the population was more scattered, regional economies were more isolated, and technological innovations were slower to make headway, life was even more localized.

The patches of British North American settlement were located on the southern edge of a northern wilderness and on the northern edge of the United States and were isolated from each other by distance, culture, and the still local scale of their technology. Conscious of their separate identities, they all lived defensively. In Northrop Frye's metaphor, they were garrison societies, each with rigid and largely unquestioned standards of behavior, deep respect for its own institutions, and a closely knit sense of identity in the face of common enemies. Perhaps this mentality was particularly characteristic of French Canadians, acutely aware as they were of their minority position amid alien and often hostile people, but it also underlay English life in the private clubs in Québec or in the remote communities on Vancouver Island, where a fastidiously British elite had reproduced many of the manners and affectations of the gentry. It characterized the four or five families hemmed by rock and sea in a Newfoundland outport, and even Southern Ontarians, who were aware of the limits of their physical environment, aware of the proximity of the Americans and French Canadians, aware of their British roots on the other side of the Atlantic. Almost wherever they lived, British North Americans defended themselves against the harshness and limitations of the land, against the restless energy of the Americans, and occasionally against the encroaching claims of other British North Americans.

The land itself was the most implacable protagonist. The settlements of fishermen and farmers around the coast of Nova Scotia backed into a rocky upland; the Shield closely rimmed the north shore of the St. Lawrence lowland; and even in Southern Ontario the maximum distance at Confederation between the lakefront and the edge of approximately contiguous farm settlement was not seventy-five miles. In Québec the

Cartouche, based on French accounts, from Hermann Moll's map of Eastern North America in 1715. The European imagination and the North American reality were still far apart.

acute shortage of land for agricultural expansion threatened a rural people's cultural survival. Parish priests extolled the economic and cultural benefits of settlement in the Canadian Shield, and thousands of French Canadians undertook the back-breaking task of making a small living from a farm lot on this unproductive land. Even in Southern Ontario a people imbued with the idea of progress and confronted with the example to the south of an expanding fee-simple empire were slow to accept the limitations of their agricultural possibilities. The Southern Ontario peninsula was just bountiful enough so that many settlers, especially those from the tiny farms of Ireland or Scotland, imagined themselves in a garden and incorporated many American values, particularly the American sense of the plenitude of land, into their own thought. Well before all the potentially arable land in Southern Ontario was occupied, colonization roads were being built into the Shield. When logger and advocate of agricultural expansion clashed over the use of the Shield the government supported the latter until well into the 1860s. Later, faced with the increasingly evident example of failure, it reversed its assessment of the Shield, but a great many young Ontarians, coming earlier to the same conclusion, had emigrated to the United States in search of land. In the western plains, settlements lined the watercourses. Even there agriculture was a precarious undertaking, while its feasibility away from a surface water supply or where heavy sod had to be broken was yet to be tested.

Because unsettled land was so close to them in time and space and because (many pioneer beliefs to the contrary) a severe climate could not be substantially altered, most British North Americans contended with the wilderness in the ordinary course of their lives. The oldest farms along the côte de Beaupré, a few miles from Québec had been conceded in the 1630s and farmed since the 1640s; still, in the 1860s the farmer who took his produce from the fields on the lower terraces near Château Richer to the open-air market in Québec could, if he wished, strike out from the back of his farm for Hudson Bay and have very little chance of seeing another white man along the way. A young Scot who in 1858 took a teaching job in Hornings Mills, a hamlet seventy miles north of Toronto, found himself amid a forest populated by wolves and bears, broken only here and there by settlers' clearings. Farmers in the Red River settlement contended with the annual probabilities of flood, drought or killing frost. Where the climate was less threatening and farms were cleared, as in parts of Southern Ontario and the Saint John valley, the land still bore the rawness of the loggers' or the pioneers' assault. Only along the lower St. Lawrence had many generations of settlement removed the scars of pioneering, but brooding over these narrow, riparian lands were the rocky, forested hills of the Shield and the Appalachian highlands. The habitants, like other British North Americans, were still enveloped by wilderness.

In these circumstances it was always a struggle to get along. Most British North Americans were farmers. They had come to the New World not in pursuit of an ideal but to improve their standard of living; their outlook was pragmatic and the wilderness was in their way. In Southern

Ontario and New Brunswick where trees were their principal obstacle, settlers had attacked the forest, and frequently had severely overcleared the land by the 1850s. When a fire burned several miles of forest and a settler's barn, the local newspaper almost invariably reported the loss of the barn. For settlers the wilderness was a threat, for many merchants an opportunity for profit, and either group was more than prepared to alter it as quickly as possible. Against this predominant attitude to the wilderness there were only two countervailing influences at Confederation. In government and to a certain extent in the largest private companies there was some sense of management. The Hudson's Bay Company, for example, managed much of the fur trade on a sustained-yield basis, competent administrators in British Columbia had controlled the excesses of the Fraser River gold rushes, and in the Ottawa valley the government built and regulated timber slides and was beginning to license the cut more stringently. Then too, the nineteenth-century cult of nature had reached British North America, although visitors were much more likely than settlers to be familiar with its attitudes. Where belief in the chastening and ennobling power of nature was actually brought into the forest, as it was by the English gentry who settled near Peterborough, Ontario, it was soon diluted by the practical reality of coping with the land. In the United States the romantic movement had found powerful indigenous expression in the writing of men such as Thoreau and Hawthorne, but to muse about nature and man by a pond near Concord, Massachusetts and on a stumpy field at the edge of the Canadian Shield were quite different experiences.

In Québec, management was largely English speaking, the values of nineteenth-century romanticism had not penetrated to the habitant population, and the very small group who had had some exposure to nineteenth-century thought tended to be preoccupied with the question of cultural survival. Although early French-Canadian life had been deeply influenced by the immediate presence of wilderness, French-Canadian nationalism in the nineteenth century was more concerned with territory—especially the seigneurial lowlands—and its particular version of the North American pastoral myth. Wilderness, which stood in the way of territorial enlargement and the perpetuation of an agricultural life, threatened not only the French Canadians' economic prosperity but also their cultural survival. Consequently they attacked the wilderness with at least as much determination as their English-speaking counterparts, and almost no French-speaking voices were raised in its defense.

British North Americans also felt the energetic and alluring presence of the United States. Many of them had come from the United States, many more relied on American technology and trade, some admired American government, and almost anyone who knew anything about the republic to the south had to admire American drive and practical achievement. But their admiration and dependence were tinged with fear. Most British North Americans felt themselves to be different from Americans, and this feeling in a relative handful of people stretched in a thin line alongside the United States created a certain uneasiness. To be sure, in the 1790s a few French Canadians still hoped for another American invasion to liberate them from the British, and after 1820 thousands of young French Canadians drifted south to factory jobs in New England. Louis-Joseph Papineau, the leading spokesman of French-Canadian nationalism in the 1820s and 1830s, wrote admiringly of American republicanism. But in the 1850s and 1860s colonization societies were attempting to repatriate French Canadians in New England and to convince young Québecers that their future lay not in the sacrifice of language, religion, and culture in an American city but on a farm lot in the Canadian Shield of the Eastern Townships. Many French Canadians in New England did return. Many young men settled in the Shield. Theirs was essentially a defense against the non-French-Canadian world, but a large part of this world for them, as for other British North Americans, was the United States. English-speaking British North Americans, sharing the language of the Americans and, in a general way, most of their dominant values, did not have the French Canadian's fear of cultural annihilation. A young man could leave a farm in Southern Ontario or New Brunswick for opportunity in the United States without the French Canadian's deep foreboding that his life would be basically altered. But there was a strong sense of being British, hence of not being American. In many areas the War of 1812 was a vivid memory, there was still fear of Fenian invasion; and the feeling that a separate British identity in North America was threatened from the south was almost inescapable.

And there were tensions within British North America. The Métis way of life, dependent on the buffalo and on markets in the fur trade, was incompatible with Ontarians' growing interest in the western plains as an area for agricultural settlement. Where Catholic Irish and Protestant Irish were both substantially represented, as in the Ottawa valley and in Toronto, brawls and even riots were fairly frequent. Remnants of the older, Loyalist society in New Brunswick resented the mid-nineteenth-century inundation of British poor, people whom they considered their distinct inferiors. But for the most part, potential cultural tensions were minimized by isolation; British North Americans were more likely to be ignorant of each other than antagonistic. Within the St. Lawrence lowland, however, French- and English-speaking people held their own deep and mutual suspicions. For many Ontarians, particularly those from Ulster, French Canadians were agents of the relentless Papish plot to dominate the Christian world. These Catholics spoke French when, at Confederation, there were still British North Americans who had fought with Wellington at Waterloo and many more whose fathers or grandfathers had done so. France was an enemy of the British empire, and the French-speaking people along the lower St. Lawrence could easily be thought of as Frenchmen. Then too, when French- and English-speaking people did come together in the St. Lawrence lowland, the French Canadians seemed to have so little commercial momentum, so little of the drive to progress materially that characterized English-speaking Canadians, that they could be written off as inferior. For their part the French Canadians' obsessive attachment to the seigneurial lands, to language, and to custom was that of a self-conscious minority feeling itself threatened. Nor were these fears unfounded when effective power in government and commerce was in the hands of English-speaking people, when some government officials and influential Protestant churchmen had looked forward to the cultural absorption of French Canadians into an English-speaking, Protestant population, when so many English-speaking settlers were fervently anti-Catholic. In some families French-Canadian and British cultural influences had blended, and in some areas, particularly in the Eastern Townships of Québec, relations between the two groups were usually cordial, but on the whole tensions between French- and English-speaking people had created a barrier within the St. Lawrence–Great Lakes lowland that in its way was as palpable as the rim of the Canadian Shield.

This, then, was Canada at Confederation: half a continent that had not excited the European imagination and was still largely the territory of Indian and fur trader, some three million people who had shown much courage in a harsh environment but little idealism, imagination, or vision. They coped with life along the northern margin of North American agricultural possibility, fended off when they wanted to and when they could the restless energy of the United States, and viewed other areas of British North American settlement with more ignorance than affection and, in some cases, with open hostility. The French-Canadian outlook had folded around family, kin and côte, around an image of a way of life along the lower St. Lawrence before 1760. English-speaking people were engaged in the practical tasks of clearing land, building barns, towns, and prosperity, and in pursuing the closely related goals of improving education and creating a stable government. Their most adventurous spirits were businessmen, men behind the Grand Trunk or the Northern railways and much of the logging in the Ottawa and Saint John valleys. Their rhetoric was often staunchly British, but their basic commitment was to individual achievement in the marketplace. The nineteenth-century fragments that had settled the English-speaking enclaves of British North America—especially lower- and lower-middleclass people from the British Isles—had achieved many of their own goals, but they had not enlarged the nineteenth-century mind, and had not developed a sense of a collective Canadian identity.

In most of the British North American colonies there had been some political talk of confederation for years, and by the 1860s a number of important British North Americans had come to see it as a mutually convenient solution for several different problems. In Ontario there was a lively popular interest in the West. But in the face of distance, cultural differences, and non-complementary regional economies, with no national consensus or national dream, confederation was not a particularly likely and certainly not an inevitable union. It was anybody's guess whether such an arrangement could last.

Confederation had been made possible by the promise of railways and the hope of expanding markets. Underlying it was the emerging technology of the nineteenth century that was rapidly undermining the different regional traditions within the North Atlantic world. Confederation, therefore, posed a problem of fundamental proportions—the reconciliation of the centralizing efficiency of technology with the preservation of cultural variety. Confederation also gradually transformed several enclaves of colonial settlement into a vast country that was likely to remain essentially a wilderness, and this gave Canadians the opportunity, lost to most other people, to explore a continuing relationship between civilization and wilderness. In these ways, Confederation posed a challenge to British North Americans of an altogether different order from the clearing of fields, the building of industry, the defense of narrow identities, or even the creation of a ringing Canadian mythology. Basically it was the challenge to find a way to balance scale and identity, that is, to find a way to live as human beings within the modern world, a quest still reflected in the tensions of Confederation today.

Bibliography

Of recent general interpretations of Canada that bear on the pre-Confederation years see especially the following: J. M. S. Careless, " 'Limited Identities' in Canada," *Canadian Historical Review* 50 (March 1969), 1–10; Northrop Frye, "Conclusion," in C. F. Klinck (ed.), *Literary History of Canada; Canadian Literature in English* (Toronto: University of Toronto Press, 1965); George Grant, "In Defense of North America," chap. 1 in *Technology and Empire: Perspectives on North America* (Toronto: House of Anansi, 1969); R. Cole Harris, "The Myth of the Land in Canadian Nationalism," in Peter Russell (ed.), *Nationalism in Canada* (Toronto: McGraw Hill, 1966), pp. 27–43; and Allan Smith, "Metaphor and Nationality in North America," *Canadian Historical Review* 5 (Sept. 1970), 247–75.

Among the rapidly growing literature on American attitudes toward the land particularly important are Leo Marx, *The Machine in the Garden: Technology and the Pastoral Ideal in America* (New York: Oxford University Press, 1964) and Roderick Nash, *Wilderness and the American Mind* (New Haven: Yale University Press, 1967).

INDEX

mals, 271; obtaining seed, 271, 272; park lots, 273–74; population, 247–48, 249;˙ out-migration, 248, 249; settlement facilities, 275–76; wood supply, 271
Red River frame construction, 276
Red River produce, 264
Regional feeling in Atlantic region, 226
Resources: Atlantic region: alienation, 176–79; investigation, 178; Western interior: investigation, 280–82
Rice, wild, 261
Richardson, Dr. John, 261
Richibucto, 218
Riel, Louis, 284
River lots at Red River, 270
Roads: in Atlantic region, 214; to Cariboo, 304; in Southern Ontario, 119–21
Robb, James, 222
Rocky Mountain Stonies, 250
Roe, F. G., 279
Rotations of land: in Canada during French regime, 49–52; in nineteenth-century Québec, 85; in Southern Ontario, 137–38
Rotures, 39, 70, 73–74
Rupert's Land, 232; administration of, 282–83
Rut, John, 3

St. Albert mission, 249, 279
Saint John (New Brunswick), 197, 204, 213, 214, 217, 219, 226
St. John's (Newfoundland), 213, 218–19
Saint Paul, 249, 266, 267, 268, 275, 278
Saint Paul route, 266–67
St-Pierre and Miquelon, 171
St. Stephen, 218
Salish Indians, 290
Salmon fishery, 308
Sarcee Indians, 251
Sawmills, 57, 145, 199, 296
Scientific reconnaissance of Western interior, 280–82

Scientific work in Atlantic region, 222
Scots: culture, 187; migrations, 186
Sealing, 206
Secondary industry: in Atlantic region, 196–97, 208–10; in Canada during French regime, 55–57; general, 322–23; in Québec after 1760, 96–98; in Southern Ontario, 144–45
Seigneurial system: in Acadia, 28–29; in Canada during French regime, 34, 42–44; in Québec after 1760, 68–71, 77–78, 86–87
Selkirk, Earl of, 16, 186, 238, 247, 268, 271, 272, 273
Settlement: of Atlantic region, 172–76, 182; in Southern Ontario, 117–23, 124–30
Shelburne, 212
Sherbrooke, 100
Shipbuilding: in Atlantic region, 197, 209–10; at Québec, 55–56
Shubenacadie Canal, 213
Simcoe, John Graves, 113, 148, 150
Simpson, Governor George, 245, 249, 257, 261, 267, 275, 293
Smith, Titus, 178
Society for Promoting Agriculture in Nova Scotia, 200
Sorel, 100
Southesk, Earl of, 268
Speculation: in Ontario land, 119, 122
Squared timber, 91
Squared timber trade in Atlantic region, 198–99
Stages, Nova Scotia, 214
Steamboats: 302–3; Atlantic region, 206, 213; Red River, 266; Saskatchewan River, 267
Stellarton, 216
Stewart, William, 12
Summerside, 218
Sydney, 226
Sydney Harbour, 216

Talon, Jean, 32, 40, 55
Tatamagouche, 31